The
Communicative
Experience

The Communicative Experience

ALLYN AND BACON, INC.

Lawrence W. Rosenfield
Hunter College

Laurie Schultz Hayes
University of Minnesota

Thomas S. Frentz
University of Southern California

Boston·London·Sydney·Toronto

P
90
,R65

Library of Congress Cataloging in Publication Data

Rosenfield, Lawrence William.
  The communicative experience.

  Includes bibliographical references and index.
  1. Communication. I. Hayes, Laurie Schultz, 1945-   joint author. II. Frentz, Thomas S., joint author. III. Title. P90.R65   808.5   75-38775
ISBN 0-205-05419-6

ACKNOWLEDGMENTS

The authors are grateful to the following for allowing their advertisements to appear in this book: Page 152, © Eric Weber, 1974. Page 269, © Pepsi-Cola Company, 1940. Reproduced with permission. Page 270, reprinted with permission of Helena Rubenstein, Inc., New York, Paris, London. Page 271, Courtesy—Drambuie Liqueur Co. Ltd. Page 273, reprinted with permission of AT&T Long Lines Department. Page 275, reprinted with permission of E. T. Howard Company, Inc. Page 276, courtesy of The Quaker Oats Company. Page 278, reprinted with permission of the William Underwood Company. Page 279, reprinted with permission of Allied Van Lines, Inc. Page 280, reprinted with permission of The Pennyrich Corporation. Page 281, reprinted with permission of Jockey International. Page 311, photo courtesy of Chanel, Inc. Page 312, courtesy of Del Monte Corporation. Page 314, reprinted with permission from Christine Valmy. Page 315, reprinted with permission from Maidenform, Inc. Page 316, reprinted with permission of The Kendall Company. Page 318, reprinted with permission of Brown-Forman Distillers Corp., Louisville, Ky. Page 319, reprinted with permission of Jean Patou, Inc. Page 320, reprinted with permission of Weyenberg Shoe Manufacturing Company. Page 321, reprinted with permission of D'Arcy-MacManus & Masius, Inc., Advertising. Page 322, reprinted with permission of Oldsmobile Division, General Motors Corporation. Page 325, reprinted with permission of Pitney Bowes.

Contents

Preface   vii

1   *Introduction*   2

The Purpose of This Book *5*   Man Is at His Best When He Is
Thoughtful, Careful, and Touched by Good Humor *7*

2   *The Game-Play Perspective on Human
Communication*   26

The Game Perspective *28*   The Play Perspective *48*   Analysis of
Opening Dialog *59*

3   *Introduction to Interpersonal Communication
Games*   68

Formality—Intimacy Continuum *72*   Interpersonal Relationship
Images *78*

4   *Recognition Games*   88

Polite Greeting: An Approaching Recognition Game *90*   Turn
Off: A Distancing Recognition Game *99*

5   *Formal Conversation Games*   112

Polite Conversation: An Approaching Formal Conversation
Game *115*   Put Off: A Distancing Formal Conversation Game
127

6   *Informal Conversation Games*   136

Personal Conversation among Friends: An Approaching Informal

Conversation Game *140*   Put Down: A Distancing Informal
Conversation Game *160*

7   **Intimate Games**   172

Love: An Approaching Intimate Game *176*   Intensity: A
Distancing Intimate Game *184*

8   **Impersonal Games**   198

Protocol: An Approaching Impersonal Game
205   Termination: A Distancing Impersonal Game *209*

9   **Introduction to Public Communication Games**   214

Relationship between Interpersonal and Public Communication
Games *216*   The Experience of Public Communication Games *228*

10   **Poetic Games**   244

Performing and Productive Poetic Games *246*   Poetic
Games: Theater *248*   Poetic Games: Advertising *264*   Poetic
Games: Mass Entertainment Dream Machines *283*

11   **Rhetoric Games: Publicity and Political Dialog**   296

Four Rhetoric Games *299*   Three Factors in Rhetoric Games
299   Rhetoric of the Marketplace: Publicity *308*   Rhetoric of the
Forum: Political Dialog *327*

12   **Rhetoric Games: Healing and Pornography**   344

Rhetoric of the Soul: Healing *346*   Rhetoric of the Sewer:
Pornography *378*

13   **Dialectic Games**   390

Dialectic/Didactic Games: Science *397*
Dialectic/Didactic Games: Criticism *409*
Dialectic/Didactic Games: History as Creative Plaything *423*

14   **Conclusion: The Answer in the Back of the Book**   436

Index   445

Preface

This book is intended to aid those who wish to understand better their own experiences upon engaging in communicative activities. It is a book unlikely to add in a major way to the reader's store of knowledge about communication (as would be the case were we to discuss such topics as electronic signal transmission or the financial structure of the broadcasting industry) or to make the reader a more facile participant in his or her daily communicative affairs. Rather, our aim throughout this book has been to encourage readers to consider (or reconsider) with some degree of impartiality and insight how they experience those communicative acts in which we ordinarily participate without a second thought. Our interpretations are meant to challenge the conventional wisdom that permits us to dismiss such activities without reflection.

One communicative activity in which the three of us participate not only with thoughtful reflection, but with care and good humor, is this acknowledgment of a special few whose impact on our own thinking and on successive drafts of this manuscript has been both substantial and beneficial. Anne Cushing; Jerry Schulman; James T. Hayes; Mildred Schneider Schultz; Frank Ruggirello; Roderick P. Hart; Sylvia, Alison, Andrew and Hillary Rosenfield; Eric Edwin Hayes; and Kathleen and Mark Andrew Frentz all deserve our thanks for help rendered in seeing this book through to completion. Some of them aided our project in ways that neither we nor they could foresee, but all of them with the sort of intelligence and good will that marks them as human beings in the finest sense of that term.

Lawrence W. Rosenfield
Laurie Schultz Hayes
Thomas S. Frentz

*The
Communicative
Experience*

1

Introduction

Why is it that you do not always know what to say when you meet an acquaintance for the fourth time within twenty minutes?

Is it ever beneficial to fill time with conversational chatter that is rather trivial?

Should you feel embarrassed when you cannot put into words the joy you feel in the presence of a special friend?

Why is it that some people can say the meanest things to each other and yet remain friends or even lovers?

What is the difference between performing in a Broadway musical and writing a critical review of the performance?

Why do some prefer to read about James Bond's detective exploits and others prefer the official accounts of an FBI manhunt for a kidnapper?

Why are you reading this book?

How often do you ask yourself questions like these? How often do you stop to consider the whys, the whats, the hows, the whatevers of the communication you experience? If you are like most people, your probable answer is "not very often." As people and events swirl around us in our daily lives we are usually too busy to stop and to question what it all

means—either we are speaking or doing what comes naturally or we are actively listening or watching while someone else does his or her own thing. If we are not too busy, if we are at all uninvolved, we tend to feel guilty because we are not "with it," we are "out of it." Not being swept up in the swirl of things is seen by some as antisocial or unhealthy: "If you stop to think about it, you'll just get a headache." "Don't worry, it will all work out." "Oh, there's Harry, over in the corner, brooding again; his life would be much happier if he wouldn't think about things so much." For others, thinking about communication is a frivolous activity to be dismissed as "idle speculation," or an "ill-mannered" activity rather like voyeurism. Regardless of whether we have the time or the inclination, few of us reflect much on our communication experiences. Why? Probably the chief reason is that we really do not know how.

It is strange, but true, that we have all been taught how to read, how to tie our shoes, how to add 2 + 2, how to feed ourselves, and how to button our coats, but few of us have been taught how to think about communication. Of course, from birth each of us has been taught how to communicate—how to talk, how to write, how to draw, how to sing—but the emphasis has always been on the doing. In contrast, few of us have been taught how to experience communication, how to consume communication, how to think about a commercial for dog food, the chatter at a bridge party, conversations at the breakfast table, television soap operas, or stock market reports. Or more specifically, how to account for Al who in one case greets Alice with "Hello, it's really nice to see you again," but in another greets Ben with "Hey Ben, how's your ass?" Or how to think about Harold Smooth who is seemingly engaged in conversation with Simon Lump but is actually leering past Simon at Betty Bulge. Or how to appreciate why it is that your friends spend hours idly humming a rather silly commercial jingle like "Buy Brian's Bread for Better Breakfasts."

If by chance you have already given these communicative events more thought than you care to, what is to follow in the pages ahead will be of no interest to you. Put the book down; read no more. If, on the other hand, you have never really stopped to consider these events other than to offer a brief opinion such as "that conversation was crummy," "I enjoyed talking to her," or "this movie is realistic," or if you do occasionally reflect on your experience of communication, but when you do you are more confused than ever, we think that you should read on. This book is for you.

THE PURPOSE OF THIS BOOK

This book is a set of exercises in thinking critically about the experience of human communication. We hope we can spark your curiosity about communicative events. We hope to stimulate your awareness of what is happening to you and others as you interact in social space. We hope that after reading what we have to say, you will consider yourself more capable of understanding and appreciating your social environment.

There are also many things that we hope will not happen. We hope that you will not consider this text as a substitute for your own experience as a participant in communication. By increasing your understanding and appreciation of communication, we can only complement your own unique experience. We cannot replace it.

We hope that you will not expect this text to improve your communication skills. Just as reading about and understanding the requirements for a professional football player does not assure that you will qualify for the team, just as learning to recognize an *allegro con fuoco* tempo does not guarantee that you will be chosen to play with a symphony orchestra, and just as reading about insanity will not make you mad, reading about and becoming more appreciative of human communication does not certify that you will be a better communicator. Of course, we would be delighted to know that your communicative experiences are more pleasurable as a result of reading this text, but such a consequence would be more a happy coincidence than the result of a professional promise.

Furthermore, we hope that you will not expect us to make all worldly confusion comprehensible, sensible, or pleasant, or to claim that our inquiry is wholly original or even that our remarks are "correct" in any final or orthodox sense. While some of our interpretations may seem like intoxicating sorcery, others may strike you as tedious, if not downright offensive. Reflecting on your communicative experiences, perhaps even holding up to the light of public discussion those personal experiences you would rather not have exposed to public gaze, might be more uncomfortable than happy. We have our biases (on which we shall elaborate in a moment) and you have yours. We do not expect that in every case our biases will be similar or that we can make them similar. We do not assume that every reader will accept everything we are about to say.

We will consider our efforts successful, however, whether you accept or reject what we say, if we have helped each of you to think for yourself about the experience of communication.

In the chapters that follow we will argue, sometimes explicitly, sometimes more covertly, that one way of communicating is better than another, that one way of viewing communication is better than another, and that one kind of communicative experience is more rewarding than another. In no instance do we intend to make value choices for others; we do not plan to force our conclusions on anyone. As we have said already, if our readers reject our interpretations that is their business. Since what we believe makes sense to us and *we* are strongly committed to our position, we feel obliged to make the reasonableness of our perspective as clear to others as possible. At the outset, therefore, we would like to profess our critical biases—to construct the framework that will support all our conclusions.[1]

---

[1] Popular wisdom has it that critics who cannot specify what systematic procedures they

In brief, we believe that man is at his best when he is thoughtful, careful, and touched by good humor; that the best communicative experiences are those that most clearly manifest the thought, loving care, and good humor that are mankind's most distinctive and precious potentials; and that the best perspective on human communication, therefore, will not be one that limits man to thoughtlessness, carelessness, and humorlessness.

These biases are not original. We can trace their source over the slender thread of humanism reaching back through the Renaissance to the Greek and Roman philosophers. They emphasize individual freedom and the development of human potential.

Moreover, these biases are admittedly complicated. In the remainder of this chapter we shall explore their contours in more detail, specify how it is that they influence what we are going to say in the rest of the book, and forecast where, why, and how we are going in this book.

MAN IS AT HIS BEST WHEN HE IS THOUGHTFUL, CAREFUL, AND TOUCHED BY GOOD HUMOR

Thoughtful

What does it mean to say, "Man is at his best when he is thoughtful"? Actually, this is not what we have said or intend to say. Our claim is that thoughtfulness is *one aspect* of man at his best. For us, thought, loving care, and good humor are mankind's most distinctive and precious potentials and *together* they characterize man at his best. In order to understand this admittedly complex combination, however, let us begin by examining each feature separately, and start with "thoughtful."

The person who is thoughtful about himself or herself, thoughtful about his or her communication with others, or thoughtful about the world in general is reflective, receptive, and responsible.

We all engage in mental activities. We daydream; we ponder our future; we recall the past. The kind of mental activity characteristic of thoughtfulness is slightly different. All human beings have (at least

---

employ in arriving at their assertions (so that every person, given similar mental furnishings, could perform equally well at the intellectual task) are a threat to national security; if they are not subversive of democratic principles of equality, they must at the very least be bards of aristocratic wickedness. We hope that our efforts here to put our cards on the table, so to speak, will be seen as a measure of our sincerity, not as yet another tactic to divert attention while we stick something up our sleeve.

potentially) the unique capacity simultaneously to experience an event (come near to it) and to reflect on that event (get distance on it). Arthur Koestler suggests this following simple example:

> You are absorbed in a game of chess; you concentrate on a stratagem to defeat your opponent. You look up for a moment to

light a cigarette, and at that moment your awareness jumps to another plane, as it were; you say to yourself "what fun I am having playing chess with old Henry on a Sunday afternoon." Then you go back to your game. It was a brief break-through from the activity in hand to the contemplation of that activity from an upstairs balcony—a vertical shift of awareness which enabled you to look down at the top of your own head. To put it in a different way, attention has been displaced from the object of the ongoing activity to the subject engaged in carrying it out—that elusive entity, the self.[2]

We are not, therefore, describing as thoughtful the abstract thinking that can alienate us from social experience. Instead, we refer to man's capacity to separate himself from his experience, to put things at a distance from himself, while all the time maintaining contact with that experience.[3]

But the concept of thoughtfulness includes more than being reflective. Suppose, in the above example, when you look up for a moment, you say to yourself: "What day is today? Oh, this is Sunday. I always have fun on Sundays. So . . . what fun I am having playing chess with old Henry on a Sunday afternoon." For us, this is not thoughtful. It may be reflective, but it is not receptive. Thoughtful people do not reflect on their experience like mail-room clerks who sort parcels into preestablished, discrete, empty bins. (All Sundays go into a "fun bin," all Mondays go into a "depressed bin," and so on.) Thoughtful people are not bound by rigid explanations of behavior; they do not need a formula before they can experience their world. Instead, thoughtful people, as we define them, are open-minded and flexible. Their most gratifying experience is characterized more by inspiration (openness to the present) than by obedience (submission to restrictions of the past).

Now, of course, there are some circumstances when obedience to convention is not suffocating. We are not proposing that the only way one can be considered thoughtful is to improvise continually. The comfort of all air travelers, for example, is markedly increased by the probability that none of them is likely to open the plane's escape hatches in a sudden moment of inspiration. Neither are we suggesting that the use of categories to classify data is symptomatic of mental illness or subhuman behavior. After all, the mail-room clerk's routine *is* useful in sorting mail.

---

[2] A. Koestler, *The Act of Creation* (New York: Dell Publishing Co., 1967), p. 633.

[3] This juxtaposition is elegantly expressed and elaborated by Martin Buber in his essay "Distance and Relation" in *The Knowledge of Man*, a collection of Buber's works edited by Maurice Friedman (New York: Harper Torchbooks, 1965), pp. 59–71.

We merely claim that those who maintain too exclusive an allegiance to any abstract system of topics immunize themselves from experiencing the world. Instead of knowing good old Leon who lives at 116 Sheridan Place, Chickasha, Oklahoma, the regional mail clerk merely knows Zip Code 73018. All he can experience is the category 73018. We would be wrong to equate such hollow data processing with thoughtfulness.[4]

Thoughtfulness, then, as we have described the concept so far, represents the human potential to be independent both from experience and from ideological restrictions. In other words, to be thoughtful is to be self-conscious and free. In human realms we are continually open to choice. We can choose to be immersed in our experience or not; we can choose to follow convention or not. It is this very unpredictability that makes human beings different from all other elements of Nature.

But this unpredictability, this freedom to make choices, is accompanied by one other feature of thoughtfulness, and that is responsibility. The thoughtful person is accountable for his decisions. When a man chooses to build his house out of sticks and not bricks, he is responsible for the consequences; the choice was his and he made it. When a beaver builds his dam out of sticks and not bricks, he is not responsible for the consequences; he had no choice to make; beavers always build their dams out of sticks. If the house washes away, we blame the man; if the dam washes away, we do not blame the beaver. If the house is an architectural masterpiece, we praise the man and give him a prize; if the dam is an architectural masterpiece, we do not praise the beaver any more than we would praise any other beaver. A beaver's freedom in constructing his dam is severely limited. The only time we can ever praise or blame the beaver is when we also invest in him the human characteristic of reflective choice.[5]

In other words, when we say that man is at his best when his attitude is characterized, in part, by thoughtfulness, we are saying that we believe in and support man's capacity for responsible choice. We

---

[4] Perhaps this distinction has been made more elegantly by Karl Jaspers in *The Future of Mankind* (Chicago: University of Chicago Press, 1961), p. 210. Copyright © 1961.

> Sticking to abstractions alienates us from reality. Abstract thinking becomes untrue thinking if a finite definition claims to be an unrelated truth—that is to say, if it is made absolute. Unlike this abstract thinking of the mere intellect, rational thinking absorbs the abstractions, transcends them, and returns with them to reality. Such concrete thinking has content and visuality. It is not self-sufficient. It uses fruitful abstraction as a means of achieving clarity and a deeper penetration of reality, but it never loses its grip on what it relates to, where it comes from, whence it draws substance and significance: reality itself.

[5] Our childhood memories of stories like *The Three Little Pigs* really tell us more about how humans ought to make choices than about the life-styles of pigs and wolves.

believe that we all should be thinking about the choices we can make (reflective), that we all have the right to make choices for ourselves (receptive), and that we all have the obligation to accept the consequences of our choices (responsible). More specifically, let us consider some communicative experience. We propose, for example, that we all have the right to choose to tell a lie, but we also insist that when we do we must assume responsibility for misleading our listeners. If the other persons are happier for our lie, it is our "fault"; if the other persons are miserable for our lie, it is our "fault." The choice is ours and if we make it, we are responsible for it.

Similarly, let us consider your communicative experience as you read this book. Are you distancing yourself from the book as you read? (Are you reading reflectively?) Have you decided that what we have to say is potentially interesting but you will have to read more before you know? (Are you reading receptively?) Are you willing to put down the book regardless of what your friends may say or are you willing to praise what we say regardless of what your friends may say? Are you willing to make a choice and accept the consequences? (Are you reading responsibly?) Whatever—if you are thinking about what you read, as you read, if you have decided to think for yourself and, come what may, finish or not finish the book—you *are* being thoughtful, aren't you?

Because we believe that thoughtfulness is one aspect of the best attitude anyone can assume toward the communication he or she encounters, we have written a text intended to encourage the reader to be reflective, receptive, and responsible.

The Thoughtful Person Is Reflective. In the many chapters to come, we will continue to remind you to be thoughtful. To help you reflect on what we are saying, for example, we will ask you to distance yourself from what we describe. One way we will do this is to force you to examine the language we use. You will notice, for instance, that we will often fracture words, like thought-ful, re-creation, and care-less. Why? We hold with Heidegger[6] that language is the congealed artifact of experience. That is, words record and yet freeze reality into inflexible linguistic forms. At one time, for example, there may have been a special reason for calling a certain red fruit "apple" or calling a certain male person "Jim," but most of these reasons are ignored or forgotten when the words "apple" or "Jim" are being used. And so part of our effort to

---

[6] Martin Heidegger, *An Introduction to Metaphysics*, trans. Ralph Manheim (Garden City: Doubleday Anchor Books, 1961), pp. 145–155.

help you understand various communication events will be to attempt to breathe fresh life into the common words we use, to capture at least a hint of the reality that the words were created to celebrate.

Our interest in the capacity of language to congeal experience is by no means an attempt on our part to be either flashy or mysterious. Those who are concerned about the present masculine emphasis of our language, for example, share our curiosity. They call attention to such examples as the following: "Man" as the symbol of our race ("Man is at his best when he is thoughtful"); "he" as the preferred third-person singular pronoun where a referent or gender is not clear ("One ought to watch his money carefully"); and generic titles such as "chairman," "congressman," "postman," "policeman," "fireman," and the like. When they do this, they too are trying to make us reflect upon the spontaneous experience (in this case, the experience of male dominance) which the words were originally created to celebrate but which is now an inflexible part of our communication behavior.

The Thoughtful Person Is Receptive.   Secondly, to facilitate your reading receptively, we will be asking you to focus on concrete, experiential incidents of human discourse rather than on abstract theoretical principles. From our perspective, a more theoretical analysis would tend to obscure the reality that the particular incident, the "in-formed object or event," could disclose. (Remember our example of the mail-room clerk's routine?) Hence, our analysis will rely heavily on anecdotes and analogies. We will examine a series of particular communication events—such as the greeting, the cocktail party, the family reunion, and the television situation comedy, to name a few. Our purpose in reflecting upon these events will not be to generate a set of universal, demographic categories. Our intention, rather, will be to experiment in reflective thinking, to employ a variety of scholarly and analytic tools (including, but not limited to, abstract categories) in seeking a "way in" to human communicative experience. In other words, we will try to give you practice in being open to the disclosure of experience, not practice in applying a theory to explain your experience. We do not want to tell you what the world means; we want you to be receptive, free to give the world a chance to explain itself.

The Thoughtful Person Is Responsible.   Thirdly and above all, we will be challenging you to become responsible readers and consumers of all communication. Heightening your awareness of what you and others say and do to each other is serious business. When you become more conscious of your communication, there are more choices that you must make: Should I continue to do things the same way? Should I change? Should I feel guilty about who I am and what I do? Should I feel proud of who I am and what I do? Should I blame my circumstances on others? Should others blame their circumstances on me? Should I help others by sharing my insights with them, or should I let them be? Or, if I disagree with the Rosenfield, Hayes, and Frentz view of man and his efforts to establish human contact through communication, what alternative should I propose? These are not easy questions to answer and many of us would prefer not to confront them. But the thoughtful reader will recognize that he or she has these choices to make and will be accountable for the decisions; the thoughtless reader will try to escape, to ignore, or to forget either his capacity for choice or the consequences of his decisions. From our point of view, the choice of such irresponsible behavior is the only "bad" choice one can make.

Careful

Another aspect of man at his best is loving care: He is careful about himself and others, careful about the world of communication, and careful about the world in general. We shall claim that careful communicators are more gratified by the communicative activity. This claim can only be confirmed by each reader's own experiences—it can never be conclusively demonstrated. We shall also claim that careful analysis of the communication of others is itself insightful. This book will attempt to illustrate this claim, although it too can never be proven to one who wishes to deny it. But the use of the word *care* in these sentences can be misleading. No matter how innocent it may appear on the surface, "care," like "thought," is a complicated concept.

The Careful Person Takes His World to Heart.   Care, for us, is an attitude of acceptance and appreciation. The careful person takes to heart what *is* in human affairs without necessarily hoping to improve on it.[7] This is not to argue that men should accept each other and their chatter indiscriminately. We risk delusion if not self-destruction if we try to love mankind unselectively, affirming everything and denying nothing. To accept something just because it exists—just because it *is*—is, for us,

---

[7] M. Heidegger, *What Is Called Thinking?* trans. J. Glenn Gray (1954; New York: Harper & Row, 1968), p. 208.

care-less. Instead, to be careful is to respect something for what *it is as it is.* For example, to accept Eileen, Danny, Peter, Pat, and Trudi because they are human beings is to show no special regard for Eileen as she is or for Peter as he is. To accept them all merely because they are human beings ("if you've seen one, you've seen them all") is to deny each the possibility of having anything unique to offer, of being a special kind of human being. To be careful is to respect another as he or she is, as an accomplished fact of Nature not to be blinked at or idealized or rationalized away.

The Careful Person Appreciates. An attitude of carefulness is not fatalistic; it is appreciative. That is, it is not based on the assumption that "men are such devilish creatures that you will never be able to do anything about them, so unless you want to be a hermit and leave them, you may as well love them." An appreciative stance, instead, relishes the details of human affairs, even those that might be considered repugnant by more fastidious tastes. The fact that much human display is often petty and scheming intrigues the appreciative person who wants to know how and why. The attitude of appreciation presumes that other people and things have so much to tell us, if we will only let them "speak" to us.[8]

Neither is a careful attitude merely that of compassion for our fellow creatures. In order to be careful it is not enough to feel sorry for others who suffer misfortune. We are not just talking about pity or sympathy. When you are sympathetic you are not really demonstrating *care* for another. Instead you are projecting yourself into the other's situation and pondering "Golly, how would *I* feel if *I* were in her shoes? If *my* son were hit by a car, *I* would feel awful." In pity or sympathy, the emphasis is still on the self, but the self as placed in the circumstances of the other.

The appreciation that is our concern in clarifying the concept of carefulness is more accurately represented by the concept of empathy. When you empathize with another, you so care for the other that you try to see the other's situation as the other sees it. To the best of your ability you leave your own worries and prejudices behind. So taken by the

---

[8] Perhaps it is helpful to recall the origin of the term *phenomenon*, which means, in Greek, "that which reveals itself." It indicates, as Heidegger has suggested, the capacity of a thing to speak for itself. William Barrett has explained Heidegger's notion rather clearly in *Irrational Man* (Garden City: Doubleday Anchor Books, 1962), p. 214: "According to Heidegger we do not know the object by conquering and subduing it but rather by letting it be what it is and, in letting it be, allowing it to reveal itself as what it is." See also, of course, Martin Heidegger, *Discourse on Thinking*, trans. J. M. Anderson and E. H. Freund (New York: Harper & Row, 1966), pp. 76–81.

other *as the other is*, you try to *be as the other is* in order to understand the other's circumstances. "I know that *Mary* so loves *her* son, how *she* must be feeling." Empathy is not only difficult to understand, it is difficult to achieve. Being careful often goes against our selfish instincts.

There are two corollary qualifications that follow from the careful person's capacity to accept and to appreciate. One is our belief that carefulness cannot be accompanied by what we might label "the planning impulse." There are, indeed, those people who care for the world, but we would not consider them careful. Their "care" is of a different sort. They do not care for what the world is, but for what the world can become once they have worked their reforms on it. ("Just wait until Harry and I have been married for a few years. He'll be more socially acceptable once I've taught him how to be a *real* gentleman.") Such an impulse to reform, such conditional acceptance of the world, is more the mark of hopefulness than of carefulness.

A careful regard for the world invites man not only to accept that world as it is, but to take responsibility for that world as it is. And it is only when we accept such a responsibility for a world not entirely of our own making nor even under our control that we can also assume the appreciative quality of thankfulness (not hopefulness) that is implied in carefulness.

The second qualification that we place on carefulness is more of a clarification—the willingness to take to heart and appreciate what *is* in human affairs does not mean that you personally have to like everything you witness or experience or every person you meet. We do not mean to suggest that the careful person "loves" all things as a man "loves" his wife and a mother "loves" her child. If, for example, you accept the existence of a particular water snake near your home, if you appreciate its existence in the balance of nature, and if you are thankful that it has helped to keep the number of pesky mosquitoes at a minimum, your attitude toward the snake is one of carefulness. There is no rule that we can think of that requires you to fondle or even touch the snake. Or, you can accept the existence of the hypodermic needle that the nurse holds, appreciate both the nurse's duty and the significance of penicillin, and be thankful for the cure that the entire process signifies, but you do not have to "like" it. Similarly, we can all care for Joseph Stalin: We can accept him for who he was and appreciate how it was that he was able to unify the highly disparate Soviet people, or even try to empathize with how he must have felt at various times during his "reign." But being careful does not mean that we personally would have liked him or would have allowed our sister to marry him, nor does it mean that we are forgetting the cruelty or ugliness of many of his policy actions. To be careful is to extend to another person or thing the right to be as it is without necessarily approving of it. To be careful is to remain *impartial* in a sense, to continue to find reality's disclosures meaning-ful, even if not always a cause for exaltation. It is what we ask of others; it is only human that they have the right to ask the same of us.

To summarize the concept of carefulness, let us apply it to your communicative experience with this book. Are you being a careful reader? What attitude have you taken toward this book? Have you let it be what it claims to be—a set of exercises in thinking critically about the experience of human communication? Or are you still trying to *use* the book to improve your success and happiness? (Are you reading with acceptance?) Even if you dislike the fact that so far your reading of this book has not improved your health, wealth, wisdom, or happiness, are you thankful for it for what it does do, profitless as that may seem? (Are you reading with appreciation?) Or do you still have a lingering need to reform it, are you hopeful for what it could become?

As we said earlier, a careful attitude is often an unpopular attitude and it is not always easy to maintain. As you read, we will be asking you to join us in accepting and appreciating the world of human communication as it is. We will ask you to suspend any impulses you have to reform or to disregard what is; we want to explore with you communicative events that you might not normally consider as important or interesting or that you might not normally consider at all. We are not suggesting that we will study only what is potentially bizarre or dull or that anything omitted is somehow worth-less. All the communicative events we have chosen are those that impinge heavily on our everyday lives, but of course our selection is by no means exhaustive. We merely hope, however, that by the end of the book we will have helped you to appreciate communication more impartially than you do now.

Good Humor

What do *you* mean when you say that someone has a "sense of humor"?

Suppose you are enjoying yourself at a party and decide to tell a joke that you recently heard. You spend several minutes setting up your listeners for what you think is a great punch line. You deliver it with the flair worthy of a professional comedian and one of your listeners responds, "I don't get it." Would you say that that person, in that instance, has a sense of humor?

Suppose that on another occasion you approach your great aunt deciding to share what you consider a delightfully naughty story. Upon finishing your tale, her response is "Hrrumpf! That wasn't funny. You should be ashamed of yourself." Would you say that your great aunt, in that instance, has a sense of humor?

Is having a sense of humor something that you put in the same category as being able to paint pink flamingoes upside down and backwards on a wire fence—namely, worth-less?

If you happen to be frustrated by people who "don't get" a joke you have told, or "don't think it's funny," if you wish that they would because for you a sense of humor is a nice thing to have, let us share with you our understanding of what a sense of humor is and why we think it is important when we reflect on ourselves, our communication, and our world in general.

It is not without a keen sense of our own audacity that we attempt to explain the essence of being touched by good humor. From the beginning we have admitted that our biases are complex, but we are not so brash as to assume that as a result of this book we will clarify the concepts of thoughtful, careful, and good humor for all time. (Paradoxically, if we *were* able to crystallize our ideas for you we would be confining at least our own potential for thoughtfulness, and possibly thwarting yours.) But neither are we so foolish to believe that we cannot offer some suggestions for your consideration. We have asked many people what they mean when they say that someone has a "sense of humor." Most of them hesitate awkwardly, unable to answer anything more than to admit that they "know one when they see one." We think we can do better than that.

The Good-Humored Person Recognizes, Relishes, and Seeks the Incongruous. For us, the person who is touched by good humor has the capacity to recognize, the willingness to relish, and the commitment to seek out the incongruous, the incompatible, or the unique. More specifically, this definition assumes, first, that we each have some idea of what is normal or usual and, second, that the person who has a sense of humor has a particular attitude toward what is normal or usual: He or she is able to detect what is *ab*normal, or *un*usual, he or she derives pleasure from reflecting on what is *ab*normal or *un*usual, and he or she is persistently on the watch for other instances of the *ab*normal or *un*usual.

In the rest of this section we would like to elaborate this definition and then explain how a sense of humor restrains and is restrained by thoughtfulness and carefulness.

Before elaborating anything more, we must emphasize that a sense of humor is a social sense. "Normal" and "abnormal" are social concepts. Their domain is the world of men, not the world of nature. More particularly, our attitude toward social events differs from our attitude toward natural events. Our attitude toward the world of nature is to try to understand it and adjust our lives to it. We insulate our homes if we live in a cold climate; we carry umbrellas if we think it might rain; we provide alternate illumination after the sun has "set." If an extraordinary event should occur, if we should detect a phenomenon that is incompatible with our expectations, our attitude is usually marked by confusion, if not by awe or fear. But do we say that the person who has the capacity to recognize natural irregularities is demonstrating that he is touched by good humor? More than likely, we would agree that a person who laughs at a hurricane because it is an unnatural event is, indeed, "touched," but not by good humor! A sense of humor makes no sense in the world of nature.

Alternatively, in the world of human affairs, one can of course recognize something incongruous, incompatible, or unique about the presence of a hurricane. What is incongruous, however, is not the presence of the hurricane but the way that men confront it. Which specific event or behavior is detected as absurd will depend on what is considered "normal." If you think, for example, that the normal way for people to prepare for a hurricane is to board their windows with heavy wood planks, you might sense as incongruous the woman who glues toothpicks across hers or uses waxed paper because it is a wood by-product. Or, if you think the normal reaction is to chant "She sells sea shells down by the sea shore" while dancing around a fire, you will sense as absurd the man who mutters obscenities, mourns his fate, boards his windows, packs up his most precious belongings, and moves inland. Normality is an idea of what *ought to* happen in the world of men. There are many norms of social behavior; some are similar, some are dissimilar, others are contradictory. Expectations about what ought to happen can be personal or they can be shared. In any event, they are the center against which something eccentric is detected.

Having the ability to recognize a social event as abnormal is not enough to be classified as having a sense of humor. Consider the judge who convicts a burglar, the priest who absolves a penitent in the confessional, and the husband who assaults a man discovered in bed with his wife. Each of these people has detected something incompatible with his view of social reality, but we would not automatically grant each the possession of a sense of humor, would we? The impulse to rehabilitate the social offender, return the prodigal to the fold, or extract one's revenge is humanly understandable and often socially beneficial. But none of these is especially characteristic of a person touched by good humor.

Instead, to have a sense of humor, one must *delight* in his discovery of the incongruous and relish its abnormality. The judge with a sense of humor will appreciate the cleverness of the burglar's robbery, the priest will find pleasure in his parishioner's transgression, and the husband will relish the image of the sneaky adulterer in bed with his plump, middle-aged spouse. Although each has a norm against which something has been seen as abnormal, each is willing to suspend his devotion to the norm, albeit temporarily, and find pleasure in whatever is incompatible with it. This is precisely what the great aunt in our earlier example was unwilling to do. The naughty story we supposedly told violated our aunt's sensibilities and she was unwilling to find, or at least to admit to finding, any pleasure in the incompatible, in the naughty. ("Hrrumpf! That wasn't funny. You should be ashamed of yourself.") If one's commitment to a norm is excessively strong, it will be even more difficult to sense humor in the abnormal.

What do we mean when we say that someone has a sense of humor? So far, we have suggested that such a person has a special attitude toward social affairs—he or she has certain expectations about social order, but he or she is willing to recognize disorder and find pleasure, however brief, in reflecting upon the chaos. Now we need to add one more variable—the person touched by good humor does not limit himself to occasional revelry or abstain whenever possible. Rather, he is characterized by his persistent commitment to detect and delight in the abnormal. We can trust such a person to sense the humorous in practically anything and everything at one time or another.

Why do we accentuate man's capacity for humor? For two (or, depending on how you look at it, four) important reasons: *He who is touched by good humor is both thoughtful and careful, and a sense of humor is a necessary antidote both to heartless thought and mindless love.*

The Good-Humored Person Is Thoughtful. If you recall, we have proposed that the thoughtful person is reflective, receptive, and responsible. These same attributes distinguish the attitude of the person who is touched by good humor.

Consider, first, how reflective distance is necessary for humor. For one thing, humor has objects. One laughs *at* something. Even when the object of humor is the self, the laughing self is separate from the laughable self. ("Oh, I'm just laughing at myself.") But a more compelling argument for the necessity of distance in humor is that, at their base, humor and emotion are incompatible. When people are genuinely emotional, when anger or fear or pity overtake them and they are caught up in their experience, there is no room for laughter. Nightmares are full of terror until we wake up and reflect on their content. Alternatively, the often heard warning, "Come on, it isn't funny, it's serious" can also be translated "Come on, you have no right to be on the outside looking in, so distant, get involved."

The person touched by good humor is not only free from experience, but free to experience. The person who senses something as humorous does not do so just because someone has told him to do so or just because he always has in the past. Recognizing something as incongruous is a spontaneous personal experience. No one can force it; no formula can guarantee it. If, for example, someone were to say to you, "Laugh at this, it's funny," could you? Unless you shared his sense of the incongruous, you probably could not. You might, indeed, eventually laugh, but by then the absurdity that inspired you would be that of someone insisting that something was humorous when to you it was not.

The person touched by good humor is receptive in yet another way: He or she is willing to relish the possible absurdity of anything and everything. No habit, ideal, or loyalty is too sacred; nothing is beyond question. Even thoughtfulness itself is not above doubt. The person who is touched by good humor delights in the possibility that reason too might be perishable.

All this freedom, so essential to a sense of humor, entails the same responsibility that is integral to thoughtfulness. If we choose to disregard convention, to seek out and derive pleasure from what is abnormal, we must be prepared to confront the consequences of our decision. One of these consequences is that when we enjoy what we once thought was absurd, we risk the possibility of our own disorientation. The "problem" with having a sense of humor is that the more we delight in what is abnormal, the more we are tempted to question what is normal. The judge who delights in the burglar's exploits, for example, might be tempted to break the law himself, or even to doubt the validity of the law. Similarly, we can laugh at those who prepare for the hurricane by chanting "She sells sea shells down by the seashore," while dancing around a fire, but perhaps that makes just as much sense, if not more, than boarding the windows of a house that will be washed away anyway. Or does it? Confronting this dilemma is the responsibility of the person who is touched by good humor.

Another consequence of a sense of humor is that when we choose to demonstrate our good-humored detachment in communicative activities, we risk the possibility of frustrating others and being labeled as *rude*.

Crassus: "Pompous, what right have you to disrupt our pleasant conversation by asking embarrassing questions? Do you think you are better than we are?"

Pompous: "Why no, Crassus; but can't you see how funny it is to find ourselves talking about septic tanks at lunch?"

Crassus: "Pompous, either you just have a crude streak or else you are trying to ruin a nice friendship."

Pompous: "Not at all, my good friend. I'm just fascinated about what sort of friendship it is that encourages luncheon partners to discuss septic tanks."

Actually, Pompous is being neither rude nor contemptuous. Nor is he refusing to take his conversation with Crassus seriously when he laughs at it. On the contrary, Pompous may be far more serious about the conversation and his friendship with Crassus than Crassus himself is. But in his continual quest for understanding, in the pleasure he derives from holding up for inspection the very actions and relations to which he is himself a party, Pompous must be prepared to accept responsibility for destroying the very things he is examining. The luncheon conversation might dissolve in laughter or at least be "damaged" by the analysis. And the participants' relationship itself might not withstand such scrutiny. Such constant analysis and disruption will be frustrating to those, like Crassus, who do not share Pompous' sense of thoughtful good humor about the commonplace communicative events in their lives.

The Good-Humored Person Is Careful.   In the past few pages we have continually referred to *good* humor. Our choice of adjectives was deliberate. We are favorably biased toward the person who *delights* in the incongruous that he has detected. In other words, we willfully exclude those whose sense of the unique is motivated or accompanied by contempt and ridicule. This is not "good" humor;[9] it is malice.

---

[9] For more on this distinction see D. H. Munro, "Humor," *The Encyclopedia of Philosophy* (New York: Collier Macmillan, 1967), Vol. 4, pp. 90–93.

Our definition of "good humor," in contrast, is that sense of humor which in the end reaffirms what is as it is. This definition is neither novel nor eccentric. Even though the people we have interviewed could not always explain what they meant when they said that someone had a sense of humor, they generally agreed that it was a nice thing to have. Why is that the case? Probably because a sense of humor is not only personally gratifying, but because in the end it threatens no one else. If you have a sense of humor, you care for the world and you are thankful for the people who occupy it. Everything, no matter how initially incongruous or absurd, is not only worthy of your attention, but uniquely appealing. You may poke fun at all kinds of social conventions and communicative foibles, but if anything your impulse is more to restore vitality and freshness than to reform. The person who is touched by good humor seeks to revitalize life as lived rather than to modify the terms of that life.

What do we mean when we say that someone has a sense of humor? We have described this attitude as the capacity to recognize, the willingness to enjoy, and the commitment to keep looking for what is incongruous, incompatible, or unique in the world of human affairs.

"So what?"

So what? The importance of our preference for a sense of humor cannot be overemphasized. Without the element of good humor, thoughtfulness and carefulness together are at worst unattainable and at best incomplete.

Because a sense of humor is both thoughtful and careful, it alone can reconcile those two conflicting tendencies. If a person is too thoughtful, he gradually isolates himself from experience. Claiming objectivity, he settles for safe, but superficial, contact with the world. If he is touched by good humor, however, he cannot be too thoughtful; he is committed to return to the world, to come near to it in order to discover and delight in all sorts of experience. Because a sense of humor is careful, it is an antidote to heartless thought.

On the other hand, if a person is too careful, he risks hurling himself headlong into experience. So seduced by the excitement of what is, he can be rendered unfit to think about it. If he is touched by good humor, however, he cannot become so excessively careful; he is committed to recognizing individual differences and commonalities from a distance and to treasuring both for their eccentricities and their banalities. Because a sense of humor is thoughtful, it is an antidote to indiscriminate, mindless love.

Perhaps even more important for us, thoughtfulness and carefulness alone are incomplete. Together they restrict man to sobriety and earnestness. These are admirable states that are, undoubtedly, gratifying. But they are no fun. And that, precisely, is the point. Play, fun, pleasure, joy—whatever terms you use—complement the serious nature of thoughtfulness and carefulness, are necessary both for the individual and for society, and are integral to a sense of humor. From our point of view, no discussion of mankind is complete without considering humor. Our moral stance demands of us an image of man as the animal who laughs. Man's capacity for humor is the spark that fuses his capacity for reason and his capacity for care into humanity.

Because we believe that a sense of humor is so important, we intend to encourage this attitude in our readers. At times we will find it necessary to depict certain conventional communicative behaviors in a form of caricature that may be rejected by more sober types as being too exaggerated for an academic text. Our purpose is only to call to mind their incongruity, incompatibility, or uniqueness, and to invite you to relish it with us. No matter how negative they may seem on the surface, the spirit of our efforts will always be careful. We acknowledge that there is, indeed, a certain rudeness inherent in subjecting commonplace communicative experiences to inspection. But the rudeness we acknowledge is not in the sense of our being arrogant or malicious. Rather, in the very act of taking pleasure from the examination of ordinary communicative phenomena, we are "rude" because we are making the communicative phenomena vulnerable to further discussion and damage.

But it is this spirit of good humor that defines the optimal way in which we hope you will read this book. It is for those of you whose minds are not bounded by the dictates of reason or convention, who retain both lucidness and a sense of playfulness, that this book is intended. Those who take this book, not as duty or doctrine, but as an invitation to join in mental play with the world will be able to share with us a few insights and a few moments of pleasure. And that is all the sincerity one can ask of any book, or of its readers.

Are you ready?

"Wait a minute! Not yet! My head is spinning. Let my mind put its feet up for just a second. Thanks to you I may become the most thoughtful, careful, and good-humored reader to be seen in these parts for some time, but . . . time out, OK?"

Seems fair to us. How about an instant replay?

This book is a set of exercises in thinking critically about the experience of human communication. We see the first exercise, which you have just completed, as a crucial conditioning exercise. First, it is designed to initiate your thinking about the communication that is taking place between us as authors and you as reader. If you do not think critically about the communication that is taking place between us, you will literally be un-fit for the rest of the book. As we proceed we will rely on your own reflexes to stop and reflect on what we say. We hope you will do this often. We will not always script dialogue between us or qualify everything we say or remind you where every alternative exists. It is important that you let this book stimulate your own thinking, not that you let it do all your own thinking for you.

At the same time, this exercise is designed to condition you to the assumptions that underlie our particular perspective. *Everything* in the chapters that follow is based on the assumption that man is at his best when he is thoughtful (reflective, receptive, and responsible), careful (accepting and appreciative) and touched by good humor (willing to seek out and derive pleasure from the incongruous): *Our purpose* in writing this book is based on the belief that people ought to be thoughtful, careful, and good-humored about the communication that surrounds them; *our manner* of writing the book is designed to stimulate these potentials in our readers; *our judgments,* consequently, tend to be more favorably inclined toward perspectives on communication that tolerate these potentials and communicative experiences that engage them.

In the next chapter we will describe and examine a perspective that we think accommodates our biases. And in the chapters that follow we will focus our analysis on the experience of specific communication events.

2

The Game-Play Perspective on Human Communication

The following is a transcript of an actual conversation. Can you make sense of what sort of communication is occurring?

E: "Batman."

A: "OK."

E: "I know what; that's Penguin!"

M: "No. I could be Space Ghost."

A: "Yeah."

E: "I'd like to be Batman."

M: "Uh-huh. And you could be Bomber Lady."

A: "OK, and I could bomb. Don't do that. You shouldn't hit girls."

E: "I turned off your button."

A: "Well, don't hit girls."

This is plainly not ordinary locker room camaraderie, but neither is it sheer gibberish. What is it? Don't worry about it; just sit back and we will explain it all in due time.

We propose that in order to understand any instance of communication, one needs to take what appears at first to be idle chatter and to bring it into focus, much as a photographer adjusts his camera lens to bring a particular field of vision into focus. In this chapter our effort will be to do just that: to select and describe a particular lens and to use it to clarify the communication between "A," "E," and "M." In the process of offering one way to bring this conversation into focus, we hope, simultaneously, to illustrate how our perspective can lend insight into the entire field of human communicative activities, while remaining true to the parameters of thoughtfulness, carefulness, and good humor that we have set forth for ourselves.

Essentially our perspective is one that views communication as a sort of game-play. That is, for us, two particular features are common to all instances of human communication. First, every human encounter involving communication displays a structure that is comparable to the structure of a *game*. As we shall shortly explain, communicative events, like games, are rule-governed rather than law-governed experiences. It is this feature that makes awareness and responsible choice so central in communication. Secondly, our emphasis on the *play* features of communication is meant to remind us of the "actorish" quality displayed by communicative participants who seem universally to relate to one another primarily by enacting, with varying degrees of skill and sophistication, a repertoire of roles. Combining these two general observations gives us a fundamental proposition: We can understand the dynamic character of communicative events such as the one among "A," "E," and "M" if we view them as dramatic plays (and replays) of game-like enactments.

THE GAME PERSPECTIVE

We shall begin to explain our perspective in more detail by considering the game dimension. In order to do so, let us clarify exactly the senses of the term *game* that concern us and acknowledge those that do not. We do this because we are using "game" in a rather specialized sense. First, when we invoke a game image, we do not mean to suggest that all communication is frivolous, trivial, or unimportant. Many communication games are serious indeed, with serious outcomes. Of course, some communication games *are* trivial, but our game-play approach should not be taken to suggest that nothing in this world is worth taking seriously. Secondly, when we invoke a game image, we do not mean to refer only to those activities that are essentially competitive battles: Although some games are in fact of the I-win-you-lose variety, we do not propose to limit our consideration to this game category. Finally, our game analogy is not intended to suggest that human communication is an essentially hypocritical activity or that it is simply a reflection of the human capacity to be deceitful. Once again, while some games do fit in this category (and have been studied with notable sensitivity by psychologists such as Eric Berne) we do not wish to restrict our study to such a limited range of examples.

In our choice of game as a metaphor for human communication, we use the game image in its widest sense. Our claim is that in their capacity as games, communicative interactions are social activities that enable us to structure time creatively. By this we mean, first, that communication games serve to *structure* social interaction. Games, for example, are to human communication in general as grammar is to language. Much as words become meaningful within the system provided by grammar, games provide a socially agreed upon system within which communicative behavior becomes meaningful for all participants.[1] For example, just as the presence of "-ed" at the end of an English verb is meaningful when one knows that "-ed" changes the time reference of the verb, the presence of "Good bye" in a brief telephone conversation is meaningful when one knows that it means that the other person is now through talking.

By our choice of a game metaphor we also mean that to engage in communication is *to create* a work of art, an enactment, a performance. We are not suggesting that communication "players" (or "actors") enter into a transaction merely (or even consciously) to create a work of art. Rather, our concern is that participants in communication play *against* each other (generating the internal tension of the game) even as they implicitly conspire *with* each other, joining forces to overcome the limitations on their action imposed by the rules. It is this covert cooperation to master the game that causes the game to disappear in the process of play and to be replaced by a new game in a continual round of renewal and re-creation.[2]

In short, the analogy of communication as game facilitates insight into two important features of human life: (1) the structural aspects of encounters that humans enjoy in common with their fellows and (2) the

---

[1] J. L. Aranguren, *Human Communication*, trans. F. Partridge (1967; New York: McGraw-Hill, 1970), pp. 19–69.

[2] See Pierre Berloquin, *Livre Des Jeux* (Stockholm: 1970); and Jean-Reve Vernes, "The Element of Time in Competitive Games," *Diogenes* 50(Summer 1965): 25–42.

aesthetic sense in which every encounter (game, communication transaction, or otherwise) is a communal creation of a meaningful social work of art.

Having indicated generally how we intend the game metaphor to apply to communication, let us examine in more detail what exactly comprises a game as we ordinarily use the term and then explore how different forms of communication resemble different forms of games. Let us start with the excerpt with which we began this chapter—those seemingly incoherent and disconnected utterances among A, E, and M. The reason these utterances may confuse you is that they appear in isolation; they are not yet placed in a meaningful ground. From our perspective, since you do not know what communication game A, E, and M are fashioning for themselves, you cannot "make sense" of their raw words. To bring the words into focus as meaningful communication, reflect if you will on a related situation. Suppose that you were assigned to assist a visitor from another planet who had landed on a college campus one fall day and by chance the two of you came upon a large stadium filled with people. What might you say to help him comprehend the strange behavior he was observing? If you felt compelled to enlighten the visitor, where would you start? You might begin by naming the activity, telling the visitor that he was watching something called *football*. But your naming the activity would be of little more help than our telling you that A, E, and M are playing "a communication game"; attaching labels to behaviors does not of itself explain the behaviors. Not only does such labeling fail to distinguish between games and non-games (football from farming, for example), but it implies that that precious moment when a dog runs out onto the field is also part of the game. Indeed, if an understanding of the activity is limited to knowing the name of the game, the extraterrestrial visitor is in no better position to recognize that eating a hot dog at half time is not part of the game than you are as yet able to recognize possible deviant or unrelated elements in our verbal transcript.

A related explanatory approach might be to go beyond a label and define the activity in terms of its observable attributes. You might, using this approach with the football situation, point out to the spaceman the distinctive dress of the players or draw attention to such aspects as the field and yard markers. But these strategies for definition will get you nowhere, for there are sandlot games that are played without uniforms or well-marked boundaries and, for that matter, even without footballs. Similarly, in the case of the excerpt from A, E, and M, if we were to rely on a sheerly empirical explanation we would risk highlighting accidental characteristics at the expense of underplaying more essential elements.

Telling you that the transcript is typical of how A, E, and M communicate when they are together is not sufficiently meaningful; like the space visitor you are still lacking concepts that will help you to understand what you witness. At this point, we propose that one way to help a witness to such understanding would be to call attention to and to distinguish among three features of all games, be they football or communication: *rules, tactics,* and *customs.*

Rules

The rules of the game may be thought of as the formal apparatus that defines any game institution and distinguishes it from other games, as well as from other social activities. In other words, the rules of football distinguish it from such other games as basketball, track, and fencing and from such other social activities as warfare and eating lunch together. Rules serve two important functions: (1) they bring the game into existence, they *constitute* the game, and (2) they *regulate* behavior appropriate to the game.

Rules Are Regulative.   We ordinarily think of rules in their regulative capacity. In this capacity, rules impose limits on the range of permissible behavior and specify penalties for violations. Thus, the rules of football limit each team on the field to eleven players; should one team in the course of play violate the boundary condition by permitting an extra man on the field, we expect the referee to enforce the rules by invoking the appropriate penalty upon whichever team exceeded its limit.

Rules Are Constitutive.   In addition to establishing limits censorfashion, rules are also (and more importantly) constitutive; they define the game that they regulate; they bring the game into existence. The rules of football are a case in point. Consider these basic rules of football:

1. The playing field is 100 yards long (marked off in 1-yard increments) and 40 yards wide.
2. Eleven men who are presumed to share a common purpose of winning (a team) can score points by crossing the opposing team's goal line with the ball or by kicking the ball through the goalposts.
3. The team in possession of the ball is given four opportunities ("downs") to try to advance ten or more yards. If they are successful, they are rewarded with four additional tries; if they

fail, they must surrender possession of the ball to the opposing team.

4. The game is limited to four 15-minute periods, at the end of which the team with more points is declared the winner. If there is a tie score, neither team wins.

These rules, together with many others, are the sum total of the institution we know as "the game of football." The rules themselves create the abstract social institution we recognize as the game. This is what we mean when we say that rules constitute particular games and set them apart from other games. So our A, E, M excerpt begins to make some slight sense when we suggest that one meaning implicit in A's remarks is a cry of "Foul" to an umpire; A charges that a rule violation has occurred. Were this rule not implicit in the conversation, A's remarks would be senseless. The rules define the context within which the communicative behavior becomes meaningful for the participants and for witnesses.

Rules Are Arbitrary. Game rules possess several qualities that facilitate their function of defining social institutions. One such quality is that they are *arbitrary* rather than natural; that is, there is a clear distinction between rules and laws. Why, for example, must a football game consist of four equal periods of play? Isn't it intuitively obvious that we might just as well have eight periods and still play roughly the same game? Indeed, the genius of sandlot games is their recognition of this arbitrariness. Subject to mutual agreement by both teams, we can imagine such variations as nine men per team, three downs to a series, and so on. This is not to say that rules are capricious, but only that no logically necessary condition emanating from outside the game makes a rule what it is and not otherwise. Consider, in contrast, how the farmer's axiom "Sow in spring, reap in the fall" is rooted in the laws of nature: It must be as it is. Farmers do not have the option of changing the laws of nature by common consent.[3] A farmers' co-op cannot get together and decide

---

[3] The distinction drawn here between rule and law is in one respect traditional: It is based on the ancient Greek sophists' contrast between the realm of natural events (*physis*) and human affairs (*nomos*) that are by their very nature temporary, dependent upon common agreement, and so upon responsible choice. Physical laws are, after all, merciless arbiters of affairs; we would no more expect a planet to reverse its orbit (and so violate a heavenly law) than we would think of indicting Mrs. O'Leary's cow for arson. One does not choose to follow or ignore a natural law, so when something happens that is contrary to the law, we correct the law, we do not punish the deviant behavior. Deviance from a natural law is simply unthinkable, and, insofar as man is a creature of this physical universe, he is no more responsible for his motion than is a planet. But in the realm of human affairs we often use the phrase "as a rule . . ." suggesting that man retains the option of disobeying the rule without in any way altering the rule. When the planet alters course we presume we wrongly

arbitrarily to reverse the precept—to sow in the fall and to reap in the spring—without taking a financial loss or without planting certain winter-hardy seeds. Farmers, in other words, do not have any choice in the matter; they merely recognize a biological law of plant growth. But game-players *do* have a choice and the game-player who cheats at least acknowledges in his deviation a prior claim on him to uphold behavior that conforms to the rules.[4] A football team so intent upon winning that it wheels an army tank onto the field and murders all its opponents might, thereby, cross the goal line, but in the process the football game will have dissolved as an activity. Because rules are arbitrary, when they are not followed, the distinct activity that they were used to define disappears.

Rules Usually Remain Constant. A second and related feature of rules that underlies their game-defining function is that although they are arbitrary and thus subject to modification, they usually *remain constant* for the duration of any given play of the game and enable the participants to share the activity on mutually acceptable terms. Imagine the confusion if during the course of a football game one team learned that the opponents had suddenly adopted a private set of rules allowing them (and only them) to wear brass knuckles. Undoubtedly the first team would insist (if they did not demand a victory by forfeit) that play be resumed only under the universally recognized rules of the game. Strictly speaking, they could argue that with the employment of brass knuckles (or tanks) a football game was no longer in progress, but some newly invented sport that only accidentally resembled football.

As we recall the A, E, and M excerpt, something of this nature may perhaps be occurring there as well. One rule that A, E, and M appear to share in their conversation game is each player's right to assume a character ("I could be Space Ghost," "I'd like to be Batman," "And you could be Bomber Lady"—"OK"). Another rule that seems to remain constant is each character's right to choose appropriate conduct ("And I could bomb," "I turned off your button"). Maybe A's claim "Don't do that. You shouldn't hit girls" is an attempt to change the rules of the game by giving one player the right to make choices of conduct for another. Strictly speaking, E and M could argue that with A's interrup-

---

understood the law; when the man violates the game rule, we hold him responsible. The most recent statement on this crucial distinction has been made by Stephen Toulmin, "Concepts and the Explanation of Human Behavior," in T. Mischel, ed., *Human Action* (New York: Academic Press, 1969), pp. 71–104. See also E. L. Hunt, "Plato and Aristotle on Rhetoric and Rhetoricians," in R. F. Howes, ed., *Historical Studies of Rhetoric and Rhetoricians* (Ithaca: Cornell University Press, 1961), p. 24.

[4] Toulmin, "Concepts . . . ," p. 87.

tion their original game is no longer in progress, that some new activity is now occurring that only accidentally resembles their first game. But since E seems to be ignoring A's comment, covertly denying the existence of such a rule for their particular game, regular play resumes and A reluctantly surrenders—but not without pointing out, in effect, that "it would have been a good rule."

Rules Are Seldom Exhaustive. A third game-defining characteristic of rules is that (with rare exceptions such as chess) the network of constitutive rules is *seldom exhaustive.* There is probably no rule in football expressly prohibiting the use of a tank by one team, though we presume that should one be brought onto the field the referees would have the good sense to interpret an established rule (contorting it if necessary) to exclude the tank from the rest of the game. Similarly, there is no football rule expressly prohibiting a player from swimming with the ball, since we assume that the game is to be played on dry land. Hence game rules are seldom precise regarding every conceivable behavior, yet they are usually flexible enough to be applied to situations for which they were not expressly written. How precise, for example, are the rules for A, E, and M's conversation? Do you know all their limits for acceptable behavior? Could it be that A, E, and M have just arrived at a costume party, and E has wrenched A's coat off in particularly violent fashion? Or could it be that A, E, and M perhaps are three actors walking along the street, and E has just poked a passing matron? Whatever the character of their specific communication game, because rule networks are seldom complete, as witnesses we can employ a range of possible rules to gain a better understanding of the possible import of A, E, and M's remarks. Furthermore, it is probably because rules tend not to be precise, because they allow freedom, that A, E, and M chose to play the game in the first place. Activities whose rules are too exhaustive tend to demand obedience rather than improvisation; engaging in them is more work than play.[5]

Rules Are Ordinarily Not the Center of Attention. This open-ended quality suggests a final rule attribute: Rules and their enforcement are ordinarily *not the center of attention* for either players or spectators. During the course of play the rules are known tacitly but seldom reflected upon; they remain implicit in the action and peripheral to it. Usually only in the face of a challenge (as when the officials fail to notice a rule violation) or when an event occurs whose status is in doubt ("You shouldn't hit girls") will players become conscious that the disregard for rule limits threatens the play of the game. Usually only then will players appeal to official arbiters ("Isn't hitting allowed when one turns another's button?"). Nor are spectators commonly preoccupied with rules or their administrators. If they were, we might reasonably expect more fan clubs devoted to following particularly adept referees and umpires.

Rules, then, both *constitute* and *regulate* the game and the behavior appropriate to it. In their constitutive capacity they

1. Are arbitrary rather than natural (and so demand responsible choice by participants to obey them);
2. Usually remain constant for the duration of any transaction and therefore enable the participants to share the activity;

---

[5] For a most insightful discussion of the distinctions between the experience of work and the experience of games, see Kurt Riezler, "Play and Seriousness," *The Journal of Philosophy* 38 (September 1941): 505–517.

3. Form somewhat loose networks that define the range of acceptable activity; and
4. Are merely the formal preconditions of a game (the game's focus of attention is the activity occurring within the limits).

Tactics

Having told the interplanetary visitor about the rules of football, you really have not told him much about what is actually happening on the field, have you? A rule book defines a game, but is it a game by itself? In other words, if someone says "what's it like to play the game of golf?" is it enough to hand him the rules for a particular golf course? Obviously, the answer to each of these questions is "No." The ability to recognize and appreciate rules is insufficient to best understand the game experience.

The second concept that would help the visitor from another planet (or any spectator, for that matter) to distinguish a football game from other activities is that of a *tactic*. Tactics are optional actions that occur within the space created by the rule network and that are directed toward deciding the outcome of the game. In order to grasp the significance of tactics, however, our visitor would also need to have at least an instinctive sense of what we will call the *teleological process*.

Teleology of a Game.   The *teleology* of a game is the logic that responds to the question "To what end is the game played?" This is the case because two elements converge in the logic of a game. On the one hand, individual games contain devices that enable them to resolve in some fashion; games have ends. Natural events like soil erosion may go on unceasingly, but a game always has a built-in mechanism that enables human action to cease.[6] Thus, sporting events are often automatically concluded after an arbitrary time (as in football) or when one side has scored a prescribed number of points (as in Ping-Pong) or after each side has completed at least the prescribed number of encounters (innings, rounds) and one side is ahead.

The second element giving a teleological cast to games is the fact that the rules create a bounded region within which room exists for many acceptable behaviors; but among these acceptable options there are some

---

[6] W. B. Gallie, *Philosophy and the Historical Understanding* (New York: Schocken Books, 1968), pp. 37–39, provides a similar account to explain the human capacity to follow a story. See also M. Csikszentmihalyi, "Play and Intrinsic Rewards," *Journal of Humanistic Psychology* 15 (Summer 1975): 41–64.

that are preferred because they seem more likely to resolve the game on its own terms. The aim in football, for example, is to demonstrate superiority over the opposition by scoring more points, and each team chooses from among its available options those actions that it is esti- mated will maximize the likelihood of accomplishing that end.[7] It is in this sense, then, that we view tactics as choices among optional permis- sible moves that at once conform to the rules and the teleology (the telos logic) of the game; the participants are all striving to resolve the play of the game in the "best" (most appropriate) possible manner.

Notice that teleology is not the same as motive ("What need is satisfied in players by their participation in the game?") or goal direct- edness ("What reward is attendant upon the outcome of a game?"). Rather, "to what end" is a matter of the logic that encourages the events themselves to unfold. It should thus be intuitively obvious that in the conversation with A, E, and M, the telos is not the same as in a boxing match where "He hit me" is never a cause for complaint, because the telos of boxing entails rules where hitting is encouraged if not required. To ask about motives in a boxing match is to ask about the boxers' personal desire to win; to ask about goals is to inquire into means and outcomes (a knockout), again in personal terms. But "what end does boxing itself serve?" (answer: to assess relative physical strength in combat) is intrinsic to the activity itself rather than the psychological makeup of the participants or the immediate payoff they seek.[8]

Perhaps the teleological character of tactical choice can be clarified with a number of illustrations. Let us begin with a tactical aberration. Imagine this non-tactical behavior (which is nevertheless within the rules) in a football game: One lineman executes a handstand prior to every downfield block he throws. No rule prohibits this, but it is some- what unusual. The coach calls the player to the sidelines and asks why he behaves so. What would constitute an acceptable response from the lineman? Wouldn't his answer be most appropriate if he could show that

---

[7] It is in this sense that "responsible choice" from among the total ground of available options takes on an added dimension. We presume, for example, that a political candidate for office will actually accept the telos of a campaign—seeking to render a public verdict in his own favor. It may happen that a candidate runs for office in order to satisfy some darker personal motive but deliberately engineers his own defeat. Although permissible, such a denial of the campaign's telos is as destructive to the institution of political campaigns as is a rigged boxing match to the institution of boxing.

[8] In this focus on the end intrinsic to a particular game our treatment of games is clearly at odds with Berne, who concentrates on analysis of personal payoffs. We are not concerned so much with the question "why is it that certain people play the games that they do?" as we are with the question "what logically happens to people who play certain games?" or "What is it in a game itself that affects the players who choose to play that game?"

his odd conduct in some manner helped him to throw a better block or similarly to contribute to the team's overall effort? Would it be acceptable for him to explain that he got a joyous sensation whenever he exhibited his dexterity to the fans? Indeed, such an explanation might account for his personal payoff, but we expect the player to justify his play with the criterion already mentioned: helping to realize the game's telos. The "best" tactics are those chosen by the players to accomplish the end of the game, not those chosen to satisfy some end extrinsic to the game.

In these terms we can now bring the seemingly incoherent excerpt of communication with which we began this chapter into much clearer focus for the *sequence* of remarks itself takes on a meaning apart from the individual verbal choices A, E, and M made. It becomes apparent, for example, that we are most likely witnessing three young children rehearsing adult-mythic roles (pretending to be Batman et al.) in much the manner of youngsters trying on old costumes in an attic. When A interrupts this verbal rehearsal with "Don't do that . . ." A is abandoning the rehearsal telos for a different game, one whose telos is the proper behavior between boys and girls. Of course, it is also possible to assume that A, E, and M are attending a sado-masochistic party; but if that were the case, then the telos of the activity would call for remarks on hitting to be uttered with more pride and with less debate concerning the legitimacy (within the rule-created region) of the tactical action. So for the sake of clarity, let us presume that the child-rehearsal telos evident in the transcript is an accurate focus.

Teleological and Personal Standards of Tactical Choice.   Notice in these two examples, the football handstand and the conversation among A, E, and M, that even within games defined by a rather loose network of rules, there seem to exist fairly clear telos-based standards of tactical appropriateness that we can use to distinguish between rule violations and tactically queer behavior. Deliberate rule violations that we call *cheating* or *foul play* evoke our wrath. "You shouldn't hit girls" is a claim of a rule violation in A's Boy/Girl game. Non-teleological actions— "pseudo-tactics" if you will—we can only dismiss as foolish or inept: They evoke our contempt. The handstand appears to make no sense in the football game just as the claim "You shouldn't hit girls" appears to make no sense in a game that involves rehearsal of roles such as Batman, Space Ghost, and Bomber Lady. (Only when we allow for a change of game and a subsequent change of telos, does "You shouldn't hit girls" begin to make sense as a communicative tactic and not a tactical oddity;

only when the lineman can explain the appropriateness of his handstand to football or to the telos of another game, do we stop dismissing his behavior as foolish.)

This *teleological quality of tactical choice* (we select among the available options those actions that are most appropriate to resolving the game in a fitting manner) lends further insight into why people play games at all. For in addition to being options defined by the bounded region created by the rules (and so injecting the element of choice into the game), it is important to understand that the region thus created has a *moral* dimension, that is, the telos of each game implies how the options *ought* to be selected so as to resolve the game properly—and so the element of responsibility enters in. It is plain, for example, that the same sort of qualities sought in a boxer (such as brute physical strength) will not necessarily be admired in other games such as chess (where physical strength is irrelevant) or tennis (where disciplined energy is preferable to mere physical power). Clearly, the standards for determining winners in various games (i.e., for terminating games by assessing which player or team is "better," which is a moral valuation), depend upon the game's telos.

This may help us to understand why some people are devoted to particular games, while others are completely indifferent to those activities. Some, for instance, are avid followers of football and hockey, mildly interested in horse races and tennis, but uninterested in golf or bridge. Others might like to swim and ski but find checkers boring and wrestling revolting.[9] The telos of a game, in other words, represents a symbolic moral universe, and an individual chooses to enjoy those games that more or less correspond to his vision of how social and natural dynamics control his life.[10] Every game, with its structural hierarchies and focus on the here-and-now in which choices must be made in accord with implicit moral values, represents a limited moral

[9] It is of course possible to claim that we come to enjoy the games we played earlier in life ("We were conditioned") or that we were once adept at ("We were reinforced"). However, such psychological perspectives really focus on the individual's history rather than his present state of mind, and so would seem to side-step the issue of either the individual's responsibility for his choices or the reality of the player's here-and-now *presence* in the game.

[10] According to Eric Berne, children's fairy tales serve the purpose of initially implanting a taste for these particular moral domains and tactical hierarchies—Berne calls them scripts—early in the child's life. We would again stress that it is just this concern for the individual's historical development that distinguishes Berne's Freudian-Behavioral analysis from our own concern for the topology of human communication in the here-and-now. See his *What Do You Say After You Say Hello?* (New York: Grove Press, 1972), pp. 203–242.

universe within which the players act out various types of ethical conduct according to each game's standards of justice (telos).

The *question of individual morality* is thus implicit in all games, since each player must adjust his or her game behavior to accommodate two contrary impulses: (1) striving to win in the game while (2) striving to maintain the integrity of the game. That is, every game-player likes to win, sometimes even at the cost of cheating. But to cheat is to defy the rules of the game and therefore to threaten the viability of the game itself. Since such "victory" is meaningless if the game has been abused, every individual has a stake in maintaining the game's standards.

Let us illustrate the moral dimension implicit in a game's telos in a number of instances by returning again in this moral sense to the overriding tactical question: "to what end?" in order to see how games (whether athletic or communicative) each display a certain unique character.

Boxing. The outstanding features that distinguish boxing from other contact sports like football are that it is a one-to-one personal encounter and that the contact is intentionally direct and brutal. Thus, a sparring match in which the participants merely touch one another does not truly symbolize the telos of the sport. Boxing therefore is a game that incorporates in its moral system a direct personal physical rivalry designed to assess superiority on the basis of physical strength employed aggressively against the person of another.

The universe symbolized in a boxing match is one in which the strongest and most pugnacious triumph. The moral axis of such a universe is the aggressive expenditure of brute physical force. Hence, anyone who relishes boxing to the exclusion of all other sports more likely than not accepts with little qualification the moral precepts inherent in the game's logic, namely, that direct physical competition and determination of superiority on the basis of physical strength are good things. He or she probably also approaches his or her own daily affairs with the attitude that social interaction is basically hostile, that the world contains considerable brutality, that only those who fight for what they want can survive, that aggression has a proper place in human affairs, that a person can trust only him- or herself. One's gratification with boxing tactics comes from the appreciation of the boxer acting in accord with the injunctions of such a morality.

Crew. Contrast the moral rehearsal for life that boxing's telos affords with the kind of character needed to excel in or appreciate the sport of competitive rowing. Here is how a renowned rowing coach once described the ideal crew:

It is the systematic men who are of the most service in a boat, as everywhere else. There are some students who are without a balance wheel. They will come rushing into the boathouse and throw their coats one way and their hats another. For these men I have no patience. The man who comes to the boathouse the exact minute he has promised to be there, who hangs up his clothes methodically, dons his rowing costume and goes out into the boat quietly and without any "hurrah" about it, is pretty sure to be the man who will do the hardest work in a race, and who can be depended upon not to go to pieces in a pinch. If you get one disturbing element in a boat, one man who is a growler or a grumbler, you will always have trouble to make that crew row well. [11]

From the foregoing, what characteristic moral domain could we say inheres in this sport? Cooperation, methodicalness, self-effacement, steadiness, punctuality: Crew rehearses the dedicated company person. To take pleasure from terminating a rowing contest in an appropriate way (with a win, achieved within the rules) one must value these sorts of character traits more than those we have suggested as necessary for a sport such as boxing.

Chess. Like boxing, chess also involves a person-to-person rivalry; but it is clear that chess is not a competition of physical strength. Instead, it values intellectual skills, and success in the game presumably depends on superior mental powers: reasoning ability, spatial visualization, calculation, etc. Oddly enough we might conclude that chess and boxing are in at least one dimension related: Chess is popular with would-be intellectual bullies rather than the standard variety of physical bully.

Bridge. If we were to lump bridge into the category of intellectual competition with chess we would immediately notice one significant difference: Besides intellectual ability, bridge also requires a certain amount of social cooperation. [12] This need for social cooperation is of

---

[11] C. E. Courtney, cited in W. T. Hewett, *Cornell University: A History* (New York: 1905), III, p. 203.

[12] Note also that inclusion of cards in games is a significant feature representing "limited opportunity": you are dealt a hand, and it is up to you (or your partner) to make the most of it. Note here (as in the case of games that employ a ball as a prop) the resemblance to Horatio Alger's myth of success: Life deals you a situation of handicap or opportunity; it is up to you to exploit the (limited) opportunities. Sometimes you are dealt a bum hand, sometimes the resources for a grand slam. Your character is shaped by your readiness to seize the opportunity. In much the same way, Horatio Alger's nineteenth-century novels typically feature a poor but ambitious young man—Tom the bootblack, for example—who gets a minor lucky break (like receiving a five-dollar tip from a prodigal) and who by shrewd investment (he buys a white shirt and applies for a job as a bank teller) and great industry parlays his initial capital into a small fortune.

course an important factor in the moral factor of many games. It is one of the main things that distinguishes boxing from football, for example. In football, it is not enough for a lineman to be a behemoth; he must discipline his strength and channel it into carrying out his assignment for the good of the team rather than simply in an effort to floor the opposing lineman.

Poker. Another illustration of the moral dimension prominent in the telos of games is offered by poker. The inherent talent necessary for poker is neither physical strength nor team cooperation nor even, to a very great extent, intellectual capacity. Most poker aficionados are proudest of those games in which they pulled off a monumental bluff. What counts here (beyond the ability to calculate the odds of holding various hands and managing one's betting accordingly as a symbol of confidence in one's calculations) is slick nonchalance and skill in misleading one's opponents. The poker fan likely acts in his strategy on the moral premise that the outward appearance of things ought not always to be what the things really are, that one succeeds in the world by being crafty and seductive rather than brazen, that deception and cool predatory behavior are valuable assets in social affairs.

We have attempted here to illustrate the moral dimension that makes the telos, and hence the selection of appropriate tactics, within various games understandable. Our effort has been primarily to clarify the notions of telos and tactic, so we have offered only a limited set of illustrations. But we mean to contend that this moral quality is inherent in all games. The games people play reflect symbolically the kinds of dynamic conflicts that are perceived between man and man, between man and nature, and between man and himself,[13] and that thus call for normative criteria if man is to make the choices necessary to confront these conflicts. In the interests of brevity let us merely assert that this moral dimension is inherent in all games (whether competitive or noncompetitive). As we progress we shall find it helpful to search out this moral factor of telos as we explore the communication games we are studying.

Summarizing the attributes of tactics, we have observed the following:

---

[13] Hence it is that one "game" that neither adults nor children play (unless they are psychopaths or autistic) is "rocks." No one plays at being a rock, standing frozen in a corner for hours on end. This fact confirms the moral quality inherent in games. The games people choose to play reflect symbolically the kinds of *dramatic conflicts* that they perceive. Games satisfy the intuitive urge to play out, in symbolic form, visions of the forces that surround us. See Jacques Ehrmann, ed., *Game, Play, Literature* (Boston: Beacon Press, 1971).

1. Tactics are those rule-bound choices open to the players.
2. Players, who as participants are committed to realizing the end(s) implicit in the game, will select tactics that in their judgment will appropriately achieve the end (telos). Not all options are equally preferable; the criterion of appropriateness is the telos implicit in the game.
3. The standards of value used to make responsible, tactical choices will invariably reflect a particular normative dimension, a commitment to the inherent worth of some human actions over others; this normative dimension will correspond to the moral outlook of those who play, appreciate, or follow the game, since it will incorporate their understanding of what constitutes a reasonable basis for action in the rule-governed world of men. Comprehending tactics in games thus represents a moral rehearsal for responsible choice in all realms involving human action.

Customs

Once he has come to understand the framework of game rules and the teleological hierarchy of tactical actions, our interplanetary visitor will still be puzzled by a residue of attendant behavior patterns that are peripheral to the essence of the football game. We call these residual behaviors *customs*. Think of the cheerleaders; they are certainly not required by the rules, nor do most people seriously contend that they are a necessary component of the team's effort to resolve the contest (although we may excuse their presence with the polite fiction that cheering encourages the team). Much the same is true of the selection of roles by A, E, and M. The effort by E, having opted for the role of Batman, to encourage one of the other participants to play Penguin (a stock villain) may be a tactical necessity if the super hero is to have a fitting opponent. A's choice of the role of "Bomber Lady" might be a similar tactic—perhaps to give Batman double trouble. If, however, we tell you that A is a female, you might see A's choice of "Bomber Lady" as related less to how the game will be played out than to A's effort to adopt a customary role (she chooses a female role because she is a female). Game-players, as we shall shortly see, readily accept a number of constraints on the range of their behavior, not because of any rule limitations, or because of the teleological end sought by the game, but simply because they have become habituated to such behaviors. In other words, over a period of time some game behavior assumes the status of convention; that is, it is automatically presumed that A (who is female) will choose a female role in the game and that there will be volunteers to lead cheers at football games.

Two features distinguish what we are calling customs[14] from what we have specified as rules and tactics.

Customs and Tradition.   First, whereas tactics are teleological (active choices made in terms of a scale of values concerning outcome), customs are justified solely by tradition.[15] Whatever its origin (and some customs may in the dim past have been originally adopted because they had tactical value) a custom is, in the here-and-now context of the game, a fossilized behavior pattern, a habit.[16] Whatever teleological vitality it may once have had is now gone. A custom is not selected deliberately. If any thought is given to it at all, a custom gains its authority from precedent because such behavior is "expected." We would feel awkward at a football game without flags, bands, sideline activity, and team huddles because our expectations would not be met. Yet we could dispense with such customary behavior and still play fooball; the logic of the game itself would not be infringed. But we have been rehearsed through previous experience to remember and thus anticipate these nonessential features (this conventional fabric) and it is in some psychological sense reassuring. When we rely on custom we turn away from the moment before us and compare it to previous similar moments we have known.

Customs and Comfort.   The comfort afforded by custom is its second distinguishing trait. Whereas rule violations if allowed to pass without penalty threaten the very existence of the game and so evoke our outrage, and whereas tactical errors betray a lack of appreciation for teleological significance and so evoke our contempt, violations of custom produce an almost irrational sense of being offended, literally a disorientation. When a custom is ignored, we feel similar to when any long-established habit is suddenly broken—we miss the security of conven-

---

[14] We wish to caution that we are not using the term *custom* in its colloquial sense. That is, when some people use the term, their reference is, in actuality, to what we would label a *rule*—a constitutive and regulating sanction that when violated results in a penalty.

[15] J. Ladd, "Custom," *Encyclopedia of Philosophy*, Vol. II, pp. 278–280; D. K. Lewis, *Convention: A Philosophical Study* (Boston: Harvard University Press, 1969), pp. 36–83.

[16] For example, it makes tactical sense to separate teams on the playing field by assigning them differently colored uniforms to wear. There is no logical necessity, however, that one team wear red uniforms and another blue, or one green and another gold. This decision is based on tradition ("we are the Golden Gophers," or "the Crimson Tide") not teleological potency.

tion, of being able to anticipate what will follow.[17] It is not the game but the participants and spectators themselves who feel abused.

To say that the fabric of customs that surrounds a game (like the fossils that comprise a coral reef) is based on habit and enacted without thought does not deny the significance of convention for the game's performance. We ought to appreciate how important such comfort is to our daily well-being. Consider, for example, the following illustration of a situation in which custom is stripped away: While you are shopping in a grocery store, a stranger approaches and begins to paw through your shopping cart, commenting on your apt choice of melons, asking you to justify your selection of certain brands, engaging you in familiar conversation about your eating habits and tonight's menu. How would you respond to this unconventional behavior? Most likely with shock and some fear that you were dealing with a madman? Now imagine you take the food home, set it on the kitchen table, and your kid brother begins to paw through the bag, commenting on your choice of melons, asking what you intend to cook for supper, asking you to justify your purchases. Who is crazy in this case? Is your brother's behavior unconventional or customary? Clearly, to say that customs comfort us is to say a lot; it is to say that we need more than logical conformity to allay our fear of the unknown.[18]

Indeed, in one respect the stable structure of suitable behaviors that custom offers makes tactical deviations more acceptable. Customs pro-

---

[17] Heidegger traces our distress in the face of violations of customs to the capacity of language itself, once congealed, to take on a kind of permanence even as it loses its meaningfulness:

A wide range of meaning belongs generally to the nature of every word. This fact, again, arises from the mystery of language. Language admits of two things: One, that it be reduced to a mere system of signs, uniformly available to everybody, and in this form be enforced as binding; and two, that language at one great moment says one unique thing, for one time only, which remains inexhaustible because it is always originary, and thus beyond the reach of any kind of leveling. These two possibilities of language are so far removed from each other that we should not be doing justice to their disparity even if we were to call them extreme opposites.

Customary speech vacillates between these two possible ways in which language speaks. It gets caught halfway. Mediocrity becomes the rule. Commonness, which looks much like custom, attaches itself to the rule. Common speech puffs itself up as the sole binding rule for everything we say—and now every word at variance with it immediately looks like an arbitrary violation.

M. Heidegger, *What Is Called Thinking?*, trans. J. Glenn Gray and Fred D. Wieck (New York: Harper & Row, 1972), pp. 191–192.

We shall return to these polarities when we consider the continuum of rapport and ritual communicative games. For now it is sufficient to note Heidegger's claim that as language becomes more habitual—we would say more customary—it becomes more rigid and less tolerant of variation.

[18] See Erving Goffman, "On Face-Work," *Psychiatry* 18(August 1955): 213–232.

vide the comfort and security of the familiar, while tactics offer the adventure of risk, novelty, and responsibility. As long as the rule network retains room for both, as long as the range of tactical options does not become subsumed under the controlled influence of convention, we can more readily experience the alertness and sense of being alive afforded by tactics. We will not be overwhelmed by the fear of too much opportunity for newness, just because there will also be room for the familiar. Thus the realm of the customary, the realm of behavior that is shaped by habit rather than the demands of the moment, is in one sense in a constant struggle with the reach of tactics, whose aim is to fulfill and resolve the logic of the here-and-now game without destroying the game itself.[19]

To the degree that we have explored our analogy properly, both you and our interplanetary tourist should now know what we mean by the concept "game" and, furthermore, you should begin to realize what we mean when we claim that the model of the game offers a helpful focus for understanding the activity of human communication. There are three facets of games that enable us to say that human communication is game-like:

1. Rules are the formal apparatus that distinguishes the game-play from surrounding activities (constitutive function) and that maintains its stability by the invocation of penalties as a means to control human action (regulative function).

2. Tactics are the strategic choices from among the range of rulebound options. These choices, insofar as they contribute to the proper resolution of the game (in accord with the telos implicit in the game's logic), will reflect the normative priorities that make the game attractive to its followers in the first place. (A person, for example, must appreciate the significance of chance in life's affairs in order to find the lottery appealing.)

3. Customs are habitual behaviors whose sanction in tradition will fill in the gap of acceptable actions between the full range allowed by the network of rules and the suitable priorities available in tactics. At the same time, tactics and customs will remain in a state of

---

[19] Marshall McLuhan has suggested that it is our tenacious clinging to the stability of custom that often gives us the illusion that we have a clear understanding of certain human activities, when in fact what we are experiencing is the assurance that comes from remaining distant from and untouched by those events. In Chapter 1, we, too, expressed our concern for such behavior which we labeled "careless thought." See M. McLuhan's book *The Medium Is the Message* (New York: Bantam Books, 1967).

tension, with tactics being constantly innovated in an effort to add vitality in the attempt to accomplish the game's telos while convention will always seek to enlarge its domain at the expense of the uncertainty that is the condition of tactical choice.

More specifically, how does this game model help us to understand communicative experience? The game perspective invites us to appreciate communication *as spectators* appreciate a sporting event, to focus carefully on the implicit structure of the events we witness. It asks us to seek out, to accept, and to enjoy what might be the constituting principles and the peculiar sanctions of a particular communicative interaction. Sensitivity to the notion of rule-governed tactics leads us to examine thoughtfully the participants' particular modes of conduct: to reflect on what the rules of the encounter permit the participants to say, to be receptive to what the participants actually do say, to evaluate the participants' choices within the morality of the encounter, and to assess the extent to which each participant appears to assume responsibility for his or her choices. The perspective also conditions us to watch for signs of habitual communication behavior, to prize such customs for the comfort that they offer, while simultaneously regretting that in their lack of inventiveness they fail to challenge human potential.

The game perspective, however, is by itself unable to provide us with sufficient insight into our own communicative experience *as participants.* Indeed, it does help us to appreciate the fact that in order to relate to each other as communicators: (1) we must learn to recognize and to internalize the rules of commonly understood social transactions, (2) we must continue to develop an expanding repertoire of communicative tactics, and (3) we must discover and adhere to those familiar communication behaviors that provide us and our associates with both comfort and security. But an understanding of the game structure alone does not enlighten our understanding of the moment-by-moment experience of creatively playing a game. Each time we play a game (when we enact a token-performance of the activity-class made up of rules, tactics, and customs), the game metaphor terminology is inadequate for describing the particular experience we have. Therefore, in order to recognize and appreciate the dynamics of communication, to view the phenomenon from within, as a game-player, we add to our game image the features of dramatistic play. It shall be our claim that the logical features of games combined with an understanding of the dynamic play of drama provide a fair notion of what the experience of human communication is all about.

THE PLAY PERSPECTIVE

If you were asked to describe what it is that constitutes a "play," how would you respond? If you are like most people, you would probably eventually construct an answer that included "actors" (people disguised as others), "scenes" (artificial situations in which the actors come together), and a "script" (the predetermined plan that guides the actors' interaction). There is nothing especially mystical about these individual features of a play. One does not need much assistance to recognize and appreciate them. What is special, however, is their combination in a particular dramatic event. That is, at any given moment during a performance, the actors, scene, and script blend together by design and yet simultaneously create a here-and-now experience that is unlike any in the past and that will never occur again. It is *this* sense of "drama," the experience of play within a framework yet the creation of a "real-life" experience that is unique to the moment, which we shall try to capture in our exploration of communication as "play."[20]

Let us begin by examining the relationship between communication and drama in more detail. In a play, the actors are assigned motivations and individual histories by the playwright and the drama is created when these "life spaces" merge or overlap. This merging can occur with varying degrees of formality. In some plays, such as Kabuki Theater, the actions and dialogue are extremely structured, stylized, well rehearsed, and memorized. In others, like the Renaissance dramas of the Italian *commedia dell'arte* players or the contemporary "happening," there are no scripts, no memorized lines or actions. The players are assigned only their formalized roles and a basic theme; their interaction is improvised at the moment of performance.

The same symbolic interaction that generates drama's internal coherence is found in human communication. Like characters on a stage, human beings have intentions, unique world views, and individual histories. In real-life performances, our internal selves generate roles; we portray characters. The communicative event occurs when the life space of our character overlaps the life space of another character and we share the experience of the moment by means of symbols.

---

[20] There is a deceptive similarity between the notion of "play" that we offer here and Kenneth Burke's popular "dramatistic" analysis of communication. Burke's thinking, however, draws heavily from Marx and Freud, influences that are far less prominent in the perspective we are proposing. See R. Ambrester, "Identification Within: Kenneth Burke's View of the Unconscious," *Philosophy & Rhetoric* 7(Fall 1974):205–216; D. Abbot, "Marxist Influences on the Rhetorical Theory of Kenneth Burke," ibid.:217–233.

At this point the analogy between drama and human interaction is most explicit. As we generate real-life roles, for example, our performances are salient to the plot of the moment. The overall stage directions have been standardized and rehearsed since childhood, but the dialogue is spontaneous. Much the same as jazz musicians, we improvise on a theme that is being played by the rest of the ensemble. We are like *commedia dell'arte* players who know the basic underlying themes, know what our parts are, and make up the script as we go along. The line between drama and "real life," therefore, is an extremely arbitrary one: A snip of real life put up on a stage becomes a drama that is being portrayed,[21] a snip of any drama being portrayed on stage has its own real life.

In developing the similarity between drama and communication, there are several contemporary views that we must, therefore, reject. The first originates with behavioral psychology and is based on the metaphor of man as rat. In this view, all human behavior is primarily determined by an incredibly complex array of environmental stimuli (food, sex, temperature, sound, and so on). Our ability to control these stimuli accounts for our ability to manipulate the behaviors of others ("condition it" is the usual professional phrase) just as we manipulate the behavior of rats that we condition to run mazes. An equally unacceptable metaphor is based on man as thermostat, a device that turns on the furnace when it registers "too cold" and turns off the furnace when it registers "just right." In this view, the human organism is pre-programmed to maintain a degree of internal and/or social consistency, a homeostatic balance, and this unconscious mechanism accounts for human behavior. The presence of pain, for example, is said to give immediate rise to pressures to reduce or eliminate that pain; the presence of familial disharmony is said to give immediate rise to pressures to reduce or eliminate that conflict. Yet another view sees man as a simple organic creature, like a plant, whose entire existence is devoted to a struggle to remain at one with the environment in order to be nurtured by the elements.

There are several deficiencies with these metaphors from our perspective. First, they leave no room in the organism for purposiveness, for imbalance, for action—except in the most trivial of senses. Second, they focus upon how forces beyond our control shape our every move. We do not contend that humans cannot be conditioned or that we cannot conceptualize an internal balance-type mechanism or that we cannot

---

[21] See Erving Goffman, *The Presentation of Self in Everyday Life* (Garden City: Doubleday Anchor Books, 1959), p. 72.

appreciate the desirability of being at peace with one's self in this world. Rather, we posit that these images of rat, thermostat, and plant do not capture the nature of man as actor—and that most essentially is what we are after.

How then do we propose that one ought to account for the act-ive mentality of a communicator? Since we contend that an individual's mind is not a blank area waiting to be filled in by signal transmission, nor is it a particular consciousness waiting either for a corrective signal or seeking satisfaction in the experience of internal psychic euphoria, we propose that individuals who engage one another in communication have minds that contain conscious images[22] and that the mosaic com-posed by these images both represents each individual's different life space and manifests itself in each individual's communicative perfor-mance. In these performances, each individual *presents* himself and each listener tries to interpret the presentation/performance of the other.[23] In the next few pages, we will discuss the five images that constitute an individual's internal image configuration, the momentary images each player brings to a performance. In so doing, we will suggest how these images affect both the individual's life space and the individual's com-municative play. We will then summarize how the perspective of com-munication as play brings the experience of a particular encounter into focus.

Scene-Image

The first image to consider is the image we have of the scene in which a communicative encounter occurs.[24] How A, E, and M picture the physi-cal situation that surrounds their conversation is influencing how they act and how they expect others to act. Their *scene-image* provides a context in which communication can be considered appropriate or inap-propriate, meaningful or incoherent.

We, too, know, for example, that the behavior expected of us in a large vacant warehouse is different than the behavior we would expect to

---

[22] For more on the significance of images of consciousness, see: R. R. Holt, "Imagery: The Return of the Ostracized," *American Psychologist,* 19(March 1964):254–264.

[23] An interesting discussion of this most complex notion is offered by T. Mader in "On Presence in Rhetoric," *College Composition and Communication* 24(December 1973):375–381.

[24] In Chapter 9 we will explore in more detail the communicative implications of private and public scenes.

display if we found ourselves in a doctor's waiting room. Our temptation in the warehouse is to shout or do something silly, to explore and try to fill the empty space with our presence. Alone in all that space we would want to explore it. In contrast, the situation provided by the waiting room calls for more refined behavior and more controlled communication. We are as suspicious of a quiet whisper in a corner of the warehouse as we are of an exhuberant shout whose presence fills the waiting room. Similarly, we all alter our grammatical patterns slightly and unconsciously in accordance with the formality we perceive in a situation. We tend to speak more "correctly" in formal scenes, saying *"for the desk"* for instance. But when we perceive ourselves to be in an informal situation, our enunciation is liable to become more casual, as in *"fur duh des'."* In other words, at any given moment we have an image of the performance area and this image focuses our communicative expectations and, to some extent, directs our communicative behavior.

Self-Image

Another salient image in a communicator's life space is the *self-image* that he or she has. The self-image is composed of beliefs and feelings that one experiences about his or her own personal characteristics. A, for example, may believe that she is overweight and clumsy and feel guilty about her self. On the other hand, E may have a mental picture of his self as plump and reckless and feel happy about his image. In either case, the particular image of self will influence the person's communicative performance. When A chooses to talk she may make disparaging remarks about her self (". . . and I could bomb") and E may never make any comments about his, or self references may be the only kind he chooses to make ("I'd like to be Batman"; "I turned off your button"). Although others may perceive A as attractive or E as obnoxious, at any given moment for A or E these perceptions are not as important as how A imagines her self or how E imagines his self. Each individual's self-image will affect what each says and how each says it.

Other-Image

Just as we have images of ourselves, we also have particular images of others ("I could be Space Ghost . . . And you could be Bomber Lady"). At any given moment the beliefs and feelings we experience about an

other may or may not correspond with the other's own self-image. (A, for example, may never have considered being Bomber Lady before but that is the way E suggests that he sees her.) What matters is that our communicative behavior is influenced by the images we have of other individuals. (If A is Bomber Lady, then E can turn off her button.) Consider, for example, how the image we have of the other influences our experience of a telephone conversation. Won't our description of a raucous Saturday night party vary depending on whether we are talking to a fraternity brother, a parent, the landlady, or a repairman? Our *other-images* are crucial. A speaker's image of his listener will condition his communication to the listener.

In a similar way, as a listener our image of the speaker will constrain how we interpret the message that we receive. It will make a difference if our other-image is a used car salesman or a garage mechanic when he tells us that a 1938 Dodge "runs like a dream." Who we imagine a person to be will influence what we think he or she says. If we are told that someone once said "I'd like to be Batman," our communicative experience will vary according to whether we visualize the speaker as (1) the actor who played Batman on television, (2) Raquel Welch, (3) Lyndon Johnson, or (4) a three-year-old boy. The other-image is a significant feature in the communicator's dramatic life space.

Topic-Image

Every conversation ostensibly springs from a "topic of concern," a state of affairs. How the communicating participants imagine the topic of concern will greatly influence the shape their conversation takes. Consider, for example, what might happen if you were involved in a conversation whose topic was your recent trip to Europe. As you shared your experiences with your listeners, you would likely envisage a series of images that you would describe to your listeners as though you were describing a film to someone who could not see the screen in a movie theater. As your listeners attended to your description, they would imagine the scenes that you were attempting to describe.

Not all *topic-images* need be sheer memories like these. At times the topic of concern may be a willful state of affairs, as when you envisage joining your listener for a snack. This image might be transformed into an imperative message, "Let's get something to eat."[25] Or again, conver-

[25] See H. S. Leonard, "Interrogatives, Imperatives, Truth, Falsity and Lies," *Philosophy of Science* 26(1959):172–186.

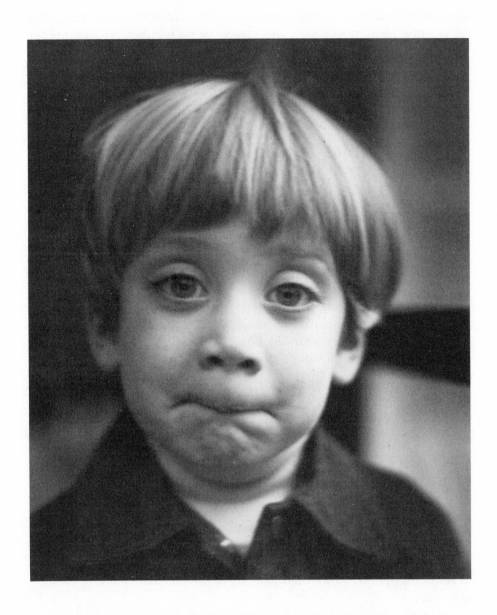

Visualizing the speaker as a little boy would influence the communicative experience.

sationalists bent on establishing a closer relationship might ransack their minds for a jointly acceptable topic of concern that could serve as a vehicle, an excuse for conversing. ("Batman." "OK" "I know what; that's Penguin." "No. I could be Space Ghost." "Yeah.")

In each of these sample cases the players' topic-images are serving as the explicit "subject matter" of the dramatic dialog. The topic of concern is a neutral ground in the interaction. It is outside the specific control of any one individual, yet it is also influenced by the topic-images that each individual has. In speaking about the world, the players imply that they share images of that world in common with each other and the rest of the community.[26]

Persona

In addition to images of self, other, scene, and topic (and perhaps because of them), we all have *personae*. That is, like actors in ancient Greek plays who wore masks large enough to depict emotions that could be seen by spectators sitting in the last rows of the amphitheater (*personae*), each of us has a costume wardrobe from which we select apparel by which to "present" ourselves in the gaze of others. We all are not as obvious about it as A, E, and M (who appear to have chosen Bomber Lady, Batman, and Space Ghost, respectively), but we all do develop a complex array of public roles, of tactical styles. We adjust to the situation and alter our play to fit the terms of personality we want to portray at the moment, to fit the image of ourselves that we hope the other will buy:

> Everyone is always and everywhere, more or less consciously, playing a role. . . . It is in these roles that we know each other; it is in these roles that we know ourselves.[27]

We want to influence how our listeners define the situations in which we find ourselves together.

Consider, for example, the woman, who on the second night of her honeymoon, is sitting at a hotel bar with her new husband. She decides to strike up a conversation with a couple sitting next to them. But how shall she do it? She has never had a conversation with another couple as a "wife" before. Up until just recently she has always been "a girl

---

[26] There are, of course, curious special cases of topic-images, such as when a patient reports a dream to his therapist and the therapist has difficulty sharing the images. But here the topic of concern is less the dream than the opportunity both players have to inspect symptoms.

[27] R. E. Park, *Race and Culture* (Glencoe, Ill.: Free Press, 1950), p. 249.

friend" or "fiancée" or "daughter" or "sister." But now she would like to suggest to her listeners that she is a "wife," but not a "newlywed." Is there a difference? For her husband, there surely is. For him, their honeymoon is a time for them to get away from everyone—a time to ignore the rest of the world and explore each other. When he sees her attempts to socialize as "the wife of a husband," he is insulted. By initiating the conversation with the other couple she immediately projects an image to him that suggests that she is not proud of the special newness of their relationship (she also wants to talk to others); the image that she projects as she talks reinforces his interpretation (she doesn't want others to see her as a newlywed either).[28] It is useless to question which, if any, of these personae the woman could have portrayed represents her "real self."[29] The significant point is that she could and presumably did consciously adapt her communication play to suit a particular image. Whatever role we decide to play on a given morning, whether we want to portray the alienated sullen intellectual or the all-American sweet young thing, that role, our *persona*, will influence our costume for the day and our entire communication activity.

Life Space

It is the unique combination of the five elements mentioned so far—scene-image, self-image, other-image, topic-image, and persona—which constitutes the *life space* that the player brings to the moment of communicative encounter. This image configuration, this life space, is unique in a double sense. First, it is unique to the individual. Although the image configurations for two individuals may become very similar, and we shall discuss this possibility in Chapters 3 and 7, the life spaces can never become exactly the same. Secondly, since the coalescence of scene-image, self-image, other-image, topic-image, and persona is momentary, and since each of these images is continually subject to variation, the life space of the individual is itself in a state of continual, if gradual, change—both during any communicative encounter and between encounters.

---

[28] We are indebted to R. D. Laing, H. Phillipson, and A. R. Lee (*Interpersonal Perception* [New York: Springer, 1966], pp. 23–24), who explore just such a situation in their efforts to clarify the fusion of projection and perception that characterizes interpersonal interexperience.

[29] Useless, that is, unless one wishes to dwell on a particular player's "sincerity" or "hypocrisy." Such judgments are usually made by speculating on the degree of discrepancy between a player's persona and self-image. Indeed the word *hypocrite* is derived from the Greek *hupo-krisis* (literally, "overdone" theatrical performance) meaning "bad actor," referring to a contradiction we detect in the hypocrite's performance.

Gap

This essential privacy in image composition suggests that there is a *gap* that separates all life spaces, a gap that poses several challenges to those who would experience human communication. First, because a gap exists between a player's own image configurations, part of the challenge of communication is *intra*personal: to recall from the reservoir of memory, from one's experiential storage systems, images that will facilitate action in the present. "Growing up" to a large degree involves learning to relate to other humans in commonly understood social transactions, and our capacity to internalize rule-governed experience and then later to recall tactics and customs at will is what enables us to consider ourselves "mature." To appreciate the communicative importance of this intrapersonal gap, consider for a moment how your experience of a given communicative encounter is frustrated or inhibited or hampered when the gap between your present and past experience is too great and you are unable to recall a former image.

On the other hand, another part of the challenge that the intrapersonal gap poses for communication is that it is often not large enough to keep one's former experiences from intruding on the present. There are many occasions when we wish that the gaps between our own image configurations were greater, that we could literally forget the past, or a part of it, and be open only to the experience of our images of the present.

A third communicative challenge, posed by the gap between different players' life spaces—the *inter*personal gap—is simply one of deciding what to do with the gap. That is, although the gap will always exist, it can be modified, accepted, or ignored. And so, in other words, our experience of any given communicative play no doubt will include one of the following: (1) the experience of attempting to bridge the gap with another, trying to share our image configurations; (2) the experience of concealing our personal space, trying to hide our image configurations, and thereby contributing to a larger gap between us; (3) the experience of protecting our personal space, accepting the gap, and using it to resist intentional or accidental invasions of our privacy; or (4) the experience of communicative events in which concern for the gap is unimportant, in which the gap is consciously or unconsciously ignored.

Finally, even as a communicator is deciding how to deal with the interpersonal gap in a given encounter, he or she is also trying to discover the extent of that gap.[30] In other words, communicators not only act as speakers who present themselves to listeners, but they also act as listeners who interpret the presentation of others. ("What is his other-image [of me]?" "Does it match the persona I have tried to project?" "How accurate is my other-image [of him]?" "Does it agree with his self-image?" "Do our scene-images really agree?" and so on.) As a means to detect these private images, listeners split the messages they experience into signals intentionally given and cues unintentionally given off, and they rely on the cues that they *take as given off* to confirm or refute the signals that they *take as given*.[31] Thus, consider the dinner party guest who wears fashionable clothes, presumably because he wishes to *give* a certain impression to others as to his taste. However, if, while engrossed in a conversation at the dinner table, he is observed stuffing his mouth, smacking his lips, belching raucously, and gesturing with his steak bone, his listeners may *take* such behaviors *as cues being given off* that bear heavily on how seriously they accept his "tasteful" persona.

The experience of communication, then, is an ongoing struggle to deal with the intrapersonal and interpersonal gaps that separate our life spaces. Intrapersonally, we wish both to remember and yet to forget. Interpersonally, we act as though it is *possible not* to communicate (that we can keep our images to ourselves), while at the same time we act as though it is *not possible not* to communicate (that regardless of the other's efforts, we claim to see across the gap either more than he intends or more than he himself knows).

In summary, an understanding of the manner in which humans dramatistically play out their encounters with one another will recognize five operative elements in such presentations:

1. How the character perceives the situation: scene-image.
2. How the character thinks about self: self-image.
3. How the character thinks about an other: other-image.
4. How the character envisages the topic of concern: topic-image.
5. How the character would like to be seen by others: persona.

---

[30] This assertion holds insofar as the players are thoughtful and careful. Later we shall consider games whose telos is obedience and lack of communication, and it could be argued that in such rituals curiosity about the participants is minimized lest it interfere with the sheer role enactment.

[31] The irony of the influence of the gap here ought not to be ignored. Our sorting of another's communicative behaviors into signals "intentionally given" and cues "unintentionally given off" is, like all our other images in and of the encounter, ultimately subjective.

Moreover, appreciation of dramatic enactments will also include a recognition of how it is that these images cohere for the individual and, for that individual, for the particular moment, and how it is that the gap that separates the image configurations is a continuing challenge for those who would experience both intrapersonal and interpersonal communication.

ANALYSIS OF OPENING DIALOG

Throughout this chapter, we have explored fragments of a specific instance of conversation among A, E, and M as part of our explanation of the general features of game-play. We are finally in a position to focus the entire game-play perspective on what started as an incoherent series of remarks. By now you have doubtless recognized that in all likelihood the remarks are those of three children and that M(Michael) and E(Eric) are boys, while A(Alison) is a girl. Let us share some other details that may help you to understand the character of this particular game-play. On the day this particular conversation took place the three children were being driven to nursery school by A's parents in a compact auto. Michael, the oldest, was just four. An imaginative child given to accommodation and compromise, Michael often directed their play. Eric, aged three, was a lively, rambunctious mimic. He preferred starring roles. Alison, also a three year old, struggled constantly to be a little girl in an arena defined mainly by and for boys. On the way to school the children were holding, as they often did, a spontaneous dramatic rehearsal, replete with stage directions, discussion of how their roles were to be performed, and sets of complex communicative tactics.

If we use the game-play perspective to focus our understanding of the A, E, M interaction, we can thus say that the game being played is or was Dramatic Rehearsal. Consequently, as the children present their television characters they are literally putting on a play within a play. We offer this conversation as an illustration primarily (1) because it is complex and convoluted, (2) because it was performed by children who, according to many behavioral scientists, are too young to have yet mastered elementary verbal skills, and (3) because it is easier for adult readers to observe the implementation of the game-play perspective itself when the object of focus is not familiar, that is, it is easier to be careful about the experience of using a particular perspective when one does not have personal experience with the object of focus. As the following game-play analysis of a more elaborate transcript should show, communication seen as game-play is complex, and these youngsters are far more sophisticated than we might believe. Their game shows amazing tactical skill:[32]

PHASE I: THE "PLAY" FOR THE DAY IS SELECTED

As the three children settle down for their ride to nursery school, they set the scene and discuss role portrayals and possible plot lines for the morning's game-play.

A: "Now what do you want to play?"	A suggests that her image of the scene invites communication; she starts the search for a topic that they can all share.
E: "Batman."	E proposes that they play out their own version of a recent television drama that he has seen.
A: "OK"	A is willing to share E's topic-image.
E: "I know what; that's Penguin!"	E's image of the projected play includes a character named "Penguin"; he assumes the persona of director and assigns that role to M, the only other male present. In so doing, E implies that his self-image incorporates both the roles of star and director of this day's play.
M: "No. I could be Space Ghost."	M prefers to be his own director; he indicates that his topic-image, includes a character named "Space Ghost" and that he identifies with that role. He yields the starring role to E. The Space Ghost role is drawn from another television program, but the children are in the process of creatively combining fragments of dialog into their own unique play—an original montage—so this eclecticism is appropriate for the game's telos.
A: "Yeah."	A suggests that she shares a

---

[32] Before proceeding, let us explain briefly our format for analysis. In the column on the left are transcribed excerpts from the conversation of A, E, and M. The ellipses (. . .) indicate that we have omitted part of the transcript. In the column on the right is a sample of the insights afforded us by the game-play perspective.

topic-image that includes Space Ghost and an other-image of M that allows him to assume the role.

E: "I'd like to be Batman."

E formally announces his choice of role and the persona of "star."

M: "Uh-huh. And you could be Bomber Lady."

M formally acknowledges E's choice and assumes the persona of "director" by assigning A her part.

A: "OK, and I could bomb."

A accepts M as director and, in assuming the role that he has assigned her, A indicates that she accepts a character of "Bomber Lady" in her topic-image and that she is confident in her ability to perform the role—she is already aware of some tactical options that accompany it.

. . .

PHASE II: TACTICAL SOPHISTICATION

As the play has proceeded, E (as Batman) and M (as Space Ghost) have come to represent the sources of Good, while A (as Bomber Lady) has come to represent the forces of Evil. In the course of the action, E and M have ganged up on A. What follows displays A's efforts to extricate herself from the Dramatic Rehearsal game, a game that she has played, but never with the creative enthusiasm that E and M share.

(E pokes A.)

E accentuates that A's character is losing in their Dramatic Rehearsal; Penguin is getting Bomber Lady; Good is beating up on Evil.

A: "Don't do that. You shouldn't hit girls."

A's tactic to maintain her self-image as a girl in a game defined by boys is not to hit back. Indeed, she has already acknowledged that she could—by admitting that as Bomber Lady she can bomb. Instead, A's tactic is to change the game to one where hitting is a rule violation. She tries to change the game from one of Dramatic Rehearsal to a game in which she has more of a chance—the Boy/Girl game. This switch allows her to chastize E for violating a rule of all Boy/Girl games—namely, that boys do not hit girls. Notice the degree of sophistication with which A already has learned the complex social relationships between boys and girls and how A expects E to accept responsibility for his action.

E: "I turned off your button."

E is no fool. He knows full well that to enter the Boy/Girl game does indeed make him responsible for his act. His

	tactic is a diversionary one; he ignores A's specific complaint and justifies his behavior within the Dramatic Rehearsal game.
A: "Well, don't hit girls."	A persists in the Boy/Girl game. Notice that she does not say "Don't hit Bomber Lady."
E: (sings jingle)	E is evasive: Singing is an appropriate tactic for both the Dramatic Rehearsal game and the Boy/Girl game. Perhaps his image of A's persistence is confusing his topic-image: "What game *are* we playing? What actions *am* I responsible for?" E's obvious reluctance to confront A directly could suggest his lack of confidence in both his self-image and his persona of "star."
A: "You know what Michael says. He says not to hit girls."	An extremely sophisticated tactic on A's part. A reveals that her other-image of M is one of the group's leader and she elicits support for her Boy/Girl game switch from M. In so doing, A puts M in a double-bind: If M agrees with A, he reaffirms his leader persona but abandons the Dramatic Rehearsal game; if he refutes A, he loses A's other-image of him as leader, but reaffirms his allegiance to E in the Dramatic Rehearsal game.
M: "Only men."	M's self-image as leader/director is more important than his role as Space Ghost. If he does not "side" with A, he cannot count on her support of him as leader, so he abandons the "old game" for A's Boy/Girl game.
A: "Yeah."	A reinforces her new alliance with M against E.

. . .

PHASE III: ALISON'S GAME
Sometime later, the children return to their Dramatic Rehearsal game. As before, M and E are much more actively involved in the play than A. As before, A switches the game to the one she prefers—the Boy/Girl game.

(General scuffle)

E: "Space Ghost, you . . ."

M: "This is a job for Superman."
(General scuffle)

M, as director, calls for another character. He has already suggested that his role of Space Ghost is more spurious than his persona of director. He now assumes the role of Superman.

E: "No, this is a job for Batman. It's Superman to Batman."
(General scuffle)

E's other-image of M allows M this flexibility—he lets M change to Superman. But E does refuse to yield his self-image as "star." His topic-image is of a Batman who beats all comers.

A: "Mom, he hitted me. He hitted me."

A tactical variation. Not only does A attempt to switch to the Boy/Girl game again, but this time she invokes the aid of Mom—the Wonder Woman in many children's game-play. This is especially strategic because A could have called on Dad instead, since Dad, too, is sitting in the front seat. A sees the Boy/Girl game as a battle of the sexes, and her team needs help.

E: "I'm the roughest boy."

A has conned E into entering the Boy/Girl game. E's entry is marked by his asserting a persona of roughness, an attribute of boys that he hopes defines a social relationship between boys (he and M) and girls (A). That is, he is willing to enter A's game, but on terms that still allow him to dominate play.

A: "No, you're not; you shouldn't be rough to girls."

A's rebuttal has its own special game-sensitive logic:
1. To be the best in any game, one must play by the rules.
2. You [E] broke a rule [you hit me].
3. Therefore, you [E] are not the best [at roughness].

M: "No, I'm the roughest boy."

M gets the best of both worlds, for once—knowingly or unknowingly, he challenges E *within* A's rules: M does not hit girls, therefore, his persona as the roughest is legitimate.

A: "No, you're not . . ."	This is a symptom of A's confusion—her other-image of M does not include his being rough [E hits girls; M does not]; yet, within the rules she has just created, M's claim is legitimate.
E: "I'm the roughest Batman."	E struggles to maintain his self-image as "star." Since A has asserted that E is not rough in the Boy/Girl game, and M is claiming that he, M, is the roughest in any game, to regain his identity E transfers the roughness attribute that both A and M have denied him in the Dramatic Rehearsal game.
A: "Huh-uh [no]."	A simply denies the legitimacy of such a transfer.
E: "Yes I am."	E and A engage in rudimentary assertion/counter-assertion, a customary communicative behavior pattern that dots many children's (and adult's) conflicts.
A: "Huh-uh [no], because you can't hit girls."	Notice that for A, E's hitting her denies him the right for *any* future star billing. At the age of three, A knows the seriousness of responsible action as well as the severity of penalty for rule violation.
M: "You know what I'm gonna . . . I'm the roughest boy and you could hit me. . . .	M tries to reconcile his self-image of leader with his topic-image of a stalemated conflict—leaders have "responsibilities"; M must do something. In spite of being only four years old, he employs a sophisticated tactic after just one false start; he offers the following compromise: Since E likes to hit, but it is against the rules to hit A, E could hit M—by A's standards M is the roughest boy; he ought to be able to take it.
A: "But I'll—but you shouldn't hit girls."	A's false start seems indicative of the difficulty she is having refusing M's compromise. The problem: If A does not do something the game will resort once again to one that tolerates hitting. Her counter-assertion, which seems

	like reliance on the security of a customary response is, more accurately, a strategic surrender—she will return to their game *if* she can set limits on hitting as it pertains to girls.
M: "I'm not going to . . ."	M approves the rule change.
E: "Only men, right?"	E tries to define the new limits; he hopes that there is still room for his kind of action.
A: "Only Daddys. . . ." *E*: "Huh-uh [no]." *M*: "Only men."	A is attempting to define the parameters of the new game with enough specificity and precision that she can protect herself.
A: "No, only Daddys; men are Daddys."	A closes the trap. Since Daddy is sitting in the front seat of the auto, A is challenging E to divert his aggression to someone able to deal with it, or at least she wants it understood that she can call on Daddy if she wants/needs to.

And so our extended analysis of this particular children's game discloses the unfolding of active human rationality. Here we have caught the rudiments of "acting man" taking form; we can see the roles and tactics that will eventually shape all communicative encounters being rehearsed, polished, and perfected. And what may be even more amazing, such development ordinarily occurs under the very noses of adults, who remain as oblivious to its subtlety as an untutored Martian might upon witnessing his first football game. Although children are constantly in the company of adults (parents, relatives, teachers, babysitters), adults seldom monitor them, that is, attend to the children's actions or words. Unless the child intrudes upon the adult world by making a request, as a rule he or she lives and plays in a world adults seldom notice. Even in the above example, where the adults were careful to attend to the children's game (enough to tape record it, so that it could be studied), the adults chose not to participate in the activity. When we take the time to recognize the game-play telos of their activity, however, such incidents become meaningful (and some of us even wish that we, too, could have played).

So far we have suggested that the most suitable moral stance for examining *human* communication is one that both relies on the examiner's thoughtfulness, carefulness, and good humor and that at the same time recognizes those as the most essential qualities in participants in communication events. In this chapter, based on these moral parameters, we have generated a perspective that combines the logical features of games with the dynamics of drama, a perspective that we hope will assist our readers in achieving a more meaningful understanding of communication events. Finally, using a particular transcript of some children's conversation, we have tried to illustrate how the sensible use of this game-play lexicon encourages insight.

However, we must not begin to worship this moral stance, lest we corrupt it through unthinking reverence. Nor should we think that just because the terms *thoughtful, careful,* and *good-humored* are rather general that they open up the possibility of any interpretation whatsoever. Although the moral terms and the resulting lexicon sound innocuous (like nostrums or clichés such as apple pie and motherhood), they are not in fact universally accepted, nor do they give us license to interpret communicative events any way we choose. Our approach is by no means eclectic. Indeed, it places a number of special restrictions on the interpretations of whatever is given to experience. These limits subtly shaded the interpretations we provided of the children's games. So before we continue, we must alert you to the fact that there are a number of unforseen implications hiding behind the effort to treat human communication in a thoughtful, careful, good-humored manner while at the same time focusing through the game-play lens. In the pages to follow you will undoubtedly feel cramped at times by what we offer you as meaningful. We hope that you confront this cramped feeling for yourself, and that you struggle with your discomfort in as thoughtful, careful, and good-humored a way as you are able. See to what extent the game-play lexicon does *not* succeed as what you would regard as the most thoughtful, careful, and good-humored interpretation. Try at those points to consider alternatives and less restrictive explications of the events we are discussing. At the end of the book we shall return to these problems and try to consider how the moral commitments implicit in the stance we took at the outset may have limited our own analysis, and to what extent they may have shaped or misshaped your own understanding.

3

Introduction to Interpersonal Communication Games

So far we have examined the elements of a game-play perspective on human communication and have explored the insights which that perspective affords us when we focus on the communication of some children. Now we shall focus our attention more directly on the kinds of communication that adults are fond of and expert in. In this chapter our purpose is to introduce, more specifically, the concept of interpersonal communication games.

Before proceeding, we should make it explicit that we use the term *communication* in its widest sense—our scope includes not merely what people say, their speech, but also what they do not say, either what they leave out or what they communicate nonverbally.

Consider, for example, the following situation: You arrive at a door simultaneously with someone else, you reach for the door, you open it, you say "After me!" and the other person walks through the door in front of you. To appreciate even minimally what has happened in this interpersonal encounter, we must extend our range of observation wide enough to include more than the specific speech communication ("After me!"). In the given case, for example, we would want to note that although the other person is responding inappropriately to the *said* (going first when you have just said "After *me!*"), she or he is responding appropriately to the *act of saying* (the polite gesture of opening the door normally accompanies the saying "After *you!*"). To appreciate the interpersonal inter-action that has occurred, we cannot limit ourselves to the sheer language of the encounter.[1]

In spite of the range of interpersonal behavior that this admittedly broad use of the term *communication* entails, it need not overwhelm us. We propose that the game-play perspective is a viable means for classifying and analyzing the "communication" that humans use to manage their relationships. Even more important than its capacity to describe and to classify, we believe that the game-play perspective, culminating in a discussion of some specific interpersonal communication games, invites us to appreciate man's sophisticated facility for interpersonal interaction.

At the outset, then, we assume that most adults are already quite proficient in what we call interpersonal game-play.[2] And because of this our purpose is not to describe a series of games and supply instructions for those who would choose to play them. Instead, our aim is to make us more conscious of the performances we already give, of the games we already play. More specifically, we see ourselves in a position not unlike that of the elementary school language teacher. Children do not learn their native language in the third grade; most children understand and know how to speak it sufficiently well by the time they are four.[3] Instruction in grammar may help children to "improve" their communication performances or it may not. Learning to recognize and appreciate that "ain't" is a colloquial contraction for "is not" may have nothing to do with a child's future speech behavior; the child may continue to say "is not" instead of "ain't" or "ain't" instead of "is not." But hopefully,

---

[1] We owe the distinction between the *saying* and the *said* as a common illusion in human affairs to Christian Metz:

> The angry lover shouts to his faithless mistress, "You don't understand me!" But she understands him only too well; the case is simply that she no longer loves him. . . . If men do not "understand" each other, it is not only because of words, but also because of what the words contain.

Christian Metz, *Film Language*, trans. M. Taylor (New York: Oxford, 1974), pp. 73–74; see also pp. 235–252.

[2] The interpersonal communication of children, as we suggested earlier, is fascinating, but for the most part is evidence of the imitation and gradual acquisition of adult communication patterns. Those adults who have not learned the games or refuse to play them—those who continuously disrupt our social gatherings and occasions—are those we put in institutions, mental or penal. See R.H. Phillips, "The Nature and Function of Children's Games," *Psychoanalytic Quarterly* 29(1961): 200–207.

[3] Eric Lenneberg, "The Natural History of Language," in F. Smith and G. Miller, eds., *The Genesis of Language* (Cambridge, Mass.: MIT Press, 1966), Table 1, p. 222.

as a result of grammatical exercises, the child learns to be thoughtful and careful about what it is that he or she does say.

Similarly, we assume that our readers already utilize a variety of communication patterns in their interpersonal relationships. As we discuss interpersonal communication as games, we hope to facilitate an understanding of what most adults already know *how* to do, not provide rules for new experience. The purpose of the game-play perspective is to direct our attention to the communication with which we are already familiar; hopefully, the "grammar" of the perspective and our communicative experience can play *against* each other even as they work *together* to make each person more aware of his or her *own* communicative experience. We are not, therefore, suggesting that game-play is the way interpersonal communication is, and/or that it is the way we ought to communicate, but that the game-play perspective is a "way into" what interpersonal communication might be.

A study of interpersonal communication as game-play explores the drama that is created when two or more life spaces overlap—when two or more persons play the same communication game with or against each other. Before we discuss in any detail the particular communication games that individuals play in their interpersonal relationships, we would like to clarify what we mean by an "interpersonal relationship image" and to specify how it is that we think such images influence interpersonal communication.

Our social fabric is composed of many interpersonal relationships. One way that we can discuss these alliances is to take into consideration how we get them, how they come to be. That is, we can divide our relationships into those we inherit and those we select.

When one person asks us how we are related to someone else and we say "He is my brother-in-law," or "She is my tennis coach," or "We are in class together," do we leave it at that? Perhaps in response to the particular question we often do limit ourselves to specifying the grounds for our association, explaining only how it is that our relationship has come to be. But then how do we account for a vocabulary that is full of such terms as *friend, lover, pal, rival, acquaintance, buddy, associate, enemy,* and *comrade?* If asked, could we also use these terms to describe our brother-in-law, our coach, or our classmate? Indeed we could, and each of us would probably discriminate among the terms thoughtfully and carefully.

These terms we have just mentioned, however, are not Other-image terms. That is, they are not terms like *handsome, rich, happy,* and *healthy,* terms that label qualities that we attribute to an Other's person. Instead, terms such as *friend, foe,* and *confidante* are labels that we use to imagine our experience in a relationship with an Other, they are labels for interpersonal-relationship-images. This is not as mystical as it may seem. What we mean, using game-play terminology, is that these terms specify how an individual imagines the gap that separates his or her life space from the life space of a "related" Other, that these terms specify the degree of distance that individuals attribute to the experience of a particular interpersonal relationship. Although physical distance is relevant to an individual's interpersonal relationship images, the distance that we believe is more crucial is the distance that we intuitively measure in order to label someone a *close friend* or a *distant acquaintance*. For want of a better label, we shall refer to this distance as *emotional distance*.

FORMALITY—INTIMACY CONTINUUM

In order to appreciate the range of emotional distance that is captured in our various interpersonal relationship images, we propose the following continuum:

FORMALITY . . . . INTIMACY

This continuum is not especially inventive. It is, rather, merely a graphic presentation of a scale that most of us already carry around more or less consciously in our heads, a scale whose ends represent the extremes of emotional distance that two people may experience in a relationship—from almost total to almost none. We say "almost total" because it is logically impossible for two individuals *in a relationship* to completely separate their life spaces—if nothing else they will have images of the few moments that they have shared. Similarly, we say "almost none" because it is logically impossible for two *individuals* in a relationship to completely share their life spaces—if nothing else, each will have images, however momentary, of times they were separate.[4] But we *can* experience a relationship that comes close to one of the poles, and probably each one of us has: A relationship is close to the Formality (F) pole to the extent that its participants imagine that they are able to become emotionally separate from each other, and a rela-

---

[4] Here we wish to distinguish ourselves from those who argue that intimacy is essentially the "melting" of individuality and the resurrection of "oneness." There may be *moments* of such transcendence and that is why we have a continuum with Intimacy as an extreme. But most intimate relationships are of the "almost, not quite" variety.

tionship is close to the Intimacy (I) pole to the extent that its participants imagine that they are able to become emotionally near to each other.[5] In other words, whether or not one relationship is more Formal or more Intimate depends upon the extent of the gap that the participants experience between them, on how fully they are "touched" by the act of relating to one another.

As a "way in" to describing the various relationship experiences that we intuitively arrange along the Formality—Intimacy continuum, we ask you to consider four qualities, varying degrees of which we think help to specify how an individual experiences the gap that separates his or her life space from the life space of another. These qualities are: accessibility, reciprocity, commitment, and spontaneity. We will discuss each feature separately, but their interrelatedness should be obvious.

Accessibility

The extent to which the participants in a relationship are willing to open themselves up to each other is a measure of the *accessibility* in their relationship. To be accessible to another implies more than a willingness to make oneself known to another; it also indicates a willingness to know the Other's world and to be influenced by it. To be accessible is to be interpersonally vulnerable. Minimal accessibility is probably that which we have with someone whom we have not seen in several years and whose address we have lost, or with someone whom we see every day but whom we try constantly to ignore. In these very formal relationships it is difficult for us to imagine that we affect or are affected by the other. We are more accessible in those relationships where we at least make ourselves "available" (physically present) to another. Even when we spend a certain obligatory amount of time with each other, exchanging polite platitudes of mutual concern, we are taking some risks, however small. But in such relationships, where accessibility is only moderate, as soon as the Other is out of sight, he or she is out of mind—we never let these acquaintances get "close" to us, to "touch" us. More extensive interpersonal accessibility, however, entails a releasement, a dissolution of the boundaries between people. Two persons' life spaces can never completely merge, but each will experience their relationship as fairly

---

[5] The *preferences* players will display for more or less intimate play is another matter. Eric Berne offers a Freudian account of their genesis in *What Do You Say After You Say Hello?* (New York: Grove Press, 1972).

intimate to the extent that each is willing to affect and to be affected by the other.[6]

Reciprocity

Another feature that helps us to specify the amount of distance experienced in a relationship is *reciprocity*, the extent to which our relationship with another is distinguished by mutual give-and-take.[7] In the most formal relationships, the only reciprocity that exists is the sharing that is prescribed by custom. The participants give only what they know they are supposed to give and take only what they are supposed to take. Military reciprocity, for example, between two soldiers of varying rank, is limited to one giving an order and the other taking it and one giving respect and the other taking it. Relationships in which the participants do not rely so heavily on the reciprocity outlined by tradition can be characterized by degrees of reciprocity, ranging from practically none (when one person dominates the relationship and all but excludes the other or one always gives and the other always takes[8]) to considerable (when each has the courage *both* to give and to take[9]).

Commitment

A third way of describing how individuals experience the gap between them is to consider the degree of *commitment* that each has for the relationship, the degree to which each imagines that he or she is engaged with the other for the sake of the unique relationship itself. In formal relationships it is difficult to experience the relationship as unique because we do not commit ourselves to another as a person so much as we commit ourselves to another as a non-person. That is, in these

---

[6] See R. Bayne, "Does the J.S.D.Q. Measure Authenticity?" *Journal of Humanistic Psychology* 14(Summer 1974): 79–86.

[7] See A. W. Gouldner, "The Norm of Reciprocity: A Preliminary Statement," *American Sociological Review* 25(1960): 161–178. Gouldner contends that while the norm of reciprocity is universal, it is not unconditional.

[8] The tragedy of unilateral giving in a relationship is emphasized by Hugh Prather in his book *Notes to Myself* (Moab, Utah: Real People Press, 1970): "As long as I'm giving you things (even 'love') I don't have to notice you." (Pages unnumbered.)

[9] It is strange, but true, that the aspect of reciprocity that is often most difficult in those relationships that we imagine as approaching intimacy, is *taking*. But when we are trying so hard to give to the other ("It is more blessed to give than to receive"), we must also allow the other the same privilege—and *take* what we are given. Ironically, Intimacy, like Formality, requires some degree of selfishness.

relationships we could substitute one person for another without too much difficulty, we do not need the special relationship itself; rather we enter into it because it is a means to some other goal—a purchase or a sale we want to make, instructions that we need to have or want to give, a job that we want done or a promotion we would like to have. A greater degree of commitment exists between two persons who need to engage in their specific relationship. In these relationships the participants are dependent upon each other as unique individuals. One person, for example, might experience considerable commitment in his relationship with his father; his image of the sacrifices made on his behalf by his father minimizes the distance he experiences in their relationship. Similarly, another might experience closeness to a certain friend because that friend is always around when needed most. These individuals are committed to their relationships. The most committed individuals, however, are not those who engage in a relationship because they profit from it in an extrinsic way or those who engage in a relationship to allay their own anxieties. Rather, the most committed individuals are those who derive pleasure from their relationship as an inherently gratifying experience; for them the unique relationship itself is intrinsically satisfying.[10] They are amateurs who work *at* a relationship, not professionals who work *through* a relationship. This kind of commitment to a relationship can be evidenced by individuals who maintain their relationship even though immediate needs have been quenched.[11] In this respect it might be possible to define love as that residue of a relationship that persists even though lust may have been gratified.

---

[10] See Hugh Dalziel Duncan, "Simmel's Image of Society," in Kurt H. Wolff, ed., *Georg Simmel, 1858–1918* (Columbus: Ohio State University Press, 1959), pp. 100–118. Especially page 102, where Duncan reports: "Sociability [we would substitute commitment] has no objective purpose, no content, no extrinsic results; it depends entirely on the actors in the moment of sociation. Its aim is nothing but the success of the sociable moment and, at most, a memory of it."

What we suggest by commitment, further, is not unlike Leon Festinger's concept of "consummatory communication"—a form of communication in which simple expression reduces the force to communicate. (L. Festinger, "Informal Social Communication," *Psychological Review* 57[1950]: 281.)

The fact that it is possible for the participants to ignore other goals that may or may not be achieved is due, in part, to what Harry Stack Sullivan calls "selective inattention." (H. S. Sullivan, *Clinical Studies in Psychiatry* [New York: W. W. Norton and Company, 1956], pp. 38–76.) The participants can be so engrossed in their interaction, so enjoying their relationship, that they are honestly (and not pathologically) unaware of matters other than the activity.

[11] Nena O'Neill and George O'Neill describe this kind of commitment to the relationship itself in their book *Open Marriage* (New York: M. Evans and Company, 1972), p. 79: "Partners know that *they* are the most important ingredients in the marriage, know that personal, immediate awareness of the self and the mate's self are more important than any future possibility."

Spontaneity

Yet another related quality present in varying degrees in the experience of interpersonal relationships is *spontaneity*, the degree to which individuals in a relationship feel free to acknowledge their experience of the moment. Each of us can imagine several interpersonal relationships in which we are either unable or unwilling to let our impulses show themselves. In formal ceremonial relationships spontaneity is against the rules and in polite relationships it is a tactic we would rather not choose. ("It's not nice to get angry in public, dear!") Our experience in these relationships is like nearly bumping into someone on the street; we literally hold our breath and/or tense our muscles so as not to touch or be touched by the other. By this we do not mean to suggest that wild, exhuberant behavior is evidence of spontaneity in a relationship or that formal relationships are necessarily quiet or that intimate relationships are necessarily erratic and boisterous. There are some formal relationships in which expansive expressiveness is the rule, and the appearance of quiet and lethargy are signs of individual spontaneity subject to penalty. Our concern with spontaneity could be interpreted more accurately as a concern for how much an individual perceives that he or she is free "to be" in the relationship.

In relationships that are less formal, where the individual participants perceive that they have some freedom, what distinguishes different degrees of spontaneity is confidence and willingness. In some relationships, this confidence is translated into willingness to confront the other with the "brutal" truth or to confess past misdeeds. This degree of spontaneity is still relatively minimal. In neither case is the individual actually acknowledging here-and-now experience; instead, he or she is indulging in premeditated destructive criticism or is preoccupied with feelings or facts from the past.[12] The interpersonal gap in these relationships is still large. The distance is less when an individual's confidence becomes willingness to trust: trust himself, trust himself in the presence of the Other, and trust the Other to respond in complementary ways. But the gap probably never disappears even between intimates because spontaneity is something we all resist. The experience of "being," even in the presence of someone in whom we have considerable confidence, can be terrifying because we know we are just imagining the Other's probable reactions to us; we can never predict them for sure.[13] When

---

[12] On pages 114–117 of *Open Marriage* O'Neill and O'Neill discuss the question "Is honesty the best policy?"

[13] Sidney M. Jourard, *The Transparent Self* (Princeton, N.J.: D. Van Nostrand Company, 1964), pp. 19–30.

individuals experience a high degree of spontaneity in their relationship, consequently, it is not so much that they always and only "do-what-comes-naturally" but more the feeling of enough confidence in the relationship that if "what-comes-naturally" does, each person will have minimal regret, and both might even enjoy the experience.

In sum, we maintain that every individual has a supply of more or less conscious interpersonal relationship images. These images are seldom, if ever, limited to historical data regarding the relationship's origin(s). Instead of dwelling on how the relationship *came to be* ("He is my father," "She is my teacher," "He is my son," "He is my doctor," and so on), the interpersonal relationship image is a picture of how the relationship *is*[14] ("He is my friend," "We are bitter enemies," "He scratches my back and I scratch his"). Furthermore, we propose that individuals can and do make meaningful distinctions among these images and that they do so by resorting to an intuitive scale that resembles a continuum whose ends are Formality and Intimacy. That is, each of us discriminates among the people we are "related" to in terms of how "far" and how "near" we experience them. Several interrelated factors contribute to the complexity of the distinctions we make. Some of these are:

How much we imagine that we are known by and know about the Other (accessibility);

How much we imagine that our knowing is coequally shared (reciprocity);

How much we imagine that we are involved with each other for the Other's sake (commitment); and

How much we imagine that we are free to be in the Other's presence (spontaneity).

These factors are obviously interdependent: Accessibility tends to increase when individuals are reciprocal,[15] reciprocity depends upon commitment,[16] commitment grows through perceived accessibility and spontaneity, and so on. Conversely, when we imagine that someone would prefer not to be touched by our life space, we tend to reciprocate

---

[14] See S. Kiesler, "Emotion in Groups," *Journal of Humanistic Psychology*, 13(Summer 1973): 19–31 for a consideration of how such images are articulated.

[15] Sidney Jourard calls this input-output correlation the "dyadic effect" in "Self-Disclosure and Other Cathexis," *Journal of Abnormal and Social Psychology* 59(1959): 428–431.

[16] Maximum reciprocity is really only possible when the participants are committed to each other. One tends to reciprocate more when he senses that his own needs are the cause of another's acts—when he sees the Other as "generous"—rather than when he senses the Other as "selfish" or "manipulative." See John Schopler and Vaida Diller Thompson, "Role Attribution Process in Mediating Amount of Reciprocity for a Favor," *Journal of Personality and Social Psychology* 9(1969): 243–250.

by withholding our accessibility; when we are less committed to our relationship, we tend to be more careful to ensure that we get what we want from the relationship, we tend to be less spontaneous, and so on.

We are not suggesting, therefore, that there is necessarily a substance "Intimacy" made by simply adding these features together: [accessibility] + [reciprocity] + [commitment] + [spontaneity], or that "Formality" is made by simply subtracting them: [intimacy] − [accessibility] − [reciprocity] − [commitment] − [spontaneity]. The concepts could never be so isolated from each other. We do believe, however, that these concepts provide us with a "way in" for estimating and describing our experience and our images of Others as more or less distant.

INTERPERSONAL RELATIONSHIP IMAGES

Let us now redirect our attention and for the remainder of this chapter begin to explore the implications that interpersonal relationship images have for communicative experience. Specifically, we shall examine first how the images affect the communication in any given interpersonal encounter—how an individual's interpersonal relationship image defines the encounter at the start and shapes his or her expectations about the nature of the interaction that will follow. Secondly, we shall reverse the emphasis to see how specific communicative encounters affect interpersonal relationship images.

For any specific encounter, we have an immediate, momentary image of our relationship with the Other(s). These images, ranging from complete strangers through casual acquaintances through rivals and friends to intimates, define our encounter at the start. Like the rules of a game, they place our experience in a meaningful context. For one thing, unless we are extremely emotionally distant from the other, or unless we consciously intend otherwise, we expect that *there will be interaction*. Our image of most interpersonal relationships is dynamic. Unlike our image of objects, our image of most relationships allows for the Other to act. When we encounter a plant, a parking meter, or a golf ball, we do so for some reason other than to engage the object in inter-action. Indeed, we may act *as though* the object could respond, but, in point of fact, we would be startled if it did.[17] In encountering a person with whom we are

---

[17] This is not to deny that persons may have special relationships with plants and golf balls, and, for that matter, even parking meters. But we, as well as those who have them, probably

somehow related, however, we at least allow for the Other to act and in most cases we even expect continued interaction. (Using the terminology we proposed in the last chapter, we are suggesting that it is not only the authors of this book who posit an act-ive human mentality, but that this assumption/projection is true of most people when they encounter a related Other.)

Because the interpersonal relationship image conceptualizes the degree of emotional distance between the participants, it also dictates the forms of address each will use or avoid when he or she begins to speak. Consider, for example, the grossly different relationship images that must be present in order to address a male person in the following ways: "Senator Robert Q. Smith," "Mr. Smith," "Senator," "Robert," "Bob," "R.Q.," "Smith," "Smitty," and "Sweet-ums." There is no way for someone outside of the relationship to designate the most appropriate term(s) to use, unless the participants reveal what their image of the relationship is. And the final choice in any given case is ultimately the responsibility of the participants themselves.[18]

But the interpersonal communicative experience is more than the experience of an encounter in which we call each other names. That is, if we look at interpersonal encounters as communication games, we can offer possible answers to such questions as "What else happens?" "How?" and "Why?" We can suggest that an individual's interpersonal relationship image not only defines an encounter with another but also influences the kind of communication he or she expects and presents.

One way that we can see interpersonal encounters as communication games is to view them as act-ivities bounded by rules that specify what kind of relationship can play. In other words, the rules of communication games like the rules for all other games specify and regulate the players. For each game-like encounter, there are certain communicative tactics that are appropriate both to these rules (to the relationship between the players) and to the encounter's resolution (the game's telos). One game differs from another in terms of its rules (who can play) and in terms of its telos (to what end the game itself is played).

In the next few chapters of this book we hope to illustrate a sample

---

still do not credit the relationships with being inter-personal alliances. If the plant dies, we usually blame ourselves for neglect, over-watering, or over-feeding—we do not blame the plant for commiting suicide; similarly, we may sometimes think the golf ball has a mind of its own, but the scores kept in the game ultimately indicate that the competition is person against person, not person against ball.

[18] In some cases, as John M. Schlien notes ("Mother-In-Law: A Problem in Kinship Terminology," *ETC.* 19[1962]: 161–170), no suitable form exists and the participants are most comfortable when no term of address is used.

collection of these interpersonal communication patterns ("what else happens?") and we shall distinguish among them in terms of their rules ("how" they are played) and in terms of their telos ("why" they are played).

In order to visualize the range of potential communication games we shall use the same Formality—Intimacy spectrum that we use to imagine interpersonal relationships. This interrelatedness is both possible and necessary because of the easily reversible way we can view interpersonal encounters as games. And there is more than one way to analyze the game. On the one hand, we can say that if it is possible for an individual to imagine a certain interpersonal relationship, it is possible for there to be a communication game that requires such a relationship between its players. On the other hand, a spectator (or a speculator) can observe a given encounter as a game-like activity whose rules stipulate that those who would play share certain relationship images. In this way, it is possible to say that the range of potential communication games requires an equally expansive range of interpersonal relationship images. Regardless of which "way in" we choose to view the communication in interpersonal relationships as games, therefore, the Formality—Intimacy continuum is a reasonable way to organize our comprehension of them.[19]

Approaching and Distancing Games

In placing interpersonal communication games on the F—I continuum, we also distinguish among them in terms of the ends to which the games themselves are played. Specifically, we will classify an interpersonal communication game as leading toward one of two different ends. A game may be such that playing it leads the players to recreate or

---

[19] A rough parallel to the analysis we are offering of the Formal-Intimate continuum can be found in Eric Berne's insightful discussion of human relations in his *Sex and Human Loving* (New York: Simon & Schuster, 1970), pp. 109–144. Berne classifies relations much as we do games, ranging from those of acquaintances and co-workers (which we call *Recognition games*) through relations of admiration, affection, and companionship through to intimacy and love. There are, however, serious differences between our explanation for the dynamics underlying these activities about which we and Berne agree as to the empirical features and the neo-Freudian explanation Berne offers. For one thing, Berne does not see individual instances of encounter as lying on a continuum. He prefers to treat each relationship on its own in terms of psychological forces at work *in* the participants. We, however, regard it as no accident that Berne placed each of the relations he discusses in the same sequence as we offer; his discussion would seem to confirm our claim that factors of authenticity are salient. For another thing, although Berne employs the notion of communication games as merely an illuminating metaphor to explain observed behavior, we prefer to treat the notion of game-play on its own terms; hence we concentrate on the logical features of observed events and avoid psychoanalytic interpretations whose basis is the past history of the players.

minimize the emotional distance in their relationship images, or a game may be such that playing it leads the players to increase the emotional distance in their relationship images. If the telos of a game is to recreate or facilitate rapport in the relationship (that is, to increase intimacy), we shall label it an *Approaching game.* If the telos of a game is to inhibit, to dissolve, or to minimize the rapport in a relationship (that is, to increase formality), we shall label it a *Distancing game.*[20]

We make this additional distinction because we do not believe that every individual is bound by and to his or her relationship images. The thoughtful individual does not take his or her image of a relationship as unchangeable; we are not trapped and ought not to be trapped by our "first impressions." If we were to let our interpersonal relationship image define and regulate our interaction in every encounter, we would always play the same communication games with the same individuals. Fortunately this disagreeable prospect is not characteristic of our actual communicative experience. Our relationship images are fragile; they can and do change. Our experience of communicative play is the continual re-creation or alteration of our interpersonal relationship images.[21]

The following series of diagrams is an attempt to portray the dramatic tension that characterizes interpersonal communication game-play.

Two persons encounter one another and they imagine their interpersonal relationship to be one of casual acquaintances. Let us assume that an image of a casual acquaintanceship would be midway between Formality and Intimacy on our continuum:

$$F \; . \; . \; . \; . \; \{ \quad \} \; . \; . \; . \; . \; I$$

They can play a game that reinforces this image, possibly minimizing perceived emotional distance (an Approaching game, or "AG"):

---

[20] Much the same distinction has been suggested by D. R. Smith ("The Fallacy of the Communication Breakdown," *Quarterly Journal of Speech* 56(December 1970): 346). Smith focuses on two dimensions of communication that for him ultimately act to facilitate social integration: "that dimension which directly facilitates social integration and that dimension which inhibits social integration."

[21] Admittedly, at this point, we would appear to be suggesting that *a player's motive* for choosing one game over another and *the game's telos* seem all but synonymous. In Chapter 2, we made a special effort to keep these two separate. And they still are: At the end of this chapter we shall mention games in which player motive and game telos are not harmonious and in such cases the "To what end?" of the game (the telos) unfolds not to facilitate the player's motive but *in spite of it.*

$$AG\rightarrow$$
$$F \ . \ . \ . \ . \ \{ \ \ \} \ . \ . \ . \ . \ I$$

Joe: "Hi Sue. How's it going?"

Sue: "Super!"

Joe: "Yeah, me too. How about an encore tonight at 7:00?"

Sue: "Fine, see you then."

Or they can play a game that inhibits this image, possibly increasing perceived emotional distance (a Distancing game, or "DG"):

$$F \ . \ . \ . \ . \ \{ \ \ \} \ . \ . \ . \ . \ I$$
$$\leftarrow\text{DG}$$

Joe: "Hi Sue. How's it going?"

Sue: "OK"

Joe: "Hey, I had a great time last night!!!"

Sue: "That's good."

Joe: "How about an encore tonight?"

Sue: "We'll see."

On one level, then, the consequences of playing certain games can be seen as ranging from the extreme emotional distance that results when people with formal, distant images of each other play Formal Distancing games (already distant, the players disallow even that much nearness), to the extreme emotional nearness that results when people with emotionally intimate images of each other play Intimate Approaching games (already emotionally near, the players encourage even greater intimacy).

$$AG\rightarrow$$
$$F \ \{ \ \ \} \ . \ . \ . \ . \ . \ . \ \{ \ \ \} \ I$$
$$\leftarrow\text{DG}$$

Incongruity in Game-Playing

There is a second way that our interpersonal relationship images are affected by the communication games we play. In order to understand the dynamics of this interpersonal communicative experience we need to consider more than the interdependence of relationship images and

Approaching or Distancing games. More specifically, our image of an interpersonal relationship can also be altered by playing a game that is incongruent with our initial relationship images. In these situations, the notion of a game's telos as the internal logic that encourages the events themselves to unfold is even more apparent. In these situations, the player's here-and-now presence in a game is more important to the game's resolution than the player's motive for playing the game in the first place.

In the two preceding illustrations we supposed that the participants (Joe and Sue) had roughly similar interpersonal relationship images at the outset of the exchange. And in a typical interpersonal communication game this is the case: The collective pre-game relationship images held by the players either match or are minimally discrepant. Complexity enters into our exchanges, however, whenever there is an initial incongruity between the players as to the general degree of intimacy they have prior to the game. In such cases players who appear to be playing a common game may, in fact, find themselves using different sets of rules (different relationship images), and this misunderstanding may give rise to various interesting and not always predictable outcomes.[22] When such a discrepancy arises, there is a tendency for some sort of equilibrium to be restored.[23] Specifically, each player will strive to resolve the play of the game in the "best" (most appropriate) possible manner.

Consider some of the more common directions that may be taken in the following games. Sam presumes that he has a somewhat formal relationship with his boss, but he finds Boss playing games more suitable for personal comrades (making enquiries into his personal affairs, for example). Or consider Sarah, who presumes that she is fairly close to her friend Betty, but discovers Betty talking to her one day as though she were a shop clerk and not a friend; the relationship has suddenly cooled. In each of these examples, where the players' initial relationship images prove to be incongruent with the games they find themselves playing, any of the following may result:

1. Sam may submit to (or be conned by) Boss's image of the game (commonly known as "seduction and betrayal" even without sexual connotations).
2. Sam may try to "enlighten" his Boss (bring Boss's understanding more into line with Sam's image).
3. Sam may permit his Boss to continue to misunderstand but avoid further situations (such as eating lunch together) in which the incongruity will manifest itself.
4. Some intermediate compromise may be established.
5. Sarah, feeling hurt, may renounce further close exchanges with Betty.
6. Sarah may react out of anxiety (being caught in an approach-avoidance trap by her warm feelings for Betty) and display unexpected or inappropriate behavior, such as shouting at Betty.

---

[22] We are for the moment presuming sincerity on the part of the participants, that is, following Erving Goffman, we are only considering those cases in which each participant believes in his own performance. There are of course innumerable variations from this, as in the case of the con man, who cheats, which are not of immediate interest here. We shall also disregard instances of spoofing, feigning, and the like except in our consideration of humor. See Thomas Szasz, *The Myth of Mental Illness* (New York: Dell Press, 1961), pp. 239–240, for a discussion of games where it is revealed that the participants are playing by different rules from each other.

[23] That is, unless all participants are engaging in hypocritical action, which is itself a congruent exchange. Two persons, for example, could both "understand" that although emotionally distant from each other, they were persisting in enacting a more intimate game as a ritual intended to fool potential casual observers.

In any event, our point here is simple: We do not usually persist in playing communication games that demand one level of emotional distance, while holding a conflicting image of the relationship. Either we stop playing the old game and start playing a game less discrepant with our relationship image, or our image of the relationship changes and conforms to the game in which we are present.

We have not attempted to account for all of the possible combinations between the games played and the images of the social relationship (before and after the play of the game). Although we welcome our readers to speculate on the consequences of any combination, we will concentrate on those "normal" or more typically straightforward exchanges where the discrepancy between the game being played and the interpersonal relationship image being affected is slight. It is certainly the case that communicative events exist in which there are gross differences between the relationship image and the game actually enacted (as in a rape), but these events are for the most part pathological and as such are not emphasized here.

We shall examine interpersonal communicative experience in terms of two merging features: the collective interpersonal relationship images players bring to the game and the communicative games they engage in as they play. We shall label each game as either "Distancing" or "Approaching" and explain why we do so. We are by no means suggesting that one game is better than any other, that intimacy is necessarily always a worthy goal, or that a Distancing game is to be avoided.

A game is "good" insofar as it achieves greater happiness for the player; it is "bad" insofar as it is counterproductive of the player's welfare (such as barroom games that end up in stabbings). In these terms, consider the situation where Bill and Joe—two nominal friends—pass each other and Bill says, "Hi, Joe," whereas Joe passes by and refuses to acknowledge the greeting. First of all, this is a Distancing social exchange; the greeting ritual has been disrupted. No matter what Joe's reason for not replying, there is no empirical evidence we can offer to claim that the interaction has allowed Bill and Joe to maintain or increase their emotional nearness to each other. On the contrary, this inter-action may be seen as increasing emotional distance in the relationship. If Bill knew Joe only slightly, he may never call out to him again. If Bill knew Joe more than casually, additional reciprocity between the two is at least handicapped.

From Bill's point of view the game is a "bad" one. If we assume that Bill enjoyed his relationship (however nominal) with Joe, Joe's refusal to acknowledge Bill's greeting causes Bill embarrassment.

On the other hand, consider what might be Joe's purpose. Suppose that Joe intended a display of hostility or at least a deliberate snub of Bill. The game is still Distancing in terms of the dissolution of rapport in the relationship, but it might be a very "good" game for Joe—Joe was able to break off a nominal acquaintance to his satisfaction.

Before examining some specific personal games, may we also emphasize our belief that a heightened consciousness of social interaction and awareness of possibilities of responsible choice need not be disruptive of our experience of interpersonal spontaneity and pleasure. There are those who lament that only innocence is bliss ("Oh, dear, now that I know what people do in that situation, how can I ever possibly enjoy myself in a similar situation again?"), or those who fear that the spectator will never be able to experience an event fully ("I couldn't possibly

detach myself from a *real* human situation; you miss so much if you make yourself distant!"). We would remind those who are apprehensive that there are different levels of conscious attention. One, the *involuntary*, is the response of our sympathetic nervous system: Our bodies jerk to a sudden loud noise, our eyes follow a bright moving light in a dark room, our noses are unable to ignore the stench of the sewage. In each case our attention is attracted unwillingly. We have no choice but to pay attention. Involuntary attention is an unlearned response.

There is also that kind of attention that we give willingly, that demands a definite effort. On this *voluntary* level of consciousness we deliberately focus on one thing to the exclusion of another. We try to stay awake and take notes during a boring lecture; a nurse listens carefully to the doctor's instructions for her patient; the young baseball fan watches and ponders his first-baseman hero's every move. We learn to give attention at this level and this is the level to which we shall direct your attention as we look at interpersonal games. We shall ask that you deliberately reflect upon specific patterns of human social interaction.

Fortunately for our interpersonal spontaneity and pleasure, there is yet another level of attention, the *non-voluntary*. At this level, our effort to attend fades away with the pleasure of participation. We may, for example, approach someone with a specific purpose in mind and yet forget that goal as we talk, only to realize after the encounter, "Oh, good grief, I forgot to ask if I could borrow her lecture notes," or "Now, why *did* I come down the hall to his room in the first place?" It is to this level of attention that even the most devoted observer of human life may escape. He may start out as the conscientious observer in the corner at a cocktail party, but if the right person comes along and engages him in conversation, the observer's pleasure will "divert his attention" and he will be fully immersed in the situation as an experiencing participant.

In sum, what have we said in this chapter? We assume that our social structure is composed of relationships characterized by varying degrees of imagined emotional distance between the participants and that the participants in those relationships will communicate themselves to each other in varying ways. Accordingly, we propose the existence of communicative games that reflect the different kinds of rapport in interpersonal relationships (F . . . . I) and that when played either minimize the players' imagined emotional distance from each other (Approaching Interpersonal Communication games) or increase their imagined emotional distance from each other (Distancing Interpersonal Communication games).

For the next few chapters, then, let us direct our voluntary attention to some interpersonal games that relationships play.

4

Recognition Games

I n the last chapter we suggested a means by which a game-play perspective could help us to appreciate the kinds of communication that affect our experience in interpersonal relationships. Now we would like to begin our discussion of some specific interpersonal games by considering the communication that we experience several times each day when we "run into" a casual acquaintance and "exchange a few words." We call these games—which demand of their participants relationship images of minimal accessibility, reciprocity, spontaneity, and commitment—Recognition games.[1]

Like all interpersonal communication games, Recognition games have Approaching and Distancing varieties. And, as in all interpersonal games, individuals may choose one game

---

[1] We need to emphasize that the games we focus on here are those that require, produce, or inhibit relationship images of "casual acquaintance." In other words, we are not suggesting that all recognitions are of the type we describe here—intimates, for example, may recognize one another by exchanging signals of affection in a mini-version of a more intimate game. It is, of course, also true that "intimates" may play the games we describe in this chapter; if they do so too frequently, however, we would be suspicious of the authenticity of their perceived intimacy or suspect that their interaction was consciously hypocritical. There are, however, assorted relationships for which Recognition games are the standard play. These are our focus in this chapter.

over another depending upon their image of the interpersonal relationship and the consequences that the play of a given game will have for that relationship, or individuals may find themselves unwitting players in a game that will lead to its own resolution.

"Polite Greeting" is an Approaching game—the telos of this game is recognition of the interpersonal relationship images of casual acquaintances or the creation of casual relationship images between strangers. "Turn Off" is a Distancing game—the telos of this game is the denial of the rapport images between two casual acquaintances or the prohibition of casual relationship images between strangers.

POLITE GREETING: AN APPROACHING RECOGNITION GAME

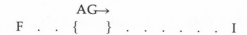

$$AG\rightarrow$$
$$F \quad . \quad . \quad \{ \quad \quad \} \quad . \quad . \quad . \quad . \quad . \quad I$$

Polite Greeting games are played by persons who imagine their relationship as rather distant or nonexistent. The consequences of a play of the game are that the image of perceived distance is maintained or somewhat minimized or that for persons who have not met previously an image of perceived distance (acquaintanceship) is created. Let us examine both types of Polite Greetings.

Polite Greeting Played by Casual Acquaintances

Consider the following interpersonal communication game between two classmates who meet on campus one day, by chance:

Bill: "Hi there, Joe! How've ya been feeling?"

Joe: "Hey Bill, you old son of a bitch! How's the world treating you?"

Bill: "Can't complain. Going my way?"

Joe: "No, have to run. Let's get together sometime."

Bill: "Sure thing; give me a ring. See ya around."

Joe: "So long."

This game should be a familiar one; we have all starred in similar productions—often many times in the same day. To see how the game affirms the interpersonal relationship image held by Joe and Bill, let us examine each conversational tactic in more detail:

Bill: "Hi there, Joe! How've ya been feeling?"

This is obviously not a request for a detailed physical report. If Joe were to respond by saying, "Well, my temperature this morning was 98.6°, but my blood pressure's a little higher than usual, and my feet are sore from walking around," it would throw everything off, for what is at stake is not Joe's specific physical condition. Instead, "How've ya been feeling?" is a signal to Joe that Bill has a polite concern for him; it indicates that Bill cares about Joe's emotional well-being but that he does not really want to know all the details.

Joe: "Hey Bill, you old son of a bitch!"

Is this a nice way for college students to talk? It would probably be inappropriate if Joe and Bill were total strangers; we rarely address total strangers in this manner. (Imagine the confused response of the man on the street who is approached and asked, "Excuse me, you old son of a bitch, do you have a match?") And yet calling someone we know a son of a bitch is not always an insult; such a remark does not always provoke hostility. On the contrary, in the current example it is a sign of some mutual trust because Joe expects that Bill will not be offended.

"How's the world treating you?"

Here, again, is another conversational gambit that is designed for the same thing as "How've ya been feeling?" It signals a reciprocal polite concern for the other. It reassures Bill, if there was any doubt, that Joe remains somewhat fond of him and concerned for his well-being. Following Bill's opening gambit, it further acknowledges that Joe has received and appreciates Bill's public recognition of him.

Bill: "Can't complain."

Of course Bill probably could complain about something, but the conversational ploy by his partner, "How's the world treating you?" is not a strong enough bid for an extended disclosure. Unless Joe were more specific or were to press the point, this comment represents no more than a "passing" bid in the game. If Joe were to follow this move with a more insistent request concerning Bill's well-being ("No, really, have you been O.K.? You look a bit tired and run down."), then perhaps a more detailed account could be presented. But in that case, Joe and Bill would leave the realm of Recognition games and progress into some version of a more intimate communication game.

"Going my way?"

On the one hand, it is obvious that Joe is *not* going Bill's way since they met while passing in opposite directions. On the other hand, though, this move is an invitation from Bill to Joe to engage in continued conversation should they be able to maintain the same scene-image for the next several minutes. Bill's tactic here is to offer Joe a choice between "Come along with me and play a more intimate conversation game," or "Let's break things off here with the Recognition game."

Joe: "No, I have to run."

Joe chooses not to engage in a less formal game at this time.

"Let's get together sometime."

Joe politely signals that parting is not pleasant; he suggests that he is not opposed to an invitation for a less formal game sometime in the future. There is no effort, however, to extend the contact, as there would be in a more formal proposal. If, for example, Joe were to say "Well listen, why don't I meet you at three o'clock this afternoon at Wally's Pub for a beer," the situation would be totally different. Such a statement is a specific proposal. But to say, "I'll see you around" or "I'll see you again sometime," is another matter. Comments like these break off the contact regretfully but indefinitely. They are remedial—designed to break contact without causing wounds. (It just would not do for Joe to say "I've spent enough time with you, considering the relative shallowness of our ties. I'm leaving now.") Adults often do the same thing to youngsters by patting them on the head.

Bill: "Sure thing; give me a ring."   Bill's answer throws the responsibility of additional contacts back to Joe.

"See ya around."   Bill signals that as far as he is concerned the formal end of the conversation has been reached. He blesses the departure. Were he a bishop he might say, "Go thou in peace."

Joe: "So long."   Joe acknowledges the state of affairs and they part comfortably.[2]

Let us review what has happened here. This game has enabled two acquaintances who were going in opposite directions to pass each other without a collision. If Joe and Bill were automobiles, we could easily arrange a standard way for them to pass each other (our traffic codes, for example, include rules that place one car on the right-hand side of the road and the other on the left-hand side). If Joe and Bill were strangers, they could pass without a collision by resorting to the informal understandings that regulate pedestrian traffic.[3] Since Joe and Bill are human beings who have past experiences with each other, since they are acquainted,[4] they are obliged to acknowledge their relationship. Persons play the Polite Greeting game because it allows for the passage of two

---

[2] An alternative analysis of similar speech gestures is offered by S. S. Feldman in "Mannerisms of Speech," *Psychoanalytic Quarterly* 17(July 1948): 356–367.

[3] See Erving Goffman, *Relations in Public* (New York: Harper Colophon Books, 1972), pp. 9–18.

[4] The preconditions of acquaintanceship that Goffman specifies are similar to those that we imply: "when each of two individuals can personally identify the other by knowledge that distinguishes this other from everyone else, and when each acknowledges to the other that this state of mutual information exists." E. Goffman, *Behavior in Public Places,* (New York: Free Press, 1963), p. 112.

"related" individuals: It enables them to confront one another, to publicly "celebrate" their relationship, and then to go on about their intended business without having a collision that would take too much
time.

This kind of interpersonal exchange is a clear case of our claim that
when we play interpersonal communication games *the said* is often not as
important as the *act of saying*, the effect the verbal gesture has on the
relationship. That is, in this instance we can accuse neither Joe nor Bill of
being uninformative. It is true that in one sense neither Joe nor Bill
communicates any new information—their exchange is fairly predictable.
It is important, however, for each of them to say something, even if each
has "nothing new to say." Each is obliged to offer covert reassurance to
the other that each still has a casual acquaintance relationship image.
(We say covert because rare is the individual who approaches an acquaintance and says, "Hello . . . I like our relationship . . . Good day.")

Similarly, the exchange between Joe and Bill cannot be regarded as a
series of lies. The participants are not making literal statements. When
Bill says, "Can't complain," he is not giving a report on the real world;
all he is trying to do is to toss out a customary remark that will enable
him to make and break the contact in a socially acceptable manner. What
is most significant in their Polite Greeting play is that Joe and Bill have
facilitated the existence of a particular relationship image; they have
played an Approaching game. What specific tactics they have used are of
secondary importance.

An awareness of the rules and tactics of Polite Greeting helps us to
understand some uncomfortable situations in which we often find ourselves. For example, why is it that when we pass someone in a hallway three
times in a period of thirty minutes we are embarrassed? This happens
because the game has a limited number of standard polite tactics. Once we
have played the game, we have used up most of the usual ploys and we are
left with little more to say. By the third or fourth time we meet someone, all
we can do is smile weakly at each other or pretend not to notice each other in
order to make the passage as swift as possible.[5]

Polite Greeting Played by Strangers

So far we have been discussing how we play Polite Greeting with people we already know. We have seen how the game has the positive

[5] See M. L. Knapp et al., on leave-taking norms in "The Rhetoric of Goodbye: Verbal and
Nonverbal Correlates of Human Leave-Taking," *Speech Monographs* 40(August 1973):
182–198.

effect of reinforcing a relationship image at a certain level of emotional distance. But often as we maneuver in public space we encounter strangers, unacquainted Others for whom we have no relationship image, persons we do not, as yet, recognize. By "stranger" we do not mean merely an unacquainted Other. Somehow we expect to greet various unknown shop clerks, policemen, and gas station attendants as we go about our daily social business. These unacquainted Others perform public service roles comparable to spear carriers in an opera, and in many ways we are related to them whether we initiate Polite Greeting or not. That is, even if we never look her in the eye, the lady at the grocery check-out will collect our money; even if we give him no sign of personal recognition, the police officer will direct us as a part of the rush hour traffic; in spite of the fact that "Fill it with regular" would be an unorthodox greeting in any other circumstances, the station attendant will pump the gas requested. So, in a sense, these people are not really strangers, they are non-persons. We are acquainted with them to the extent that they perform a defined social role; within a given range, we can predict how, in conforming to their roles, they will interact with us. We shall discuss our communication games with players like these in Chapter 8.

But what about the person pushing the grocery cart ahead of us, or making a left turn in front of us, or getting out of his car at the ethyl gas pump along side of us? Can we anticipate how, if at all, these unacquainted Others will interact with us? Probably not. These fellow users of public space are strangers. Interaction with them involves some risk, some uncertainty.[6]

There are several reasons for allowing ourselves to be minimally accessible, reciprocal, spontaneous, and committed to strangers.[7] The game that we have learned for initiating contact is the Polite Greeting. For players who are strangers, the Polite Greeting game encourages the creation of relationship images.

One reason we retain some readiness for potential Polite Greetings is in order to honor an acquaintance we already have by allowing him to

---

[6] Consider this example of an all-too-frequent situation in which at least one party wishes in retrospect that some strangers had taken such a risk:

Would the person or persons who saw the accident between a white 1972 Buick and a green 1968 Mustang at University and 15th Avenue SE at 5:25 P.M. on March 13th, please call 373–4144 as soon as possible?

Many witnesses of the accident must have chosen to preclude their emotional involvement in the accident by not stopping and risking uncertainty with strangers.

[7] As Goffman so aptly notes: "One might say, as a general rule, that acquainted persons in a social situation require a reason not to enter into a face engagement with each other, while unacquainted persons require a reason to do so." (E. Goffman, *Behavior in Public Places*, p. 124.)

introduce us to other acquaintances of his. And thus it is that we have a panoply of customary introductions. Pages of etiquette books and columns of advice in newpapers and magazines are devoted to the protocols of polite introductions for situations as various as State Department diplomatic receptions, PTA open houses, and grandmothers visiting communes.[8] Being accessible to such Polite Greetings is doubly functional. Not only are we able to christen a new social relationship, but we also reaffirm our "old" relationship by allowing our friend to officiate, to "do the honors." We may not enjoy being introduced to a particular stranger, in which case the game is a "bad" one for us. But because this variation of the Polite Greeting game permits the creation of one social relationship while reinforcing another, we can consider it an Approaching game.

Understanding how the Polite Greeting game can possibly affect two different relationships might help to explain why we are sometimes uncomfortable when a friend is about to introduce us to someone we have already met. We want to give our friend the pleasure that accompanies his enactment of the public rite of introduction, yet to indulge him is to deny the existence of the other relationship. To flatter one relationship is to insult the other. Usually we end up mumbling something like "I'm sorry, but we've already been introduced." An apology of sorts seems somehow necessary.

Polite Greeting games with strangers are not always mediated by a mutual acquaintance. That is, we have reasons for initiating a relationship with a stranger beyond that of honoring a friend. One selfish, but sensible, reason is that we can serve our own interests.[9] If we are accessible to strangers we will let them tell us that we have dropped a glove on the ground or have left a package at the counter; we will let them tell us that the bridge down the road has been washed out by high water. If we choose to ignore the efforts of these people to contact us, we will be without a glove or a package, or we will find ourselves wasting time because of an unanticipated detour.

Our awareness of the fact that we should be ready for this kind of

---

[8] We might also note why most of us are uncomfortable during formal introductions, despite their acknowledged functional character. For when the already customary behavior of greeting games becomes completely ossified in the pages of Emily Post, Ann Landers, or *The Playboy Adviser*, the game becomes little more than a series of preprogrammed moves and countermoves that preclude thought, care, and most certainly good humor. It is little wonder that we resent this denial of our humanity; there is no room for creative choice. All decisions are binary—either right or wrong. Our resentment arises when social pressure makes us concentrate more on the "rightness" or "wrongness" of our move than upon the players with whom we should be establishing interpersonal relationships.

[9] Goffman, *Behavior in Public Places*, p. 104.

helpful information and that others are ready to give it, can lead us to use the Polite Greeting as a less innocent and more deliberate tactic. On the one hand, we know that it will be acceptable for us to stop and ask someone for directions or to bother a stranger with a polite request to find out the time. On the other hand, there are more indirect uses of the game. We are reminded of the romantic heroine who drops her handkerchief in hopes that the dashing hero will pick it up and have a reason for a Polite Greeting. Or, consider the innovative man-about-town who, equipped with his own reserve supply of lace handkerchiefs, drops one of them, and then has the excuse to say, "Pardon me, miss, is this yours?" The handkerchief, an informal search warrant, gives the hero the social right to initiate the Greeting game and, thereby, hopefully to justify the creation of a relationship image.

A second, more altruistic reason for being open to potential Polite Greetings from strangers is that we can serve as a relay between those who are present and those who are not present.[10] We can be a link in a human chain. It is not unusual, for example, to be approached by someone in the park who says, "If you see a little blonde boy, about this tall, wearing blue jeans and a red and white striped shirt, would you tell him that his mother will meet him back at the car?" The woman's reason for initiating the relationship is primarily selfish; she is not especially committed to her imagined relationship with us except that she would like us to do her a favor. The extent to which we reciprocate beyond acknowledging her right to speak to us is also somewhat selfish. How much we will become committed to the woman and her search will depend on such self-concerns as how much we will be inconvenienced (How much time will it take to pass the message on to the boy? If we want to leave the park, will we feel obliged to wait around until we see him? Will we have to struggle with the boy because he might resent being informed by a stranger?) and how much of an investment we want to make in the "Golden Rule Social Bank." (By initiating a relationship with us, the woman opens herself up to reciprocal requests from us. Will we want to take advantage of the opportunity? Or do we see our altruism as a more general investment in our social future; will we accumulate relay credits and hence earn the right to withdraw from someone else at some other time?)

Perhaps the least self-serving reason we have for being ready participants in the Polite Greeting game is to allow someone else the right to make social contact. Goffman describes the constraints of this situation well:

---

[10] Goffman, *Behavior in Public Places*, p. 104.

When this opportunity to participate is proffered by another, it ought not to be refused, for to decline such a request is to reject someone who has committed himself to a sign of desiring contact. More than this, refusal of an offer implies that the refuser rejects the other's claim to membership in the gathering and the social occasion in which the gathering occurs. It is therefore uncommon for persons to deny these obligations to respond.[11]

Goffman does not mention it, but we would propose that this reason for Polite Greeting is the least tolerated as strangers move through public space. We indulge the efforts of children and old people to engage us in this way—we let the small child stop us on the street to show us his new shoes or to demonstrate how far he can spit; we let the old lady sitting next to us on the bus show us her bracelet or tell us about her grandchildren. We see small children and the elderly, like domestic animals, as having a special need for social contact or as not knowing any better, or both. We are startled, however, by strangers whom we perceive as "mature peers" who try to greet us merely for the sake of making contact or, if we let them, greet us and thereby allow ourselves to be accessible to them, we are suspicious that they must have some other "real" reason. Why is that? We tend, as a rule, to disallow such strong commitment to the relationship for its own sake from those we choose to recognize merely as casual acquaintances.

We have discussed two kinds of Approaching Recognition games called *Polite Greetings*. First, we explored one kind that reaffirms the interpersonal relationship images of casual acquaintances. Second, we considered those games that allow strangers to engage each other in relationships characterized by minimal emotional involvement. Having engaged in such game-play, all Polite Greeting players are obliged to and are given license to recognize each other in the future.

TURN OFF: A DISTANCING RECOGNITION GAME

$$F \quad . \quad . \quad \{ \quad \} \quad . \quad . \quad . \quad . \quad . \quad I$$
$$\leftarrow DG$$

Knowledge of the Polite Greeting helps us to understand the Distancing Recognition games that we call *Turn Off*. Recall that earlier we

---

[11] Goffman, *Behavior in Public Places,* pp. 104–105.

specified that we would label interpersonal communication games "Distancing" if they contributed to greater emotional distance between the players. Turn Offs are Distancing because they signal, accidentally or intentionally, denial of the relationship images between casual acquaintances or the unwillingness of strangers to establish casual relationship images. In both of these situations, while playing Turn Off may be "good" for the mental and physical well-being of the participants, as we will show, the communication patterns have an inhibiting effect on the relationship images of the players.

Turn Off Played by Casual Acquaintances

Where the players involved share images of an established acquaintanceship, there are at least two appropriate tactics that will lead to the game's resolution:

1. One or more of the players will completely fail to recognize his or her relationship image.
2. One or more of the players will fail to recognize his or her relationship image appropriately.

Let us examine these in more detail.

The first Turn Off tactic we mentioned is, essentially, a nongreeting. It is an encounter that should have taken place, but for some reason did not. The participants know each other, approach each other, but instead of recognizing each other they pass on by. The outcome of the failure to offer relationship recognition where it is expected or anticipated is to diminish the degree of emotional nearness between the individuals.

We illustrated this variety of Turn Off earlier, when we were clarifying our bases for evaluating interpersonal communication games as "good" or "bad." Recall the situation: Bill and Joe pass each other on the sidewalk; Bill says "Hi, Joe," and Joe walks by without acknowledging Bill's greeting. Regardless of Joe's reason for not replying, we have no empirical evidence to suggest that the "inter-action" increased Bill's emotional nearness to Joe. If and when Bill and Joe next meet, the encounter will be marred by Bill's recollection that Joe once refused to recognize their relationship.

In describing the failure of acquaintances to greet each other, we do not mean to include those instances in which two or more "related" people

pass each other literally like ships in the night. That is, we exclude those situations in which the possibility for greeting is high, but neither party knows that the other is present. Frequently we are physically near someone with whom we are acquainted and yet we are unaware of the proximity unless we eventually collide, or unless someone else reports the potential collision to us, or unless at some later time our conversation is punctured by at least one round of "Oh-were-you-there-too?" Such failures to recognize are *not* instances of Turn Off. Interpersonal relationship images cannot be tarnished by unknown circumstances. The inherent logic of relationship recognition seems to be that if neither person in a relationship knows that the other is present, then neither can be accused of deliberately refusing recognition to the other and, hence, the status of the relationship remains undisturbed.

But consider how often we play the Turn Off game deliberately. We often choose not to recognize a relationship image we have. It is true that such behavior increases imagined emotional distance among the players, but we are pleased at such a prospect because for some reason disruption or destruction of our emotional involvement with another is precisely what we have in mind. We blatantly disregard the shouted "Hello!" of an acquaintance whose intimacy we are trying to discourage; we refuse to acknowledge an unwelcome written invitation boldly marked "RSVP" or, as a more extreme measure, return the invitation unopened. In cases like these, we openly communicate to the other our decision to discard our acquaintanceship image.

In more subtle, but no less deliberate, instances of Turn Off we refuse to recognize an interpersonal relationship image but we do not communicate this intent to the other. In situations such as these, we rely on the earlier mentioned "what-you-don't-know-can't-hurt-you" logic of relationship recognition. Consider our actions when we see an acquaintance approaching and, presuming that we have not yet been noticed, we decide that we have neither the time nor the interest to play Polite Greeting. Turn Off provides us with at least two options in this instance. We can quickly move away in another direction, hoping that a drastic change of course will preclude a collision. ("If she doesn't see me, she's none the wiser that I chose not to see her.") Or, we can divert our glance—look at our feet, pick up a book, engage another in conversation. ("If she sees me, she won't know that I saw her, so she can't blame me for offending her.")

Earlier when we alluded to the intricate ways in which we all manage our social affairs, did you suspect that an action that appears as simple as a greeting between acquaintances could be so complicated?

Perhaps even more amazing is the fact that most of us have become expert players of these complex games without formal training. Few of us have been presented with organized lessons on how and when to recognize and not to recognize others. As a matter of fact, most of us have learned the tactics of these games even without a high degree of conscious awareness,[12] yet we are remarkably adept.

As evidence of our adeptness, consider not only the various ways that we disrupt a relationship by failing to recognize an acquaintance, but consider, too, the many ways we prevent intimacy by recognizing an acquaintance with inappropriate tactics. To understand how a tactic can be inappropriate, it is not necessary for us to propose a grid system whereby a given tactic could be looked up as in a dictionary and then considered appropriate or inappropriate. Even if it were possible to prepare such a complex chart, there is no way that we could predict with any accuracy that it would apply to all people at all times even within the same subculture. Once again, we return to our original claim that whether a game is good or bad for the welfare of its participants is a matter only the participants can decide. Similarly, the final judges of whether a recognition tactic is appropriate or inappropriate to the norms for a relationship are the participants themselves.

At the same time, however, we can provide some examples of situations in which the "wrong" recognition tactic (in terms of the participants' expectations) was employed, with the result of decreasing images of rapport in a casual relationship. One instance of what might be an inappropriate tactic is to use a spoken greeting when a nonverbal one is customary. Each of us no doubt has a few nominal relationships the image of which we regularly recognize with reciprocal nonverbal cues. We nod our head and, perhaps, smile to recognize a recurrent fellow passenger on the bus, a lady who usually sits near us in a cafeteria, or the student who shares our table in the library reference room. But in spite of what may be the strength of such relationships, since they have been established with silence, they often have a limited tolerance for tactics other than silence. To use a verbal greeting with a nominal acquaintance might be seen as a demand for more accessibility

---

[12] In discussing vicarious learning, Mark Abrahamson notes: "Without realizing it, individuals observe people punished for talking too loudly in certain situations or praised for showing difference in others. [His footnote: How many people, for example, have to ever be told to talk softly when they are in a funeral parlor? Almost everyone knows this, but few people are aware of how or where they learned it.] Future behavior is then planned accordingly, though the individuals are often unaware of the observations which originally led them to make such behavioral adjustments." Mark Abrahamson, *Interpersonal Accommodation* (New York: Van Nostrand Reinhold Insight Book, 1966), p. 14.

than the person wishes to give us. At a later date we may find ourselves "abandoned"—our "former acquaintance" no longer takes the same bus or eats in the cafeteria. You can verify the impropriety of this recognition tactic experientially by using it. That is, stop and speak to someone you regularly greet with a nod or smile and see whether you can detect a trace of discomfort in their response. If we are right, you will even find it difficult to initiate such a game; you will feel somewhat inhibited. We submit that your inhibitions are signs that you too sense the possible inappropriateness of the tactic.

We are not suggesting that all relationships that were formed in silence are doomed to a future of minimal intimacy. Many of us can cite a lasting friendship which was formed in silence but which can now tolerate both verbal and nonverbal reciprocity. We mention this kind of Turn Off merely to illustrate that many relationships expect nonverbal recognition; any other tactic is seen as inappropriate and a threat to the future of the relationship.

A second instance of an inappropriate recognition tactic occurs among those acquaintances for whom the only appropriate greeting is a verbal one. To greet such an acquaintance nonverbally is to play Turn Off. Consider, for example, the shock of the society matron who, expecting a formal "How do you do, Madam?" from her butler, receives, instead, a bear hug and a juicy kiss on the cheek. Unless the butler can provide a quick explanation for his unexpectedly intimate behavior (or unless we have seriously misinterpreted the relationship between matron and butler), the astonished matron will probably dismiss him (either from the room, from her employ, or both) for fear of additional relationship image violations.

At the other extreme, imagine a girl who sees someone walking in her direction and recognizes him as a fellow she has met just moments before. For him then to greet her with a quick smile and pass on by—to offer a brief nonverbal recognition when she would naturally expect at least minimal verbal contact—could communicate something to her other than his interest in pursuing their acquaintanceship. To be sure, unless the coed knew that he was in some special hurry, or had some other reason not to speak to her, she could and would probably consider the future of their relationship endangered.

In addition to all those situations in which one acquaintance uses a verbal recognition when a nonverbal one is anticipated, or a nonverbal recognition when a verbal one is anticipated, consider the Turn Offs that occur when acquaintances use the "right" medium (verbal or nonverbal), but the "wrong" tactic. A familiar example of this Distancing game is to address someone by the wrong name. Our names play important roles in our lives; more than labels they are a significant part of who we are.[13] We are often pleased when people know us by name because this symbolizes a more "personal" relationship. We are reminded here of the disdain of students for academic administrators who deal with students as numbers, not as individuals with names;[14] or the public relations adviser who admonishes his managerial trainees both to learn and to use the name of each and every business associate. Hence, when we think someone knows us by name and then he or she passes by and addresses us incorrectly (Fred to Jim: "Oh, hi Bob! How's it going?"), we sense a sudden drop in the rapport of our relationship. Using the wrong name can even cast doubt on the legitimacy of the relationship image itself. ("Since he calls me 'Bob,' how do I know that he recognizes *me* at all?") Similar inhibiting consequences can occur when someone greets us and uses the wrong form of our name.[15]

We need not catalogue all the unanticipated nonverbal tactics that are used in the Turn Off game. The following samples should be sufficient to illustrate how the "wrong" nonverbal tactic can upset the

---

[13] The disgrace implied by the statements "using his name in vain" or "soiling his good name" is not attributable to the name itself, but to the person who has the name. Interesting insight into the way people use their names and nicknames and the names of others has been gained by a study of the public written language (graffiti) of black and Puerto Rican urban youth in New York City. See Herbert Kohl, "Names, Graffiti and Culture," in T. Kochman, ed., *Rappin' and Stylin' Out* (Urbana, Ill.: University of Illinois Press, 1972), pp. 109–133.

[14] Any situation in which we are assigned a number object-ifies us; it puts us on a par with automobiles, toasters, television sets, and irons. We will explore the full import of this dehumanization when we examine extremely formal interpersonal relationships and again when we analyze many dehumanizing public games. For now, it is sufficient to notice that in denying us our name, a fundamental attribute of our humanity is denied as well.

[15] Arthur L. Smith (*Transracial Communication* [Englewood Cliffs, N. J.: Prentice-Hall, Inc., 1973], p. 113) narrates the "story of the bank president who slaps the Chicano parking-lot attendant on the back, 'Hi, Carlos.' Carlos responds in a similar manner by slapping the president on the back and saying, 'Pretty well, Johnnie, old buddy.' The president's reaction to the reply is usually one of consternation. Not in his most unguarded moments could he conceive of a Mexican-American slapping him on the back and calling him by his first name. And a parking-lot attendant, at that!"
Herbert Kohl, in T. Kochman, ed., *Rappin' and Stylin' Out*, pp. 126-127, reports a similar problem:
I'm called "Mr. Kohl" by my pupils, "Herbert" by my parents, "Herb" by my wife, "Herbie" by childhood friends, and "Kohl" by some colleagues. The differences are not so slight as they may seem. They embody a whole range of social relationships which we all participate in, ranging from the most intimate to the most formal. We may not institutionalize forms of address as rigidly as some cultures (e.g., the Japanese), yet violations of the conventions of which name to use in which social situation are often regarded by us as serious, even insulting. To be called "Herbie" by a stranger or "Kohl" by a close friend are both insults and signs of the disruption of ordinary social relations.

rapport in a relationship: embracing an acquaintance who has reason to expect a firm handshake; offering an obscene gesture to an acquaintance who would prefer not to be so recognized; greeting with the Black Power salute instead of giving skin;[16] or initiating contact with a business associate by invading his personal space (a distance of one and a half to two and a half feet).[17] In each of these situations a preexistent relationship is recognized, but with an inappropriate tactic; a Distancing game is played.

Turn Off Played by Strangers

We have just considered two types of Turn Off that occur among players linked by the image of a preexisting casual relationship. We turn now to Turn Off as a game played by strangers, a game whose telos is the prevention of a casual acquaintanceship.

There are at least two appropriate tactics that will lead to the game's resolution:

1. Two or more strangers will refuse to recognize each other.
2. At least one stranger will refuse an invitation of accessibility from another.

Earlier we mentioned that we exclude from the category of Turn Off those instances in which "related" people are physically near to each other but fail to recognize their relationship because they are unaware of their proximity. The prevailing logic being "what you don't know can't hurt the rapport in your relationship." There is a similar situation, however, that we *do* include as a variation of Turn Off. In this situation, strangers who are physically near to each other *are* aware of their proximity (they imagine themselves to be "related" in physical space), but they choose to avoid each other—to deny as much intimacy to each other as the situation permits. The logic here seems to be "what we know about each other could be a basis for establishing a relationship, but let's not."

There are many reasons why playing such a Distancing game can be desirable for the participant(s). Being accessible to Polite Greeting has

---

[16] Benjamin G. Cooke, "Nonverbal Communication Among Afro-Americans: An Initial Classification," in T. Kochman, ed., *Rappin' and Stylin' Out*, pp. 32–64.

[17] See Edward T. Hall's description of the four distances in man—intimate, personal, social, and public—in *The Hidden Dimension* (Garden City, N. Y.: Doubleday and Company, Anchor Book Edition, 1969), pp. 113–129.

the advantages we cited above (honoring an acquaintance by permitting him to introduce us to someone "new," being open to new relationships that can serve our own interests in the present or in the future, or being open to new relationships in which we can gratify another's need for human contact). But this accessibility is accompanied by risks. Being open to strangers can make us vulnerable not only to false information, but to physical or psychological assault. To acknowledge a stranger's Polite Greeting may be to invite all kinds of undesirable consequences.[18]

To avoid these potentially undesirable consequences, strangers frequently choose to avoid each other. Their withdrawn behavior signifies an unwillingness to seize the opportunity of temporary physical nearness to develop emotional nearness. During rush hour on crowded buses and subways, when people are forced to exist physically in close contact with strangers whom they are not sure they would like to know, "riders lower their eyes and sometimes 'freeze' or become rigid as a form of minimizing unwanted social intercourse."[19] Preparing to pass each other, oncoming pedestrians scan the scene—they give each other brief visual notice and apportion sides of the walk. Then, preferring greater distance than the space allows, they withdraw their attention, divert their glances, and pass on by. Similar advice is often given to a "foreigner" who must walk through a potentially hostile urban ghetto. He is cautioned to establish his distance by watching his feet and walking fast.

Perhaps a more complicated instance of this type of Turn Off, where the strangers are not only physically close, but have temporary privacy as well, occurs in elevators. Thrust momentarily into closer physical proximity than we would like with a group of strangers, we tend to do two things: (1) arrange ourselves in the elevator to allow the maximum space between ourselves in the limited area of the elevator (it would be rather odd for three strangers occupying an elevator to all crowd up against one side of the compartment for the duration of their ride) and (2) withdraw into ourselves, assuming a blank, absent-minded state in which we seem either to be "somewhere else" or disconnected robots. By thus refusing to acknowledge our physical closeness we maintain our emotional distance. This is why people often—in fact usually—seem to be entranced

---

[18] In this regard Goffman describes the intriguing concept of the "relationship wedge":
  Once an individual has extended to another enough consideration to hear him out for a moment, some kind of bond of mutual obligation is established, which the initiator can use in turn as a basis for still further claims; once this new extended bond is granted, grudgingly or willingly, still further claims for social or material indulgence can be made.
  E. Goffman, *Behavior in Public Places*, p. 105.
[19] Robert Summer, *Personal Space* (Englewood Cliffs, N.J.: Prentice-Hall, 1969), p. 29.

by the passing numbers as they register on the plate above the door, as if by a collective act of will the strangers could somehow make the elevator go faster.

This is not to suggest that we are always silent on elevators, buses, subways, trains, or the like. Two friends can talk to each other and still play Turn Off with strangers. In a subtle way, the pair communicates to the others nearby that they imagine themselves to be a pair and that they would like to exclude the strangers from their acquaintanceship. The primary tactic of this game is to be cryptic. The pair maintains the conversation begun prior to entering the elevator, bus, or subway, but as they ride they try not to give away any information. That is, the two friends communicate to the strangers that they are indeed a pair, but since the strangers are physically intimate and can hear every word of their conversation, the friends try to deny emotional intimacy to the strangers by not really saying much.[20] Imagine two women whose conversation includes such cryptic remarks as:

Geraldine: "Did you do it?"

Hilary: "No, but I'm thinking of doing it, but I've got to see you-know-who first."

Geraldine: "Oh, Hilary, you're so adventurous! I wish I had your courage to do things like that."

Hilary: "Well, as you know, it took me over two years to justify doing something like this. It wasn't easy."

The subject of this conversation does not matter. What does matter is to note the exaggerated stress in the conversational rhythm. Like stretching out a piece of taffy in order to pass the time, Geraldine and Hilary are trying to keep a kind of verbal dance going just between themselves until they can get away from the strangers and recapture the mood and content of their private conversation. Until then their pronouns and indirect references make the game intelligible only to Geraldine and Hilary. What we have here is a tactic that "codifies" a game thereby "protecting" the relationships of the players from outside intervention.[21]

---

[20] An exception here is the case of a pair speaking a foreign language. They might assume, correctly or incorrectly, that the strangers do not understand the language and hence continue to speak with no noticeable distortion in the content of their conversation.

[21] This Turn Off tactic is called by the British sociologist Basil Bernstein, a "restricted language code." By *restricted* Bernstein means the code is intelligible only to those who share a great deal of background information about each other, the topic of conversation, etc. In this way, restricted codes are means of protecting cultural groups from invasion

During Geraldine and Hilary's conversation, the nearby strangers, presumably, are also playing Turn Off—they are trying to give the appearance, at least, of being disinterested in establishing a relationship with the women. If, by chance, one or more of them *were* interested, each attempt to establish an acquaintanceship would be considered a play of Polite Greeting.

Similarly, if the women were to offer to include their fellow passengers in their conversation, directly or indirectly, theirs would be a Polite Greeting. The strangers could respond by playing Polite Greeting—facilitating a casual relationship with the women—or they could respond by playing Turn Off—indicating, directly or indirectly, that they were not interested in pursuing such emotional contact.

For the most part, up to this point, the discussion of Turn Off has concentrated on its *offensive* tactics—the choices players make when they wish to communicate to physically near but emotionally distant strangers that they prefer not to establish rapport with them. We should also mention the *defensive* Turn Off tactics. These are the choices players make in response to a stranger's request for accessibility, choices that communicate their unwillingness to become involved in a relationship with a rapport seeker.

Above we stated that one of the reasons for being open to Polite Greetings from strangers is to allow someone the right to make social contact. But we also proposed that we usually tolerate this request for rapport only from the very young or the very old. Perhaps we indulge these people because we do not see temporary involvement with them as being a risk to our physical or psychological safety. Neither do we see them as reliable sources of information, so they are unable to mislead us. But as we move around in public places with strangers who are "mature peers," not only do we wish to avoid the undesirable consequences of Polite Greeting with them (assaults, pleadings, insults, misinformation, and the like), but often we are in a hurry to get somewhere or to accomplish some task. Under this combination of circumstances, we tend to avoid emotional contacts with physically proximate strangers. Generally we presume that if given the choice most strangers would prefer to resort to offensive Turn Off tactics, to play mutual avoidance.

Subsequently, it distresses us when a stranger violates these expectations and sends us familiar or "uncalled for" or "vulgar" messages.

---

from other cultures; they are a way of preserving a culture's identity. See Basil Berstein, "A Sociolinguistic Approach to Socialization: With Some Reference to Educability," in Frederick Williams, ed., *Language and Poverty: Perspectives on a Theme* (Chicago: Markham Publishing Company, 1970), pp. 25–61.

This "ungrammatical" behavior (like saying "ain't" in the presence of someone who prefers "correct" grammar) is irritating if we would rather ignore strangers from the start. Such behavior forces us to make a choice where we wish no choice to exist—we are forced to choose between encouraging or discouraging further emotional advances. It is additionally frustrating because to acknowledge such an invitation for rapport is especially risky—one who violates public syntax may do other unexpected things. (In the same way, Portnoy's mother always implied that someone who *ate* just anything was capable of *doing* anything.[22])

Usually, therefore, we choose not to take such a risk; instead we play Turn Off—defensively. As an example, consider the wide range of ungrammatical tactics used every day by bored or ungratified men who ride the subways and buses and attempt by nonverbal means to invite more intimate relationships with female passengers: turning to stare momentarily at the female's face, moving one's body to attract the female's attention, taking a seat next to the female when there are other seats near males available, following the female off the vehicle for a step or so. These varied tactics are intended to achieve one of two outcomes: either invite the female to engage in other games, or, failing that, to derive pleasure from any fearful, flustered, or other emotional reactions she may display. The female for her part, if she is a seasoned mass transit rider, will counter with a totally blank performance, refusing to respond in the least to the gambits. She chooses to play Turn Off, not Polite Greeting. By her icy demeanor, her refusal to offer even a negative response (and this refusal is in itself a response), she is establishing the greatest degree of emotional distance between herself and her anonymous admirers—drawing an emotional cloak, as it were, around herself.[23]

The Turn Off is by no means confined to public transportation or to the response of women. Just as there are construction workers who enjoy "cheating" by speaking familiarly to passing females, there are drunks, panhandlers, and confidence men who accost us on the street. Women approach men in waiting rooms, at luncheon counters, and in bars. Women address other women in beauty salons, dress shops, and public rest rooms. Each of these strangers attempts to catch the attention of another stranger; each attempts to evoke a direct response. Each, while playing Polite Greeting, also risks being "turned off."

The tension between Polite Greeting and Turn Off is momentarily tolerable. However, after the initial move, some resolution is required.

---

[22] Philip Roth, *Portnoy's Complaint* (New York: Random House, 1967), pp. 22–39.
[23] See F. J. Prial, "On Finding a Subway Seat," *New York Times* (3 June 1972): 31.

Just as one cannot continue to play tennis while his opponent plays golf, one participant cannot continue to play Polite Greeting while the other continues to play Turn Off. Turn Off is a game whose initiation and resolution are almost simultaneous. If the player who first hoped to play Turn Off continues to interact with the stranger who chose to play Polite Greeting, each is offering accessibility, reciprocity, spontaneity, and commitment to the other and, however undesirable, is minimizing the emotional distance between them. As a matter of fact, the players are no longer enacting Turn Off but the inhibiting counterpart of some more intimate personal communication game. (We will discuss this kind of interaction in the next chapter.)

We have elaborated at length on what on the surface appears to be the simple process of recognizing or not recognizing acquaintances and strangers:

POLITE GREETING is an Approaching game in which casual acquaintances reaffirm their relationship image of each other.

POLITE GREETING is also an Approaching game that creates casual acquaintanceships among strangers. We examined several reasons why strangers seek to engage each other in relationships that sustain minimal emotional involvement.

TURN OFF is a Distancing game that denies rapport in a casual acquaintanceship. We examined how the end of this game is achieved when one or more of the participants fail to recognize their relationship at all or when one or more of them fail to recognize the relationship with the appropriate tactics.

TURN OFF is also a Distancing game that prevents casual acquaintanceship between strangers. We examined how the end of this game is achieved when strangers mutually avoid each other or when one decides to refuse another's demand for accessibility.

5

Formal Conversation Games

. . .They stood for some time without speaking a word; and she began to imagine that their silence was to last through the two dances, and at first was resolved not to break it; till suddenly fancying that it would be the greater punishment to her partner to oblige him to talk, she made some slight observation on the dance. He replied, and was again silent. After a pause of some minutes she addressed him a second time with,

"It is your turn to say something now, Mr. Darcy. I talked about the dance, and you ought to make some kind of remark on the size of the room, or the number of couples."

He smiled, and assured her that whatever she wished him to say should be said.

"Very well.—That reply will do for the present.—Perhaps by and by I may observe that private balls are much pleasanter than public ones.—But now we may be silent."

"Do you talk by rule, then, when you are dancing?"

"Sometimes. One must speak a little, you know. It would look odd to be entirely silent for half an hour together, and yet for the advantage of some, conversation ought to be so arranged as that they may have the trouble of saying as little as possible." [1]

Formal Conversation games involve players whose relationship images are more intimate than the casual acquaintanceship that is required for Recognition games. Players of Formal Conversation games are minimally spontaneous or emotionally accessible to one another, but they are also

---

[1] Jane Austen, *Pride and Prejudice* (New York: New American Library, 1961), pp. 79–80.

committed to a certain degree of reciprocity over a given amount of time: Instead of briefly recognizing their relationship, they expect to and are willing to devote some time to an encounter. Furthermore, instead of resorting to a limited number of standard ploys, the participants have a more extensive list of appropriate tactics from which to choose in order to keep the conversation moving.

The excerpt provided from Jane Austen's novel suggests in some detail one scene for Formal Conversation. Other possible scenes include office parties, ceremonial family gatherings, neighborhood teas, meetings with classmates before class and with professors or city officials in their offices; idle chatter with a barber, a secretary, a boss; passing the time with a person on a bus or in a laundromat or a clinic waiting room. In each of these situations there is a specific amount of time that one can fill with conversation (the party is to last for two hours, the class bell will ring in five minutes, it only takes twenty minutes for a haircut, the woman will get off the bus in ten blocks). In each of these situations, silence can be uncomfortable, if not alarming,[2] but too much intimacy is also uncomfortable, if not dangerous (family reunions are not the time for violent arguments, city officials need not know all one's personal details and vice versa, one probably should not be too candid with the boss or take emotional risks with a man on the bus). Therefore, in each of these situations, if we do not play Polite Greeting or Turn Off, we normally play Formal Conversation games.

Just as there are Approaching and Distancing Recognition games, so, too, there are Approaching and Distancing Formal Conversation games. We call the Approaching variation "Polite Conversation." The telos of this game is the facilitation of moderately close acquaintanceship images. The Distancing variety of Formal Conversation is "Put Off." The telos of this game is the inhibition of moderately close acquaintanceship images. The game encourages those who play it to imagine greater emotional distance between them without explicitly turning each other off.

POLITE CONVERSATION: AN APPROACHING FORMAL CONVERSATION GAME

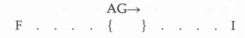

$$AG\rightarrow$$
$$F \quad . \quad . \quad . \quad \{ \quad \} \quad . \quad . \quad . \quad I$$

---

[2] Robert L. Scott, "Rhetoric and Silence," *Western Speech* (Summer 1972), pp. 146–158. "And I feel danger in the isolation your silence rings about me; for what might you do, if you will not say? There is something threatening in the silence of another, and silence may be used to threaten."

In brief, the object of this Formal Conversation game is to be in complete control of a variety of conversational ploys and to display by those ploys an ability to function with a minimal amount of intimacy in the company of others. That is to say, the experience of Polite Conversation is the experience of exercise in small talk. Much of the conversation has little personal significance for the participants. The players continue to imagine a sizeable gap between their life spaces. What is significant is the participants' ability to maintain control of the situation by signalling support, affiliation, and wit *in the proper degree*.

Bronislaw Malinowski, who labeled this form of social intercourse as *phatic communion*, proposed that it is "in use as much among savage tribes as in a European drawing-room."[3] He described its nature thus:

> After the . . . [breaking of silence] there comes a flow of language, purposeless expressions of preference or aversion, accounts of irrelevant happenings, comments on what is perfectly obvious. Such gossip, as found in Primitive Societies, differs only a little from our own. Always the same emphasis of affirmation and consent, mixed perhaps with an incidental disagreement which creates the bonds of antipathy. Or personal accounts of the speaker's views and life history, to which the hearer listens under some restraint and with slightly veiled impatience, waiting till his own turn arrives to speak. For in this use of speech the bonds created between hearer and speaker are not quite symmetrical, the man linguistically active receiving the greater share of social pleasure and self-enhancement. But though the hearing given to such utterances is as a rule not as intense as the speaker's own share, it is quite essential for his pleasure, and the reciprocity is established by the change of roles.[4]

Let us examine a particular example to clarify what is involved in a Polite Conversation. Consider this scene: A businessman enters a coffee shop where he has breakfast two or three times each week. As he browses through the morning paper, a waitress approaches to take his order. Since these morning breakfasts have occurred for over a year now, we can assume that Harry, the businessman, and Shirley, the waitress, know each other at least casually. This is their conversation:

Shirley: "Hi Harry. What'll it be? The usual?"

---

[3] Bronislaw Malinowski, "The Problem of Meaning in Primitive Language," Supplement I in C. K. Ogden and I. A. Richards, *The Meaning of Meaning* (New York: Harcourt, Brace and Company, 1948), p. 313.

[4] B. Malinowski, pp. 314–315.

Harry: "Naw. Gimme two eggs, over easy, today. It was a tough night."

Shirley: "Yeah, I know those nights. Had a few myself."

Harry: "I'll bet you have. Did your sister ever arrive?"

Shirley: "The witch! Said she'd 'Met a guy on the way and got delayed.' "

Harry: "Heh, heh, heh. I'll *bet* she got delayed!"

Shirley: "Probably so. Listen, I'll check with you later. My orders are up."

Although this example is condensed and abbreviated, note several things. First, both players seem to be in control of the situation; they have some time to fill and so they engage one another and keep their conversation moving. Notice also, however, that their spontaneity and accessibility to one another are still rather limited; that whereas several potentially "intimate" subjects were mentioned (e.g., Harry's "tough night" and Shirley's sister "the witch"), both players interpreted such topics in the context of the Polite Conversation game and did not pursue either topic. That is, Shirley did not push Harry on the nature of his "tough night," and Harry, although guilty of a naughty innuendo, did not seriously question the morality of Shirley's sister. Both of the tactics that follow the introduction of these potentially more intimate topics— Shirley's "Yeah, I know those nights" and Harry's "Heh, heh, heh. I'll bet . . ."—suggest their unwillingness to pursue either topic in more detail. To get more involved with the specifics of each other's situations would be to invade the limited accessibility that characterizes their pre-game relationship image. If their conversational tactics were to pursue more potentially risky topic-images, Shirley and Harry would be playing a variety of a more intimate personal game. We will discuss examples of these in the next chapter.

Polite Conversation is not a game that everyone can play well. A person adept at the game is quite an artist. We have a certain amount of admiration for a person who is able to maintain that "comfortable" feeling among a group of casual acquaintances; in many instances we appreciate the presence of some one who can help us to avoid silence, but who also can help us to avoid intimacy. In a sense, we admire even more the person who is able to do this at a cocktail party or a rock festival because he or she can take part in the elaborate choreography required for a group as small as 35 or as large as 600,000 under deliberately handicapping conditions. That is, the person who can still perform this game while drinking, smoking grass, or popping downers distinguishes himself or herself as a genuine virtuoso of Polite Conversation.

Admittedly, for some people such proficiency is worthless. For them, Polite Conversation is both unsatisfying as a participant and distasteful as an observer.[5] How many times have you heard or said something like this: "I don't play those games! With all the important problems in the world and all the serious issues to be discussed, why should I waste my time making noises with shallow-minded fools in bars and at parties?"

In spite of the fact that we may not enjoy this kind of interaction and/or we may not perform very well, Polite Conversation is still a viable means to facilitate images of moderate intimacy in a relationship. Polite Conversation not only provides a way to structure time and a chance to be in the company of others at a distance, but it provides the arena within which one picks and chooses acquaintances as candidates for friendship.[6] In other words, playing Polite Conversation provides the propinquity, the physical nearness, that so many researchers consistently document as a powerful influence on the formation of friendship images.[7] Few people create friendship images merely on the basis of playing Polite Greeting; Polite Conversation provides the necessary staging grounds.

Perhaps nowhere is the nature and scope of Polite Conversation easier to isolate than in the adult cocktail party. The formal elements of the playing field itself and the tactics that the players use in this situation provide a paradigm case of extended Polite Conversation game-play. Let us elaborate.

---

[5] John Powell, S.J. (*Why Am I Afraid to Tell You Who I Am?* [Chicago: Argus Communications, 1969], p. 54) labels this kind of interaction as *cliché conversation* and claims that it "represents the weakest response to the human dilemma and the lowest level of self-communication." He condemns what he sees as the superficiality and conventionality, the "noncommunication" of this kind of interaction.

[6] Eric Berne's interaction concept of a "pastime" posits a similar function: "At the end of the party, each person will have selected certain players he would like to see more of, while others he will discard, regardless of how skillfully or pleasantly they each engaged in the pastime. The ones he selects are those who seem the most likely candidates for more complex relationships." Eric Berne, *Games People Play* (New York: Grove Press, 1964), pp. 44–45.

[7] See, for example, R. H. Abrams, "Residential Propinquity as a Factor in Marriage Selection," *American Sociological Review* 8(1943): 288–294; D. Barnlund and C. Harland, "Propinquity and Prestige as Determinants of Communication Networks," *Sociometry* 26(1963): 467–479; D. Berne, "The Influence of Propinquity and Opportunities for Interaction in Classroom Relationships," *Human Relations* 14(1961): 63–70; J. Gullahorn, "Distance and Friendship as Factors in the Gross Interaction Matrix," *Sociometry* 15(1952): 123–134.

First we need to examine the nature of the playing field, which is broken into three major parts: vestibule, onstage, and backstage. Have you ever wondered why so many homes or apartments have a vestibule (foyer or front hallway), a seemingly useless area separating the main entrance and the living room? It is because American homes are designed to facilitate Polite Conversation games. The vestibule serves as a kind of decompression chamber, enabling guests at a party to make a graceful transition from their roles as travelers in public space to cocktail party actors.[8] Notice how most vestibules are furnished: coat rack, umbrella stand, large mirror (to check costumes before stepping onstage, as when a newly arrived guest checks his or her hairdo), and useless table (useless, that is, unless the guest has brought a small gift for the host and needs a place to set it while straightening a tie or a hem). The guest, in the course of greeting the host in the vestibule and removing his or her travel costume (coat), will often also try to garner some hints as to the nature of the game being played onstage. Peering around the corner into the living room and making remarks such as, "Hope I'm not late"; "Has the fun begun yet?"; and "Hey, I *sure* can tell old Chris Kerbs is here! Listen to that laugh"; are tactics that enable the guest to gain some information about the specific game that is being played—tactics that enable the guest to assess the appropriateness of the persona that he or she would like to assume and present.

The backstage area consists of those sections of the home that support the party (kitchens where food is being prepared, bathrooms where appearances are overhauled or tuned up, storage areas where spare liquor is kept) but which contradict the smooth onstage performances (for instance, bedrooms where the host hides his argyle socks or pantries filled with dirty dishes and ugly food scraps).[9] Backstage in fact serves a number of functions in addition to supporting the official performance; these added functions can be called the setting for the "party improper" (in contrast to onstage, where the "party proper" occurs). If the hostess wishes not to interact with the guests, she will banish herself for the

---

[8] In other scenes where Polite Conversation is played, even though there are no specific vestibules, players still act as though there were one—straightening a tie or a hem before walking in to see the boss, for instance. Each player hesitates a moment in order to prepare his or her character.

[9] E. Goffman, in *The Presentation of Self in Everyday Life* (New York: Doubleday, 1959), p. 112, defines this back region as "a place, relative to a given performance, where the impression fostered by the performance is knowingly contradicted as a matter of course." See also, E. Berne, *The Structure and Dynamics of Organizations and Groups* (1963; New York: Grove Press, 1968), pp. 150–169.

bulk of the evening to the kitchen, where she will assume a non-person status as food preparer. Various guest wives who wish to take a recess from the stage action will call time out with the remark, "Oh, let me help you with that." In fact, they are helping themselves off the field.[10] Then too, bedrooms and closets serve as suitable alcoves for personal scandal to occur (swapping mates, throwing tantrums, and other things grown-ups do when they take a recess from adulthood). Thus, the party improper is a lively and ongoing activity in the course of the evening. Theoretically backstage is a support area for the Formal Conversation game field, but it often contains numerous games of its own.

But, of course, the main event is onstage, in the living room and its adjacent areas (those curiously proper rooms with the "good" furniture, where the youngsters are never allowed to play, being relegated in the course of their growing years to the recreation room and the backyard). Onstage features a number of props (indirect lighting to signal a "cool" performance, perhaps, or a stack of records to set the mood for the evening) and two essential pieces of equipment. The first of these is some sort of sofa that serves as a penalty box. Here a would-be swinger dumps a partner whom he or she fears will crimp his or her style— perhaps a non-aggressive, giggling, or inebriated mate. As the party warms up, you may notice these rejects lined up like pigeons on the sidelines, some struggling amidst the foamy cushions to twist sideways to give the illusion of interaction and others lapsing into their assigned or assumed roles as spectators to the action.

This is not to suggest that anyone on the sidelines or sitting down is either an inept player or necessarily out of the game. Indeed, an especially lively and assertive female or honored guest at the party (such as a local celebrity) may create an additional piece of onstage equipment by sitting in a centrally located chair (usually the big "easy" chair, although a stool is also good if the guest does not want to resort to an ostentatious throne) and holding court, with admirers strewn in a semicircle. In short, the sofa may well be a vehicle for skilled players to rest momentarily before taking up the game again. Our point is that the sofa is primarily the party magnet that gradually attracts pieces of extraneous party metal during the course of play. If the importance of this piece of equipment seems a bit overstated, try these simple tests: The next time you attend a cocktail party (or whatever its equivalent is in your area), make a mental

---

[10] If too many intrude on this backstage area, however, it can become another onstage area of the party. The fugitive hostess or player may then seek another backstage area where she/he can relax out of character.

note of those persons who are sitting on the sofa when the party breaks up. If we are right, most of them will be those you identify as "losers." Alternatively, imagine where it is that *you* go in situations like these when you are tired and/or would rather not leave the field altogether, but also are not interested in playing for the time being.

The second essential prop for a cocktail party is a "swapping post," any piece of furniture near which players can swap off those they have been playing with for someone else. Usually, the refreshment table is this prop, because hunting for food ("Can I get you something to eat?") or drink ("Let me re-freshen my drink.") are legitimate tactics for switching players. The same social message underlies both tactics—beneath *the said* is the *act of saying:* "I've spent enough time with you; let me go." The momentarily detached player approaches the bar or canapé table like a diplomat approaching a rajah. In the case of food, there are several stately "oohs" and "mmms," a good deal of lip-pursing, and a few mumbled comments relating to the lavishness of the spread. This is usually followed by a slow, painstaking, examination of the herring tidbits before the exquisite selection is made. This guest is not so much a gourmet as he is "idling"—in the momentary state of suspension wherein he gives the appearance of being engrossed at filling his plate, while in fact he is monitoring nearby game-play trying to decide which he will join next. Other idling tactics include staring at the guppies in the fish tank or intently toeing a mythical piece of lint on the carpet or giving the appearance of waiting for an imminent arrival.[11] Of course, the bar/food prop is a good location in which to be unengaged since other detached players are also more likely to be found there.

If you doubt the essential function of the swapping post, try this simple test. Next time you give a party, place the refreshment area offstage; perhaps in a logical place like the kitchen. If our interpretation of the significance of this prop is correct, your party will eventually end up in the kitchen with at least half the people having converted the kitchen into an onstage area in its own right. This will occur because the swapping post is an essential ingredient in the extended Polite Conversation game.

---

[11] E. Goffman, in *Relations in Public* (New York: Harper & Row, 1972), proposes that social situations are not organized in terms of individuals but in terms of interaction units. He suggests that a "single" ("a party of one, a person who has come alone, a person 'by himself' " [p. 19]) is relatively vulnerable to contact from others. But a "with" ("a party of more than one whose numbers are perceived to be 'together' " [p. 19]) offers mutual protection. Often, then, to "save one from being seen as unaccompanied" (p. 21), we assume the stance that communicates "I'm with someone" and hold ourself in abeyance.

Keeping in mind the formal scenic elements of the cocktail party as an example of the playing field for extended Polite Conversation, let us now examine more specifically some of the players' conversational options. Three tactics seem most characteristic of satisfactory experience in playing the Polite Conversation game: aficionado, obligatory incantation, and swinging. Each tactic enables a player to maintain control of the situation by keeping the conversation moving and by signalling support, affiliation, and wit in the proper degree.

Aficionado

Aficionado is a Polite Conversation tactic that consists of exercising expertise in all the trivia of a popular topic, such as rattling off the names and roles of all the movie stars in 1930's films, mentioning all the "right places" in town for various meals or entertainments, extensive baseball lore, or displaying exquisite taste in camp furniture. We call these kinds of topics *trivia* precisely because they are trivial; for more serious pursuits they are a waste of time. But they are well-suited to a person who wants to say something without risking too much accessibility or spontaneity, for a person who wants to "waste time" in the company of others.

This tactic is most fun when two participants discover that they share the same area of expertise and engage in an impromptu jam session. Their conversation becomes animated, and they are committed enough to their topic and each other that their conversation is involving. But, at the same time, at the end of the conversation, neither participant has a necessarily more accessible image of the other than before they played their game. Except for the fact that they now, perhaps, recognize each other as people willing to engage in a particular "trivia" topic, they have not really taken any risks that necessarily change their relationship image to one that is more intimate: Neither is there any reason why, in the future, either should expect to play more intimate personal communication games with the other. Each has kept himself or herself open, but neither has made any special disclosures.

Obligatory Incantation

Obligatory incantation is a tactic of Polite Conversation that consists of reciting all the safe, but necessary, topics. "Safe" topics are those that reflect values presumably shared by the group. In reciting them no participant risks any personal disclosure other than the wish to be affiliated with the group that shares the values. But the reasons that make the topics "safe" to discuss also make them necessary to discuss. Merely being with the group is insufficient. One must also demonstrate that he or she belongs to the group. Reciting the topics is like wearing a membership badge. In a college town, for example, such safe conversational topics might include "the weather we're having" with special reference to its effects on everyone's tomato plants or this week's "big game." In large metropolitan areas fashionable talk might include at least one round of paeans to a special department store's current sale or various anecdotes about incredibly fine apartments discovered by a friend of a cousin at pre-1948 rents. These conversations indicate that all participants share certain common values or hold the proper local idols in suitable awe.

A variation of the obligatory incantation is making sure that one converses at some time during the gathering with all the "right" people. If the purpose of engaging in Polite Conversation in the first place is to confirm an image of moderate emotional closeness with acquaintances, then those acquaintances should be included in the conversation at one time or another. Primary on the list of "right" people would be the host and/or hostess and any other special guests. Tolstoy captured the essence of this conversational tactic in the following excerpt from *War and Peace:*

> Anna Pavlovna's drawing-room gradually began to fill. The people of the highest distinction in Petersburg were there, people very different in ages and characters, but alike in the set in which they moved. The daughter of Prince Vassily, the beauty, Ellen, came to fetch her father and go with him to the ambassador's fete. She was wearing a ball-dress with an imperial badge on it. The young Princess Bolkonsky was there, celebrated as the most seductive woman in Petersburg. She had been married the previous winter, and was not now going out into the great world on account of her interesting condition, but was still to be seen at small parties. Prince Ippolit, the son of Prince Vassily, came too with Mortmart, whom he introduced. The Abbe Morio was there too, and many others.
>
> "Have you not yet seen, or not been introduced to *ma tante*?" Anna Pavlovna said to her guests as they arrived, and very seriously she led them up to a little old lady wearing tall bows, who had sailed in out of the next room as soon as the guests began to arrive. Anna Pavlovna mentioned their names, deliberately turning her eyes from the guest to *ma tante*, and then withdrew. All the guests performed the ceremony of greeting the aunt, who was unknown, uninteresting and

unnecessary to every one. Anna Pavlovna with mournful, solemn sympathy, followed these greetings, silently approving them. *Ma tante* said to each person the same words about his health, her own health, and the health of her majesty, who was, thank God, better to-day. Everyone, though from politeness showing no undue haste, moved away from the old lady with a sense of relief at a tiresome duty accomplished, and did not approach her again all the evening.[12]

Obligatory incantation need not always be such an unpleasant communication experience. Consider, for example, those occasions when you have the opportunity to speak, however briefly, with someone you are rather pleased to keep on your list of "people I know who also know me."

Swinging

Swinging is one of the most popular tactics in Polite Conversation and in many ways is the primary reason for the cocktail party. Swinging allows everyone to engage in a bit of coy flirtation: The amateurs can experiment, the professionals can polish their style, and the old pros can come out of retirement to repeat their best plays. For the most part, swinging consists of the first two stages of courtship: gender signalling and pre-courtship. Stage 1, *gender signalling*,[13] consists of those behaviors that bear witness to one's sexual maturity: They are not yet invitations to "engage" on a sexual basis, which is actual courting. Gender signals consist of various symptoms of "maleness" (such as showing interest in the female by one's posture, preening to adjust one's socks or hair, or assorted methods of drawing attention to one's genitals such as tight pants or jiggling change in one's pocket) or "femaleness" (cocking one's head to one side while seemingly engrossed in another's conversation, assuming a stance that emphasizes the breasts, or thrusting a hip or thigh forward). Gender signals express without inviting response.

Should the initial signals "take" between two individuals (and we confine our discussion here to heterosexual interaction), the couple will enter stage 2 and begin a slow kind of *flirtation dance* in which the visual displays begin to become more and more coordinated into a

---

[12] Count Leo Tolstoy, *War and Peace*, trans. by Constance Garnett (New York: Random House, Inc., n.d.), p. 5.

[13] A. E. Scheflen, "Quasi-Courting Behavior in Psychotherapy," *Psychiatry* 28(1965): 245–257; R. L. Birdwhistell, *Kinesics and Context* (Philadelphia: University of Pennsylvania Press, 1970), pp. 39–46.

particular rhythm. Stage 2 is an invitation to a duet that is counterpoint to the general group rhythm. It is important to note here that almost everyone engages in gender signals when meeting someone of the opposite sex. In fact, the only people who do not are those whom we perceive as being somehow "cold" or standoffish (and it is this absence of gender signals that makes us perceive them as we do). In other words, gender signals alone cannot be read as invitations in any sense. If, on the other hand, it is said that Bertha's hubby got overly chummy with a blonde in the foyer during the evening, what is probably meant is that the two culprits had begun swinging at stage 2, that mild flirtation (pre-courting) dance that takes a given couple anywhere from twenty minutes to ten years to reach the mutually suitable tempo to move on to clear courtship. Thus pre-courting is a symptom of mutual availability,[14] an invitation to move onto games appropriate to players with more intimate relationship images.

It is impossible to itemize the specific behavioral features of pre-courting since (1) they vary from culture to culture and (2) it is not so much the features (a raised eyebrow in the proper context, the exposure of wrist and palm to the partner in the proper context) as it is the general rhythmic pattern that is at stake. It is the case, however, that when the rhythm and intensity of pre-courting dancing is right, the participants will experience a kind of "melting" of reserve or of "distance" in one another. They will feel a "kind of closeness" and the genuine courtship will begin.

Given this sketchy knowledge of the swinger's dance, it is possible to note performance flaws at the cocktail party. For example, at times one will run into a player who seems to be trying for the title of "Miss Gender Signal"; she is giving off all the female signals, like a pipe organ with all the stops out. Unable to engage in the sedate maneuvering needed in the entire group synchrony, she is communicating seduction messages to one and all in an inappropriate context. At other times one may come across a clumsy swinger, one who leaves out one stage of the entire courtship ritual. Just as a child learning to walk must pass through a developmental sequence (sit up-crawl-stand-toddle-walk) so it is with swinging. The young woman who reports that "We were just having a nice talk, and suddenly he began to paw me," is probably describing a young man who fails to appreciate that the necessary sequence is gender signal-flirtation-courtship.

It should be apparent that swinging, like other conversational tac-

---

[14] See A. E. Scheflen, *Psychiatry* 28(1965): 245–257.

tics, can both spice up the game and endanger the ensemble if overused to the exclusion of other ploys. We often engage in gender signal duets in the course of an evening with friends, but when the group finds two participants moving on to more sustained flirtation the ensemble rhythms are liable to suffer at the expense of the side play.

We have used the cocktail party, an informed particular, as a paradigm for understanding the general category of Formal Polite Conversation. Although the cocktail party is to be appreciated for some of its own unique characteristics—and our discussion admittedly has indulged in what might seem to be some of these incidentals—it also serves to highlight the major features of the communication we experience when we encounter acquaintances with whom we are committed to a certain degree of reciprocity for a given amount of time. On one hand, the formality of the cocktail party playing field—its division into the vestibule, onstage, and backstage areas—symbolizes the formality of all Polite Conversation scenes. In the communication that we experience as Formal Conversation, our spontaneity *is* overshadowed; as participants we are aware that we are performing but our attitudes may still be genuine. In Polite Greetings, which are so fleeting, we may not be as conscious of the scene, but in those interactions that have the formality of Recognition games accompanied by additional time, we are especially conscious of the scene and the personae that it will allow us to present. Secondly, the tactics that are available to cocktail party hosts and guests typify the tactics that all Polite Conversation players have at their disposal. When we discuss a recent lecture with a classmate before class, when we allude to the weather as we pass the time in a laundromat, or when we flirt with each other in the factory cafeteria, we usually resort to the same tactics appropriate to the cocktail party communicative experience; we exercise our expertise in "trivia" (aficionado), recite necessary, but safe, topics (obligatory incantation), and/or express our sexual maturity and engage in pre-courtship synchrony (swinging).

Before turning to those Formal Conversation games that are more Distancing than Approaching, see if you can apply what we have just said about Polite Conversation as a "way in" to understanding some of your own communicative experience. Consider, for example, what happens when a large, geographically scattered family gets together for a reunion. Many of the relatives may be strangers to one another for all intents and purposes and so will be unable to establish instant intimacy. Thus they will explore one another using polite conversation strategies appropriate to their actual degree of closeness in order to keep alive what contact they have and to gradually seek out a comfortable level of intimacy. We talk with one another in such encounters about the family milestones: the recent marriages and illnesses, the children's achievements; we also play with the dog and in general fill air time in a "holding pattern," waiting to see if we wish to remain polite acquaintances for the duration of the reunion or perhaps develop a deeper fondness for one another.

Think about the gatherings like this that you have experienced. What did the scene look like: What did you talk about? How did you fill air time in an "idle" condition? Did you remain polite acquaintances, or did you sometimes develop fondness for one another and move on to more intimate games?

PUT OFF: A DISTANCING FORMAL CONVERSATION GAME

$$F \: . \: . \: . \: . \: \{ \quad \} \: . \: . \: . \: . \: I$$
$$\leftarrow DG$$

Recall if you will the excerpt from *Pride and Prejudice* that we offered at the beginning of this chapter. Is the Formal Conversation game that the participants seem to be playing an Approaching game or a Distancing game? Do the participants seem to be confirming and encouraging images of moderate emotional closeness between them or are they refusing greater nearness with each other? Of course, we cannot say for sure how "he" and "she" are experiencing one another as they interact; how they are "touched" by the act of relating to each other during their communication is something known, if at all, only to them. But suppose that you were one of them, how would you experience the communicative event? Or, to make the example more specific, how would you feel if someone were to say to you, "You're not talking enough as we dance— please say something, however inconsequential, so that others who might be watching us won't think we're odd"? Is it possible that you might feel "put off"? After all, there you are, dancing with someone—a situation in which you are at least physically accessible if not especially emotionally accessible to each other and committed to being that way for a given amount of time (at least until the dance is over)—and your partner is telling you to talk merely for the sake of talk. Somehow this does not seem quite the same as the "flirtation dance" we discussed under stage 2 of swinging, does it? Isn't it doubtful that continued experience of this kind would encourage you to want to dance with this partner again? Why?

What does it mean to feel "put off"? We have chosen the term *Put Off* for several reasons.[15] One reason, probably more stylistically clever than intrinsically meritorious, is that we are trying to label the communicative experience that is neither as intimate as Put Down (which we shall cover in the next chapter) nor as formal as Turn Off (which we discussed in the last chapter). Hence, in trying to symbolize the kind of distancing communication that occurs between casual acquaintances—in relationships whose level of familiarity is midway between friends and strangers—we have combined the names of "Put Down" and "Turn Off" into "Put Off."

A more important reason for our use of the term *Put Off*, however, is our effort to describe in common terms both the feeling of postponement and the feeling of evasion that characterize the experience of Distancing Formal communication. When we feel "put off" we feel set aside, ignored, or insulted; we sense that someone is trying to keep a high degree of emotional distance between himself and us. But the distance we sense or intend another to sense is not the distance that characterizes the Turn Off. In the latter case, you will recall, the participants deny or disallow the relationship; they fail to recognize each other at all or one fails to recognize the relationship with appropriate tactics or one overtly refuses another's demand for initial accessibility. In the Put Off, casual acquaintances can and do communicate their refusal to become more intimately involved with each other, but at the same time they refuse to break off the relationship completely. They postpone the question of intimacy in the relationship, while they evade responsibility for the alternative— cancelling the relationship altogether. Their minimal commitment keeps them talking to each other, but their minimal spontaneity keeps them from "telling it like it is." In other words, the Put Off is a cop-out: It is a denial without actually saying no, a rejection of the other without actually turning him off. Put Off players reject intimacy without the risk entailed in authentic disclosure of feelings. The best players of Put Off are virtuosos of camouflage.

Let us return, for a moment, to the excerpt from *Pride and Prejudice*. There is a sense in which it is possible for us to say that these characters

---

[15] Our use of the term *put off* is not to be confused with the "put off" that A. H. Chapman describes in his book *Put-Offs and Come-Ons* (New York: G. P. Putnam's Sons, a Berkley Medallion Book, 1969). Chapman's focus is on "put-off forces"—all "the forces which drive people apart from each other." Our use of "put off" is less broad.

are experiencing Put Off communication. They are casual acquaintances who are communicating with each other for a given amount of time. Neither is taking any special emotional risks with the other. He, for example, risks nothing when he assures her "that whatever she wished him to say should be said," because, of course, he does not actually say any of it. In other words, he suggests that the risks, if any, are hers to take. Her response "Very well—that reply will do for the present," indicates her similar reluctance to become any more accessible to her partner. Furthermore, each seems, in effect, to be prohibiting the spontaneity of the other—she gives him directions for what he ought to do next and he continues to objectify her communicative behavior. As they dance, they are touching each other, but their contact is primarily physical, not emotional. Each is evading the other and the here-and-now status as well as the future of their relationship is ambiguous.

Put Off is a Distancing Formal Conversation game. As with its counterpart, Polite Conversation, the object of the interaction is to maintain control of the situation by functioning with a minimal amount of intimacy in the company of others. But unlike Polite Conversation, the telos of Put Off is not an invitation but an admonition. Casual acquaintances who engage in Polite Conversation leave themselves open for more intimate advances; casual acquaintances who engage in Put Off discourage greater intimacy.

A careful concern for communicative experience will allow us to appreciate the advantages of knowing how to play Put Off. Whereas Polite Conversation provides us with the means to be in the company of acquaintances in order to select candidates for friendship, Put Off provides us with the means when we *have* to be in the company of others to refuse them as candidates for friendship.

Let us consider some more examples of Put Off. As you read the following, notice how in each case one or more players either postpone the possibility of more intimacy in a relationship or evade the obligations of authenticity already imposed by the degree of intimacy in the relationship. The specific Put Off tactics we will focus on are distraction, ambiguity, silence, and jabber.

Distraction

Consider what is happening, when in response to her date's inquiry about whether she is enjoying the dinner he is treating her to, the sweet young thing answers, "Do you know where the ladies' room is?" Is it possible for us to conjecture in this case that he is asking if she enjoys sharing a pleasurable experience with him and she is refusing his invitation to greater accessibility? If so, her distracting response places him in a dilemma: How should he respond? If he accuses her of not answering his question, of denying him ("Eileen, why didn't you answer my question?"), she can reply that she was not doing that at all, but was merely putting more immediate needs first. Furthermore, *she* can then accuse *him* of doubting her interest in him ("Why, Charlie, don't you think I'm having a good time?"). If he does not accuse her of not answering him, he will not know for sure if she is enjoying her evening with him. Hence, because of her distraction, he is tempted to postpone additional gestures toward more intimacy in their relationship (which is probably what she wanted) and she has evaded responsibility for the rejection.

Ambiguity

Whereas the Put Off in the previous example is obvious, insofar as the girl has not answered her date's question, consider the following examples of Put Off in which acquaintances are asked similar kinds of questions, each inviting greater intimacy, but each receiving an equally evasive, ambiguous response:

> A noted art critic is asked to comment on the painting done by the wife of a friend. The critic responds, "My, isn't that something!"

> A new mother proudly displays her infant to a neighbor. The neighbor comments, "Oh, dear! What a baby!"

> A businessman attends the premier performance of a play in which his secretary is the heroine. The next morning in the office, when other co-workers ask how the opening went, the secretary urges her boss, "You were there; you tell them." The boss replies, "It was every bit as professional as I thought it would be."

In each of these cases, the commitment that the participants have for the relationship obliges them to say something, but, at the same time, the minimal spontaneity that characterizes their relationship keeps them from the risks entailed in more authentic disclosures of their feelings. Each of the above examples could be interpreted as a positive *or* a negative response. The Put Off is characterized by this ambiguity. Unless one participant wishes to risk the possibility of being hurt by

pursuing the issue and unless the other wishes to become more open and hence more involved with and responsible for the relationship, each heeds the admonition of the Put Off—"hands off; for the time being don't pursue this."

Silence

The Put Off is also experienced when at least one casual acquaintance is characterized by his or her apparent unwillingness to get involved in the conversation at all. This person is not quiet—he or she participates—but the other players sense what seems to be his or her growing indifference to the conversation. It is a Put Off tactic because it forces the others to do more in the conversation than their minimally intimate relationship obliges them to do. The unwilling participant forces the others either to get more involved or to reject him or her. Consider the following exchange:

> *Ida:* "What did you think about last week's movie, Jeremiah?"
>
> *Jeremiah:* "I didn't see it."
>
> *Harold:* "Did someone tell me you are a history major, Jeremiah?"
>
> *Jeremiah:* "Yup."
>
> *Ida:* "Oh, that must be very interesting."
>
> *Jeremiah:* "Yup."
>
> *Harvey:* "Is it very difficult?"
>
> *Jeremiah:* "Nope."

Now it may indeed be the case that Jeremiah is merely inept at Polite Conversation ("Better to remain quiet and be thought stupid than to speak and remove all doubt!") and not deliberately trying to sabotage the communicative relationship. Regardless of his intent, the experience of the other participants is the experience of Put Off. Unless they are especially committed to their relationship with Jeremiah, the game's logic will lead to its resolution—the other players will sense the futility of their conversation and soon try to put him off, too.

We are not suggesting that everyone need reply to every question with a virtuoso performance. But we are suggesting that participants in a communicative relationship must meet their responsibility to reciprocate. When we evade the obligations imposed by the degree of intimacy in our pre-game relationship images, we are engaging in inhibiting maneuvers. When this happens between participants whose relationship is fairly formal we consider the interaction Put Off.

Jabber

This popular tactic of the Formal Conversation Put Off is the polar opposite of silence. The person who jabbers so floods the conversation with words that he or she does not allow the other participants to reciprocate. This is a Put Off tactic because not only does it postpone greater intimacy in a communicative relationship, but it actually keeps the others from communicating—the only way that others can talk is to look and wait for that point at which the jabberer takes a breath. Unless the participants are especially committed to their relationship with the person who jabbers, the logic of the game will encourage the remaining action to unfold—the other players will sense the futility of their efforts at conversation and soon try to put the jabberer off, too. How many times have you been in conversation with someone whose talk was incessant? How did you feel? Alternatively, have you ever used this tactic yourself to keep others at a distance from you?

This tactic is not to be confused with the behavior of the person who cannot contain his or her enthusiasm over a particular event or topic and so literally bubbles over and through the conversation. Our communicative experience with this kind of person is usually characterized by curiosity, if not delight, in the other's spontaneous disclosure. Instead, we are trying to describe the communicative experience of babble, interminable small talk.

As the previous examples suggest, Put Off can occur any time two or more persons share moderately formal pre-game images of each other. Put Offs are especially prominent in situations in which the amount of personal involvement is not a voluntary matter, where persons who share moderately formal images of one another are forced to share physical proximity. Some adolescent siblings, for example, may not in fact be very close to each other or to their parents, but they must share the same household facilities until they are old enough to strike out on their own. To avoid bringing their rather formal relationship images of each other into the open, they avoid those topics or acknowledgements that might upset the surface calm. The tension one feels upon regularly visiting one's in-laws also often stems from the fact that one is required to spend a good deal of time in a "close" scene with people with whom one would rather be distant. We can imagine Arnold, who detests his brother-in-law and sister-in-law, reluctantly going for his monthly Sunday visit and slouching down for the afternoon with his brother-in-law Stanley to watch two football games on television. Their conversation will avoid personal matters and dwell on the football games.[16] Meanwhile Arnold's wife Sybil will rush off into the kitchen to help out in getting dinner ready. She has never been especially fond of her sister, Mellanie, but feels obliged to continue in some sort of familial contact. Instead of engaging one another with images of perceived intimacy, Sybil and Mellanie can discuss recipes and food preparation and so go through life with the illusion that they are close, when, in fact, they act like mere acquaintances.

In this chapter we have discussed in some detail the kinds of communication that mediate relatively formal interpersonal relationships; we have examined the communicative experience of people engaged in interpersonal relationships that are defined and regulated by expectations of relatively low degrees of accessibility, reciprocity, spontaneity, and commitment. We have divided this Formal Conversation into two categories according to the two major consequences that the communication can have for the relationship of its participants.

> POLITE CONVERSATION is an Approaching game played by casual acquaintances who wish to function in each other's company with a minimal amount of intimacy. Tactics such as aficionado, obligatory incantation, and swinging allow the participants to maintain their pre-game images of each other as casual acquaintances who are possible partners in more intimate games.
>
> PUT OFF is a Distancing game played by casual acquaintances who also wish to function in each other's company with a minimal amount of intimacy. While tactics such as distraction, ambiguity, silence, and jabber enable the participants to keep the conversation moving, they are also means of denying closeness and involvement in the relationship and of doing so with a minimum of responsibility and anxiety. We have identified this as a Distancing game at the same time that we have acknowledged that such communication can be personally gratifying when the participant's intent is to deny further intimacy to an acquaintance.

---

[16] It may be the case that the great popularity of weekend televised sports is just that it serves in countless homes to avoid "unnecessary" emotional contact with one's relatives.

6

Informal Conversation Games

Alex: "You've missed the point completely, Julia: There *were* no tigers. That was the point."

Julia: "Then what were you doing, up in a tree: You and the Maharaja?"

Alex: "My dear Julia! It's perfectly hopeless. You haven't been listening."

Peter: "You'll have to tell us all over again, Alex."

Alex: "I never tell the same story twice."

Julia: "But I'm still waiting to know what happened. I know it started as a story about tigers."

Alex: "I said there were no tigers."

Celia: "Oh do stop wrangling, both of you. It's your turn, Julia. Do tell us that story you told the other day, about Lady Klootz and the wedding cake."

Peter: "And how the butler found her in the pantry, rinsing her mouth out with champagne. I like that story."

Celia: "I love that story."

Alex: "*I'm* never tired of hearing that story."

Julia: "Well, you all seem to know it."

Celia: "Do we all know it? But we're never tired of hearing *you* tell it. I don't believe everyone here knows it."

[To the Unidentified Guest]

"You don't know it, do you?"

Unidentified Guest: "No, I've never heard it."

Celia: "Here's one new listener for you, Julia; and I don't believe Edward knows it."

Edward: "I may have heard it, but I don't remember it."

Celia: "And Julia's the only person to tell it. She's such a good mimic."

Julia: "Am I a good mimic?"

Peter: "You *are* a good mimic. You never miss anything."

Alex: "She never misses anything unless she wants to."

Celia: "Especially the Lithuanian accent."

Julia: "Lithuanian? Lady Klootz?"

Peter: "I thought she was Belgian."

Alex: "Her father belonged to a Baltic family—one of the *oldest* Baltic families with a branch in Sweden and one in Denmark. There were several very lovely daughters: I wonder what's become of them now."[1]

In this excerpt, T. S. Eliot has captured the sense of yet another kind of interpersonal communication that we all experience at one time or another—the interaction of people who imagine themselves to be less emotionally distant from each other than polite acquaintances. These individuals develop topic-images of a personal nature (accessibility); they seem to enjoy conversing together about whatever, for its own sake (commitment); they seem to appreciate cooperative participation more than thematic continuity (reciprocity); and they seem confident in expressing and confronting interpersonal praise and blame in their conversation (spontaneity). We shall return to this conversation at various points throughout this chapter as we explore some of the ways that individuals who share this kind of relationship image engage in communication, and we shall specu-

---

[1] T. S. Eliot, *The Cocktail Party* (New York: Harcourt Brace Jovanovich, Inc., 1950), Act I, Scene I, pp. 9–12. Copyright 1950 by T. S. Eliot. Reprinted by permission of Harcourt Brace Jovanovich, Inc. and Faber and Faber Ltd. We should be careful not to confuse the title of this play with the paradigm of Polite Conversation presented in the preceding chapter. For us, the game enacted by Eliot's characters, the play within the play, is a paradigm of a less formal conversation type.

late on how their communication, seen as Informal Conversation games, influences their relationship images.

Our use of the word *informal* is not intended to suggest that this communication is any less rule-governed than the other interaction we have already investigated. As participants in these activities we have expectations about the definition of the encounter and the appropriateness of certain tactics that are no less important than the expectations we have when we play Polite Greeting, Turn Off, Polite Conversation, and Put Off. When we imagine our relationship with another as reasonably intimate, we expect our understanding of the relationship to be shared.

For us, "informal" refers more to the tactical freedom that the participants experience. Because the players have reasonably intimate images of their relationship, because each imagines the Other(s) more as a unique individual than as a stranger or a non-person, the range of possible options in one's Informal Conversation repertoire is considerably larger than in one's Polite Conversation repertoire. In the latter, where we do not "know" the other as well we resort to safe topics or ambiguous, evasive references. We acquire a list of routines that we can re-enact from time to time either to encourage an acquaintance or put off a person whose communicative behavior toward us we suspect is or would be maladaptive. In more informal conversation we are more daring: We think we know more about the other and we act accordingly. As a matter of fact, one of the reasons we engage in this kind of interaction is the challenge—the challenge to know and be known by someone whom we trust will respond to us in certain ways.

As in previous chapters, we shall divide our discussion of Informal Conversation games into two varieties depending upon the end to which the game itself is played. An Approaching Informal Conversation game is one that facilitates images of friendship in a relationship; a Distancing Informal Conversation game is one that inhibits images of friendship in a relationship. Individual players choose to play one game over another according to their image of the relationship and the imagined consequences that a play of the given game will have for the relationship. Individuals may also find themselves unwitting players in a game *not* of their choosing (Approaching instead of Distancing or Distancing instead of Approaching), in which case, if the players do not withdraw, the game will lead to its own resolution in spite of the player's own motivation. (That is, white flags of peace are often ignored in war games and potentially damaging insults are usually seen as playful jests among friends.)

The Approaching variety of Informal Conversation we shall call "Personal Conversation Among Friends"; the Distancing variety we shall call "Put Down." In the former, the participants trust each other to respond as friends;

careful attention to each other's personally felt adequacies in order to discourage feelings of inadequacy encourages a bond of reciprocal affection. In Put Down, the participants trust each other to respond in "enemy" fashion; careful attention to each other's personally felt inadequacies in order to discourage feelings of adequacy encourages a bond of reciprocal disaffection.

PERSONAL CONVERSATION AMONG FRIENDS: AN APPROACHING INFORMAL CONVERSATION GAME

$$\text{AG} \rightarrow$$
$$\text{F} \quad . \quad . \quad . \quad . \quad . \quad . \quad \{ \quad \} \quad . \quad . \quad \text{I}$$

Imagine inviting several fairly congenial friends to your home. The interaction you expect, although similar in its surface aspects to the cocktail party (you will probably engineer the environment again through the use of peaceful lighting, perhaps soothing music, and casual snacks), will differ in one crucial respect: Unlike the constantly shifting revelry common to the cocktail party, your entering guests will expect a sustained period of ensemble interplay among the group as a whole.[2] Or, imagine those scenes that you cannot and do not engineer so specifically (a drugstore booth, a picnic table in the park, a street corner on a warm muggy night) but in which you have experienced extended interaction with people whose presence you enjoy.

We would like to suggest that one reason these encounters are gratifying is that they provide each of us with an opportunity to demonstrate and to develop personal verbal virtuosity while simultaneously engaging in a display of interpersonal teamwork. In other words, unlike our experience of Polite Conversation, an experience in which the participants literally *inter-act* by *exchanging performances* (the participants who are not speaking being more concerned with resolving the question, "Now what can I say next that will keep the conversation moving?" than with carefully listening to the other's speech), Personal Conversation is the

---

[2] Various studies have attempted to specify how large a group may be before this kind of interaction is no longer possible. The results are inconclusive because the composition of the specific group is an important variable in the decision. It is generally agreed, however, that as the number in a group becomes larger than seven, the group will break up into smaller groups or the discussion will centralize more and more around a few people. In groups of five or less, all participants generally speak to one another. See Ernest G. Bormann, *Discussion and Group Methods* (New York: Harper & Row, 1969), pp. 3–4.

experience of *collaboration, a co-active performance*. Where the specific relationship is important to its members, they want to help that relationship to do well and are pleased when it does.

Perhaps we can explain the spirit of this collaboration by likening it to the verbal equivalent of a mixture of cross-country romping and soccer. On the one hand, one of the delights of cross-country romping (running, hiking, or whatever) is the scenic variety afforded, literally, by being off the beaten track. The activity of encountering irregular terrain can be a pleasurable challenge, both to discover and appreciate the uniqueness of the specific locale and to discover and appreciate one's own ability to survive the unexpected. In other words, Personal Conversation allows us to experience the verbal equivalent of this challenge: We can "go out on a limb" in our search for topics, we can take risks in exhibiting our own uncertain intellectual capacity, we can delight in the discovery of our own dexterity ("I didn't think I had it in me to . . . "), and we can learn about ourselves by assessing those topics we can handle, those which make us anxious, and those in which we tend to get bogged down.

By blending some features of soccer with this image, we add both the presence of other individuals and the exhilaration of sustained rhythmic play. The challenge in the experience of soccer is the exertion required for keeping the ball rapidly moving between teammates and out of the hands of the opponents. The more challenging the opposition, the more the players are asked to "test their limits," the greater the feeling of accomplishment and pleasure at the end of the play. We have all seen or participated in such moments when teammates collapse into each others' arms, full of affection for one another and full of pride in their accomplishment as a team.

In our image of Personal Conversation as a cross-country soccer game, we project this spirit of combined play not against another team, but against the elements of the terrain. That is, each team creates its own conversational course even as it tries to perform it well. The competition is not against another similar group of individuals ("Nyahh, nyahh! *Our* Personal Conversation is better than *yours*."), although any one person may make mental comparisons between this team's play and the play of another team of which he is a member. Instead, the game is played across time. As a relationship of friends we compete against ourselves. ("That wasn't as much fun as last time; Susan wasn't in good form tonight"; or "Remember the time we were discussing such and such, and such and such happened . . . and how we worked our way around that one?!") We try to create discussions that are interesting to pursue and intrinsically satisfying when adeptly sustained. We participate in the creation of a communicative event that could not be accomplished without our mutual cooperation. This capacity for enhanced synchrony encourages images of closer friendship. Personal Conversation is an Approaching game.

There are several categories of tactical options available to the players of Personal Conversation Among Friends. In the next few pages, let us investigate some of those that are most commonly employed: arabesque, presto, flooding out, sounding, diplomacy, cheerleading, shared silence, and courting.

Arabesque

One of the many tactics that can be used to good advantage in Personal Conversation is the *arabesque*. The arabesque lends a bravura tone to the game: A player takes the ball and dribbles it for a time on his or her own; if the player is especially adept he or she may even pass off the ball behind his or her back. In other words, there may be improvisations or variations on the topic of the moment as one player "picks up the ball" with a piece of gossip or keeps everyone breathless with her cliff-hanging expertise on the matter at hand. Another person may perform an arabesque by sharing an amusing anecdote. ("Do tell that story you told the other day, about Lady Klootz and the wedding cake," . . . "And how the butler found her in the pantry, rinsing her mouth out with champagne. I like that story."[3]) Yet another may want to reminisce about a past event that is of interest to the rest of the ensemble. ("Remember that time we all went on that fantastic picnic . . . ?") In these circumstances, one player might literally engage in a monologue for a while and the others will adapt to the mood that he sets—his "style of play" or altered rhythm. The others will cheer him on and position themselves to receive the ball at a later point in the game.

A clear illustration of the arabesque occurs when a group of college alumni gather to celebrate their thirtieth reunion. Consider, for example, how old Standish Potts may be called upon to retell to a small gathering of chums the story of how he and old Milhous were caught smoking grass in the office of the Dean of Women. Of course, the chums were all in college at the time, and they have all heard the tale retold several times (in fact, its retelling is one of the popular moments of each of the reunions), but once again, Potts is prevailed upon to tell the story "as only he can tell it." ("And Julia's the only person to tell it. She's such a

---

[3] T. S. Eliot, *The Cocktail Party*, p. 10.

good mimic."[4]) By this last remark, we mean that Potts has developed a "number" over the years; he has added various embellishments to the story (which may be true or may be mere exaggerations—it really does not matter). As the storyteller begins to unfold the familiar theme, his various virtuoso turns are met with friendly chuckles, rather like small cries of encouragement to the jazz soloist, urging him on to greater heights of inspiration while they relax in the comfort of the familiar. ("*I'm* never tired of hearing that story."[5])

If an arabesque is a "number" that the group has heard before, it reinforces the perceived relationship of the players by reminding them of topic-images that they willingly share in common. If the arabesque is a "new trick," it also reinforces the perceived friendship, because it is symptomatic of the others' trust in the individual performer—they are willing to be responsible for sharing in the new images that the performer is about to present and are willing to continue the conversation from wherever and whenever the arabesque is finished.

Presto

The *presto* tactic of Personal Conversation is related to the arabesque in that both tactics have a magical quality about them. Whereas the arabesque can be an enchanting monologue, the presto is a quick sleight of hand, often catching even the performer by surprise. The presto is an abrupt shift in the conversation.

When it is a deliberate tactic, the presto is announced with a verbal flourish like "Oh, before I forget . . ." or "That reminds me, did you hear . . ." or "You'll never believe this, but . . ." In a flash, one player transforms the topic of conversation. To use our cross-country soccer analogy, the player has suddenly taken the ball and is running with it up a side path. Ordinarily the others momentarily suspend their play, blink once or twice to see where their fellow player and the new path are, check to be sure of their own footing, and then follow the lead. If the other player has found an especially interesting path to explore, the game will be enhanced. If the path is a dead end, they will quickly retreat for a more rewarding direction of play. In any event, they will have maintained their group rhythm and rewarded the other's inspiration, however productive, with their trust.

---

[4] T. S. Eliot, *The Cocktail Party*, p. 11.
[5] T. S. Eliot, *The Cocktail Party*, p. 10.

When the presto is less deliberate it often goes unnoticed until later in the conversation, if at all. But occasionally the players suddenly do stop mid-play or during a break to ask themselves, "Now, how did we get on this subject? Why just a minute ago we were talking about tigers and being up in a tree with a Maharaja and now we're discussing Lady Klootz's Lithuanian accent!" The really curious players sometimes even enjoy recounting the details of their conversation, like watching family movies backwards, hoping to find the origin of their conversational tangent.

At any rate, Personal Conversation Among Friends tends to be full of prestos. Whether consciously intended or not, they are additional evidence for our claim that in this kind of communicative interaction cooperative participation is more important than thematic continuity. The players are most interested in playing with each other; getting somewhere specific is more a happy coincidence than a predetermined goal.[6]

Flooding Out

Another tactic found in Personal Conversation that often contributes to a satisfactory play of the game is *flooding out*.[7] Like presto, flooding out is a temporary challenge to the even flow of the conversation. But unlike presto, the challenge of flooding out is more compelling than the group's chase after an elusive teammate—flooding out has potential for capsizing the entire conversation because it literally leaves "every man to sink or swim for himself."

Returning to our metaphor of the cross-country soccer romp, flooding out occurs when one player suddenly picks up the ball and tosses it into a pond. The players must then get wet, recover the ball, and keep the game moving. In the conversational equivalent, the players find themselves right in the midst of a "touchy" topic, and everyone has to take some risks so that harmony may be restored to the encounter.

Various topics can be "touchy" even among those who perceive each other as fairly close friends. One player, for example, may disclose some

---

6 "Committee meeting," therefore, is a variation on the game of Personal Conversation Among Friends. Those who seek the most efficient path for the group to reach the end of a course, in order to finish the business and adjourn the meeting, might consider presto more a bothersome interruption than a potentially productive inspiration.

7 The term comes from E. Goffman, *Encounters* (Indianapolis: Bobbs-Merrill Co., 1961), pp. 55–61. Goffman, however, uses "flooding out" to describe when a person is "momentarily 'out of play.'" We use it here as an ongoing tactic in a play of the game.

personal information about his or her self that the group had never had access to before. ("Well, I think *I* understand because I tried to commit suicide once myself" or "I lost *my* virginity when I was 16" or "Loved Rebecca? I hated her.") Willingness to make such disclosures is symptomatic of perceived interpersonal trust, but it also challenges the group to reciprocate either with similar disclosures or at least with acceptance of the original disclosure.

Another player may flood out the conversation by suggesting that the group discuss a topic that is not in the group's repertoire of commonly shared topic-images. Suppose, for example, that four friends gathered for the evening are planning what to do next. One of them suggests, "Let's go to an adult movie theatre. There's a double feature at the Erotica Exotica." This proposal could be considered a flood out if the group members have never shared their personal opinions on the value of adult movies or if they have shared them in the past, but the group is sensitive to the fact that the opinions are not all the same. Even if the friends choose not to follow the suggestion and go, one player has proposed that the movies are a topic worthy of the group's discussion— either for the first time or once again—and the rest of the group must respond.

The value of flooding out to Personal Conversation is that the capsized conversation offers a challenge to the ensemble to get the conversation back on course with a new tempo. There is pleasure afforded to players who are reminded that they are playing a teamwork game and who are challenged to seek additional evidence for their friendship images. Much the same fun derives in a rowboat filled with teen-agers when someone begins to rock it playfully. Although some on board may squeal, "Oh, Andrew, stop that!" they do so gleefully, and everyone laughs as the boat tips over and one and all get dunked. There is then the added joy as confusion reigns amidst the general grabbing for the overturned boat and the effort to return to stability: "No, tip it up this way!" "No, no, we're going to go under," and so on. Just as these individuals enjoy testing their ensemble skill in righting the boat, so the personal conversationalists welcome such a mild test of their teamwork in recovering the ball from the conversational thicket of a menacing topic.

Sounding

In Personal Conversation Among Friends, *sounding* is a verbal teasing tactic that players use to test both group trust and self-control. Sounding is literally a depth charge that measures the extent of both group and player vulnerability. In the cross-country soccer game analogy, it could be likened to one player's bumping into another, throwing the other off balance. Everyone else watches hoping that the one doing the bumping "didn't mean to hurt the other," that the one bumped "can take it," and that play can continue with renewed confidence, not handicapped by injured players.

To a passerby, such shoving and poking might seem more to inhibit than facilitate teamwork. If we were to come upon a group of players who were sounding, we might note that seeming friends were tossing out insults such as "Your mother eats rat heads" or "What kind of a fathead goofball are you, Henry?" or "Where'd you get all that kinky hair, Nigger?" Indeed, what is *said* may be very offensive. Insults, by definition, are not compliments. But, once again, what is *said* in this communicative experience is not as important as the *act of saying*—what the tactic itself says about and for the interpersonal relationship images of the players.

The friendship readings that are being taken in sounding are incredibly complex. We do not intend to elaborate them all here, but let us suggest a few. First, we can consider the features of the tactic from the perspective of the person who does the sounding. The sounder could be checking, however consciously, to see how accessible he and another person are to one another and how willing the other is to allow personal information to be shared for the sake of the relationship. That is, when the sounder says, "Boy, Jerry, are you ever a loser! Can't you do *anything* right?" he is also saying, "I imagine that I know you well enough that what I am saying *could* insult you, but I also imagine that you know me well enough to trust that I am merely playing with you— that I am enjoying our relationship for its own sake."

The sounder's intentions could also be therapeutic. Relying on a certain amount of accessibility in a relationship, sounding can also serve as an innoculation: In an atmosphere of perceived trust, one player might try to desensitize another in order to prepare the other for times when the insults might be more real. "I imagine that I know you well enough that what I am saying *could* insult you, but I also imagine that you know me well enough to trust me that I am merely playing with you for your own sake to give you feedback, to help you test your own limits, to challenge your own self-control." Consider, for example, the case of a pregnant thirteen year old in a reformatory. Every day the girls in her cabin, some of whom were also pregnant, made fun of her, often reducing her to tears. When the cabin mates were asked by a counselor why

they did this, they responded, "She's got to learn how to take it. If she can't take it now, among us, her friends, she's never going to survive outside." Verbal sparring can be intended to train a player to be able to "take it" when the situation is real.

The responsibility that the sounding tactic implies for the object of the remarks is equally, if not more, complicated. The "sounded" has to choose how to interpret the remarks and how to respond. The first part of the interpretation is probably an implicit acknowledgement of the potential legitimacy of the insult: "You're so right; you do know me well; that is a sore spot of mine." Simultaneously, the sounded must also acknowledge that the other has the right and/or the duty to express the remark: "You are a friend whom I trust so I know that you are probably playing with me and/or I would expect you, as a friend, to have my best interests at heart and tease me for my own good if I deserve it."

Once the sounded affords the other this sounding license, admitting to a certain level of friendship between them, then it is necessary to respond—reciprocity being an inherent feature of the nearness of this kind of a relationship. (To ignore the sounding would be to play Put Off—a game played by acquaintances, those who cannot take risks with personal vulnerabilities.) The sounded cannot deny the insult ("That's a lie! . . . Oh, no I'm not!"); to indicate that the comment hurt would be to admit that it was taken literally, that the other's teasing intentions were not interpreted that way. Some other response is therefore necessary so that the player can indicate both his or her trust in the sounder and his or her ability to "take it," to "keep cool." Often, then, the sounded sounds back, displaying trust, self-control, and maybe even verbal virtuosity—giving verbally as well as taking. The complexity of the interaction multiplies.[8]

All the while the "sounder" and the "sounded" are testing the depth of their friendship, the trust and control of the rest of the players who are present are also being challenged. From their point of view, they are trusting that their image of the group's friendship is legitimate, that the sounding is a symptom of group solidarity. Each trusts that the person

---

[8] For some friendships sounding is a very popular Personal Conversation tactic and players develop a special reputation for their virtuosity. Linguistic studies report regional variations of such elaborate ritualistic insult exchanges as having names like "woofing," "joning," "the dozens," "signifying," "cutting," "chopping," "ranking," "jamming," "cracking," "blintzing," and "pimping." We would refer our readers to the following sources as an introduction to this kind of communication study: Roger D. Abrahams, *Deep Down in the Jungle*, rev. ed. (Chicago: Aldine, 1970); Thomas Kochman, ed., *Rappin' and Stylin' Out: Communication in Urban Black America* (Urbana, Ill.: University of Illinois Press, 1972); Frederick Williams, ed., *Language and Poverty: Perspectives on a Theme* (Chicago: Markham Publishing Company, 1970).

doing the sounding is teasing for the sake of play or helpful concern, not for the sake of violence. Each also trusts that the person being sounded will trust the validity of these implicit intentions and respond accordingly. As a rule, the complex display of group loyalty and personal strength that accompanies sounding encourages better teamwork in future play.

Diplomacy

In terms of the cross-country soccer game, we have great respect for someone who can negotiate difficult parts of the terrain (ponds, streams, thickets, or whatever) with agility. We admire the player who can avoid obstacles and direct the game around them or the player who can gingerly maneuver through the swamp if necessary or even, as in the case of flooding out, set things straight once again.

In Personal Conversation Among Friends, a player can exercise diplomacy in two ways: He or she may simply avoid potentially menacing topics such as politics and religion and steer the conversation around them, or he or she may discuss the topics carefully using the quality we call *tact*. Either way, the diplomat helps his friends meet and overcome uncomfortable situations. ("Oh do stop wrangling, both of you. It's your turn, Julia. Do tell that story you told the other day. . . ."[9])

This is not to suggest that controversial subjects should always be avoided. On the contrary, as we continue to emphasize, experienced conversationalists thrive on variety, and without such occasional challenges any conversational ensemble may become rather dull. But also without the presence of diplomats to ensure that variety will not become violence, the group tends not to be especially daring. The players may find themselves "in a rut," covering the same safe topical ground with little change of pace.

Cheerleading

Those who are not as agile as diplomats often perform an equally important support function for the group by *cheerleading*—offering praise and encouragement both for what is said and for the people who are doing the saying. Cheerleaders applaud both the game and its players. Think of the times you have experienced when friends supported one another in conversation—laughing at each others' jokes, expressing sympathy at tales of woe, listening attentively to arabesques, constantly assuring each other that they are

---

[9] T. S. Eliot, *The Cocktail Party*, p. 10.

all "on the same wave length" regarding the conversational topic. ("But I'm still waiting to know what happened. I know it started as a story about tigers.")

Since, for the most part, the players are responsible for their own conversational path, praise for the topic is easily translated into praise for the players themselves. ("And Julia's the only person to tell it. She's such a good mimic." "Am I a good mimic?" "You *are* a good mimic. You never miss anything."[10]) Soon the laughter and cheers stir the players to perform better and better. Like a jam session with a jazz combo, the enthusiasm and excitement can be contagious and inspiring.

Shared Silence

Support need not always be noisy, however. Sometimes a group of friends can be most inspired and comforted when the players pause and share a few moments of *silence*. Being able to be quiet together comfortably is symptomatic usually only of functional non-person relationships (cab driver and passenger, servant and master), or of interpersonal relationships whose members are highly confident of their mutual commitment and are willing and able to enjoy re-creative rest as well as recreational play.

Courting

The last tactic we shall include in our by no means exhaustive list of tactics that appear in the Approaching Interpersonal Communication game of Personal Conversation Among Friends is *courting*. This tactic could also be called *duet*. During a play of the game two players manifest signals of willingness to relate as a pair. Unlike swinging, however, which is a flirtatious rehearsal of ploys without invitation, courting *is* a come-on.

As is true for the pre-courting behavior of Polite Conversation, it is impossible to itemize the specific communicative features of Personal Conversation courting. The signals that say "come a little closer" vary from culture to culture, from subculture to subculture. In our uncertainty about which signals are "right" or which will be "right" for us, we turn to all kinds of authorities to tell us what is customary. Novels, plays, movies, television, advertising, religion, astrology, politics, philosophy,

---

[10] T. S. Eliot, *The Cocktail Party*, p. 11.

psychology, and tales of "real-life experience" are but a few of the "authorities" who compete to answer such intrapersonal questions as: "How should I behave?" "What should I say?" "How can I attract the

'right' other(s)?" "Who are the 'right' other(s) I should try to attract?" (And, paradoxically, our assertion that courting styles can, do, will, and ought to vary is part of yet another competing authoritative tradition that will be accepted by some and rejected by others.)

Whatever its features, if a duet proves mutually gratifying during the course of Personal Conversation Among Friends, the couple may decide to establish more private arenas (a "date"). Two-Handed Personal Conversation is inappropriate in the presence of the ensemble. A group of friends may, indeed, be pleased and proud of the various special relationships among its members, but when they are together they expect to play together as a team. Just as the group delights in arabesque, it will also give acting space to duets, but it will not allow a duet to steal the ball and run away with it.

Having courted as much as is suitable in the presence of their friends, then, a couple will meet under a variety of circumstances that enable them to continue—now as a two-person team—the same tactics we have seen in Personal Conversation Among Friends: arabesque ("Actually, the whole thing started when I was in fourth grade in Detroit. Even then, as a 9-year-old child, I was directing plays. Why I remember one spring day out on the playground when . . ."), presto ("Oh! I don't know why or how, but that reminds me—cheese! I'm sorry for interrupting, but after you finish your story, don't let me forget to add cheese to the grocery list for the party . . ."), flooding out ("Let's go up to my grandparents' cabin for the weekend; this time we'll have the place all to ourselves . . ."), sounding ("Good grief, Susan, you smoke like a factory; how many packs of those cancerous things do you put away in a day?"), diplomacy ("Maybe tonight isn't the time to talk about this, Charles, you look so tired . . ."), cheerleading ("I'm very pleased with all the nice things you said to my folks as we were leaving, Tom . . ."), and shared silence (" . . ."). Personal Conversation Among Friends played by two people adds the experience of tennis practice to the cross-country soccer analogy—the players derive pleasure from sustaining the rhythm of a volley with no concerted effort to score points but with emphasis on improving each other's capacity to play the game.

It goes without saying that this is not all there is to courting, although for many couples the exchange of come-ons becomes the core of their relationship and no effort is made to go beyond the come-on tactics (which admittedly are flattering and help the participants raise each others' self-esteem) and become more intimate. It is even possible for a couple who do not actually imagine each other as intimates but who court exceptionally well together to mistake the come-ons for love and to get married. Thus, one sometimes meets a married couple who are little more than acquaintances; upon questioning as to why they married, one spouse may remark that "He (she) was such a good dancer, and I loved to go dancing." Odd as this may sound in retrospect, it more often than not reveals two players who performed customary courting tactics in good faith but were unable to distinguish the come-on of Personal Conversation Among Friends from a more intimate game.

The relationship expectations that individuals bring to Two-Handed Personal Conversation Among Friends, therefore, are no less important than those that regulate any other communicative experience. These expectations will have to be met if the game is to prove mutually gratifying. And if the play of the game is successful, if the players do experience each other as "closer" friends as a result of their communicative experience, they will seek additional opportunities to play, to encourage ever more intimate synchrony of action and communication.[11]

The foregoing discussion of tactical options that are typically available to personal conversationalists is not intended to suggest that each player performs only one role or that each must limit his or her choice to a single persona. We need personal variety as well as conversational variety. And among friends we can try on numerous kinds of conversational costumes, some of which, we may discover, we would never wear again, at least not in more formal circumstances, and some of which, we may discover, suit us rather well. That is, if we are unable to perform any one of these tactics especially well, our "friends" will not hold our performance failure against us. To the extent that we imagine each other as "friend" we continually try to put the best construction on everything. Neither do we claim that our list is exhaustive. It is merely representative of the numerous verbal gestures that individuals use to facilitate images of friendship in interpersonal communication.

Personal Conversation facilitates increased emotional nearness because it offers a climate in which the participants feel encouraged to cooperate as a group in the use of tactics aimed at maintaining and enhancing mutual rapport. Unlike Polite Conversation, where the action is more transitory and the goal is to rehearse oneself in gambits in order to pass the time, the object of Personal Conversation is to listen to others, to hook remarks on to what they have said, to demonstrate not

---

[11] Later in this chapter we will suggest what happens when, for whatever reason, one of the players emits come-on signals without being prepared to act on them responsibly. A play of that Distancing game, although potentially physically intimate, will keep the players emotionally separate.

facile style but considerable interpersonal accessibility, reciprocity, spontaneity, and commitment.

As a paradigm illustration, let us look at some expert players engaged in Personal Conversation. Let us glance once again at the dialogue offered by T. S. Eliot in his drama *The Cocktail Party*. Hopefully, by viewing the dialogue through the game-play perspective of Personal Conversation Among Friends we can better see where and how the players listen to one another and hook on to one another's comments. We should also be able to observe the interplay of tactics and customs as the participants meander through the conversation course, adeptly tossing the ball back and forth.

Alex: "You've missed the point completely, Julia: There *were* no tigers. *That* was the point."

Possibly an instance of sounding; Alex, at least, is trusting that Julia will not be personally insulted by his demonstrating that she has missed the point.

Julia: "Then what were you doing, up in a tree: You and the Maharaja?"

Julia trusts Alex; does not show offense. Instead, she seeks clarification from a friend.

Alex: "My dear Julia! It's perfectly hopeless. You haven't been listening."

Sounding once again; perhaps marking time in hopes that some one else will pick up the conversation.

Peter: "You'll have to tell us all over again, Alex."

Peter diplomatically invites an arabesque, giving Alex "the floor" if he would like it and taking Julia "off the hook" too—"tell *us* all over again."

Alex: "I never tell the same story twice."

Coy—courting some reinforcing cheers.

Julia: "But I'm still waiting to know what happened. I know it started out as a story about tigers."

Julia, still confused, offers some encouragement.

Alex: "I said there were no tigers."

Alex, fearing that his performance will, once again, go unappreciated, does not begin.

Celia: "O do stop wrangling, both of you. It's your turn, Julia. Do tell us that story you told the other day, about Lady Klootz and the wedding cake."

Celia, diplomatically recognizing that Alex would prefer not to continue down what to him is a dead end, prestos the conversation to Julia, reminding Julia that she is not unloved or seen as completely stupid just because she missed the point of Alex's tale.

Peter: "And how the butler found her in the pantry, rinsing her mouth out with champagne. I like that story."

Peter chimes in cheering for what no doubt is a customary arabesque that they all enjoy.

Celia: "I love that story."

Celia encourages Julia to play with the ball she is being tossed.

Alex: "*I'm* never tired of hearing that story."

Alex, glad not to be the focus of attention, invites a bravura performance from Julia.

Julia: "Well, you all seem to know it."

A coy flood out from Julia. Perhaps she does not completely trust that Alex's earlier sounding of her was for its own sake. Maybe the group would be happier if she were quiet?

Celia: "Do we all know it? But we're never tired of hearing *you* tell it. I don't believe everyone here knows it."
[To the unidentified Guest]
"You don't know it, do you?"

Celia hastens to recover the conversational situation. She diplomatically reports the results of an intuitive opinion poll and, in case that is insufficient encouragement, seeks additional proof that *everyone* has not heard Julia's arabesque.

Unidentified Guest: "No, I've never heard it."

The stranger verifies Celia's suspicion and indirectly signals that he would not be opposed to Julia's presentation.

Celia: "Here's one new listener for you, Julia; and I don't believe Edward knows it."

Celia announces her new proof—and suggests the possibility of more.

Edward: "I may have heard it, but I don't remember it."

Edward offers encouragement; but it could also be a flood out—the story must not be very exciting if he thinks he's heard it, but he cannot remember it for sure.

Celia: "And Julia's the only person to tell it. She's such a good mimic."

Once again, Celia to the rescue. Just in case Edward *is* a little sour on the *topic* of Julia's arabesque, she reinforces Julia's arabesque *style*.

Julia: "Am I a good mimic?"

Checking to see what the cheers are for. Maybe she, too, is tired of the story itself but *is* proud of her style and if that is what the group wants, she will perform.

Peter: "You *are* a good mimic. You never miss anything."

Once again, Peter rushes to Julia's side.

Alex: "She never misses anything unless she wants to."

Alex *could* be cheering, but he might also be flooding out—reminding Julia and the others that his wounds caused by Julia's earlier ineptness are still sore, handicapping his play.

Celia: "Especially the Lithuanian accent."

Celia is especially quick, not letting the possible flood out even happen. She recalls a special flourish of Julia's. Celia suggests that at least *she* remembers both the topic of the story *and* Julia's special style.

Julia: "Lithuanian? Lady Klootz?"

Whoops! Celia was trying too hard. She too seems to have missed this time.

Peter: "I thought she was Belgian."

Checking out his image of the topic.

Alex: "Her father belonged to a Baltic family—one of the *oldest* Baltic families with a branch in Sweden and one in Denmark. There were several very lovely daughters: I wonder what's become of them now."[12]

Hurray! Alex is back in old form. His wounds seem to have healed enough to permit a new arabesque.

So far they have swiftly passed the ball back and forth. Now they are off on a side track to explain Lady Klootz and her background. Notice what has happened to the opening story about the tigers: The subject changed without disrupting the conversation. The group has roamed afield over topics that allow for the *maximum participation* without needless sacrifice of thematic continuity. At this point they all want to go over familiar terrain—the story about Lady Klootz. Let us watch them a little while longer and continue our play by play commentary.

Julia: "Lady Klootz was very lovely, once upon a time. What a life she led! I used to say to her: 'Greta! You have too much vitality.' But she enjoyed herself."

Alex has joined the group and so Julia begins her arabesque, making sure to include the stranger in their team play.

[To the Unidentified Guest]

"Did *you* know Lady Klootz?"

---

[12] T. S. Eliot, *The Cocktail Party*, pp. 9–12.

Unidentified Guest: "No, I never met her."

He plays, but not especially well. Almost breaks the conversational rhythm with an inartistic return.

Celia: "Go on with the story about the wedding cake."

But here is diplomat Celia again, cheering for a special part of the story, trying to stabilize the rhythm of the conversation.

Julia: "Well, but it really isn't my story. I heard it first from Delia Verinder who was there when it happened."
[To the Unidentified Guest] "Do *you* know Delia Verinder?"

Julia, encouraged, continues but not without risking the rhythm once again. Perhaps, for her, equal participation from one and all is worth the sacrifice not only of thematic continuity, but of her own arabesque as well.

Unidentified Guest: "No, I don't know her."

Another polite response, albeit an ungraceful return.

Julia: "Well, one can't be too careful before one tells a story."

Julia, now being her *own* diplomat, accounts for her repeated attempts to include everyone in her conversational negotiation.

Alex: "Delia Verinder? Was she the one who had three brothers?"

His strength renewed, Alex makes an effort to contribute to the developing topic.

Julia: "How many brothers? Two, I think."

Julia interprets Alex's comment as a fair play.

Alex: "No, there were three, but you wouldn't know the third one: They kept him rather quiet."

Oh dear, perhaps we guessed too much too soon: Alex is either especially disagreeable tonight or his injuries still ache. He will not let Julia be competent even in her own arabesque. Presto! He knows more about it than she does.

Julia: "Oh, you mean *that* one."

Julia responds next—not letting Alex carry the ball away from her too far—and furthermore she lets him know that he is not hiding anything either.

Alex: "He was feebleminded."

Since Alex cannot presto the ball away from Julia, how about a flood out?

Julia: "Oh, not feebleminded: He was only harmless."

Julia, ever more the diplomat, indicates *both* her knowledge of the topic's details and her ability to be tactful.

Alex: "Well then, harmless."	Alex gives in and tosses the conversation ball with no special challenge.
Julia: "He was very clever at repairing clocks; and he had a remarkable sense of hearing—the only man I ever met who could hear the cry of bats."	Julia prestos the conversation away from its embarrassing potential into an elaboration of the harmless brother's virtues.
Peter: "Hear the cry of bats?"	Peter reenters with a short volley, courting Julia's attention.
Julia: "He could hear the cry of bats."	Julia volleys back in the same rhythm.
Celia: "But how do you know he could hear the cry of bats?"	Celia turns the duet into a trio.
Julia: "Because he said so. And I believed him."	Julia calls a halt to the trio.
Celia: "But if he was so . . . harmless, how could you believe him? He might have imagined it."	No longer the diplomat, Celia is challenging, almost sounding Julia. Is she now doubting Julia's intelligence, accusing her of being gullible, or is she just checking up on the details of the story?
Julia: "My darling Celia, you needn't be so skeptical. I stayed there once at their castle in the North. How he suffered! They had to find an island for him where there were no bats."	Julia does not take Celia's question as a sound. She responds as though Celia were trying to verify the story's details; she does not try to defend her own gullibility or respond by sounding Celia.
Alex: "And is he still there? Julia is really a mine of information.	Keeping in the play—it is difficult for outsiders to guarantee, however, whether Alex is cheering Julia on or sounding her.
Celia: "There isn't much that Julia doesn't know."	The same goes for Celia—cheer or sound?
Peter: "Go on with the story about the wedding cake." [Edward leaves the room.]	Peter, at any rate, although perhaps personally interested in Julia, moves the conversation away from her personal style (which the others now could possibly be questioning) and

back to the story she was telling. (Not only was Edward uninspired by the story in the first place, but he now seems to have cast his vote against Julia herself by leaving the playing field.)

Julia: "No, we'll wait until Edward comes back into the room. Now I want to relax. Are there any more cocktails?"

Still preferring full participation (taking no affront at Edward's departure) to personal fame, Julia calls time out.

Peter: "But do go on. Edward wasn't listening anyway."[13]

Peter would like Julia to get some glory, he does not want her to yield to the others, and yet in his enthusiasm he floods out her arabesque by commenting on Edward's inattentiveness and obvious disinterest.

Surely these are virtuoso personal conversationalists. Their display of teamwork and control by means of verbal contact as they meander through a variety of topics indicates that they are seasoned players of Personal Conversation Among Friends. But for the most part, their expertise is no different than that which most of us display when we take time to enjoy ourselves in conversations with friends.

We now turn from this game that facilitates images of friendship, to its reciprocal Informal Conversation game—Personal Conversation Among Enemies or Put Down.

PUT DOWN: A DISTANCING INFORMAL CONVERSATION GAME

$$F \quad . \quad . \quad . \quad . \quad . \quad \{ \quad \} \quad . \quad . \quad I$$
$$\leftarrow DG$$

So far in this chapter our efforts have been to describe the communicative experience of individuals who imagine themselves as relatively accessible, reciprocal, committed, and spontaneous with each other. We have suggested how it might be when people who view the interpersonal gap in their relationship as reasonably minimal communi-

---

[13] T. S. Eliot, *The Cocktail Party*, pp. 12–15.

cate across that gap which separates their life spaces and, in some cases, even minimize the extent of the gap.

Now we would like to consider what might be the communicative experience of individuals who imagine an equally minimal degree of emotional distance in their relationship but who are bound to communicate as enemies because of a bond of reciprocal disaffection. We shall consider this kind of communicative activity as a game called *Put Down*. Put Down is a game whose telos inhibits images of friendship among fairly intimate players.

Everyone is capable of engaging in an enemy relationship. A complex social fabric that tolerates a range of short-lived as well as enduring sympathies also includes a range of short-lived and enduring aversions.[14] We are not suggesting that every kind of relationship is equally sought after and equally enjoyed. Enemy relationships, for example, are uncomfortable for people whose upbringing emphasizes verbal politeness. That is, many people would rather play Put Off with an antagonistic acquaintance or just ignore potential enemies altogether (Turn Off). But, for better or worse, when we take the emotional risks necessary to play Informal Conversation games, we may be facilitating the development of friendship images with some players, but we are also committing ourselves to the possibility of becoming accessible to someone whom we find disagreeable. Distancing ourselves from the other in these kinds of relationships is not always easy, but we can and we do and in the rest of this chapter we shall explore both possibilities of "escape" that the Put Down facilitates: hustling and hassling. As you read you might compare what we say with your own experience. How is it that *you* deal with *your* hostility and derive gratification from *your* enemies?

Before examining these communicative experiences explicitly, let us elaborate what we mean by the bond of reciprocal disaffection that binds those who play Put Down. We would like to suggest that two elements converge in the interpersonal relationship image of "enemy." These elements are competition and vulnerability.

Why disagreeable relationships exist at all is a compelling question. And we should probably avoid the traps in which such a philosophical, historical, theological, and/or psychological discussion would surely catch us. It does seem safe to say, however, that interpersonal antagonism does exist and that it usually occurs whenever or wherever we encounter a situation whose resources are limited and we perceive that

---

[14] "And in this complex, the sphere of indifference is relatively limited." Georg Simmel, *Conflict*, trans. Kurt H. Wolff (New York: Free Press of Glencoe, 1964), p. 20.

the Other would prefer to compete with us for them rather than to collaborate in their acquisition.

In some relationships the nature and extent of the competition is ambiguous. Where we think that the Other might be engaged with us hoping to gain through us but not at our expense we tend to have "mixed feelings" or "mixed motives." If we think we can gain in a similar fashion from the relationship, we do not challenge the Other; we just put the Other off, inhibiting the possibility of increased intimacy where we may indeed lose. Recall our previous Put Off example of the girl and her date at dinner. His gain may be to be seen in a fashionable restaurant with an attractive girl and her gain may be enjoyment of an elegantly prepared meal. In this case, neither of them is gaining at the Other's loss. To keep it that way—perhaps to avoid the possibility of embarrassing intimate advances in public—the girl evades her date's overtures for greater accessibility by playing Put Off. And since a public "scene" between them would be a loss for him, he too plays Put Off and avoids pursuing the issue.

In other relationships, however, we do not perceive the extent of the competition as so ambiguous. That is, in some relationships where we think we know more about the Other (where the Other is more accessible to us) we sense both that the Other is committed to us because of what he or she stands to gain from our relationship and that the Other's gain will probably be at our loss. In other words, such relationships *are* disagreeable; we imagine that the Other is trying to put us down.[15] In these relationships, then, the only way we can possibly gain is to reciprocate, to compete in kind. That is, if we ignore the Other (play Turn Off) we can possibly lose. The Other knows so much about us that we fear what he or she will do with his information in our absence. Furthermore, if we evade the Other (play Put Off) we may also lose. To communicate our wish to postpone the issue signals weakness to an antagonist who will then take advantage. ("Hey! You! . . . Don't you evade me . . . Answer me . . . Right now . . !")

In other words, because the Other is accessible to us we perceive his or her competition as disagreeable, but because the Other is accessible to us he or she is also vulnerable to reciprocity. Whoever "started" the disagreeable relationship is not the issue at question, even if it were

---

[15] At any rate, in such situations, it is "safer" to distrust the Other than it is to trust him or her. Morton Deutsch reminds us about the pain of misplaced trust by suggesting that when trust is not fulfilled the trusting individual suffers an unpleasant consequence that is greater than the gain that he or she would have derived if the trusted person had proven to be reliable. Morton Deutsch, "Trust and Suspicion," *Journal of Conflict Resolution* 2(1958): 265–279.

possible to locate the origins of our mutual animosity (which it often is not). What *is* significant, however, is that enemies are committed to each other as actively as are friends[16] and that in such a bond of reciprocal disaffection *winner* and *loser* are not especially meaningful terms.

Stop for a moment and consider the image of an enemy in international politics. Isn't it true but also strange that we tend to have or try to have the most agreements with those we fear the most? We do not exert ourselves in communicating with those countries whose competitive capacity is minimal or whose intentions are not suspect. The grand gesture of cutting off communication with a country is really not as courageous as it seems. Either the country is not really seen as a capable competitor in the first place, or else we just increase our supply of "secret" communication channels (spies, counterspies, reconnaissance flights, "unofficial" meetings between various heads of state, and so on). Those we fear the most are those whom we know the most about, those who know the most about us, and those whom we suspect do not have our best interests as their goals. This inflationary spiral of distrust keeps us enemies *and* keeps us in contact. To continue to confirm our suspicions that someone is an enemy, we cannot avoid him or be evasive in his presence, we must interact, and we must continue to behave contrary to each other's goals. An enemy relationship image is meaningful only if there is conflict and this conflict can only be known if there is communication.[17]

The communicative enactments of persons related by reciprocal enemy images are games that we have labeled *Put Down*. Two major strategies are manifest in these communicative experiences. In one, hustling, the players engage in hypocrisy—each knowingly contradicting what he or she says with what he or she means. That is, the players communicate intimacy but deny responsibility for emotional nearness. In the other strategy, hassling, players confront each other in a continual

---

[16] "The more players act together, despite competition, to produce a common game, the closer is the bond unifying them all." Paul Weiss, *Sport: A Philosophic Inquiry* (Carbondale, Ill.: Southern Illinois University Press, 1971), p. 246.

[17] "Social conflict is a term we assign to particular human communicative behaviors. Two assumptions are implicit in this statement. First, social conflict is communicative behavior. There can be no conflict without verbal and nonverbal communication. Humans define their relationships by communication, and a relationship characterized by conflict is a relationship—hence, a form of communicative behavior. Second, social conflict is *not* a 'thing' in the language of General Semantics. Conflict exists when the parties involved agree in some way that the behaviors associated with their relationship are labeled as 'conflict' behaviors. Thus, conflict is not an external reality, but conflict is associated with an attitude determining perceptions and behaviors held by members of a relationship." Fred E. Jandt, *Conflict Resolution Through Communication* (New York: Harper & Row, 1973), p. 2.

exchange of hostility—each saying what he or she means and eventually altering the explicit nature of the physical intimacy as well. That is, these players openly express their frustrations, but they also hope to avoid being disgraced in physical confrontation.

Hustling

One of the most obvious examples of the Put Down tactic of *hustling* occurs in the interpersonal communicative relationship known variously as "pimping," "whoring," and "the oldest profession."[18] In this hustle, a prostitute, usually female, engages in sexual intimacy with a client in return for money. In the version played in contemporary America, the Distancing counterpart of Personal Conversation Among Friends, there are usually at least three players: the Ho (the prostitute), the Pimp (the prostitute's booking agent), and the Trick (the customer). Although on the surface the game would seem to be a strictly financial matter (the Ho offering come-ons and sex in return for a fee), the rip-off exchange that binds the participants together as a team is much more complicated,[19] just as complex, as a matter of fact, as the relationship among Alex, Julia, Celia, Peter, Edward, and the Unidentified Guest.

Ho⇌Trick. The relation of Ho to Trick is self-evident. The Ho invites the Trick to pay for sex. In this barter, the Trick pays the Ho for the opportunity of using her body; he purchases power over her, and this submission gives the Trick a kind of self-image gratification. But in taking the Trick's money, the Ho rips him off—she engages in come-ons and sex without herself being turned on sexually by the Trick; that is, in spite of her behavior she, as a professional, only gives the appearance of intimacy. She moves but does not act. The Trick understands this rip-off and will sometimes try to rip the Ho off by getting her to enjoy the sexual union in spite of herself (thus increasing his ego satisfaction with his own sexual abilities). Of course, the Ho fully realizes the value of this bonus and is prepared to fake her own sexual stimulation with a well-paying or steady customer in order to retain his regular business. In one

---

[18] There is no way that communication is *not* a part of this experience, yet there is also no way that describing the specifics of what *is said* will add any special flavor, except for those with prurient interests, to our analysis.

[19] In what is to follow we have relied heavily upon Christina Milner and Richard Milner, *Black Players: The Secret World of Black Pimps* (New York: Bantam Books, 1972), although we have modified several features of their sociological study to meet the needs of our communication orientation.

sense, then, one hesitates to say that these come-ons for profit are distancing, but in another sense it should be clear that such careful calculation of relative advantage goes a long way toward maintaining the interpersonal emotional gap between the players.

Ho⇌Pimp. The Ho, in her turn, plays a game with her Pimp in which she suffers the larger rip-off. The emotional exchange here is two-way: In return for her turning over to him the Trick's money (or in some cases, giving him his manager's commission), the Pimp provides the Ho with the emotional security of a steady male and perhaps living accommodations. However, because in most instances the Pimp has a fundamental disregard for women,[20] he measures out his emotional support to the Ho in a fashion that maximizes her financial payoff to him while allowing him to retain a maximum emotional dominance over her. The Pimp thus replenishes his stable of Hos with his come-ons in order to rip them off financially, and because he knows that the Ho needs him for the come-ons he offers her, the Pimp is gratified both in his self-image and in his wallet.

Pimp⇌Trick. Finally, the Pimp and the Trick rely on each other as teammates even though they may never actually communicate with one another. First, the Pimp makes an emotional profit on the Trick; he knows that the Trick, in spite of his overt disgust with Pimping as a profession, secretly envies the Pimp's ability to "get it free," to dominate the Ho, and not have to pay her for her come-ons. It is clear that the Pimp is gaining just that rip-off gratification from the Ho that the Trick seeks, and it is clear furthermore that the Pimp is getting the genuine article from his Ho rather than the surface behavior the Trick must settle for. But the Pimp in his turn knows that to maintain his own flashy life-style, of fancy clothes, cars, and lavish entertainment, he must ulti-mately enslave himself to the straight world that is owned by Tricks (salesmen, store managers, etc.). The Pimp not only sees himself as dependent for his material gratifications upon the straight world inhab-ited by his own customers, but also, in forcing him to pay exorbitant prices for products, the Tricks are ripping him off as part of the natural financial cycle.

The Pimp rationalizes this subservience to the straight world in the belief that the salesman is actually a kind of Ho insofar as he too must submit to a "boss" (Pimp) who doles out a paycheck in return for work. The Ho, too, rationalizes her circumstances by claiming that even the

---

[20] Milner and Milner, pp. 55–58.

most intimate relationships are hustles, that, for example, a housewife is a Ho who does not know it insofar as her husband keeps her supplied with material goods in exchange for her sexual favors. What matters for *our* purposes in this consortium, however, is not psychological consider-ations of this order, but the simple recognition that hustling is a tactic that paradoxically provides continual communicative opportunities for players who would choose to keep their distance from, while ripping-off, those whom they disrespect. In this way, hustlers are communicative pickpockets who continually victimize each other.

Hustling, of course, is not limited to the Pimp-Ho-Trick relation-ship. In passing we might reflect momentarily on the communicative experience that occurs in a few other relationships. Similar bonds of disaffection develop in situations where players exchange signals that they are willing to engage in authentic friendship but also recognize that they are *giving off and taking cues,* that each is not willing to assume responsibility for his or her actions. In some families, for example, the parents and children display symptoms of affection and security all the while ripping each other off emotionally—inhibiting the experience of authentic affection among them.[21] Likewise, the relationship between a married man, his spouse, and his mistress or that between a married woman, her spouse, and her paramour can be equally full of fairly intimate reciprocal communicative duplicity.

Hassling

For many individuals the duplicity involved in hustling is difficult to maintain in relationships with perceived enemies. The Put Down tactic that is probably more characteristic of their communicative experience, therefore, is *hassling*. Hassling involves expressing one's felt hostility all the while hoping not to lose at what is an inevitable physical confronta-tion.

The tension of hassling is the same tension that pervades all com-petitive negotiation and bargaining:[22] No player wants to lose, yet,

---

[21] A telling example of this kind of hustling is provided by A. H. Chapman's discussion of "Divide and Rule," a stratagem in which a child plays his parents off against each other. *Put-Offs and Come-Ons* (New York: Berkley Publishing Corp., 1969), pp. 56–60.

[22] Although the goals of Put Down are relatively clear-cut there is a strong similarity between the strategy of hassling and the competitive communicative strategies that occur in mixed-motive interaction. See Thomas Beisecker, "Verbal Persuasion Strategies in Mixed Motive Situations," *Quarterly Journal of Speech* 61(April 1970): 149–160.

because each player is trusted to respond competitively, no player wants to reveal, and therefore exhaust, his or her strengths too soon. Hence, play moves more slowly. For purposes of discussion, we have divided the progressive hassling—from the first expressions of hostility all the way to a conversation run amuck with physical violence—into a five-stage chronological sequence.

Repartee. The first stage is what we shall call the *repartee* stage. Here, the players first verbalize their antagonism for one another in the form of wisecracks and efforts at one-upmanship. Each person tries to top the other with a witty retort. This stage lasts a relatively short time either because the participants are not skilled in "ready wit" or because they are not interested in controlling the situation with verbal ploys. The typical kind of comments we should expect to hear in this first stage would be something like, "Well, here comes the 'ladies man.' " "Hey Joe, are you going on a date all dressed up like that?" Joe's response, in trying to be one-up, might be, "Wouldn't you like to know?" The remark hooked onto Joe's response could be, "My, she must be something special for you to be getting all dolled up like that," or "Why, I'll bet you even took a bath." The objective here is to hook on, as in Personal Conversation, a rejoinder to whatever is said. It is not unlike the "last tag" play of children. Each participant tries to be the last one to hit. A requirement essential to this stage, therefore, is that each must listen to the other's remarks while veiled insults are exchanged.

Cliché. This is the turning point in the conversation for it is here that the first sign of communicative destruction appears. The participants no longer engage in an exchange of original remarks. They readily resort to "canned" retorts, such as "So's your old man," and the like. Efforts to hook on remarks and best one another in spontaneous witty repartee are abandoned and replaced by a simple test of recollection in the face of mild conventional jibes. In other words, the participants try desperately to keep the conversation going. To desist, to stop answering, is humiliating: It signifies a lack of wit to any witnesses and to the other participants. To give up in public is not only to lose the play but to lose face in general.[23] Having run out of especially creative things to say, therefore, the players quickly try to recall something to say that will make it appear that at least they are still playing.

The *cliché* stage may be the longest. If neither participant desires

---

[23] J. Dollard, "The Dozens: Dialect of Insult," *American Imago* 1(1939): 3–25.

continued confrontation, it may dissipate after a while into remarks such as "Oh, yeah?" or "Very funny." The conversation then becomes filled with blank retorts: "Very funny." "Oh, yeah?" "Yeah." "Very funny." The players gradually lose interest. They fill air time, but fail to move the conversation any further. Neither has lost his image of the other as "enemy," but also neither has decided to act on his image at this time.

On the other hand, the interaction may become progressively more personal, pungent, and tangential. If one of the participants in this situation wishes to press for a fight, he will persist in the face of the "oh, yeah's" and become more and more vitriolic. This will lead, after a prolonged length of time, to the next stage. Therefore, although the cliché stage begins with the desire to hook on any rejoinder in order to stay in play, as time passes, and the players exhaust their stock of standard responses, the remarks become increasingly irrelevant to one another. The players are no longer listening to their conversation.

Name-Calling. In the *name-calling* stage remarks such as "Dago," "Sure glad I don't live in a Jew neighborhood," or "Didn't I see your mother with a Spic?" are tossed about and are intended as a kind of psychological assault. They are an effort to expose an individual's personal inadequacies to public scorn. The presence of witnesses during this stage is important. By holding up the things a person is born with or those that he simply cannot escape, the name-caller stigmatizes the object of his insult. The objective of his remarks is to try to humiliate the target by calling into public view his innate shortcomings as a person. The name-caller suggests that because his target belongs to the class of "dago" he is somehow outside the pale of humanity, that he is a subhuman species and does not belong, that he is lacking in honor.

At this point, the communicative interaction has become a symbolic fight. As the slurs are thrown back and forth a confrontation is present in everything but a physical sense. Unanswered insults are repeated much as one would repeat a successful punch. One player, for example, might say "Gee, I wish I had slanted eyes," and if the target player does not respond for a moment, his next remark if "Say, where'd you get those slanted eyes?" The same remark used over and over in this way serves two functions: It enables one to "hurt" his opponent (the fact that the comment is unanswered says something about its potency), and, at the same time, it is a way to conserve ammunition (it is best to use one's supply of painful insults sparingly and only when necessary).

Occasionally, fear of a physical beating will prompt one player to regain his senses at this point. Realizing that his opponent is stronger or that there are too many antagonists present, he might try to abort the entire encounter and "bail out" of the situation. One way is to leave, claiming a previous appointment; another is to indicate boredom with the interaction and try to shift from Put Down to Put Off; still a third is to be assisted by a witness who intervenes and "coaxes" the player to leave ("Aw, come on, Joe; don't hang around with these guys.") with his pride scruffed but intact. However, extrication from a name-calling contest is not an easy matter, and it becomes increasingly difficult as the name-calling continues. Unlike the leisurely meandering of Personal Conversation, hassling conversations increasingly limit the communicative options open to the players.

Provocation.   The *provocation* stage is a very short and rapid degeneration of the verbal sparring, which may take as little as ten seconds. At this point the very strongest invective is used. In terms of the cultural background of participants, the worst possible things are said and, because of the relatively intimate nature of the relationship between these enemies, each knows where the other is most vulnerable. In other words, these insults not only "sound" that way but, unlike the teasing of Personal Conversation, they are perceived as real. They serve as personal signals that things are out of control. In much the same way as wild animals that are about to fight engage in ritual motions, or give off musky odors, these remarks signal that the verbal punching is over and that a scuffle is in the works. The actual list of terms depends upon the specifics of the players involved. An illustration, however, of a remark that is commonly used in this way is, "Why you mother-loving'. . . ." This may be meaningless in the context of the conversation in which it appears. Nevertheless, for some it is an utterance of a taboo oath from which one may retreat only by risking extreme humiliation and shame. In this case, one is expected to take great affront at the suggestion of incestuous relations with his mother. Of course, if the previous sequence of remarks makes it obvious that no affront is intended, this comment may be one of endearment: "Rory, you mother-lovin' . . . ; I haven't seen you in ten years. It's good to see you." When this provocational remark is uttered after the interaction has passed through this much hassling, however, it is a clear sign that at least one of the participants is ready to fight.

Another telling illustration of the communication characteristic of the provocation stage is provided by the interaction in a girls' reformatory. Frequently, a provocational remark is, "You slut!" If one of the girls says this to another it is an immediate challenge to a fight, comparable to a slap in the face as an invitation to a duel. In a very limited sense all the girls present could be "sluts." There is really nothing unusual about the comment. But given that the appropriate sequence of events has occurred, the utterance of the remark becomes a very serious business. It leads immediately to the final stage of hassling.

Physiological Degeneration.   At this point the changes that occur are not verbal, but physical. The eyes of the participants about to fight dilate. Their faces become set; the facial muscles tighten into a kind of mask. That is to say, just before they begin to fight, the faces of the players resemble the Greek personae masks. Using the masks as emotional shields, they cut off all social contact. Their faces give off no social cues. This stage lasts only a few seconds and usually precedes and is a part of the transition into a fist swinging brawl.

Looking back at this sequence of communicative events it is apparent that the participants are vulnerable to each other (accessible), are willing to shift the responsibility for each move back and forth (reciprocal), are willing to carry the encounter as far as necessary (committed), and are "free" enough to allow their polite verbal control to degenerate into fisticuffs (spontaneous). The fact that the interaction progresses through several successive stages also suggests that each player trusts the potential strength of the other and that neither especially wants to lose in the interaction, either verbally or physically, in the eyes of the opponent(s) or the witnesses. Each proceeds cautiously hoping to gain wherever possible whenever possible.

It is also readily apparent that although this kind of interaction demands images of considerable intimacy from the participants, there is no empirical evidence to suggest that the encounter facilitates greater intimacy between them. Indeed, for those persons who see most of their social relationships in such a profit-loss light,[24] Put Down may be an especially gratifying, "good" game. But those who continue to exploit personal encounters for profit, those who encourage rip-offs, still derive satisfaction from the abuse of others. Such inhibiting exchanges can only be labeled as *Distancing*.

---

[24] Some people are brought up assuming that all giving and getting of affection operates within a limited emotional economy: If my sibling receives attention from my parent, then I must perforce lose my parent's attention. The premise of exchange thus comes to dominate one's efforts to establish intimacy. Love becomes a matter of barter; do not just give your love away—wait until you have guarantees, such as a ring and a legally binding contract. You must not squeeze the melon till you get the melon home.

The purpose of this chapter has been to engage in thoughtful appreciation of the communication we all experience with those whom we imagine as friends and enemies. In both of these interpersonal relationships, the gap that separates our image configurations is relatively small. Such perceived intimacy poses challenges to our efforts at communication: On the one hand we would like to share our privacy with our friends and on the other we would like to conceal or protect our personal space from our enemies. We have suggested that one way of reflecting on what it is that we do to meet these communicative challenges is to consider the possibilities of two decidedly different kinds of communicative encounters—Personal Conversation Among Friends and Put Down.

PERSONAL CONVERSATION AMONG FRIENDS is a game-like activity entered into by those who perceive themselves as friends. Communicative tactics are selected from among those that contribute both to the expectations of friendship and to the possibility of increased intimacy. The play occurs in customary places and the conversation often moves through familiar topics. But the game also provides an arena in which personal risks may be taken and group satisfaction is enhanced when the communicative play is sustained through such special efforts.

PUT DOWN is a game-like activity entered into by those who perceive themselves as enemies—persons bound by reciprocal disaffection. In this case, communicative tactics are chosen from among those that allow persons to gain from and/or not lose to those with whom they are personally vulnerable. Some people who prefer the customary familiarity of their enemies to the risks involved with separating from them, engage in hustling, an "escape" tactic that allows some emotional distance in exchange for physical intimacy. Others, who prefer to risk separation from their enemies, engage in hassling, an "escape" tactic that allows the expression of emotional frustration but that ultimately leads to physical injury.

7

Intimate Games

In the past few chapters we have been demonstrating how a game-play perspective can be used to reflect on various kinds of interpersonal communicative experience—we have been noting how interpersonal relationship images affect and are affected by communication seen as games played. Now we come to those enactments that demand of their players relationship images of the most accessibility, reciprocity, commitment, and spontaneity.

One would surely think that the games that approach most near the Intimacy pole must be those in which a mutual feeling state that we call *love* is reached. But even here, as is the case for all interpersonal communicative experience, Intimate games have Approaching and Distancing varieties. That is, the very privacy that makes "Love" possible as an Approaching game also makes "Intensity" possible as a Distancing game. In this chapter we shall discuss the communicative experience that facilitates interpersonal sharing between intimates and that which permits and relies on emotional retrenchment between intimates.

LOVE: AN APPROACHING INTIMATE GAME

$$F \; . \quad . \quad . \quad . \quad . \quad . \quad . \; \overset{\text{AG}\rightarrow}{\{ \quad \}} \; I$$

What is "love"? Is it possible that any of these pictures have captured, or can capture, your perception of the interpersonal communicative experience called "love"? For us, the word *love* itself is an uncomfortable word to use. In an age when so many people have become highly suspicious of abstract terms (like *wisdom, patriotism, honor, virtue,* and, we should probably add, *thought, care,* and *good humor*), "love" seems either too grand or meaningless for our daily pursuits. Yet, paradoxically enough, like these other exploited terms, although love is often denegrated, it is universally, if sometimes only covertly, sought.

What is "love"? In spite of its ambiguity, we believe that it is possible for us to use the term *love* to refer to that form of human communication that is most gratifyingly intimate. We recognize that love manifests itself in a wide array of human interactions.[1] And we also recognize that in each case it involves a process of forging one of the most enduring bonds that can exist between human players.

As a way to initiate consideration of this communicative experience, let us first explore the relationship characteristics that constitute and regulate the communication of those who would claim at a given moment to be experiencing love. Because loving communication is so prized, examining it impartially is a ticklish matter. In Chapter 3 we cautioned that the concepts of accessibility, reciprocity, commitment, and spontaneity are highly interdependent, and nowhere is their fusion more complete than in the Approaching communication between intimates. Nevertheless, in the following discussion we will use these individual concepts as probes in our analysis, hoping all the while that our surgery will be seen as a beneficial exploration, not as an autopsy.

Accessibility

This most intimate form of communication is characterized, first of all, by the high degree of risk that is involved. The participants entrust

---

[1] The ancient Greeks, for example, admitted several forms of relationships, all of which had elements of loving intimacy as an essential ingredient: lustful attraction, fondness, comradeship, high regard, passionate caring, love of wisdom, and an extensive list of "loving feelings"—parental, filial, conjugal, fraternal, patriotic, heterosexual, and homosexual. See G. Boas, "Love," *Encyclopedia of Philosophy*, V, p. 90.

accessibility

reciprocity

commitment

spontaneity

themselves with each other. Entrusting, the logical extension of accessibility, involves daring to disclose extremely personal things, daring to make oneself vulnerable, daring to share one's most private images and experiences.

Entrusting should not be confused with the sort of personal exposure that often occurs when a couple of persons who have settled into an extended performance of Personal Conversation Courting (have begun to "go steady") sit down in a secluded spot for a "serious" talk modeled after the fashion of beach-party movies starring Annette Funicello and Frankie Avalon. The revelations they share are not especially intimate images but gossip—a series of carefully rehearsed declarations reciting past misfortunes. Insofar as these are revelations at all, they are rather like the hospital patient who shows his visitors the scars from his operation. What is a scar, after all, but an ugly, numb artifact of a *previous* wound? Its most distinctive characteristic is that it currently lacks feeling.

Thus some of the "golden oldies" in the scar-gossip realm include such comments as "Virgil, on the outside I'm tough, I've had a hard life; but deep down inside I'm soft—I need love, comfort, warmth," or "Oh, Muffie, my wretched upbringing, my cruel parents; I just don't know if I can ever break out of my cold shell." In both of these examples it is possible to say that we are confronted with something other than openness or intimate disclosure. In the first, perhaps, we can see the customary "Tart-with-a-heart-of-gold" scar; in the second, we are shown the "I-can't-help-it-that-I'm-selfish, it's-all-my-parents-doing" scar. Indeed, the common maneuver to expose scars does ensure one's security and comfort. Allowing someone to poke a scar is not the same as handing over a scalpel. If the relationship comes unglued, the Other cannot do much harm. But the unwillingness to risk also precludes the sort of closeness essential for the experience of love.

The high degree of openness in love is interwoven with a complete confidence in one's image of the Other as trustworthy. We imagine that the Other will not abuse the power he or she is given; we trust that the Other will not use his or her license to scrutinize our personally felt flaws in a manner that would make them any more painful.[2]

---

[2] Under these conditions of accessibility, the participants both experience a willingness to disclose their immediate feelings, to make themselves vulnerable, to *share* their images and experiences rather than trying to control the encounter (and each other) by releasing only selected information or by managing the Other as one would a piece of property. "Complete surrender," said Nietzsche, "(not merely devotion) of soul and body, without any motive, without any reservation, rather with shame and terror at the thought of a devotion restricted by clauses or associated with conditions. In this absence of condition [our] love is precisely a

But accessibility should not be likened merely to opening one's own flood gates so that the water can run out. Interpersonal openness involves more than self-disclosure and the risk of what the Other may or may not do with the exhibition. Accessibility also involves backwash—the risk of being open to the Other's exposure and to responsible management of the Other's trust. (Somehow the following comment, heard while passing a couple strolling along an icy walk, suggests that at least one party recognized the risks of entrusting himself to the Other: "Let go of my hand; what do you expect me to do—break *my* neck when *you* fall down?")

In addition, the risk taking in love is multiplied by the fact that the gesture of accessibility is an indefinite one. When one opens his or her self so completely to the Other, he or she becomes vulnerable not only to that person, but also to the effects of time, namely, aging and death. Accessibility in love is the risk of potential harm and grief.

Commitment

The second characteristic of the experience of loving communication is that the players are committed to their relationship for its own sake, not for some extrinsic profit.[3] That is, love is not a calculated risk. One does not "decide to risk" an intimate relationship like one decides to risk the purchase of property (by estimating potential gain against potential loss). Those who engage in these computations merely end up with "love objects" whose value can only be measured selfishly in degrees of personal gratification. Similarly, the ongoing experience of love is not the fulfillment of self-interest *through* the Other. Those who find themselves asking of a communicative relationship "What needs in me are being satisfied? How is she/he helping or assisting me?" are not, in those moments, likely to be experiencing the necessary commitment for loving communication. Maneuvering for self-gratification and power are uncharacteristic of the experience of loving communication.

This is not to suggest that love is blind, that the risk of love is irrational. Rather, we would claim that the nature of the commitment by those who would experience the communication of love is a commit-

---

faith." (F. Nietzsche, *Joyful Wisdom,* trans. T. Common [New York: Ungar Publishing, 1960], 363.) Copyright ©1960 by Frederick Ungar Publishing Co. In these terms, the act of playing a love game stands directly opposed to power manipulation, whether for dominance or defense.

[3] "Only in the love of those who do not serve a purpose, love begins to unfold." Erich Fromm, *The Art of Loving* (New York: Bantam Books, 1956), p. 40.

ment to *sharing the pleasure of the unique relationship with the Other*. Just as the especially exhilarating moments of sustained teamwork facilitate pleasure in Personal Conversation Among Friends, consummatory communication enhances the experience of an intimate relationship.[4] The irony of the interpersonal commitment in an intimate relationship therefore is that one *can* profit from the experience of intimacy, but only if one does not first seek that profit.[5]

Spontaneity

As a result of and inexorably bound up with our perception of the Other as entrusted and committed, comes the interpersonal experience of freedom. That is, when we imagine that someone knows us well and is committed to us for the sake of our unique relationship, we develop confidence in being ourselves in their presence. In the ideal moment of loving communication, there is no reason for the experience of pretense.

Loving care is the acceptance of the Other on his or her own terms.[6] This sort of concern goes beyond the normal interest we show in our daily acquaintances. There are many people whom we know and care for, but on our own terms. We maintain our relationships with them until their terms inconvenience us or make us uncomfortable.

In the experience of love, who and how the Other is does not distress us. The Other, literally *as is*, is a source of pleasure. Loving care, therefore, is not a desire to reform the Other. We have all heard the tape from the blushing bride: "I know Sidney isn't much, BUT I'LL MAKE SOMETHING OF HIM." This sort of compulsive desire to help the Other to help himself demands not a mate, but a lump of clay. This person is looking for a run-down house she can refurbish. In later years she will get her payoff in two forms: She will take credit for the salvage operation she

---

[4] The anthropologist Ruth Benedict and the psychologist Abraham Maslow have studied the dynamics of this experience as the concept of "synergy." The special adaptation of this process to one kind of intimate relationship, the open marriage, is explored in some detail by Nena O'Neill and George O'Neill, *Open Marriage* (New York: M. Evans and Co., 1972), pp. 260–269. In general, synergy "occurs when the combined action of two things produces a more beneficial and greater effect or result than the sum of their separate individual actions. It is a process by which the whole becomes more than the sum of the parts, while at the same time those parts retain their individuality."

[5] Once again our concern for the development of human potential separates us from those transcendentalists who would see commitment in intimacy as the self-sacrificing experience of oneness. For us, the *together* experience of interpersonal intimacy does not allow a loss of individuality, but invites enriched individual potential.

[6] See Aristotle, *Nichomachean Ethics*, 1159a10.

did on Sidney, and she will derive a special perverse pleasure for not being thanked by him for her efforts ("What would he be without me? But do you think I get any gratitude from that wretch?" Obviously, her task is not yet completed). But the pleasure she will experience will not be the pleasure she could have derived had she let Sidney be, had she been committed to Sidney and not to her own demonstration of power.

We do not mean to imply that it is easy to facilitate spontaneity in a relationship. Unconditional acceptance is not only difficult to extend to another, but it is also difficult to imagine that the Other would extend it to us. We have the same reservations about spontaneity that we do about accessibility and commitment. But as we noted in an earlier chapter, lovers are amateurs who *work at* their relationship. Since the life space of the individual is itself in a state of continual, if gradual, change, those who would experience intimacy must engage in the labor of love. To the extent that they feel free to be in a relationship and are willing to extend the same privilege to the Other, they are able to experience loving intimacy.

Reciprocity

Reciprocity is, of course, a significant variable in the accessibility, commitment, and spontaneity we have already described. It is hard to imagine how one can experience these relationship features without simultaneously imagining the willingness of the Other to give and take in the relationship. The experience of intimacy is not a unilateral challenge.

In the communication of love, however, reciprocity takes on a special character. The reciprocity of intimacy culminates in a regression to preverbal physical contact. As a genuine love relation grows, the static character of language proves too clumsy and the participants, growing ever nearer to each other, find themselves "melting" into one another's emotional regions. Evidence for this increased closeness is the increasing need lovers have to whisper with one another rather than to talk aloud; whispering cuts down on physical distance. But even whispering eventually proves too much of a barrier for felt nearness: "Vocalization at intimate distance plays a very minor part in the communication process, which is carried mainly by other channels. A whisper has the effect of expanding the distance. The vocalizations that do occur are largely involuntary."[7] In this light, the Biblical expression "to become one with"

---

[7] E. Hall, *The Hidden Dimension* (Garden City: Doubleday & Company, Anchor Books, 1969), p. 117.

is not so much a physical but an experiential description of how it feels as the emotional boundaries that separate individuals liquefy and dissolve. The love participants begin to respond with pleasure rather than fear[8] to sensual signals of each Other's presence (including the tactile and olfactory cues that we normally regard as socially unacceptable).

You may have witnessed such moments of loving communication if you have ever noticed a parent's gentle caress of a child too young to speak. Even for those who can speak, preverbal physical contact seems the most adequate means to express the tenderness of felt emotions. Such tender touching is a symptom of a loving state of affairs; it occurs as loving reciprocity encourages two humans to increase their emotional contact and to realize their interpersonal warmth and intimacy in preverbal gestural form.[9]

Let us summarize, to this point, what we have proposed as the characteristics of the relationship image required by the rules of the communication game we call *love*. The players must be willing to entrust themselves with each other (accessibility), willing to engage in the relationship as a unique and inherently gratifying one (commitment), willing to be as they are in each other's presence (spontaneity), and willing to express the tenderness of felt emotion by exchanging preverbal physical contact (reciprocity).

We can achieve yet another perspective on loving communication if we view the "melting" just mentioned as the developing congruity of the life spaces of two persons. Complementary image patterns emerge as He comes to trust that She shares his image of himself (that his self-image closely approximates her Other-image of him). Likewise, his image of his beloved merges with her own self-image and the enduring vision of their love itself (their topic-image) unites into an intersubjective form held in common.[10] That is, part of loving another involves sharing the

---

[8] See F. Nietzsche, *Joyful Wisdom*, p. 372.

[9] For an elaborate dissertation on the importance of the skin as a tactile organ, see Ashley Montagu, *Touching: The Human Significance of the Skin* (New York: Harper & Row, Perennial Library Edition, 1972). We are indebted to Montagu's calling to our attention the following from W. Ong, *The Presence of the Word* (New Haven: Yale University Press, 1967), pp. 169–70: "By the very fact that it attests the not-me more than any other sense, touch involves my own subjectivity more than any other sense. When I feel this objective something 'out there' beyond the bounds of my body, I also at the same instant experience my own self. I feel other and self simultaneously."

[10] Much the same state of affairs was recognized by Saint Augustine, who claimed that because this enhanced congruity of images causes us to become whomever we love, we would be best off loving God and thus becoming more saintly (St. Augustine, *Confessions*, Book viii, chapters 8–10). Note that where some Eastern faiths hold that in the ultimate transcendence

happy realization of being similarly loved by the other. This fusion produces that enduring bond that serves to "couple" the players.

Players who are able to achieve such congruity ordinarily become comparably oblivious to their scene-images and are overwhelmed by the momentary liberation they feel from the constant loneliness unique image systems bestow on all human players. And this sense of liberation, this discovery of a life space identical in almost all respects to one's own, is the love game outcome we refer to as ecstasy. Ecstasy is experienced as a passionate condition (because it takes such full hold of us), but it is clearly more than the sum total of sensuality and emotions. It is, in other words, more than simply intense desire because insofar as it is a reciprocal condition it remains responsible. Indeed, were the love game simply a matter of eros (i.e., sexual gratification without the congruity of internal imagery) it would seek its expression only in the privacy of lustful acts. But authentic lovers experience a mutual desire to celebrate, to make permanent in some fashion, the release afforded by their congruity. Thus, lovers carve their initials on a tree or they memorialize and make permanent their gratification with a marriage ceremony or they feel a primal urge to concretize the congruity of their images through reproduction, as though a child born of such a thorough union might be invested with the ecstasy as a way of preserving the shared imagery through time.[11]

We are not being naïve in describing this nonverbal condition in which the experience of totally loving communication is manifested in the act of producing a child. We appreciate that we are describing the ideal state of affairs; but to say that loving communication is an ideal is not to say it is nonexistent (literally "utopian"), only that as a form of human interaction it is relatively rare and certainly difficult to achieve in an authentic form. There are, of course, many partial variations, such as couples who settle for the empty ritual of marriage in hopes of finding ecstasy at some later private moment, or homosexual marriages in which the urge to memorialize through reproduction may be as strong as in heterosexual unions but sociologically taboo and biologically impossible.

Seen in terms of authenticity of communication and merging of

---

all four images in each player merge into a single primordial oneness with the divine, we, with Saint Augustine, hold that although complementary and congruent, the four images in each player retain their integrity even as they come to fit more harmoniously together with each other and with the phenomenal view of another.

[11] For a profound exploration of this primal urge in the face of otherwise distracting scene-arenas see the novel by Edward Whittemore, *Quin's Shanghai Circus* (New York: Holt, Rinehart & Winston, 1974).

personal images into a common shared imagery we can draw certain corollaries about the love game. We can for instance (without any partisanship regarding contemporary political issues) understand abortions as symbolic denials of the significance of an intimate relationship. Likewise illegitimate children who are ignored by their parents after birth represent parental refusals to acknowledge that such a shared imagery ever existed (as indeed the sharing may not have existed if the players were hustling and a biological foul ball occurred in the course of play).

And we can understand further in what sense all those players who can only swing or hustle, but who are, for whatever reason, not prepared to celebrate their love game, are called *adolescent* in the sense of having a stunted emotional development. All such players are limited to reaping a profit from the game; they are not prepared to *feel with* the Other but only to *react toward* the Other. In a word, because the politics of their play remains re-action-ary, they remain dependent in their relation with the Other. That is, each is dependent upon the Other's responses to continue to shape his or her own distinct and isolated images of self, Other, scene, and topic. The adolescent player is one who is bound to play communicative games in which, for example, he says to himself, "If she smiles at me fondly, I can permit myself to like her." The player authentically engaged in the communicative experience of love, however, does not need to monitor his performance; he can afford to acknowledge his feelings regardless of the Other's responses. The love player has enough confidence to say "I like her, and I hope she likes me in return; but if she doesn't, although I will feel sad, I will still accept the fact that I like her."[12]

In many respects, people who resort to Distancing games when loving communication is possible do so because they are not entirely at peace with themselves and so need to shield the pattern of their self-, topic-, Other-, and scene-images from exposure to too great an influence by another. Let us now consider such Distancing cases.

INTENSITY: A DISTANCING INTIMATE GAME

$$F \; . \; . \; . \; . \; . \; . \; . \; \{ \quad \} \; I$$
$$\leftarrow DG$$

---

[12] It was very likely this capacity to consciously accept this complete congruence of images we

As we said at the beginning of this chapter, the very privacy that makes "Love" possible as an Approaching game also makes "Intensity" possible as a Distancing game. In other words, there are those intimate relationships in which the participants *could* experience ever increasing interpersonal synchrony, but they do not. When the tenderness of love is absent but love's energy remains, the game liable to be played will be "Intensity." In such a case, though ecstatic gratification will be sought, each play of the game will only result in frustration and anger for the players.

Have you ever heard someone say of his stormy domestic life, "Sure we fight a lot; but that's only because we really love each other with such passion. After all, blood is thicker than water"? Chemical analyses aside, we would argue that whoever claims that the song of love includes fighting in the rhythm section is confusing ecstasy with uproar.

The examination of the Intensity game is a full-time occupation for thousands of psychiatrists and therapists, and we would not presume to supersede the entire Helping Industry in a few short pages. It is possible to offer a few insights, nevertheless, if we continue to illustrate various communicative experiences as games. First of all, we can see why Intensity is necessarily a two-person game. Although many people can play Intensity, at any given moment a play of the game is really one against one. In describing the way intimates distance themselves from each Other, we must necessarily be talking about how two people who are especially close are continually keeping the gap between them.

Secondly, in using the game-play perspective we can consider some typical Intensity tactics. We have previously suggested that persons who are unwilling or unable to achieve interpersonal image congruity will relate in a stunted or adolescent fashion. We could, therefore, enumerate all the potential conflict interactions that emerge when specific images are not congruent in the participants. Since our purpose is more to speculate on the varieties of communicative experience than to catalogue them all, however, we shall confine our discussion to two typical tactical procedures that follow from incongruity of self- and Other-images: placating and tyranny.[13]

---

are here examining that Aristotle meant when, in Book ix of the *Nichomachean Ethics*, he claimed that the most important thing in life was for a person to be friends with himself, that the unhappiest person was one—whom we have labeled *adolescent*—in whom reason and desire were at war, such that the individual might create troubles in the world in an effort to forget the internal self-hatred within himself.

[13] We are grateful to Professor Paul Friedman for suggesting the placating-tyranny distinction.

Placating

Some Intensity players prefer to diminish their own Self-image and to be influenced by a predominant image of the Other. The archetype Placator is the Sacrificing Mother: "Whatever you want is fine with me dear; I only want you to be happy. My needs aren't important; for you I'd do anything. Go out and have a good time and don't worry about me; I'll just stay here and pick up after you." Typical qualities characteristic of the *placating* maneuver are the player's deferential manner, readiness to give in on arguments, tendencies to shyness and timidity, ingratiating patience, and unassuming agreeableness. The Placator lacks confidence in his or her own taste or judgment, so continually submits to the Other. The player using the placating tactic in intimate relationships can be relied upon to laugh at all the Other's silly remarks, to go wherever and do whatever the Other wants, to clean up the dirty coffee cups after the Other leaves, and in general to tend to the messy tasks that the Other would prefer to avoid. This Other-centered behavior may initially sound both loving and appealing ("Whither thou goest . . ." and so on). We all enjoy a little solicitous concern from someone else for our well-being, we like to have our jokes appreciated, and we are really not all that fond of dirty coffee cups.

Nevertheless, contrary to what we might initially expect, Others are seldom pleased to find themselves caught up in an intimate game with a Placator. The Placator's timid, self-effacing efforts to be a "good-old-Joe" encourage the Other both to be thoughtless and careless *and* to feel guilty about being thoughtless and careless. Consider, for example, "Placator Franklin." He thinks so little of himself that he does not let his partner Olivia think about him! She cannot be receptive because he hides his Self-image; she cannot be reflective because she cannot get distance on her own shadow. Furthermore, since Franklin is so careful, showing concern only for Olivia's needs, he does not let Olivia care for him. If Olivia accepts and appreciates Franklin, she literally cares for herself. Olivia not only appears selfish, but that is all she can be. Supposing, then, that Olivia *is* thoughtless and careless about Franklin, what next? He forgives her, comforts her, even reassures her. ("That's all right. I really enjoy cleaning up around the house. Besides, it's one of the few things I'm any good at.") In short, Franklin's tactic can only frustrate Olivia. He encourages her to take advantage of him as a person and to exploit their relationship for her satisfaction alone, and then he refuses to allow her to be responsible for such irresponsible behavior. He constantly expresses a sense of helplessness and inadequacy in coping with the world but he simultaneously denies the legitimacy of these messages and the necessity and/or capacity of the Other to do anything about them.

Tyranny

An opposite Intensity tactic is that of *tyranny*, used by a person who enters an intimate relationship thinking only of Self and not at all conscious of the Other. We recognize this tactic by several identifying features. Its user tends to be loud and truculent; his or her opinions are often judgmental: "They (college kids, minorities, the opposing team) are just a bunch of lousy bums." The Tyrant eschews inquiry in favor of bullying: "In my relationships, the man is boss; the woman does what she is told." Unimpressed by the Other's image, this player seeks dictatorial control. He or she wants to have things a certain way and is unable to tolerate ambiguity or a gracious concession: "As long as you live in my house, you do as I say; if you don't like it, get out!"

Sometimes a player who lacks brawn will try to seduce or nag others until he or she achieves dominance. The whining child (of whatever age) who resorts to tantrums or impertinence is using an embryonic form of tyranny to get his or her way. Conflict is all but inevitable with those who favor tyranny as a tactic—they thrive on it and prefer to engineer all encounters into contests over who is responsible for shortcomings. Such upsets as are thus created enable the Tyrant to triumph over an Other of whom the Tyrant is largely oblivious. We shall assume that we need not elaborate why the Other experiences frustration when confronted by such communicative tactics.

Both placating and tyranny are distancing tactics. They work in diametrically opposite ways but achieve the same effect: The Placator distances himself from the Other through self-denial, backing away from the Other in repeated acts of deference. The Tyrant distances himself from the Other through Other-denial, pushing the Other away in recurrent gestures of deprecation. In either case, the Placator or Tyrant denies himself the opportunity to have the other satisfy his personal needs in a loving exchange. Whereas the communicative experience of Put Down is hypocritical, the communicative experience of Intensity is paradoxical.[14]

A substantial number of communicative experiences can emerge from encounters involving just these two Intensity tactics. Because Intensity tends to be noisy, it leaves more meaningful traces in verbal communication than does love. Let us therefore examine a particular

---

[14] For a complementary discussion of paradoxical communication see P. Watzlawick, J. H. Beavin, and Don Jackson, *Pragmatics of Human Communication* (New York: W. W. Norton & Company, 1967), pp. 187–229. Their careful distinction between contradictory and paradoxical communication informs our analysis. Whereas a contradiction may have an unhappy result, choice is at least possible. Paradoxes are frustrating because they provide no choice—any position is untenable.

dialogue as a play of Intensity. The following exchange between George and Martha[15] can be seen as a game in which two players who would seek the intimacy of love are unable or unwilling to achieve such congruity because both employ tyrannical tactics:

Martha: "Hey, put some more ice in my drink, will you? You never put any ice in my drink. Why is that, hunh?"

This petulent order reduces George to a tool submissive to Martha's whims.

George: "I always put ice in your drink. You eat it, that's all. It's that habit you have . . . chewing your ice cubes . . . like a cocker spaniel. You'll crack your big teeth."

George refuses to respond in the terms laid down by Martha's demands. To do so would be to deny the self-respect he seeks for his own self-image. Instead he denies Martha not only the ice she seeks (and the personal recognition its giving would symbolize) but he mocks *her* self-image by comparing her to a dog. (He does not call her a "bitch" or a "cur" outright—George's tyranny is subtle.)

Martha: "THEY'RE MY BIG TEETH!"

Martha's tyranny is loud and truculent.

George: "Some of them . . . some of them."

George's tyranny is also more seductive—he nags Martha by calling attention to her shortcomings.

Martha: "I've got more teeth than you've got."

Martha retaliates by calling attention to George's shortcomings.

George: "Two more."

George's response does not allow Martha to gain very much.

Martha: "Well, two more's a lot more."

Martha wants to make an issue out of what little George *has* given her. She desperately seeks affection, but she continually forces George to remain closed off and invulnerable to her.

George: "I suppose it is. I suppose it's pretty remarkable . . . considering how old you are."

Since Martha has responded to George's meagre attempt to acknowledge her by bullying him (albeit an admission that the Other has more teeth is not a

---

[15] The following dialogue has been taken from Act I of Edward Albee's play *Who's Afraid of Virginia Woolf?* (New York: Atheneum House, 1962). Copyright © 1962 by Edward Albee. Reprinted by permission of Atheneum Publishers. We do not intend our remarks to be seen as an interpretation of Albee's play, and we hope that prior experience, if any, with the play will not prohibit response to this segment as a compelling example of the communicative experience we label *Intensity*.

significant personal concession), George retrenches and throws another of her shortcomings into Martha's face.

Martha: "YOU CUT THAT OUT! (pause) You're not so young yourself."

More truculence, with some retaliation for extra measure.

George: "I'm six years younger than you are . . . I always have been and I always will be."

George admits, once again, that he *is* conscious of Martha—but he is only willing to acknowledge her in terms of her shortcomings.

Martha: "Well . . . you're going bald."

Martha offers as a trade her recognition of one of George's flaws.

George: "So are you. (pause . . . they both laugh) Hello, honey."

George first "gets" Martha in a double fashion: He denies her—*she* of course could not be bald; but if she *were* bald (and he were to call attention to it) he would be highlighting a personal flaw. (We are tempted to wonder if in their laughter they are possibly approving the complexity of George's artistry.) After their brief recess, George initiates another round. A seemingly gentle serve.

Martha: "Hello. C'mon over here and give your mommy a big sloppy kiss."

Martha responds to George's serve with a more direct signal for some affection: instead of ice, she demands a kiss. But they (ice and kiss) might as well be the same thing because she trivializes this request, couching it in such terms as "Mommy" and "a big sloppy kiss." She almost seems to suggest that George would be less of a person if he *were* to respond; she challenges him.

George: ". . . oh, now. . . ."

George seems to recognize the bind in which Martha has just placed him: she will not respect him if he does not kiss her and she will not respect him if he does.

Martha: "I WANT A BIG SLOPPY KISS!"

Recognizing George's momentary incapacity to retaliate, she takes advantage of his weakness and repeats her challenge.

George: "I don't *want* to kiss you, Martha. Where *are* these

George responds to Martha's challenge with an explicit denial. But, perhaps unwilling to assume responsibility for

people? Where are these *people* you invited over?"

direct confrontation. George quickly evades Martha; he returns to his more subtle tyrannical style by insulting the as yet unarrived guests and blaming Martha for inviting them.

Martha: "They stayed on to talk to Daddy. . . . They'll be here. . . . *Why* don't you want to kiss me?"

Martha does not *always* bully without listening. Here she actually answers George. Perhaps she hopes that *her* recognition of *him*, will force *him* to recognize *her* and answer her question. . . . But what kind of question has she asked? How can George answer this question and "win"?

George: "Well, dear, if I kissed you I'd get all excited . . . I'd get beside myself, and I'd take you, by force, right here on the living room rug, and then our little guests would walk in, and . . . well, just think what your father would say about that."

George has regained his wits; he goes outside the box Martha has put him in—and traps her: He indicates that he knows the behavior of a passionate lover, that he could satisfy Martha's hunger if he wanted to, but he evades responsibility for his rejection of her by couching his denial in a very complicated way: *Martha* of course would not want to be embarrassed in front of her guests or by the effect such behavior would have on her father. . . . But to admit to George's "logic" is to be denied the affection she "wants" as well as to accept the fact that even as George is using the "little guests" and her father to make his point, he is belittling them as audiences of dubious merit anyway. George's sardonic retaliation serves as much to manipulate Martha as it does to fend her off.

Martha: "You pig!"

Martha bids for a restoration of the more blatant insult duel—her tyranny is more successful in such circumstances.

George: "Oink! Oink!"

George is happy to oblige. But in his response he mocks Martha's charge—he "becomes" what Martha has called him. (In so doing he also forces Martha to recognize him—"better to be seen as a pig, I guess, than not to be seen at all. . . .")

Martha: "Ha, ha, ha, HA! Make me another drink . . . lover."

Does Martha appreciate George's cleverness? On what level? Regardless, she initiates round 3.

George: "My God, you can swill it down, can't you?"

Once again, George refuses to respond in the terms laid down by Martha's demands. He not only refuses to satisfy her need but he mocks it as well.

Martha: "I'm firsty."

Perhaps "Martha-the-helpless-child" will get a drink *and* some more affection.

George: "Jesus!"

No way!

Martha: "Look, sweetheart, I can drink you under any goddamn table you want . . . so don't worry about me!"

"Martha-the-helpless-child" quickly becomes the dictatorial shrew. The seductive whining of a child is obviously *not* her tyrannical style!

George: "Martha, I gave you the prize years ago. . . . There isn't an abomination award going that you. . . ."

George even undercuts Martha's claim that she is the "best shrew around." That's old hat, he says; besides that, she's even more abominable than she claims to be.

Martha: "I swear . . . if you existed I'd divorce you. . . ."

An outright admission: Of course you do not exist—so I will not divorce you. But even more important to an increasing understanding of the nature of Intensity: Martha admits her dependence on George—how she is "caught" by her need for him. By tyrannical fiat she has disallowed his ability to leave her, too. ("Since you don't exist, you can't divorce me.")

George: "Well, just stay on your feet, that's all. . . . These people are your guests, you know, and. . . ."

George does not debate the issue of their mutual dependence, but his unwillingness to break off even conversational contact when he has the opportunity suggests that the bond forged between them is an enduring one.

Martha: "I can't even see you. . . . I haven't been able to see you for years. . . ."

George: ". . . if you pass out, or throw up, or something. . . ."

Martha: ". . . I mean, you're a blank, a cipher. . . ."

George: ". . . and try to keep your clothes on, too. There aren't many more sickening sights

Quick exchange of fire—not unlike the rapid run-through of lines by actors just prior to appearing on stage.

than you with a couple of drinks in you and your skirt up over your head, you know. . .''

Martha: ''. . . a zero. . .''

George: ''. . . your heads, I should say.''

(The front doorbell chimes)

Martha: ''Party! Party!''

George: ''I'm really looking forward to this, Martha. . . .''

Martha: ''Go answer the door.''

Even in their rapid preparation for their guests Martha doesn't abandon her efforts—however petty—to get George to reveal an awareness of her. She is sufficiently ravenous for human contact to invite conflict in the absence of warmth.

George: ''You answer it.''

Martha: ''Get to that door, you. I'll fix you.''

Why should George break his record and oblige now?

George: (fake spits) ''. . . to you. . . .''

(Door chimes again)

Martha: (shouting . . . to the door) ''C'MON IN! (To George, between her teeth) I said, get over there!''

Quick exchange of vulgarity and/or mutual disrespect. (How unlike the reciprocal tender touching of love!)

George: ''All right, love . . . whatever love wants. Just don't start on the bit, that's all.''

Additional evidence that George *is* just as dependent on Martha as she is on him. Although he belittles her affection —''whatever love wants''—he obviously *needs* her presence, in whatever state of conflict, because he mounts yet another attack in their communicative experience—''the bit.''

Martha: ''The bit? The bit? What kind of language is that? What are you talking about?

George: ''The bit. Just don't start in on the bit.''

Martha: ''You imitating one of your students, for God's sake?

Martha must not be used to a challenge from George, whose tyranny is normally more subtle; but rather than let him get away with a domineering challenge, she retaliates.

What are you trying to do?
WHAT BIT?''

George: "Just don't start in on the
bit about the kid, that's all."

Martha: "What do you take me
for?''

George: "Much too much."

Martha: "Yeah? Well, I'll start in
on the kid if I want to."

George: "Just leave the kid out
of this."

Martha: "He's mine as much as
he is yours. I'll talk about him
if I want to."

George: "I'd advise against it,
Martha."

The sheer bulk of Martha's litany is a special form of manipulation—it constitutes a constant reminder to George of the futility of his aspiration to gentility.

Martha: "Well, good for you.
(*Knock*) C'mon in. Get over
there and open the door!"

Still not comfortable with George's new style, Martha reverts to hers.

George: "You've been advised."

A "less meaty" counter-challenge.

Martha: "Yeah . . . sure. Get
over there!"

Martha discredits George's move explicitly and then bludgeons him with yet another command.

George: "All right, love . . .
whatever love wants. Isn't it
nice the way some people have
manners, though, even in this
day and age? Isn't it nice that
some people won't just come
breaking into other people's
houses even if they *do* hear
some sub-human monster
yowling at 'em from inside
. . . ?''

Checkmate.

In reflecting on this particular dialogue between George and Martha we have tried to be open to the disclosure of the communicative experience of Intensity. Our efforts have been to capture the state of affairs that exists when players who perhaps set out to play a game of love find themselves caught up in spite of themselves in the distancing counterpart of love—to see how players like George and Martha employ angry, tyrannical tactics with just those people most available for love games.

George and Martha *are* intimates, but, every time they act on this image of their relationship, their communication inhibits the experience of intimacy between them. They are *accessible* to each other's needs, yet each refuses to acknowledge the needs of the other and/or to be responsible for them. They are highly *reciprocal*, yet the volume of their exchange is limited to verbal conflicts designed to undermine each other's self-image—they use their privileged accessibility to belittle both the beliefs and feelings that each experiences about his or her own personal characteristics. They are *spontaneous*, in that each not only lets the other be, but each encourages the other to be a Tyrant. Each trusts that the other will respond as a Tyrant, and, at the same time in escalating each play of the game or continually challenging a re-match, each does not allow the other to respond in any other way. They are *committed* to their unique relationship, and occasionally enjoy their shared interaction, but whatever pleasure they experience comes only from being able to survive their mutual dependence—each player is "caught" in his or her relationship with the other. Each does satisfy one crucial need that the other has—each has a *need for the other* as someone to tyrannize.

Ironically, the only way that intimacy can be facilitated between such players is for one or both to risk severing the powerful bond of their relationship in a more authentic disclosure of feelings. But in the case of George and Martha neither player is capable or willing to take such a risk. Each would rather *react to* the other, being dependent upon the other's responses, and experience "the known" (however uncomfortable) than *act* on his or her own terms *with* the other and experience "the unknown." Together they behave as if having personal integrity were incompatible with intimacy. Hence, their intimate communication discourages both self-disclosure and personal growth. Yet their intimate communication also thwarts intimacy itself. Because they are unable to *feel with* each other and to explore the unknown together, they are unable to discover additional evidence for their intimacy and to experience the ecstasy of a more elaborate shared imagery. Hence, their relationship stagnates as they constantly fabricate abrasive moments to fill a mutual emotional void. Communicative Intensity fossilizes the gap, however small, between its players.

In this chapter we have explored the contours of intimate communicative experience as they are disclosed by the game-play perspective and we have noted two distinct forms: Love and Intensity. Although the rules of each communicative game require of the players relationship images of a high degree of accessibility, reciprocity, spontaneity, and commitment, the Intimate games we have described differ in terms of the ends to which each is played.

What is LOVE? Seen as an Approaching Communication game played by intimates, Love is an enactment in which each player chooses communicative tactics that maximize the likelihood of the experience of ecstasy. Each player's initial impulse to communicate culminates in the tender expression of preverbal physical contact. A play of the game has as its end the players' *momentary liberation from* the essential loneliness of their unique life spaces, a *temporary* *"melting"* of the emotional gap that separates them.

What is INTENSITY? Seen as a Distancing Communication game played by intimates, Intensity is an enactment in which each player chooses communicative tactics that maximize the likelihood of the experience of acrimony. Each player's initial impulse to communicate culminates in the hateful expression of verbal self and/or other denunciation. A play of the game has as its end the players' *momentary retreat into* the essential loneliness of their unique life spaces and a *temporary "freezing"* of the gap that separates them.

8

Impersonal Games

S o far we have seen how we play communicative games that maintain or modify our relations with people whom we have previously imagined as strangers, acquaintances, friends (or antagonists), or intimates. In each instance a degree of involvement with the other players is at stake, and our game-play articulates, enhances, or otherwise alters the experience we share with the other.

In this chapter we shall move back across the Formality—Intimacy continuum and examine some of those instances of interpersonal communicative experience that approach the extreme Formality pole of the continuum, interaction that we shall label Impersonal games. Impersonal games are no more or less regulated by player expectations than any other communicative encounter. The interaction types we shall consider as some of the most formal in human communicative experience are placed where they are because in them players experience the maximum degree of emotional distance possible between people playing the same game (see the table at the end of the chapter). That is, with the introduction of Impersonal games we shall focus on the kinds of communication we experience with Others who are so distant that we do not even grant them the status of strangers. In order to appreciate this communicative experience more fully, let us first examine the nature of the impersonal relationship that the participants share.

The proposition that game-players can be more emotionally distant than strangers is not as nonsensical as it may seem. In Chapter 4 we suggested that a "stranger" is a player we encounter whom we do not as yet recognize as a person: An anonymous Other we pass on the street, meet at a filling station, or sit next to at the bus depot. Now we want to suggest that we also encounter people who are more emotionally distant than strangers. We *do* recognize these people but they have no personal identity for us beyond their social position. In these relationships, interpersonal *accessibility* is minimal. We regard the other players as though they were robots, objects moving along socially predetermined paths without personal volition.

In our daily lives we often encounter Others whom we imagine in this way. We recognize them not as particular individuals but as "waitress," "sergeant," "teller," "clerk," "priest," and so on. We engage these players impersonally, as performers of objectified institutional roles who intrude on us in various service capacities, but who lack any salient presence as unique players in our life space.[1] Of course, it is possible that repeated exposure to one of these non-person players, such as the girl who has worked at the local grocery check-out counter for several years, may cause us to imagine her as more than a role—we may get in the habit of exchanging a friendly word with her now and then and invite her to join us in more intimate communication game-play. But then again we may also continue to remain as oblivious to her as an individual as we are to a well-functioning vending machine.[2]

Imagining the Other in a relationship as a non-person has a special consequence for the relationship's *reciprocity*. To the extent that we

---

[1] And, as Roger Brown and Marguerite Ford are careful to note: "Where contact and concern are minimal and distance greatest, titles alone are likely to be used in address. To call someone Miss or sir is to address the person on a categorical level which does not establish the addressee's individual identity." Roger Brown and Marguerite Ford, "Address in American English," in Dell Hymes, ed., *Language in Culture and Society* (New York: Harper & Row, 1964), p. 239. We might add, in passing, that Brown and Ford also comment on an individual's tendency to have multiple names for those imagined as intimates.

[2] We are reminded here of some merchandising establishments that even make their patrons responsible for maintaining the robot-like behavior of the clerks. Recall the signs, "If our clerks don't say 'Thank you for shopping at . . . ,' report them to the management." The patron is then encouraged to tattle on the clerk, just as one does when a pop-machine malfunctions. Preferring not to be punished for unbusinesslike conduct, the clerks dutifully drone their "Thank you's" like so many prerecorded messages. We doubt really that many customers "turn in" such "malfunctioning" clerks, however, because such involvement is usually more embarrassing or time-consuming than the trading stamps (or whatever bonus is offered as a reward) are worth.

objectify the Other, we also objectify ourselves.[3] Not many people are willing to become involved with a non-person (after all, precious few of us play interpersonal communication games with parking meters), and so most of us literally "do-unto-ourselves-as-we-do-unto-others." That is, when we imagine ourselves in an impersonal relationship, we accord ourselves robot status as well. When we choose to treat another as a non-person, we expect or invite reciprocal non-person treatment. Think about your relationships with people you engage as non-persons. Don't you invite, if not expect, similar impersonal behavior from them? Whenever you want to regard the grocery check-out clerk as a vending machine, do you want her to respond by commenting on your assorted purchases and by inquiring about your activities of the past week, or do you just want your groceries and the correct change? When you are annoyed by such polite concern, isn't it because you are thinking, literally, "That's none of your business"? And, in this case, what *is* her business—to regard you as impersonally as you have her and imagine you only as the socially predetermined object called *customer?*

In Chapter 4 we discussed some reasons for being accessible to strangers, and we suggested how the Polite Greeting, although admittedly formal, *is* a gesture of relationship. It signals polite concern for the other person's welfare. Here, however, we are suggesting that impersonal relationships are those in which we expect reciprocal inaccessibility. We presume we are invulnerable to personal contact by the Other.[4] Hence, we may even shrink from inconsequential polite overtures in such a relationship. For example, although it may be proper for a person we imagine as a stranger to ask us for a match, we would probably consider it impertinent if someone we imagined as an anonymous waiter were to do so. ("Who does he think he is?" "Boy, he's got some nerve!") When we let an Other approach us as more than a non-person, when we allow the Other to have presence as a unique player in our life space ("I guess he has a right to ask me for a match"), our relationship is not an impersonal one.

As distant as these impersonal relationships may seem, there is still some interpersonal *commitment* in them. Most people are committed to

---

[3] For a complementary and more elaborate discussion of the activity of achieving and bestowing "personhood" and its reciprocal, the activity of treating the Other as an object and diminishing one's own personhood, see Douglas Ehninger, "Argument as Method: Its Nature, Its Limitations and Its Uses," *Speech Monographs* 38(June 1970): 101–110.

[4] Using Goffman's terms, reciprocal impersonal relationships are those in which the participants refrain from expressions of or refuse to acknowledge the Other's expressions of role distance. For an extensive analysis of the way players convey detachment from the roles they are performing, see E. Goffman, "Role Distance," in *Encounters* (Indianapolis: Bobbs-Merrill Company, 1961), pp. 83–152.

the relationships as a means to an end—to buy a loaf of bread, to sell a car, to be served a meal, to cash a check, and so on. In this sense, players need to engage in the relationship because it provides an extrinsic gratification.

There is also a sense, however, in which engaging in such relationships can be inherently gratifying. To the extent that the relationships are static, highly formalized social structures, they bring some order and predictability into our lives: The waitress will not be shocked when we ask for "two eggs over easy," we can ask the barber to "trim a little around the ears," and the motel clerk will not mind when we drive up at 3:30 in the morning and ask for one of his vacant rooms. Imagine how much personal energy would be required if every time we wanted someone to fix us some eggs, cut our hair, or provide a place for us to sleep we would first have to explain why we thought we had a right to make the request and why we thought the Other was obliged to honor it. Fortunately, every interpersonal encounter does not involve repeated personal risk, or so we imagine. (We presume that we need not provide a list of all those who have taken advantage of an Impersonal relationship—ranging from poor service and embezzlement to unpaid bills and wiretapping.) Engaging in these communicative relationships, customary behavior, brings, if nothing else, the security that comes with the familiar.[5]

When players with impersonal relationship images encounter one another, therefore, *spontaneity* of play is severely limited. Participants restrict their conversation to impersonal exchanges that preclude the potential for them to know one another as humans apart from their social position.[6] In their encounters tactical option (human choice) is minimized and formal standing (status) replaces personal experiential engagement. The freedom extended to each individual is minimal: "Play your part or don't play at all." Players of Impersonal games, therefore, try to *master* the occasion—to pick a part (if they have such a choice), play it

---

[5] Such, therefore, is the pleasure that can still be derived from the twenty-one-day prepackaged tour of a dozen European countries. Although the tour is so carefully structured and rehearsed in advance that the tourists never "experience" Europe—they could just as well roam from airport to motel to airport to motel in the USA—such a tour does serve the important function of minimizing contact with the unknown ("If we do not experience the real flavor of the natives, at least we will not suffer any potentially troublesome consequences of involvement").

[6] We accept as the rule that non-person relations will be of this indifferent order. Thus, the news media occasionally feature a "human interest" story that is an exception to the rule: When a waitress who has worked many years in one establishment becomes ill and the regular customers, most of whom do not even know her name, take up a collection in her behalf, they "prove" thereby that they all had a certain minimal human interest in her in spite of her anonymity.

well, and reject all impulses to act outside the customary expectations. Actually, when behaviors become so stylized, rigid, and inflexible, it is probably less proper to say that the players *play-act* than it is to say that they *go through the motions.*

A relationship in which the participants distance themselves from each other as persons is not play-full in another sense: Such relationships have no room for humor.[7] By definition, the person involved in mastering impersonal relationships is not free to disregard convention, to delight in and seek out incongruity. Impersonal relationships are serious business. The player who stops to hold up for inspection the very procedures of which he or she is a part spoils or dissolves an impersonal relationship.

Another consequence of engaging in a relationship that is governed "by the book," is that, unlike all the other relationships we have studied so far, once a player has chosen or been chosen to participate impersonally, he or she is freed from personal responsibility. The burden for the relationship is shifted away from the players and on to some outside authority that has set the rules, established the procedures. The exemplar for such behavior is the officious bureaucrat who announces his or her ignorance or inability to help you in a difficult situation, "I'm sorry, this office has just closed; you'll have to come back and get in line again after lunch."[8] The effect of this shift of responsibility is to depersonalize the encounter even more and to minimize the possibility of a face-to-face (person-to-person) confrontation.[9]

So far, then, how can we summarize the nature of a communicative relationship in which the participants are more remote from each other than they would be if they were "only strangers"? We can say that players of Impersonal games are accessible to one another as individuals in a relationship that does not allow reciprocal human emergence but facilitates the accomplishment of goals extrinsic to the relationship.

---

[7] Hugh Duncan makes much the same point in his discussion of the relationship between comedy and the survival of social order: "When the office and the man are so identified that ridicule of one becomes ridicule of the other . . . humor becomes impossible. . . ." Hugh Duncan, *Communication and Social Order* (New York: Bedminster Press, 1962), p. 414.

[8] More elaborate instances of this impersonal irresponsibility are those who defer to "Dear . . ." columns on matters ethical or those who seek the help of an outside "expert" such as a marriage counselor to mediate family disputes. Or the authority may take the form of dependence upon a set of impersonal rules such as the Bible or the Army Code of Conduct. In this sense, turning to an authority to regulate the relationship has the effect of impersonalizing the relationship.

[9] William Labov emphasizes that such freedom from responsibility is an important part of the impersonal ritual exchanges that are used to manage challenges within various peer groups. See William Labov, "Rules for Ritual Insults," in T. Kochman, ed., *Rappin' and Stylin' Out* (Urbana, Ill.: University of Illinois Press, 1972), pp. 265–314.

When people with impersonal relationship images encounter each other they play one of two varieties of Impersonal Communication games: Protocol or Termination. "Protocol" is an Approaching Impersonal game whose telos is the preservation of an impersonal relationship. That is, although a play of this game sharply limits the opportunity of the players to experience one another, it does preserve their particular impersonal relationship and may possibly facilitate additional plays of more personal games. "Termination" is a Distancing Impersonal game whose telos is the destruction of an impersonal relationship. That is, a play of this game not only limits the opportunity of the players to experience one another, but it also facilitates the transformation of non-person players into non-beings.

Since the play of these games is dominated more by customs than tactics, the games themselves are less revealing to students of communication performance than they are to anthropologists, sociologists, and other botanists of human affairs who can treat them as cultural artifacts of social institutions. But students of communication can nonetheless derive some insight even from these limiting cases by considering how communicative experience can be when deprived of its playful component.

PROTOCOL: AN APPROACHING IMPERSONAL GAME

$$AG\rightarrow$$
$$F \quad \{ \quad \} \quad . \quad . \quad . \quad . \quad . \quad . \quad I$$

Protocol[10] is a communication game played by two or more persons who have impersonal relationship images of one another. A play of this game, whose end is the preservation of the relationship, however impersonal, involves the players moving through customary routines characterized by three major features: a specific context, specially qualified players, and adherence to a special interaction formula. We shall not

---

[10] It is interesting to speculate on the origins of this word. Although it commonly denotes ceremonial custom and regulation, the Greek prefix *proto* (meaning "first," "foremost," "earliest form of") when used in chemical terminology, denotes those compounds that contain the minimum of an element (we might suggest that the minimum in our use of the term is human contact). An earlier form of the word—*protocoll(um)* in Latin and *protokollon* in Greek—referred to a first leaf glued to the front of a manuscript that contained notes as to the manuscript's contents. In this case one *could* tell a book by its cover. Everything a potential reader needed to know about the manuscript was on the surface.

attempt to catalogue all Protocol play, but let us explore these three general features by reflecting on some examples.

Specific Context

First, unlike most other communicative encounters, Protocol is *context bound*. That is, the scenic circumstances must be appropriate or the entire encounter will regress to gibberish. Just as it would not do for a baseball umpire to approach someone on the street and shout, "Strike three! You're out!" the communicative behavior of Protocol is absurd outside the specific context of the game. For example, would it make any sense for someone to approach you on the street and to say "That will be $4.95 please"? Even though the Other may be attractively attired as a waitress, in order for you to engage in some kind of *impersonal* business, the context has to be correct. Protocol players must recognize the context before they can act their parts or understand their positions. When the situation is not socially defined, players cannot engage each other as "recognizable non-persons." Instead, they are forced to engage each other at least as unacquainted strangers (and play Polite Greeting or Turn Off).

Specially Qualified Players

Another general feature that informs our experience of Protocol is that the *participants must be qualified to assume their position* in the game. Just as a milkman cannot officiate at a marriage ceremony unless he is qualified to do so, and someone else must have some sort of institutional authorization in order to christen a ship (otherwise he or she is merely breaking bottles on boats), one cannot engage in impersonal Protocol play without the correct qualifications. For example, have you ever stood and waited for what seemed an unbearable amount of time at a department store counter waiting for a salesperson to arrive? Although too ethical to shoplift, why didn't you step up to the register and ring up your own sale? Or, when the salesperson arrived, why didn't you say, "Here, let me do that"? Did you feel unqualified to assume the position? (Even the impatient but honest customer who cannot wait for the cashier will leave money *by* the cash register: In so doing, the customer does not usurp the cashier's obligation to keep inventory and does not assume responsibility for the Pandora's Box that the cash register represents.)

To appreciate the range of qualifications necessary to play Protocol, we can, of course, consider the training and certification required for such social positions as doctor, coach, teller, policeman, teacher, and garbage collector. We should, however, also consider the requirements for the players who complete the assorted impersonal relationships. For example, to be a patient you must be sick, to be an employee you must want to work for a boss, to be a student you must want to learn (or want credits or a degree), to be a passenger you must want to go somewhere, to be a customer you must need service or products. (Who calls up the washing machine repairman merely to engage him in conversation, or who waits in a long line at the bank just to chat with the teller?) In Protocol games the player roles are well defined and individuals must be qualified, have the authority, to assume them.

Special Interaction Formula

Finally, most play of Protocol is constituted not only by context and designated performers, but by *adherence to a conventional formula and/or the recitation of specific words.* That is, in most impersonal relationship encounters we know *when* we are supposed to say something if not exactly *what.* The maidservant speaks only when spoken to, the priest stops his chant, and the pharmacist says "Who's next, please?" Protocol players almost always know when it is their turn to move.

In some cases they even know *what* to say, *how* to move, because in those cases saying the correct words is necessary for the game itself to exist. Two anonymous players may, for example, encounter each other at a racetrack on either side of a window. If one says to the other, "Yesterday I bet $5.00 on Hotsy Trotsy to show," the other will probably say "That's none of my business fella' . . . move on." If the player says, "I'll bet $5.00 on Mighty Fred to win," however, the other will take the money and the wager is on. That is, the very act of saying the formula "I'll bet" consummates their Protocol play.[11]

Another example quickly comes to mind by reflecting on one's experience in a thirty-one-flavor ice cream store. Here if one player does not say *exactly* the right words although the game *will* take place it will be a

---

[11] J. L. Austin, *How to Do Things with Words* (New York: Oxford University Press, 1965).

disappointing one for at least one customer. ("Well, if you *wanted* jamoca almond peppermint cheesecake sherbet, why didn't you *say* so?") And if the "right" words *are* said, but to the "wrong" person ("Well, what do I care, buddy—I don't work here."[12]) the game will not even take place. Similarly, the "right" words said in the "wrong" context will be seen as gibberish ("I don't care if you want *vanilla*, this is a shoe repair shop, sir").

As a summary of Protocol, let us consider the classic impersonal setting found in military organizations. The military is a total hierarchy: Each member occupies a distinct place in a chain of command that specifies who can (and must) command whom, where, and how. Although the participants may fraternize (literally behave like brothers toward each other) in their off-hours, when they are performing their military roles, they are Protocol players who can communicate only by giving and/or receiving orders. Thus it is that when a private passes an officer he or she must salute regardless of who the officer is or whether the officer *personally* merits such recognition and respect. (Indeed, new recruits are reminded, "Never forget, you are saluting the uniform, not the man.") The salute is a signal that the person initiating it can be a recipient of the other's orders. Regardless of the large interpersonal gap that military players experience, their encounter, like every play of Protocol, actively congeals[13] the social system that authorizes their impersonal relationship, and each individual's appearance in the encounter maintains his or her own non-person status. In a very real sense, Protocol game-play is "empty"—deprived of players acting in concert to nourish any personal relationship it lacks a core. In Protocol the suppleness of life gives way to hardness.

---

[12] Why is it that in situations where we mistake another customer for the clerk, we feel compelled to apologize? And why is it that if and when you are mistaken for a clerk you feel somewhat insulted? Isn't it because we intuitively suspect that such recognition is nonpersonal?

[13] Like bones that lose their suppleness as they age, this congealing means that such formalized relationships become ever less likely to change unless the communicative game itself is shattered. The effort to shatter Protocol in order to free the players from formal restrictedness often takes the form of profanity or obscene behavior intended to negate the very grounds of the ceremony. We might even define the obscene as that which is offensive because it shatters the superstructure that governs behavior and leaves players alone and without sufficient control of their conduct. It is in this sense that we can understand the blasphemy of student radicals who scatter cigarette ashes over the college dean's spotless rug and then ask innocently "Why is the dean so uptight?" They are in fact claiming that the dean has become overly inflexible in his assessments of correct conduct. The problem with such behavior, as with all blasphemy, is that it usually leads to sectarian or religious cult wars and other plays of Termination rather than to more intimate contact.

TERMINATION: A DISTANCING
IMPERSONAL GAME

$$F \ \{ \quad \} \ . \quad . \quad . \quad . \quad . \quad . \quad I$$
$$\leftarrow DG$$

Termination is a game played by two or more persons who have impersonal relationship images of one another. A play of this communication game involves players moving through customary routines that end in the players' transformation from non-persons to non-beings. That is, in Termination play individuals who are already as emotionally distant as non-persons engage in procedures that deny not only personhood but being,[14] as when one person murders another.

There are several reasons why we cannot and shall not say much about Termination game-play. First, because ours is a fundamentally humanistic society that seldom tolerates institutional sanction for such Distancing games, not only will few readers have had such communicative experience, but we can offer only a few examples to inform the future experience of others.

This is not to claim that humanistic societies lack their share of heinous outrages from time to time. It is only to say that we generally regard cruel and inhumane conventional procedures as out of keeping with our social experience and so seek to suppress their popularity as game-types. We prefer instead to develop all sorts of Approaching Impersonal games that surround and/or try to prevent the occasional instances of Termination—which culminate in such arenas as a courtroom, social work case file, prison, funeral parlor, and so on.[15]

---

[14] Readers might be inclined to see this game-type as the least desirable for anyone to play. For a thorough-going exploration of a social system that has literally reversed the Formality—Intimacy continuum, with Protocol if not Termination games as the cultural ideal, see Colin Turnbull's *The Mountain People* (New York: Simon and Schuster, 1972). According to Turnbull, the primary goal of the Ik, a small tribe of African hunters, is *individual* survival. For purposes of survival, the Ik have no compassion, concern, love, or affection: They abandon the old, the sick, the young, and the crippled; they steal food from each other's mouths and derive pleasure from each other's misfortunes and misery.

[15] Hence, most of these Protocol games would not even be legitimate without occasional instances of Termination. But "fortunately" it is precisely the impersonality of Protocol, the refusal to sever human contact but the unwillingness to get personal, which ironically facilitates repeated instances of Termination and guarantees job security. Perhaps even more paradoxical is the fact that if some Termination games were tolerated, given the chance to develop ceremonial rigidity, humanistic societies would not be so chaotic. But humanistic societies could not allow this, not only because of their concern for human fulfillment, but also because such societies need a little chaos as a measure of insuring personal freedom.

Termination play does exist, however, where social systems have institutionalized violence and have authorized such Distancing games as self-immolation, human mutilation and sacrifice, concentration camp torture, and other practices that display a lack of respect for human flesh. The players who choose or are forced to play these games have impersonal relationship images of one another. They are *reciprocally inaccessible* non-persons who display no unique presence. Usually each is stripped of any personally identifying characteristics (jewelry, teeth, hair, glasses, clothing, or whatever), and/or each dons some special costume or makeup. Often, to guarantee that they will betray no emotion, the participants may even wear masks to hide their faces.

Termination players are minimally *spontaneous;* they are not free to be in their relationship: The game prohibits tactical choice both for the moment and thereafter. (The sacrificial victim may only move through the rite and can never act again; the individual who ignites himself disallows the contact of others then and forever; the executioner has no option in his procedure and after carrying out his part he voids any future choice in the relationship—literally, in terms of the particular impersonal relationship, "He who lives by the sword, dies by the sword.")

Finally, the participants are *committed* to the relationship's encounter not so much because it is inherently gratifying,[16] but because it offers extrinsic rewards—battle ribbons, promotion, immortality, justice, rain, relief from suffering, good crops, and so on.

Another reason why we cannot and shall not examine the specifics of Termination game-play is that violence is, after all, *mute.* It begins where speech and free action cease. The Formality—Intimacy continuum that we have been using to inform our reflection on interpersonal communicative experience spans the entire range of interpersonal speech communication activity: The telos of the game at each pole discourages speech. In the last chapter we suggested how the static character of language is too clumsy for those who would play the most Approaching Intimate games. The communication in these games regresses into preverbal tender touching.

---

[16] Those who find inhumane activity inherently pleasurable do not play Termination, a game that denies them tactical freedom and is over too quickly. Generally, torture games are plays of Intensity. The torturer and his "victim" become greatly accessible to one another. The torturer needs to know his victim's every vulnerability in order to display his tactical virtuosity; yet because his activity itself is pleasurable, he cannot allow the game to end or the other player to stop playing. Likewise the "victim" becomes a willing accomplice in developing the intimate relationship—seeking to know the torturer's particular vulnerabilities in order to minimize discomfort through retaliation, threat of retaliation, threat of escape, or escape. Often, for the victim, escape is more threatening than continued incarceration by a familiar tormentor.

For Termination, the most Distancing Formal communication game, speech is both inappropriate and ultimately unnecessary.[17] It is inappropriate, from our perspective, because in order to separate their life spaces, individuals should not even share topic-images in common. Furthermore, speech is unnecessary, because as a human activity, it is tactically queer in a game whose end denies human being. Unlike Turn Off in which players prevent communicative contact with another for the moment, Termination players incapacitate the communicative relationship permanently. In Termination, therefore, verbal transaction is replaced by sheer physical process. The study of such a violent, inhumane process, like the study of how lightning destroys trees, may be socially significant, but it is communicatively uninteresting.

This chapter has introduced Impersonal games—those communicative activities in which individuals encounter one another as non-persons. While in one sense we can say that players with such impersonal relationship images interact, we can also say that in these relationships human contact is at a minimum.

PROTOCOL is an Approaching game that preserves the players' imagined non-person relationship; it maintains a maximum emotional distance between related individuals. In a play of the game, the participants go through a set of prescribed motions, each objectifies the Other and rejects all impulses in self to play-act for a moment, but no player erases the possibility of human interest in the future.

TERMINATION is a Distancing game that extinguishes particular non-person relationships. In a play of the game the participants go through a set of prescribed motions and one or more of the players is irrevocably shoved an infinite distance away from the human family, never to play interpersonal communication games again.

---

[17] Alternatively, if players of violent Distancing games *are* involved in some kind of speech behavior, what *is said* is of little consequence. The 822-page report submitted to the National Commission on the Causes and Prevention of Violence by Hugh Davis Graham and Ted Robert Gurr, *Violence in America : Historical and Comparative Perspectives* (New York: Bantam Books, 1969) implies this same conclusion by its neglect of discussing what people say, if anything, while they do violence.

Table 1.

	IMPERSONAL GAMES	RECOGNITION GAMES	FORMAL CONVERSATION GAMES	INFORMAL CONVERSATION GAMES	INTIMATE GAMES
	Protocol	*Polite Greeting*	*Polite Conversation*	*Personal Conversation Among Friends*	*Love*

FORMALITY ... } .... } .... } .... } .... } ... INTIMACY

	↑	↑	↑	↑	↑
	↓	↓	↓	↓	↓
	Termination	*Turn Off*	*Put Off*	*Put Down*	*Intensity*

Every individual has a supply of more or less conscious interpersonal relationship images that inform his or her communicative experience: These images are pictures of how "close" (ranging from Formal to Intimate) an interpersonal relationship is; they define an encounter with the related Other, and they regulate what kind of communication is expected and presented. Viewing relationship encounters as game-like activities allows observers to speculate on what it is that participants may say and do and to consider how it is that some communicative activities encourage the participants to recreate or minimize imagined emotional distance in their relationship (Approaching games) and how other communicative activities encourage the participants to increase imagined emotional distance in their relationship (Distancing games).

9

Introduction to Public Communication Games

W hy are you reading this book? In this chapter, as before, the question is a crucial one. So far this book
has had little to do with what it has been talking
about. To show you what we mean, let us, here and now,
experiment and play the Polite Greeting game. We'll serve:

"Hello!"

What happened? After you responded, did you find the game
ending abruptly or did the conversation become rather one-
sided? Or did you not respond at all?

Perhaps the example is a bad one. It's silly to play Polite
Greeting when persons know each other fairly well. Let's play
Personal Conversation Among Friends instead. This time you
start:

What's wrong? Why is your communicative experience with
this book, or its authors, not the same as your experience of
playing Polite Greeting at a neighborhood party or your experience of exchanging obscene expletives with an acquaintance
in the back alley? Or is it all the same to you?

RELATIONSHIP BETWEEN INTERPERSONAL AND PUBLIC COMMUNICATION GAMES

Throughout the preceding chapters we have explored the communication that we all experience during our encounters with family, friends, and strangers. We have referred to this communication as interpersonal games, and we have suggested that two variables influence our experience of interpersonal game-play: (1) the images that players have of the relationship between them (each relationship image being a momentary encapsulation of how an individual imagines the gap that separates his or her life space from the life space of a "related" other and each image ranging from formal to intimate), and (2) the consequences that the play of a given communication game has for the relationship between the players (Approaching or Distancing).

How does your experience of this book fit in this scheme of interpersonal game-play? We can begin to answer this question by exploring the nature of this relationship between us, the authors of this book, and you, the reader. If we were to use the Formality—Intimacy continuum, where on it would you place your image of our relationship? What immediate image reminds you of how emotionally near we are to each other? In what way do accessibility, reciprocity, spontaneity, and commitment characterize the relationship between us? Let us propose how we—Rosenfield, Hayes, and Frentz—imagine our relationship with you and you see if it agrees with the image that you have.

Accessibility

There is some degree of accessibility in our relationship. We, as authors and readers, are knowingly engaged in an interpersonal relationship. We have met as sovereign parties, each determining his own emotional accessibility to the other, each choosing whether or not to open himself up to the other's influence.[1] We have chosen to share with you some ideas

---

[1] We are grateful to Carroll C. Arnold for facilitating our understanding of this knowing engagement. (See C.C. Arnold, "Oral Rhetoric, Rhetoric, and Literature," *Philosophy and Rhetoric* 1 [Fall 1968]:191–210.) In the paragraphs that follow, he is also responsible for our insight into the reader's standards for the author's sufficiency and the author's responsibility for sustaining and directing the author-reader relationship. We must acknowledge, however, that we are extending the domain of Arnold's conceptualizations. His concern is with the public speaker-listener alliance. He may or may not agree with our transposition to the author-reader relationship. See also Dwight Van deVate, "The Appeal to Force," *Philosophy and Rhetoric* 8(Winter 1975):43–60.

that are important to us, and you, as you read, have indicated that you are willing to know our ideas and perhaps be influenced by them.

On the other hand, as we, the authors, write, we are controlling what you may know specifically about us, and, in turn, we know little specifically about you, our reader. We have generalized the concept of "reader" and hope to "touch" as many of you as we can, but in our generalizing we have sacrificed the opportunity of developing a uniquely accessible relationship with any one of you. Therefore, many boundaries still remain between us.

Reciprocity

One factor that limits the potential for our becoming especially accessible to each other is the physical distance between us. Indeed, as we stated earlier, physical distance and emotional distance need not coincide. It is possible to have a fairly intimate relationship with someone who is not immediately present as well as it is possible to be a stranger to someone crowding next to us on a bus. Nevertheless, in our author-reader relationship, physical distance *is* a significant variable. For one thing, unlike some intimate but physically distant relationships, most of us have never met each other personally. We are using this book to inaugurate our relationship.

Even more important is the fact that because our relationship is extended through both space and time, we have little opportunity for genuine exchange. Our imagined conversations between authors and readers began as early as 1967, but what time is it now? Does it matter that our relationship is spread across time? In other words, in order to extend our message to a greater number of readers, we have sacrificed the opportunity for a high degree of reciprocity. We are writing and you are reading; for the most part, we are giving and you are taking.

Spontaneity

Because the roles in our relationship are stabilized, because there is a clear distinction between the role of author and the role of reader, our relationship is characterized by a low degree of spontaneity. Each of us tends to conform more to the expectations that accompany our particular roles than to our own particular momentary impulses. When you picked up this book, for example, you knew that you were expected to be the reader, not the author. No doubt, many of you were uncomfortable when we asked you to play Polite Greeting and Personal Conversation Among

Friends with us. Your discomfort was probably due to your assumption that there are limits to the range of acceptable and reasonable behavior for your role as reader: No reader talks to a book unless he is a poor reader who cannot internalize his speech, unless he is learning a foreign language, or unless he is engaging in oral interpretation. You know what your role involves; you know how to behave.

But your spontaneity as reader is not as limited as ours is as authors. After all, you may, indeed, throw darts at this book, rip it to shreds, or write obscene phrases in the margins. Authors are less free. Of course, as individuals—as Rosenfield, Hayes, or Frentz—we can each be as spontaneous as we wish; in other situations, in other relationships, we may have so much courage that our impulses are showing all over the place. But as authors, there is a range of acceptable behavior with which we must comply: Editors and publishers have lengthy lists of manuscript specifications and production deadlines, censors have lengthy lists of prohibited vocabularies and potentially libelous references, and readers have at least minimum standards of sufficiency. Our impulse may be to throw darts at our manuscript, rip it to shreds, or replace every other word with an obscenity, but unless we ignore these impulses, or deliberately select publishers, censors, and readers who expect them, we cannot, literally, be authors.

Commitment

The last factor influencing our relationship's position on the F—I continuum is commitment, the degree to which the relationship itself is the focus of our interaction. In one sense, our commitment as authors is strong. Because we have initiated the relationship, because we are doing all the "speaking," we assume responsibility for sustaining and directing our alliance. If we are successful, you will read the entire book and perhaps be informed, excited, and amused. If we fail to meet our commitment, you, our reader, will turn us off.

In other words, your commitment as a reader need not be as strong as ours. Should you find yourself determined not to accept what we say, you can refuse to "engage" us. At the very least, you can elect to turn off yourself to us much as one turns off a television set when the program is boring. You might, out of fear or outside pressure, submit to us (as by reading and taking notes reluctantly in anticipation of an exam). But you may still choose whether or not you will allow us to influence you. What happens now depends upon your commitment. It would be foolish for us to believe that for the majority of you, reading this book is an inherently gratifying experience. But neither are we willing to discount the possibility of a reader who is committed enough to read with thought, care, and good humor.

In all honesty, however, our commitment as authors extends beyond our immediate relationship with you, our reader. Although our awareness of you continues to influence what we say and how we say it, our awareness of other relationships is also significant. Because our comments are on the "public record," where we continue to be held responsible for them ("But Rosenfield, Hayes, and Frentz say on page 234 . . ."), we are committed to the sources of our information; we must be careful to give them credit where such credit is due. We are committed to our editors and publisher; they must not be unnecessarily inconvenienced by what we say. We are committed to our own best interests because what we say now we may be asked to defend or recant at some other time. We must continue to think beyond the immediate relationship between author and reader.

If we were to place our image of our relationship on the Formality—Intimacy continuum, we would place it as follows:

$$F \quad . \quad . \quad \{ \quad \quad \} \quad . \quad . \quad . \quad . \quad . \quad . \quad I$$

We have willingly chosen to take some risks with you, our reader, and you have knowingly chosen to be exposed to some of our ideas. To a certain extent, then, we are mutually accessible. Because we are separated in space and time, however, our relationship is not especially reciprocal. Since we do not "share" the here and now of our relationship at any given moment, it is difficult for us to be spontaneous with each other. It is difficult for us to establish the kind of trust that is necessary for a high degree of spontaneity because we have no way of checking to see if our images of self, topic, Other, and scene overlap even slightly. We trust, instead, our specialized roles of author and reader and rely on the socially accepted behavior that is appropriate to these roles. As a result, we are more committed to our social roles than to each other, than to our own unique relationship. In addition, to the extent that we are "using" our relationship—to learn, to teach, to improve our communication with others, and so on—to the extent that we are not enjoying our interaction for its own sake, the degree of commitment in our relationship is not especially high. This combination of minimal accessibility, reciprocity, spontaneity, and commitment suggests a relationship that is

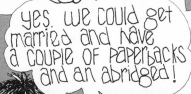

more formal than intimate. Notice, however, that we have not placed our image of our relationship at the Formal pole of the continuum. We do not think that our relationship is bound by a customary formula, severe role restrictions, or a certain context.

Earlier we asked, "Why is your communicative experience with this book, or its authors, not the same as your experience of playing Polite Greeting at a neighborhood party or your experience of exchanging obscene expletives with an acquaintance in the back alley?" In sharing our image of our relationship with you we have just demonstrated that the nature of the interpersonal relationship between the participants is not the key to understanding why your communicative experience with this book differs from your communicative experience with any of your friends, enemies, or intimates. We can bring to the author-reader relationship the same criteria (accessibility, reciprocity, spontaneity, and commitment) we have used to examine other more formal or more intimate interpersonal encounters.

But wait a minute! In discussing the interpersonal relationship that emerges between authors and reader, we are not really being fair, are we? Indeed, although a relationship between us does come to the surface, how many of you are reading this book in order to develop that relationship? How many of you had even thought about it before now? Why are you reading this book? Why are we writing this book? Are you using your reading skills to increase your emotional nearness to Rosenfield, Hayes, and/or Frentz? Are we writing carefully in hopes of developing a strong bond with you, our readers? Or, if you politely ignore some of the book's chapters, will you make our relationship more formal?

In asking these questions, we are suggesting that although your experience of reading this book is related to your experience of interpersonal communication, one of the variables that influences your experience of interpersonal game-play is missing. We *can* describe our relationship in terms of its formality or intimacy, but to describe our writing and your reading as "approaching" or as "distancing" makes little sense. Unlike interpersonal communication game-play that culminates in rewards or penalties for the relationship between its players, any consequence that reading this book has for the relationship between us (reader and authors) is purely coincidental. *Our relationship is not our focus.* As participants in this communicative experience we each have personal motives for interacting that extend beyond our relationship. Each of us knows that we are together for some reason other than our relationship and we assume that the same is true for the others. Some of you, for example, may even be uncomfortable at the seemingly "personal" tone of our present narrative. Do you wish that we would let you alone and "get on with it"? We agree. Our relationship is not our focus. "It" is. Let's move on and see what "it" might be.

Beginning with the title of this book, through Chapter 1 and on up to the present page, we have continued to use the word *experience*. We have proposed to "spark your curiosity about communicative experience," to help you "to reflect on your own communicative experience," and to explain how, for us, "the best communicative experiences are those that most clearly manifest the thought, loving care, and good humor that are mankind's most distinctive and precious potentials." Nowhere does our use of the word *experience* become more crucial than in this chapter. Here we want to argue that the human communicative experience is more diverse than the experience of interpersonal emotional nearness or distance. We want to turn our attention to different kinds of communicative experiences, experiences that are provided by the communicative events we call *public games*.

One crucial difference between our experience of what we have called "interpersonal communication games" and what we shall examine as "public communication games," is that whereas in interpersonal games we are participants in the creation of a gathering, in public games we affect or watch the transactions that occur in an arena.

Participating in the Creation of a Gathering

In interpersonal games, we participate in the creation of a gathering. By "gathering" we mean the momentary congregation of individuals who share each other's immediate, physical presence. We experience a gathering when we play Polite Greeting at a neighborhood party or when we exchange obscene expletives in the back alley (or even when we exchange obscene expletives at a neighborhood party and when we play Polite Greeting in the back alley!). In a typical interpersonal gathering we are physically close enough to one or more other persons that we can touch each other if we so desire. Our remarks are extemporaneous; we adapt them to the moment. At one moment, one of us is a speaker and another is a listener; at another moment the speaker-listener roles shift without much difficulty. At one moment the gathering changes with the inclusion of fewer or more participants; at another moment it disappears altogether. The most gratifying and consummatory communication play in a gathering occurs when an element of happy accident, or serendipity, attends the action. It is in this transitory sense of play-in-the-here-and-now that interpersonal games represent communicative works of art that come and go in a regular tide without leaving traces of their individual existence. It is because of this ephemeral quality that we discuss interpersonal games primarily in terms of the participant's momentary images. In any given case, these images, as we have seen, are hard even for the most perceptive witnesses to specify with any certainty; any specific relationship is something known, if at all, really only to its participants. It is in these senses that interpersonal games are most accurately called *participation games.*

Affecting or Watching the Transactions in an Arena

In public games we affect or watch the transactions that occur in an arena.[2] When we experience the arena we are assembled in a designated place—a concert hall, a football stadium, a museum, in front of a television set, a class, or a magazine. We expect certain experiences in each of these places. We go to the concert hall for the concert or recital, the television studio or set for the situation comedy or the variety show, and so on. The arena does not come and go as the gathering does. The arena is intended to persist over time and players and spectators return to the common place to re-enact or observe their favorite games. It is not a happy accident that players encounter and play out their favorite games; it is intentional. Likewise, it is not an intrusion when spectators appear to watch.

Some people argue that arenas were created to avoid or to escape the intimacy of interpersonal communication; to conduct the affairs of a complex society; to provide highly motivated, but superficial people, with interaction without having to confront man's *real* needs and problems; or to restore those facets of our spiritual resources which have been eroded by our continual abrasive contact with the world of men. We do not wish to take a side in this controversy. Questions dealing with the existence and necessity of social organization are beyond the scope of this book.

We will speculate on *what is as it is* in the world of human communication. Given this perspective, we begin by looking around, and, when we do, we note that in many societies designated public arenas do exist, that games have been developed to be played in them, and that the

---

[2] The origin of the word *arena* is the Latin word *arena* or *harena*, meaning "sand," "sandy place," specifically "areas sanded for combat."

games are invested with experiential satisfactions that supplant those derived from private interaction.[3] Societies that choose to provide such arenas are often called *public-minded*. The arenas they create to replace the gathering as the setting for communication are known as *public institutions*,[4] and the games most appropriately enacted in these settings entail *public address* communication rather than interpersonal utterance.

A public institution, be it a political party or a repertory theater group, which manages to generate messages that retain formal consistency over a long time, is likely to be providing its participants with a generally common experience. It shall be our task in the pages that follow to examine some of the more notable public address forms of our time, and to consider what experiential gratification the games they represent offer their participants as a replacement for the intimacy enjoyed in interpersonal utterance.

The existence of the arena has special consequences for the experience of those present. First, as participants we are usually aware that we are, essentially, standing before the community as we act. The arena has not been designated merely for our personal benefit; it is public property. As a public place, it demands of its participants greater self-consciousness, greater tactical deliberateness, greater care. We have already considered

---

[3] There is, of course, no logical necessity that a society provide public avenues to happiness. Throughout history there have been societies in which public arenas simply did not exist— such as those of the Philistines and the Babylonians. And there have been other, more despotic, regimes that actively discouraged public arenas. Such societies have left few cultural records or artifacts, so that the little we know of them comes from the reports of others who came in contact with them. (It is from the commentaries of the Old Testament Israelites, for example, that we know what we do about the Canaanites.)

Such privacy-oriented societies establish the Intimacy pole of the interpersonal game continuum as an absolute standard of happiness: For them the telos of all communication games is to achieve Intimacy. These societies are doubtless pleasant, insofar as their members are content to eat, drink, and be merry, but this also means, as Arendt notes, that their members "avoid disputes and try as far as possible to deal only with people with whom they cannot come into conflict." (H. Arendt, *Men in Dark Times*, [New York: Harcourt Brace Jovanovich, 1970], p. 30.)

Paradigms of such societies are, of course, Sodom and Gomorrah, where the populace became so intimate that they began to trade pals, spouses, and other family members in ever greater sexual intimacy. They did not see themselves as sinful; they were merely striving for gratification in communities where the only legitimate human gratification came from eating and snuggling up to one another. It is only "civilized" societies (that is, societies that encourage gratification in civic enterprises as well as in personal relations) that enjoy the sorts of games we are about to consider.

[4] The very word *institution* suggests the sort of permanence essential if society as a whole is to have the opportunity to experience public address games. "Institution" is derived from the Latin *stare* ("to stand"), and it literally means "to stand up, to make publically apparent." Related words are *stance* ("posture"), *statue* ("congealed posture"), *institute* ("set up"), *restitute* ("restore," i.e., "re-stand"), and *constitute* ("stand with"). So, an institution is a standing place, a publically designated place where everyone in the community knows certain games can be re-enacted.

how our awareness of the scene influences what we say and how we say it. Somehow, however, when we appear in an arena, before or among a group of people, our image of the scene has an especially strong influence. For example, even though the house lights may be off in the theater, we are usually aware of ourselves as part of a public audience—as witnesses of a public event; or even if no one else is around, when we speak on an empty stage we tend to restrain our spontaneity. The person who does not demonstrate the care appropriate to the arena is considered uncivilized or uncultured.[5]

A second, related experiential consequence of our presence in an arena is our awareness that we appear either as a speaker or a listener, as an actor or as an observer, as a performer or as a spectator. In a public arena there is a clear distinction between the roles of the players, and we are highly conscious of which role is ours. Most often the division is created because one player possesses access to amplification devices and another does not. Such obvious devices as microphones, speakers, platforms, print, radio, television, and film are often integral parts of a public arena. Each enables one or more players to trans-act, to extend a communicative message across space and/or time, and another player or players to receive the message or to watch the performance. Since one party controls these devices, it is unusual for a listener to become a speaker without much difficulty.

Using the criteria we have suggested to this point, let us consider the experience of this book as a public communicative experience. You may not have thought of this book as an arena, as a common place, but it is. Even though you may read it anywhere, any time, dressed as you like, eating or drinking what you wish, when you do, you enter a public arena. It is not a happy accident that we are engaged with each other. This book is designed to persist over time, permitting you to return to it wherever you wish, whenever you wish. If you should leave for a moment, the book will not disappear; if and when you return we will not have forgotten what we wanted to say, or, in your absence, have decided that we do not want to talk to you anymore. Furthermore, because we are the speakers and control the amplification devices, there is no way that something you mutter can suddenly change our game or that you can transform the book into a movie.

Some borderline situations are difficult to classify neatly because they fall in the grey area between what would now seem to be public arenas and

---

[5] We use the term *culture* in its original sense of "caring" for others (*colere* is a Latin verb meaning to "till," "cultivate," "guard," "protect," "revere"), as in terms such as "agriculture" which denotes a generalized caring for the land as a whole and not just tending a discrete land parcel. The cultured person cares; he is additionally civilized—he cares for the public well-being.

what would now seem to be interpersonal gatherings.[6] Consider, for example, a telephone conversation. Clearly, the immediate, physical presence that characterizes a gathering is missing, but the speaker and listener roles shift rapidly and the conversations are fairly extemporaneous. Is the experience one of a "public communication game"? Or what about the time that a parent was giving you a scolding. You were very conscious that your role was to listen and that anything you would say would be held against you, yet somehow you also felt the immediate physical presence of the "gathering." Public experience or private experience? There are also some small, relatively informal face-to-face groups in which a listener may become a speaker very quickly, but we are tempted to label their communication "public." Such groups as juries and town councils "gather" like this, but they also carry on public business and their communication is extended over time and space by a secretary who keeps a public record of the transactions. Is their communication experience public or interpersonal?

Clearly, then, the criteria we have so far proposed for differentiating interpersonal and public communication are insufficient. Once again, a key to minimizing our confusion is to try to appreciate the experience of the participants. Consider, for example, the just mentioned telephone conversation. Which would be more personal: if you were talking to a person making a nationwide survey on choices among brand-name peanut butters or if you were describing to an acquaintance the addition of peanut butter sandwiches to a proposed picnic menu? Which would be more public: the town council's discussion of responsibility for the next meeting's refreshments or discussion of responsibility for the next year's highway maintenance?

We are not suggesting that the content of the communication is a differentiating criterion. Censors to the contrary, the same range of content we have seen in interpersonal games is found in public arenas, from the very intimate to the very formal. Similarly, like much personal utterance, public address frequently functions in a non-informative fashion. Coronations, christenings, inaugurations, installations, retirement banquets, anniversary celebrations, wedding ceremonies, and the like, are all characteristically as void of "news" as is the polite interpersonal exchange: "Hi! How's it going?" "Fine, thanks, and you?" "Oh, just fine."

What *does* make a crucial difference between our experience of interpersonal communication and our experience of public communication, however, is *the presumed intentions of the participants by the participants.* We mentioned above that as participants in this communicative experience

---

[6] We will be analyzing some important examples in Chapter 12 on the rhetoric of healing.

(author-reader-book), we each have personal motives for interacting that extend beyond our relationship; each of us knows that we are together for some reason other than our relationship, and we assume that the same is true for the others. Such a "match" of presumed motives is important.

Let us imagine, for example, that we go to an avant-garde theater in expectation of an evening's entertainment. Once seated among the audience we see various bizarre figures in costume come out on the stage and hurl insults at the audience; perhaps these "actors" also charge up and down the aisles physically threatening the audience. We come away from the evening excited by the daring theatrical experience—unused to such abuse directed at ourselves, we are grateful to the cast. On our way home, however, we come upon some drunks who lurch up to our party, uttering abuse and threatening to come into physical contact. Here, under identical circumstances (except we are no longer in a "theater" and we have not paid the price of admission), we are appalled, angered, frightened—we hurry away from an awkward situation with a mixture of embarrassment and disgust. What has changed? Not the sheer event. Instead, we recognize that we lack an appropriate "match" of motives in the participants. We do not presume that the drunks have the actors' good will in offering us an evening's entertainment; we presume that the drunks' intent is more personal. If, however, we see the drunks as wandering minstrels whose intent is entertainment, we might not be so frightened. Or, alternatively, if we see our own intentions as personal, we might be pleased at the drunks' personal assault because it provides an outlet for our altruistic impulses. In either of these latter cases our presumed motives match. What we are proposing, then, is that in public communication games, our experience is influenced by what we presume is the intention of the Other and we presume that the focus is something more than our immediate interpersonal relationship.

Before discussing what some of these different emphases are, let us review for a moment. The purpose of this chapter so far has been to ask you to focus on the question, "Why are you reading this book?" and to demonstrate how the experience of interpersonal communication described in the first half of this book is not what you actually experience when you read this book. We have proposed that we can discuss our communicative relationship's position on the Formality—Intimacy continuum, but that the approaching/distancing distinctions of interpersonal communication make little sense. This book occurs in an arena, not a gathering, and the arena limits both physically and emotionally the interpersonal nearness that is possible in informal gatherings. And furthermore, readers and authors of this book presume that the relationship between them is purely coincidental to something else. In the main, we either have a relationship or we do not; you either read this book and imagine our relationship as F . . { } . . . . I, or you do not read this book and cannot imagine our relationship.

THE EXPERIENCE OF PUBLIC COMMUNICATION GAMES

We propose that one way to distinguish among the various kinds of public communication that we experience is to use the categories established by the Roman, Cicero. Cicero contended that the bulk of public address communication served at least one of three primary functions: to entertain or to persuade or to instruct an audience. In other words, adapting these categories to facilitate our understanding of public address experience, we would argue that quite regularly we enter public arenas expecting to entertain or to be entertained, expecting to persuade or to be persuaded, or expecting to instruct or to be instructed.

Since Chapter 1 we have professed our distrust of thoughtless reliance on formal category systems. And in this case, we do not intend to force all public communicative experience into one category or another. A thoughtful use of the categories is as a "way in" to understanding public address experience, not as "the way" to understand public address experience.

Obviously, under some circumstances, a given communicative event may satisfy more than one of these three expectations. Just as there can be hybrid games like water polo, which can be appreciated both as a ball game and as a coordination game, many institutional forms are of sufficient latitude to admit hybrid public address events. We can have propagandistic plays that operate in the entertainment arena but which function persuasively; we can have lively television shows that blend instructional and entertainment features. Similarly, other communicative events may even be unclassifiable insofar as they induce some public experience outside this triad of entertainment, persuasion, and instruction. We shall mention some of these alternatives toward the end of this chapter.

Each of these three communicative experiences can be associated with a cluster of public messages that tend to generate it. Those messages whose main function is to entertain, we call *poetic*—they appeal to our senses. Those messages that function to persuade, we call *rhetorical*—they appeal to our wills. Those messages that function to instruct, we call *dialectical*—they appeal to our intellects. In the succeeding chapters, we shall explore in more detail the range of public communicative experience generated by poetic messages, rhetorical messages, and dialectical messages, and we shall see how the play of a specific Poetic, Rhetoric, or Dialectic game, of which a particular message is a part, can enhance our potential for thought, care, and good humor. The major purpose of the rest of this chapter is to clarify the general distinguishing characteristics of each game/message category.

Poetic Public Games Are Those Whose Telos Is Affirmation: The Messages Generated Invite the Participants to Experience Aesthetic Intent

Poetic games are those in which the messages employed are invested with aesthetic import: Their significance lies with the sensuality they engage in the participants and spectators rather than in literal or indicative references to the world. By this we mean that poetic messages are those that invite us to rejuvenate our passions. This is by no means true for all public communication games. Some messages give priority to the reality of their reference. If, for instance, the local weatherman reports that the weather is fair and mild, he is stating what he presumes is fact. As we walk around outside we soon confirm for ourselves the factual character of his statement: The weather is indeed fair and mild; his statement referred to a condition in the world independent of us or his remarks: It was a correct (or "true") statement.

But the poetic message functions more to express than to denote. A still life painting of bananas and oranges can be considered a public message, but it is not a message *about* bananas and oranges. Though the painter may have used real fruit as a point of departure, his painting does not refer to the fruit in the same sense that the weather report refers to climatic conditions outside. His picture of bananas and oranges is not a report about fruit he has at home or some incident that occurred while he was eating fruit. The painting artifact functions to invoke feelings or states of mind in us, and we (insofar as we are people who prize involvement in games of poetic experience) regard our well-being as enhanced, our perception enlarged, and our soul nurtured for having the opportunity to have our passions thus stimulated. In any event, we cannot accuse the painter of telling a lie should he paint purple bananas and black oranges. His paintings are not about reality but about the ultimate well-being of the painter and his audience for having thus engaged their perceptions and allowed their feelings to be touched by the aesthetic object/event.

I'm the unluckiest orange in the world.
Why's that?
Yesterday my wife left me.
Gee, I'm sorry to hear that.
My daughter's pregnant and doesn't know who the father is.
Oh wow. that's awful!
My house burned down and the insurance company won't pay
Oh God, what a rotten break!!
and my car was repossessed. In short, I'm going bananas
You fruit!

At the other extreme, paintings, or poetic messages in general, are more than decorative pieces. Many people treat paintings as if they were designed to be functional, to serve some purpose. Without too much difficulty we can imagine an elderly lady commenting, "Well, I've just got to find a painting that has some streaks of red in it that will match my drapes and offer contrast to the couch below." This lady seems to have less need for a painting than for something to cover her wall. She might as well purchase wallpaper. Painting is neither of these extremes—poetic messages are neither about reality nor merely decorative.

In poetic messages the form as articulated is the most important thing. In other words, it is not what is said, but the way it is said; it is not always what is painted, but how it is painted. It is the emergent patterns in the message itself that are important and that themselves exercise the senses. The focus in music is usually not the similarity of the notes to the sounds of nature or the city, but harmony and rhythm, the pattern created by the notes. Likewise, the emphasis in a Shakespearean play is not on the probability that the characters ever lived, but rather on the relationships among the characters and on how they speak and act.

What, then, is the poetic "function"? It is to provide through words, images, textures, tones, and other sensual or aesthetic components, emblems that will fire the participant's mind in expanding directions. Poetic discourse serves as an expanding comment on reality. One who experiences a poetic moment may feel a momentary child-like delight that causes him to respond with a "Wow!" and an impulse to chortle, as his soul is tickled by the sensations imparted from the poetic object/event. In our daily lives we tend to shut ourselves off from sensual possibilities and from knowing reality by getting nearer to it. We brush past people; we involuntarily tense our muscles so as to derive no pleasure from tactile contact with another human. We may even catch ourselves holding our breath as we get "too close" to a stranger. Poetic messages operate to relax and comfort us, to extend our sensory awareness, to bring us nearer the elements of reality, and thereby to exalt in Being rather than cutting ourselves off from it. They serve to affirm for us *what is*, to engage us with Being, to make reality more vivid to us than the drab contact we so often have with reality in our daily schedule of events. For by offering us affirmation of Being, the poetic experience serves to reaffirm the reality of our own existence (our own *well-being*); it wakens us to life in much the same way that a moment of loving contact with another human can serve to make our surroundings more intense, our minds and bodies more alert, our reactions to the environment more "lively." In much the same way that we may suddenly be overwhelmed by the presence of another person to whom we are attracted, so poetic messages can overwhelm us with their nearness and open us to receive some dis-closure of reality contained in the aesthetic pattern offered to us.

For an example of poetic affirmation, consider a typical Western horse opera. The drama begins as a good-natured harmless hero is riding out to inspect his ranch. All of a sudden he comes upon a covered wagon that has been attacked, overturned, set afire, and its owners massacred. From amidst the smoking ruins our hero hears the cry of a small child. Somehow someone has managed to survive! And lo and behold he soon discovers that not only is the survivor a little girl, but she is blind! This is the predicament. What shall he do? There are no women on his ranch to take care of her and no orphanages in the vicinity.

The rest of the drama reveals how our hero solves his problem and how the play affirms something. The resolution might lead an audience to agree that early ranchers were warm men, tough when necessary, but generally men to be trusted, and so on. This conclusion is not a necessary conclusion as is the conclusion to a syllogism. The "truth" of the "conclusion" is not the main justification for poetic performance.

The affirmation that a poetic message seeks, the justification for the drama, can be contradicted. Let us suppose that a playgoer on one night draws a "conclusion" from Arthur Miller's *Death of A Salesman* that a family man is a happy man, that Willy Loman would have been far more happy had he been on better terms with his sons and not had mistresses, and on the next night draws the opposite "conclusion" from Harold Pinter's play *The Homecoming* that the family man is an unhappy man, that Teddy was unhappy precisely because he brought his wife home and literally shared her with his father and brothers. Although the "conclusions" drawn are opposite, the playgoer does not contradict himself. It is possible to accept the messages of both of these plays. In each case, the affirmation "celebrates" or "shakes hands with" (or in some other manner acknowledges) a reality with which men are familiar. To so acknowledge even an unhappy truth in this fashion is to offer our appreciation that this, too, is a valid part of human experience, that it contains the seeds of existence that characterize "human beings."

Poetic messages are not appropriate for all situations. At a criminal trial the determination of who is guilty and who is innocent is scarcely compatible with the issue of which lawyer can versify the best. We want the lawyers to address themselves to claims about the reality of the case. Similarly, a scientist who writes an enchanting report of an invalid or impossible experiment cannot defend his results on the basis of their written form alone. We demand that his data conform to the object-ivity of the world. When they do not, we call the writing science fiction—a poetic message. Other types of public address are more appropriate for legal and scientific contexts.

There is one final feature that can help us understand our experience of Poetic games. When we hear different types of public messages we refer to an intuitive scale to determine how salient or "real" they are to us. Although we are seldom conscious of this scale, it is always operating. We have already suggested that poetic messages do not attempt to describe "reality." This is not to say, however, that such messages have no relation to reality; that they are total fantasy forms. Intuitively, this could not be. If the patterns of poetic messages bore no resemblance to any dimension of the reality we all experience, then such messages would be totally incomprehensible to us; just as in encountering the script of a foreign language for the first time, we would have no point of reference from which to understand the messages' significance.

Poetic messages, however, exist in the realm of the *possible*, rather than in the probable. Since we expect all kinds of situations and statements, we are reluctant to commit our belief. Although we may, for example, be entertained by a short story about the invasion and overthrow of the planet Earth by miniature Martian cyclops, if given a dollar to bet, few of us would be willing to wager a quarter, if that much, that the event is imminently probable. In this age of interplanetary exploration, nevertheless, we are willing to admit that almost anything is possible, so we suspend our disbelief for a time and allow ourselves to be drawn into the "what if?" of the story.

Or consider the Western hero mentioned earlier. Given what we know for a fact about the "real Wild West," is it probable that we ever would have confronted a big hulk of a man as mild mannered as our hero? Would such a man as he have survived? Probably not! In the "real West" it would be more *probable* for the man who found the little blind orphan to be realistic and shoot her as he would a wounded helpless animal or leave her eventually to die. Still it is *possible* that such a man in such a situation did exist, so we willingly suspend our doubts and get involved with the story's predicament.

In effect, there are two levels of belief within poetic messages. First of all, we have to be willing to accept the possible moral universe within which the poetic predicament and resolution take place. Secondly, once this universe is established we demand that it be internally consistent.

By this we mean that we put some limits even on what we will accept as being possible. If the Martians of the science fiction short story arrive in a flying saucer, we will not accept their departure in time machines. Or, if we follow our Western hero through an hour-and-a-half motion picture or a 450-page novel only to see him unsuccessful in his search for a home for the blind orphan, few will then believe in murder or abandonment as possible resolutions. True, these are possible poetic solutions in general, but given what we have come to know about the character, they are impossible—a man such as he would never do those things—and we are no longer able to suspend our disbelief. Such a story, in effect, would probably not even claim two cents of our hypothetical dollar. Although a poetic message is not required to utter the truth, we demand that it must at least be honest to itself.[7]

Rhetoric Public Games Are Those Whose Telos Is Consensus: The Messages Generated Invite the Participants to Experience Political Intent

Rhetoric games are those in which messages are employed to willfully influence the actions of others. Public debate in which opposing sides do battle with symbols over such topics as civil rights, taxation, urban renewal, welfare, or military conflicts are examples of Rhetoric games. Each participant asserts that his view of reality is the most accurate. One can claim, for example, "Sex education is the moral responsibility of the home and not the domain of the public schools"; while another can argue, "It is vital that sex education be included in the public school curriculum because evidence demonstrates that parents are not adequate teachers." Each position is an assertion about the way things are or ought to be, and the participants engage in discussion in order to arrive at a satisfactory consensus for action. As the public listens, they are not concerned with evaluating the form of the statements as much as they are with assessing the compatibility of the interpretations with their own civic judgments. The persuasive speaker invites his listeners to join him in putting a common pattern on events, a single face on reality, and in so doing to reach a "consensus" (or common sense) as a basis for response. In its turn, public awareness of this consensus constitutes "community."

---

[7] For an excellent discussion of the philosophical implications of poetic and "real world" truths, see Harrington Ingram, "Truth and Fiction" (unpublished Ph.D. dissertation, University of Southern California, 1973).

Hence, we can say that Rhetoric games generate a literature of assertions, rather than a literature of affirmation, and that they expand our range of willful common action whereas Poetic games serve to enhance our perceptivity by exercising our passions. Societies that favor political action will thus encourage Rhetoric games among their citizenry.

Another means of understanding rhetorical messages is in terms of their belief quotient. Recall that poetic messages operate in the realm of possibility, that is, participants demand of such messages, first, that they bear at least some resemblance to "real world" experience, and, secondly, that they be internally consistent. By contrast, rhetorical messages operate in the realm of the *probable*. There are certain kinds of topics about which we can never be certain, but for these kinds of topics we would be willing to bet at least forty to sixty cents on the accuracy of the speaker's assertions. These contingent topics, which could always have been other than as they are, are the material out of which rhetorical messages are created.

In a trial, for example, we can never be absolutely certain about the guilt or innocence of a person. Even if we knew all there was to know, we could never be completely sure that we were correct. The best we can do is to try to get the most likely interpretation, and decide what probably happened.

Because doubt is inherent in rhetorical situations, conflicting standards are often present. When legislators determine the priorities for a new budget, there is no one absolute answer, there is no definite reason for giving more money to education, or to welfare, or to highways. In the same way, no exact amount of money makes a perfect or ideal budget. There is no rule that states that $24,002,198 is the precise amount that should be allotted for education. In such situations, the legislators' decision will be based on the nature of their objectives, whether they are trying, say, to be humanitarian, political, efficient, or economical. In other words, they can have conflicting standards, and what is right under one set of standards may be completely wrong under another set. And so they try to mediate between the varying interests and pressures and arrive at the most reasonable settlement.

This is also the crux of collective bargaining and international diplomatic negotiations. In both of these situations no one single answer exists. The best that the mediator or diplomat can do is to work things through and have everyone agree that he is probably right. The participants may not be convinced, but they will find the decision acceptable within the circumstances.

Dialectic Public Games Are Those Whose Telos Is Intellectual Understanding: The Messages Generated Invite the Participants to Experience Philosophical Intent

Dialectic games are those in which messages are employed to deal with reality, but instead of trying to interpret reality their intent is to reason through reality's structure to "objectify" it. The concern of these messages is for the "essence of things." (We are, in fact, playing a Dialectic game as we try to clarify for you the "reality" of Dialectic games.) Where poetry touches our perception in order to encourage our sensuality, Dialectic touches our intellect, our capacity to know and understand, in an effort to encourage thought.

Dialectic was a game played by the Ancient Greeks. In Plato's Socratic dialogues we have transcripts of men attempting to resolve controversy by getting as close to reality as possible. Out of their games arose the rules for logic and valid inference. Much scholarly writing and criticism fit into this category of public address. Where poetic discourse seeks to free the mind of its conventional procedures, Dialectic submits the mind to a kind of coercion, or disciplined rigor. Note how the mathematical statement "2 + 2 = 4" is received by the mind: There are no options (as there would be with the rhetorical assertion, "We should despise all assassins," or with the poetic affirmation, "Television is chewing gum for the eyes"); our minds are forced to accept the correctness of the calculation. In the face of the tyranny of logic (and math and logic are both types of Dialectic), there can be no enchantment, only acceptance.

The function of dialectical messages, as we know them, is neither aesthetic nor political but philosophic. That is, where poetic messages stimulate sensual awareness and where rhetorical messages stimulate our fraternal sense (our appetite for political action in common with others), the experiential consequence of playing a Dialectic game is to encourage us to enjoy our rational faculties and, hence, ultimately to love wisdom itself. We often have heard it said of accomplished scholars or scientists that they were lackluster students in their youth until an exceptional teacher excited their curiosity concerning a particular discipline or puzzle. In our terms, such reports are recollections of a Dialectic game that was particularly gratifying to the students and set their minds off toward particular intellectual careers.

This is not to say that Dialectic games need be totally lacking in imagination or originality—far from it. Indeed, mathematicians claim that in the advanced stages of mathematical reasoning a sensual vividness comparable to poetic ecstasy can occur. But we are surely justified in suggesting that for most players, engaging in logical or mathematical proving serves far more to control, direct, force, our minds along "correct" paths and spur our reason to manipulate abstractions rather than the more common poetic experience in which creator invites his audience to enter into a playful relation with reality. Dialectic encourages respect for the wisdom of a sage or gospel where Rhetoric encourages fraternal feelings and Poetic encourages sensuality.

As with poetic and rhetorical messages, we can add a further dimension for clarification by considering the realm of belief in which dialectical messages operate. Dialectical messages are those in which the subject practically demands our near-total belief, a complete commitment to the statements offered. Intuitively we rarely question these kinds of public messages. If given a dollar to bet, we would be willing to wager at least ninety cents that the statements were, indeed, "true."

The scientist, for example, strives to discover the universal laws of nature. When he makes statements, we tend to commit ourselves to them and to regulate our lives by them. When he says that the correct time is 10:45 A.M., we set our watches. When he predicts a lunar eclipse, the movement of the tides, and chemical reactions, we regard his predictions as inevitable. Scientists prefer to deal with *certainties*, which are most often found in most abundance in nature.[8]

Similarly, logicians are concerned that there be no inherent flaw within their arguments. They want to be able to bet ninety cents or more that their conclusions are valid or that their opponents' arguments are invalid.

In mathematics, another branch of Dialectic, the objective is to start with certain basic assumptions or postulates and to derive absolute proofs about the nature of the quadratic equation, the binomial theorem, and so on. Once the mathematician arrives at a certain conclusion based on the assumptions, nothing can shake the conclusion. As long as we accept his assumptions, we believe the mathematician's statements without question.

To this point we have sought to contrast the different experiences provided by three sorts of public communication games. We have argued that our experience in these games is influenced by something more than our immediate images of the relationships between the players. In these

---

[8] It may be worth noting in passing that one of the functions of statistical inference is to provide the scientist with a means for assuring himself that the statements he makes about reality can be accepted with maximum certainty.

games our experience is also influenced by what we presume is the intention of the players and the messages that they generate, namely, to entertain the senses (poetic messages), to persuade the will (rhetorical messages), and to instruct the intellect (dialectical messages). And insofar as we are willing to engage ourselves in the games, we claim, we have the potential to experience affirmation of human being (Poetic games), consensus of human action (Rhetoric games), and respect for human understanding (Dialectic games).

Each of these public games is *recreational*, in the original sense. Each game can re-create its participants, each can restore or enhance its participant's human potential for passion, action, or thought.[9] Recreation of this type has become especially important in modern industrial societies, where the monotonous pressures of daily living in a world dominated by production and commerce threaten to wear away the distinctive features of both men and machines.[10]

The implications of the claim that these public games are restorative are far reaching.[11] For one, we can appreciate that the best games will be those whose communication enables the audience to become thoroughly involved in the experience offered to it, although the nature and extent of that involvement is, of course, multi-faceted. For another, since different communities contain pressures and forces that erode their members in different fashions, we can expect to find a variety of public games that recreate the citizenry, each played out on its own civic platform and each generating its own variety of public messages. In the succeeding chapters, as we consider the sorts of games played, we will have an opportunity to elaborate in greater detail the recreational forces that each game embodies.

---

[9] These distinctions are explored in detail in Richard McKeon, *Thought, Action, and Passion* (Chicago: University of Chicago Press, 1954). It is also true that the categories of thought, action, and passion closely parallel the tradition in psychology known as *faculty psychology*. As will become apparent later, our use of these terms in no way implies endorsement of the faculty psychology tradition.

[10] F. Nietzsche, with his notion of a "devaluation of values," recognized just how pernicious industrialism had become for the scale of human existence. When men and commodities come to be treated completely alike and interchangeable rather than in any respects unique, then neither men, nor products, can be taken seriously. They then derive their "value" merely as entities of exchange. And in passing from hand to hand they gradually wear down like old coins, until finally they are taken out of circulation. But if men and their products are so unimportant that we can replace one with another with no more concern than we would change pants, then values themselves threaten to become trivialized beyond recognition. Cf. Hannah Arendt, *Between Past and Future* (New York: Viking Press, 1968), pp. 32–33.

[11] For an in-depth rationale for the biological necessity of generating and experiencing the "recreative," see S. Langer, *Philosophy in a New Key* (Boston: Harvard University Press, 1942).

Three Other Public Communication Games

Before going on, we need to acknowledge, clearly, that Poetic, Rhetoric, and Dialectic are not the only public communication games that a given society can play. They are common games found in many cultures, ours included, but they do not account for all the public messages that public institutions generate. We would like to admit that there are at least three other intentions that the participants may presume that they share with each other when they enter the public arena. These are not as interesting for us to explore in as much detail because their manifestations are not as various as those of entertainment, persuasion, and instruction. But their inclusion, however minimal, is necessary in order to provide context for the poetic, rhetorical, and dialectical messages that we shall investigate.

Anticipation.   First of all, many messages that are generated by public institutions invite us to experience *anticipation*. The presumed intent of messages in this category is merely to keep the communication channels open. There are frequent periods when a group or society may have no pressing issues to discuss. But this does not preclude communication. Every fraternal business meeting need not solve a crucial financial problem, and even when the President addresses a joint session of Congress he need not be declaring war. Nevertheless, clubs and committees still meet at regular intervals essentially in order to remind the members that they have an outlet for important communication if it is ever needed. Many public messages, therefore, function like the technician's repetition of "Testing; one, two, three, four" on the public address system. He has nothing important to say and for the most part those attending to his remarks do not see them as invitations to be entertained, persuaded, or instructed. He is making sure that the equipment is operational for the possible transmission of some significant information at another time.

Association for Its Own Sake.   Other public messages invite the participants to celebrate their *association for its own sake*. In a sense we can say that such messages as the Pledge of Allegiance to the Flag, a school Alma Mater, a chorus or two of "rah-rah-rah; siss-boom-bah; yeah team!", or a fraternity password are not invitations to appreciate form, agree to some action, or to consider the essence of things. Instead, participants presume they are invitations to recognize a common bond, to acknowledge the worth of their association as such.

In another sense, admittedly, these same messages could be seen as inviting the participants to affirm the Being of their and other groups, to experience a particular consensus of spirit from which they could act in common, and to experience respect for the essence of their particular group. In Poetic, Rhetoric, and Dialectic games, messages of this type might be seen as having this additional import. In others, however, they are something that seem necessary to the participants only as emblems of solidarity, such as the singing of the national anthem prior to sports events.

Some public messages are, therefore, essential just to the general maintenance of social institutions; they keep the communication channels open and the participants ready. Georg Simmel, a sociologist whose concern was the existence and necessity of human association, calls our attention to the ambiguity of public communicative events when he notes that a given game "is played not only *in* society as its outward bearer but that *with* the society actually 'society' is played."[12] In other words, people often enter a public arena merely to validate the arena's existence as a potential source of recreational public messages, and to profess their loyalty to the society that has established the arenas in the first place.

Recuperation.   A third additional category of public messages invites its participants to experience *recuperation*. These messages allow their participants to rest after work—to overcome fatigue and to rest to prepare to return to work—to restore vigor. They are not demanding; they are not stimulating. There is no action in rest, merely sensation, reception. This is not to deny the value of rest. Such public messages are essential to the general maintenance of game-players; the qualities of rest are inherently gratifying. In the pages that follow, however, we shall argue that steady participation in such "mere amusement" at the expense of recreational play is unwholesome. More specifically, there is nothing wrong with reading the labels on jars of instant coffee, but reading and rereading them every morning as a way to escape boredom during breakfast can make one thoughtless and careless and more the object of good humor than a participant.

What next? We shall abandon, except for occasional references, the communicative experiences of anticipation, association for its own sake, and recuperation and focus on the recreational experiences provided by Poetic, Rhetorical, and Dialectical games. We shall also abandon the

---

[12] G. Simmel, "The Sociology of Sociability," *The American Journal of Sociology* 55 (November 1949):258.

Formality—Intimacy continuum in favor of a scheme that more effectively describes the experiential character of these games. For where interpersonal communication games enable participants to move a potentially infinite distance together or apart, public communication games tend to enhance recreation only if successful. That is, they cannot seriously deplete us, they can only fail to recreate us. Thus, a diagram of public games requires a zero point of origin on a scale rather than a continuum with two infinitely distant poles. Because the understanding we bring to public address events grows out of our understanding of interpersonal utterance, however, we shall propose that the zero point of origin for recreational games be at that point on the F—I continuum where for the most part we experience the relationship among participants in a public address event, namely, more in the realm of Formality than Intimacy. We shall consider the three facets of recreational experience as if they were vectors moving off the interpersonal utterance continuum, filling the void of sheer Formality with communally desirable recreational experiences:

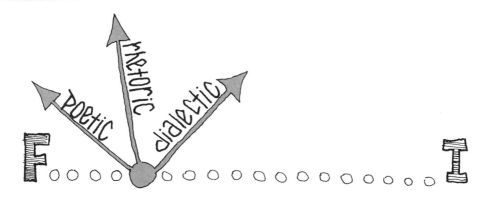

In the pages that follow, as we examine some of the more notable public address forms of our time and consider what experiential gratification the games that generate them offer to the participants, we will limit our discussion to the experience of those who receive the messages or watch the performances. That is, we will focus on the experience of being entertained, of being persuaded, and of being instructed. Our intent is not to provide— for those who wish to know how to entertain, how to persuade, and how to instruct—the appropriate rules, tactics, and customs.

We have already mentioned how it is that one experiential consequence of our presence in an arena is our awareness of the clear distinction between the roles of the players. In a gathering, agent and spectator are one and the same, but in an arena they are separate. We have written this book, as we said at the outset, because few of us have been taught how to be intelligent consumers of communication. The remainder of this book continues to be devoted to developing consumers of communication whose experience is informed by an awareness of the choices available to them.

We began this chapter, as we began this book, with the question, "Why are you reading this book?" In this chapter we have added two more questions: "Why is your communicative experience with this book not the same as your experience of playing Polite Greeting at a neighborhood party or your experience of exchanging obscene expletives with an acquaintance in the back alley?" and "Or is it all the same to you?"

"Or is it all the same to you?" Hopefully by now, if not before, your answer to this question is "No."

"Why is your communicative experience with this book not the same as your experience of playing Polite Greeting at a neighborhood party or your experience of exchanging obscene expletives with an acquaintance in the back alley?" Hopefully your answer to this question is at least easier to provide—we have suggested six different categories of public communicative experience in order to assist your reflection.

"Why are you reading this book?" Hopefully, you would now like to share with us in our reflection on public communication experiences outside our author-reader relationship, which are generated by messages other than this book.

10

Poetic Games

Poetic public games are those whose telos is affirmation:
The messages generated invite the participants to ex-
perience aesthetic intent.

I n this chapter we shall consider a few instances of an im-
mense class of public communication games that invite
public spectators (consumers) to experience aesthetic
recreation. That is, although we can consider such communicative activities as television talk shows, daily tabloids, situation
comedies, comic strips, drama, opera, hit records, fiction, symphony concerts, and museum objects as instances of individual aesthetic play that are gratifying for the participants, it
is also necessary to appreciate that an art object or event has as
its main social significance the aesthetic satisfaction of the
spectators. Unlike interpersonal communication games in
which the same participant acts both as performer and spectator alternatively, public games, and notably poetic ones, are
distinctive for being performed in an arena to impress a particular group of spectators. Thus as we continue to examine
the experience of game-play in the public arena, we concentrate our analysis on the experience of the consumer-
spectators, the witnesses. When we later come to discuss the
game of criticism (Chapter 13), we will consider the role of the
consumer-spectator who is not passive, but who, like the avid
sports fan, is responsively engaged with the public performance in a way that is thoughtful, careful, and good-humored.

For the present, however, we will devote our critical approach to devising some ways to analyze how the poetic message seems to act upon its surrounding audience. Our focus will thus be on how the radiance from a stained glass window washes color over the congregation for the sensual benefit of those spectators, rather than how it may give satisfaction to the window's creator. Meanwhile, if our readers wish to learn more about how to play the role of the performer—the artist, or perhaps the actor in a theater—then they are best advised to take an acting course; if they wish to learn about creating ads they might take a journalism course or work for an advertising firm. Our interest must be to investigate that part of the performance that spectators experience, based on the messages they behold as a result of the publicly performed game. In the process, we will devise some analytic models to explain how poetic messages are aimed at the experience of spectators.

PERFORMING AND PRODUCTIVE POETIC GAMES

The shift in focus just described will become more apparent after we distinguish between the two basic types of Poetic games: performing arts and productive arts. Performing arts (such as playing a musical instrument, dancing, and live theater) are *action*-oriented for the creators, whereas productive arts (including sculpture, creative writing, film making) are *fabrication*-oriented when viewed from the creator's perspective. That is, production implies a creative process that comes to an end when an object is made, an object behind which the creator disappears (once the table is made, for instance, we seldom give any thought to the carpenter); performing arts, on the other hand, do not of themselves leave artifacts.[1] The act of dancing, for example, is itself the artistry.

From the viewpoint of spectator experience, it can be seen at once that a corollary difference between performing and productive Poetic games is that the consummation of a performance requires an audience immediately at hand while the artist acts; performance thus relies on virtuosity with respect to other acting humans. Making, however, places no such demand; ideal fabrication entails one man working in relative isolation, free from interference. It is only after the artist has acted (the words are on paper, the paint is on canvas, the images are on film, the carving has ceased) that the spectator has contact with the object. Hence, the distinction between performing and productive Poetic games is cru-

---

[1] There are obvious complications with this formulation insofar as ours is an age in which fabrication—video tapes of live performances, for example—threatens to engulf performance. We shall treat this problem more extensively in Chapter 13.

cial insofar as we seek to understand how the message functions aesthetically for an audience. We shall rely on this general division, although we shall not press it too far, given the changes modern technology is making in this traditionally simple distinction. Nevertheless, its significance remains as an aid to understanding the sense in which aesthetic games are recreational.

As we can compare interpersonal games in terms of the degree to which they facilitate formality or intimacy, so we can compare aesthetic games, both performing and productive, in terms of their capacity to renew or re-create us. When the topic of public games was introduced in the last chapter, we proposed that Poetic games are those with a special potential to fire the auditor's mind in new and sometimes unexpected directions, that this ability to make reality more vivid and induce flexibility inspires appreciative and renewed involvement with the world—affirmation. Such an engagement of auditor and message is thus rejuvenating: The stimulation of Poetic games is a special kind of nutrition. Humans crave the newness poetry offers, crave the creative stretching from *now* back to *then* and the wholly new linkages by which *soon* is joined to both. Friends upon meeting often ask "What's new?" Our inner hunger for the new, for a sensual extension of our known surroundings beyond the reach of our sense organs into the realm of *perhaps,* is as natural and as insistent as our hunger for food.

The ability of poetic illusion to extend our aesthetic awareness of the world, to disclose the new, is provided by the following examples:

> How many ever noticed that the shadows cast by sunlight on snow were colored blue, until the impressionist painters showed us so? How many ever looked at decaying doorways and abandoned houses until photographers like Walker Evans taught us how? How many ever took seriously the environment of neon and billboards which is our natural habitat until the pop artists rubbed our noses in it?[2]

Without the renewal that aesthetic involvement invites, humans stagnate. Simple repeated recognition of the conventional numbs the mind. Soon no "experience" is distinguishable from the rest. Boredom for lack of Poetic games is thus a kind of spiritual malnutrition that in extreme cases eventuates in starvation—the empty repetition of formal rituals devoid of personal gratification, the capitulation to the tedium of customary ("norm-al") behavior.

---

[2] Eric Larrabee, "Op/Ed," *New York Times* (2 September 1973), 37. © 1973 by The New York Times Company. Reprinted by permission.

Poetic games are thus most recreationally powerful and can do the most to renew our experience when they help us to overcome the boredom of mindless habit, when they provide the stimulation and vitality of newness in our lives (even when that stimulation is rendered within the formal constraints of aesthetic convention) by tickling our sensibilities. Such recreation replenishes us and overcomes our fatigue. When Poetic games fail to recreate, as when we encounter mere "amusements" (surrogate recreations that encourage us simply to *rest* by *escaping* the daily cycle of sleeping and working) that are unable to restore our human vigor,[3] we can claim that those amusement games offer less recreational potential and are more closely related to ritual.

The problem with amusement is not that it is sinful but that it cannot re-create or restore us. It leaves its audience in a condition of passive reception, and there is no experiential involvement in rest. This is not to deny the value of rest, for rest, too, can satisfy. It is only to suggest that amusement at the expense of recreational play (which is a necessary feature of the life cycle if we are to live whole lives in the world of men) is unwholesome if not toxic. Just as a steady diet of junk foods such as potato chips can produce a nation oddly malnourished in the midst of plenty, a steady diet of processed "amusement" encourages lack of thought, care, and good humor and thereby contaminates one's aesthetic experience.

Let us explore further this aesthetic vector in Poetic games, beginning with some illustrations of the performing arts and then moving to consider how audiences engage certain modern productive arts. As we go, we shall consider how, for each poetic institution, the bulk of message-games created meet modern recreational needs and to what extent the messages fail to fulfill those aesthetic potentials and in consequence retreat toward the region of impersonal or ritualistic activity.

POETIC GAMES: THEATER

We shall begin our study of Poetic games with theater.[4] What is there about going to the theater as a performing art that is so consistently appealing for some people in ways that attending carnivals and eating ice cream are not?

---

[3] Regarding the difference between recreation and amusement, see Aristotle's *Politics,* 1334a15-20; *Nicomachean Ethics,* 1776b27. Ernest Barker's translation (New York: Oxford University Press, 1958) includes a special note on the Greek concept of recreational leisure (*schole*), and contrasts it with "the sort of thing children do" (*paidia*) as amusement.

[4] We do not mean to suggest that a dramatic message can never be rhetorical or dialectical.

Clearly, such stock explanations as "It relaxes me" or "It helps me escape daily anxieties" are not adequate answers. There are many other activities, including taking a dip in a pool, going for a walk, having friends by for an evening of gin rummy, or whatever that would serve these two purposes far more adequately. If we were to choose a means of relaxation, more of us would probably prefer to take a nap, listen to a favorite record, or go for a leisurely walk than to get dressed up on a rainy night, try to park the car, and arrive at the theater on time, only to sit for two or three hours in an uncomfortable seat. Or, if we want to escape from the humdrum realities of everyday life, most of us would daydream or read a book before we would fight ticket lines and babysitters in order to see a play. There are many other ways to escape and entertain our senses.

What does theater have that is especially intriguing? Theater is *histrionic*. It is a live performance. In the theater the spectators have the privilege, as it were, of witnessing a public reenactment of human interpersonal game playing. This is its unique characteristic: Theatergoers enjoy being spectators; they like to observe the experiences of others. In other words, in the theater we find *actors* consciously doing the kind of things we do all the time—they are assuming different roles to achieve different objectives.

It is in this sense that theater (as distinct from dramatic literature[5]) is histrionic at its core. It is a performance, an enactment, a public display of human action. It is thus this "actorish" quality of impersonation that distinguishes theater from other forms of poetic experience. None of the other paraphernalia of theater (costumes, director, lighting, props, even playwright) are in fact necessary:

On the contrary, we can cite several occasions when theatrical performances fit those categories as well. Notice, for example, the persuasive elements in Shakespeare's *Hamlet* in which Hamlet uses the Player King and the Player Queen to vilify his uncle, the "real" King, and his mother, the "real" Queen; or recall how frequently the pre-Civil War performances of Harriet Beecher Stowe's play *Uncle Tom's Cabin* won converts in the North to the antislavery position and simultaneously aroused new resentment in the South. Similarly, there are times when theater has been used to objectify reality. We can look for such dialectical elements in the numerous Passion plays or in dramatic reenactments of Revolutionary War battles. We can also see how psychodrama stimulates people to reveal the "truth" about themselves, specific events, or their relationships with others. But each of these examples is an exception rather than the rule. Few of the plays we see motivate us to immediate action, appeal merely to our educational interests, or produce major changes in our personalities or life-styles. It is more accurate to say that the demands that theater makes on an audience correspond to those we have attributed to poetic messages. Successful theater engages our passions through our senses. If unsuccessful, we claim that a given play has left us "untouched."

[5] Although characterization is basic to dramatic literature, dramatic literature itself is not performance: "Drama is literature *intended* for performance, and dramatic works *can be* performed because the actors have something to act." P. N. Campbell, *Rhetoric/Ritual: A Study of the Communicative and Aesthetic Dimensions of Language* (Belmont, Calif.: Dickenson Publishing Company, 1972), p. 166.

> By gradually eliminating whatever proved superfluous, we found that theater can exist without make-up, without autonomic costume and scenography, without a separate performance area, without lighting and sound effects. . . .
>
> We know that the text per se is not theater, that it becomes theater only through the actor's use of it. . . . Theater only ceases to exist without the actor-spectator relationship of perceptual, direct, live communion.[6]

This posture captures the logical essence of the theatrical experience: It can be poorer than film (though not by that token impoverished); it can be more austere than television; it can renounce the technical spectacle of carnival.

What we are then left with at the heart of the theatrical experience is the spectacle of impersonation. We watch Richard Burton impersonate Hamlet, and thereby consciously perform the role of prince. But for the shell that is the character Hamlet, there are also roles to be assumed, and the character must himself portray roles much as we do in everyday life. We thus witness Hamlet don a lover role, throw off a son role, even consciously perform the madman role (just as we have witnessed Burton assume the Hamlet role).

What, then, is so consistently appealing about going to the theater? This histrionic quality of theater—this "actorishness"—re-freshes us. From our experience in interpersonal communication, we bring to the theater expectations about the way men relate to each other and to the world. Through the aesthetic experience of theater, through the virtuosity of the actors' performances, we extend our awareness of the potential for human interaction. "By showing us what we have in common, they increase our command over what we have and hold alone, single to each."[7] Theater games are, indeed, games of affirmation.

If the genius of theater is the actors' virtuosity, we are in a position to redefine theater in a way that will lend further insight into traditional theatrical elements; we can propose a useful way of analyzing theater, seen now from the perspective of communication. In this method of analysis theater becomes *the spectacle* (since we view it as spectators) *of a character assuming different roles* (which assuming constitutes the plot) *to achieve dramatic ends* (the play action).[8] Our analytic model will be con-

---

[6] J. Grotowski, *Towards a Poor Theater* (New York: Simon and Schuster, 1970), p. 19.

[7] Eric Larrabee, "OP/ED," *New York Times* (2 September 1973). © 1973 by The New York Times Company. Reprinted by permission.

[8] The following analysis was inspired by L. Manfull, "Drama as Role-Playing: A Technique for Analysis" (unpublished Ph.D dissertation, University of Minnesota, 1961). See also Martin Buber, *Pointing the Way*, trans. M. S. Friedman (1957; New York: Schocken Books, 1974), pp. 63–73.

cerned with the kinds of roles that spectators are invited to focus upon. Let us proceed from this definition to explore the variety of overlapping and interacting roles that are necessary for a Theatrical game to occur.

The Anatomy of a Play

We propose three different roles that enable us to classify various Theatrical games: personal role, social role, and impersonal role.

Personal Role.   The *personal role* encompasses the character's innate human qualities, the nature of the character as it has been defined by the playwright and the director. Those qualities that a character starts out with prior to any action on stage, which we call his personal index, include such things as his sex, age, physique, race, nationality, mental capacity, and emotional sensitivity. All these qualities define who the character is.

Social Role.   Another set of characteristics that affect the actor are those we label the *social role*. Social roles are actually those that are demanded of the character by the context, and, in effect, constitute the plot. In other words, a given character with a certain sex and age, and certain personality and emotional traits, is placed in a social situation and we watch how he interacts with others. In the process of interacting he dons various personae. A play, for example, may require that a character perform a variety of family games, that he be a son, a husband, and a father. The nature of the character's dialogue and behavior, therefore, will depend upon whether he is in a scene with his mother, or his wife, or his children. Another typical social role is one's occupation. A character's profession will influence how he confronts others just as his religion will influence how he confronts his God. Or, consider a character's civic role: Is he a leader, a follower, an agitator? Or, his "love" role: Is he a seducer, a fiancé, a wallflower? All these are social roles. They are not something that is innate in the character as we find him. Instead, they constitute the way in which the character confronts social reality. In other words, the social roles reveal to us how a character is going to play his games.

Impersonal Role.   Finally, the *impersonal role* corresponds to the action or the theme or to the telos of the play. Usually there is something of importance that the character wants to accomplish. This is what we mean by impersonal role. When, for example, the ghost in *Hamlet* tells

Hamlet that the kingdom of Denmark is in danger, Hamlet sets out to restore order to the realm. Fearing possible anarchy, Hamlet's impersonal role, his basic objective, is to save the kingdom. Whereas the plot of the play consists of a series of little episodes such as Hamlet's murder of Polonius, his trip to England with Rosencrantz and Guildenstern, and his duel with Laertes, the action or theme constitutes the underlying psychic energy that is the focal point of the play. The impersonal role is the direction that the hero is taking in his moral universe.

The Physiology of a Play

To understand the relationship between these three dramatic roles, and to see how they affect a spectator's theatrical experience, we can conceive of a play in terms of three concentric rings.

Inner Ring.   The *inner ring* is the personal role of the characters as the play begins. It represents the nature of the personalities being portrayed on the stage.

Outer Ring.   The *outer ring* represents the impersonal role. At the outset of every play some sort of chaos or disequilibrium is defined, and the characters in the play, sensing this imbalance, set out to restore order. The horse opera hero discovers the blind orphan; Hamlet sees a ghost; Oedipus is confronted with famine and pestilence in Thebes; Joan of Arc announces her spiritual orders to raise the seige of Orleans; Louisa and Matt vow eternal love in spite of the wall their fathers have built between them; Romeo meets Juliet.

Middle Ring.   The *middle ring* represents the social roles. This is a series of social encounters in which the various characters play their games in an attempt to achieve their objectives. Bridging of the gap between the inner and outer rings constitutes the bulk of the play, the plot. Without this interaction there is no play. It is not enough to watch one character whose personal role we know attempt to achieve his impersonal role that we also know. It is doubtful that many of us would classify as a play the portrayal of a young dentist who, hearing a drippy faucet, rises to turn it off, does so, and returns to bed; or the aging medieval knight who, wishing to prove his fortitude, retreats to the desolate wilderness in voluntary exile. As the main characters reconcile their abilities with the disequilibrium that they face, their interaction constitutes the drama as we know it.

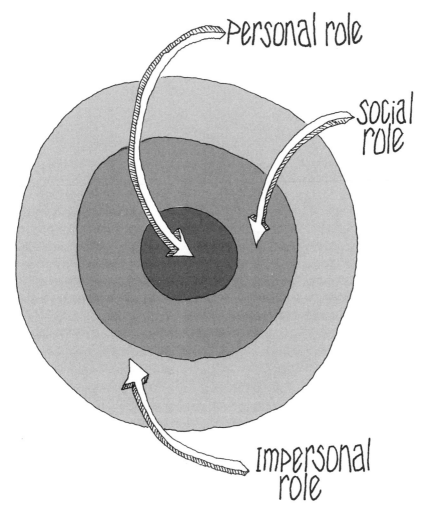

To summarize briefly we might say that theater is a poetic portrayal of life. It is not intended to be "real," but to express something about what is "real." It does this by reproducing different possible forms of human interaction in order to affirm certain human qualities and objectives. Its histrionic nature distinguishes it from other poetic forms; drama is a public reenactment. And at the heart of theatrical communication as a public game is the actor's impersonation.

Using the three concentric rings in the figure above to represent the facets of dramatic character, we are able to differentiate the basic tactics of Theatrical games. It is fruitless for us to argue that these definitions or the examples we use will be universally accepted. Instead, we suggest that they provide the student of communication with preliminary guidelines to distinguish among the numerous theater games he or she confronts and the consequent aesthetic experiences they open to the audience.[9] The four tactics that we shall describe are: tragedy, comedy, melodrama, and farce.[10]

Tragedy

The tactic of those Theatrical games we experience as *tragedy* is to emphasize the outer ring. The disruption in the universe is serious and our attention is focused on how the hero achieves or fails to achieve his impersonal role. Failure of the hero in his personal and social roles is a by-product of a moral universe that determines his impersonal role; his personal and social failures (or successes) are only symptomatic of a larger conflict. It is as though we discover inherent contradictions in the constitutive rules that define the character's entire life space. For example, a tragedy could be written concerning the futile struggle of blacks to achieve human dignity in a racially repressive society.

In this respect Arthur Miller's play *Death of a Salesman* can be approached as an example of tragedy. Willy Loman, the salesman, is given to us at the beginning of the play as a questioner of false coinage— pollution, over-population, capitalistic competition; he criticizes them all. But by the time he has experienced all the agonies that the corporate system inflicts on him, Willy is transformed into an advocate of false coinage—he lives in a daydream world, has a mistress, and eventually, unable to face his life and himself, commits suicide. In other words, a substantial change occurs in Willy in the process of trying to muddle through the serious contradictions that exist in his life. As we watch him encounter one obstacle after another, we sense that ultimately he is going to fail whatever his personal virtues. The "tragedy" of *Death of a Salesman* is that Willy cannot alone rectify the universe, nor can he escape it so long as he plays the game.

Classic Greek tragedy depicted the same titanic conflict. The basic theme of many Greek dramas was the recognition and acceptance of one's fate in a world of inherently contradicting forces. In Sophocles's

---

[9] On occasion we may exemplify a particular point by referring to a character or the plot of a film or a television program. This reference is only intended to clarify a theatrical game, not to equate film and television with theater. Theater is an actor's medium; the aesthetic form of film and television are due, not to the actor, but to the editor or the director. Actors need not be the focus of film or television; actors are the *only* focus of theater.

[10] This standard typology is similar to, but not identical with, the one drawn by Northrop Frye in his *Anatomy of Criticism* (Princeton: Princeton University Press, 1957), pp. 169–239.

Oedipus the King, for example, Oedipus starts out as a particular kind of person with a number of noble qualities. As he is forced to confront the realities of the situation in Thebes, as he gradually comes to learn the horrible truth that he had actually killed his father and married his mother, his noble qualities are stripped away from him and he is reduced to a pitiful figure. He becomes an object lesson in the futility of resisting destiny as marked out by the gods. He differs from Willy Loman in his "nobility"—he is enough of a man to recognize and accept his mortal fate (Willy finally comes to recognize his fate, but he is unable to accept it, so he commits suicide).

Similarly, consider Shakespeare's *Romeo and Juliet.* In this tragedy we watch how two innocent but immature characters try to transcend the fact that they are the children of feuding families and try to find happiness in love. We sense that they will not achieve their goal, and yet we watch as the dramatic pitfalls transform them from naïve adolescents into imprudent adults.

In all of these cases it is the hero's attempt to outdo himself, his innate-personal characteristics, and his habitual games in order to achieve an impossible impersonal objective that transforms and lends dignity to him. Tragedy is the charting of the change that occurs in the characters as they confront these double-bind features of the universe they inhabit.[11]

Comedy

Throughout the history of dramatic theory, *comedy* has been offered as an alternative tactic to tragedy. Whereas tragedy is often presented as "serious" theater and subjected to intense study, comedy is usually considered "entertainment" theater and often left on a par with amusements such as vaudeville. Although it is true that the experience of "comic" theater differs from tragedy in several ways, this does not discredit or lessen the importance of its own distinct focus. Comedy, moreover, need not always be equated with laughter. First let us look at how comedy differs from tragedy.

For one thing, the disruption in the world of comedy is a relatively minor one. It does not entail inherent contradictions in tribal or national psyche; the moral universe that is disrupted is far more limited. Indeed,

---

[11] See R. Conville, "Northrup Frye and Speech Criticism: An Introduction," *Quarterly Journal of Speech* 56(December 1970):419.

the play may be limited to the problems of one family in such a way that the predicament is of no great significance outside the immediate family.

Secondly, since the moral disruption in comedy is not catastrophic (that is, the civilization's fabric remains intact), it is not really significant for us to see whether the hero is able to achieve any impersonal objective. In other words, since the world will not come to a standstill if the hero fails, we turn our attention elsewhere—toward the kinds of pratfalls that the characters take as they engage in their social roles. In comedy, the greatest emphasis is on the middle ring.

The third distinctive feature of comedy is that change, if it occurs at all in the characters, will be in their social standing or relative hierarchy. In *The Taming of the Shrew*, the impersonal role is the uncertainty whether Kate (and hence Bianca) will ever get married, given her horrendous temper. The play unfolds as her suitor, Petruccio, gets her to engage in the sort of games that transform her into a suitable wife. The upshot is that at the end of the play the two sisters are both affianced, and we are assured that their father's wealth will be properly inherited (thus making everyone happy). The tag line, ". . . and they lived happily ever after" is a shortcut claim that the characters have now mastered a set of mutually gratifying games and have acquired the material trappings necessary to enable them to indulge in those games henceforth. Similarly, in Molière's *The Misanthrope*, the changes wrought at the end of the play are not in anyone's character; nor has anything resembling an impersonal theme been resolved (indeed, the situation remains exactly as it was at the outset of the play). What has changed is that Alceste has vowed in a pout to leave the arena and live in isolation (not play any more games)—he will not marry his love.

Another clear illustration of a comedy message is Mary Chase's play *Harvey*. In this play a rather odd man named Elwood Dowd claims to have a six-foot-tall rabbit named Harvey for a companion. No one else can see Harvey, but Dowd takes him wherever he goes. The appeal of the play is not in discovering whether or not Harvey really exists or whether or not Dowd will get rid of Harvey in the end (both impersonal themes). Although these are potentially interesting questions, we are more attracted by the social awkwardness that is raised in the various episodes of the plot, and what games Dowd must play as he confronts them.

This same social emphasis is true of a performance of Noel Coward's *Blithe Spirit*. The focus of the spectators' attention in this comedy is not to question the existence or power of mediums like Madame Arcati or the ability of wives to return from the dead to haunt their husbands.

Instead, we want to see what embarrassing things will happen when one wife, Elvira, returns and Charles has to explain her presence to Ruth, his current wife, or we enjoy watching the scatterbrained Madame Arcati conduct her unorthodox séances.

The emphasis on social roles was also characteristic of Shakespearean comedies, many of which revolved around the problems of mistaken identity. In *Twelfth Night* Viola is able to disguise herself as a young man and then is mistaken for her long-lost twin brother Sebastian. Or, similarly, Rosalind in *As You Like It* disguises herself as a boy with whom her real lover Orlando practices courtship. And Portia in *The Merchant of Venice* disguises herself as a skillful lawyer who frees her lover's faithful friend, Antonio, and traps the moneylender Shylock. In these plays we are not concerned with the feasibility or ethics of mistaken identity, or whether Malvolio, Jacques, and Shylock each receive what is coming to them, or whether love does, indeed, conquer all. Instead, we are captivated by the predicaments that the deceptions create and follow anxiously to see when and how they will be unveiled in the end. In sum, comic theatrical performance emphasizes the social encounters that occur within a minimally disrupted social setting.

Melodrama

This third dramatic tactic represents the bulk of poetic messages that we experience in American theater today. Although it can be serious or comic, all *melodrama* shares certain distinctive features.

The first characteristic that we have to recognize about melodrama is that the characters never change. There is no essential change in their attitudes, conduct, personalities, or social relations from the beginning of the play to the end. In other words, the characters in melodrama are static. The villain starts out as a bad guy and often ends up dead. In contrast to tragedy or comedy, the emphasis in melodrama is not on the changes that occur in the leading characters as they strive to achieve their impersonal objectives or confront awkward situations. Rather, our entire focus of attention is on the innate personality of the character as it is given to us at the beginning of the play. Consider, for example, this partial list of characters from Dunstan Weed's *A Fate Worse Than Death; or Adrift on Life's Sea:*

CARLOTTA FLOWER, our beautiful young heroine, who is more sinned against than sinning

RODNEY RAMSGATE, owner of the palatial home known as "The Crossroads"

FELICIA RAMSGATE, Rodney's aristocratic wife

DOROTHEA RAMSGATE, their daughter, cold and snobbish

CASSIUS CARSTAIRS, skilled in the ways of villainy, a dyed-in-the-wolf rogue

SLICK CARTER, a noted detective

BURGESS LENDAHAND, our brave and clean-living hero[12]

Many of our most popular fictional heroes, including John Wayne characters, detectives like Mannix or the radio sleuth Sam Spade, Tarzan, and others, all conform to a single archetypal personal model: They are all Batman without the leotards. The virtues they reveal are those of the samurai warrior or the knight errant, operating outside the law, preferring direct action to the intrigues of political interaction. The characters in such melodrama (and we have occasion to explore some of them further a bit later) thus personify for us the "chivalric" virtues of honor, courage, and adventure. As archetypal figures, they do not grow in the course of an episode (or even over the course of a series); rather, they exemplify those virtues and admirable qualities.

A second characteristic of melodrama is that, unlike comedy and tragedy, it never questions either the moral (impersonal) or social order. Whereas a comedy such as Albee's *The American Dream* may call into question our habits of family games and a tragedy like Miller's *Death of a Salesman* may examine the consequences of accepting a purely commercial ethic, melodrama takes both the moral universe and our ordinary interpersonal games for granted. Indeed, by so accepting such realms it affirms them and implicitly instructs the audience that the conventional values are the best. It was no accident that the current generation of college students grew up on beach party films that cast as heroes characters who were sincere, honest, cuddly, and more interested in "good clean fun" than in thinking, while the villains (usually adults—think of Mrs. Robinson in *The Graduate*) were cold, calculating, sometimes violent. Melodrama, thus, *rehearses* the audience in conventional morality and lines of thought.

The third characteristic of melodrama follows from the first two— given that the characters are static and that both social and impersonal roles are those we know and take for granted, of what interest is melodrama to us? Our interest centers on the characters' personalities. Mary

---

[12] Dunstan Weed, *A Fate Worse Than Death; or Adrift on Life's Seas* (New York: Samuel French, 1946), p. 5.

Tyler Moore (or Batman or Mannix) is our friend. We do not expect or want Dick Van Dyke to change; we want him to be there always, the same. We are less interested in what games he plays, or with what consequences, than that he remain the same sweet guy, making no demands on us when we are watching our electronic friend play his usual games. With a melodramatic hero (especially one so readily available as on a weekly television series), we have the ideal friend; we never have to be tactful with him, he remains oblivious to our moods and tantrums, we do not have to show him consideration. All we need do is check in on him once a week (if we have the time), the way a housewife might drop by for a morning cup of coffee with a next-door neighbor; we check in to reassure ourselves that our friend is the same as ever, that all is right with the world (that virtue continues to triumph, that vice is punished), that the world does indeed appreciate warmth, affection, and honesty. So we establish a para-social relationship with the character.

This third quality of melodrama helps us understand why the networks know after two weeks of the new season which shows will be popular. By then the nation has picked its friends (surely they are not watching an adventure show or situation comedy because they are in suspense about the outcome). It also explains why such a furor arises nationally when a popular character on a weekly show is replaced by another character. The public is not interested in the show—and they feel cheated when a friend (such as Chester on the "Gunsmoke" series) is removed.

Serious Melodrama.   There are two basic melodrama tactics that correspond in tone to tragedy and comedy. The first we call *serious melodrama*. Here the relationships (especially the social-personal ones) are static, and there is an absence of any view of impersonal-moral qualities. Most television drama falls into this category. Serious melodrama is primarily judicial or punitive theater. It relies on fear and hatred of evil to maintain excitement. Such drama is really no different than medieval morality plays. The same plot week after week represents the struggle of good versus evil, and the basic impersonal theme is an affirmation that virtue should be rewarded and vice should be punished. In courtroom sagas such as Perry Mason we are presented with lawyers and their assistants who are the good guys, the predictable, stereotyped characters whose antics we approve week after week. The bad guys, on the other hand, are replaceable. They get convicted, murdered, or disposed of in some way. The plot represents Good coming in contact with Evil and Good emerging triumphant. The lawyers never lose their cases nor get killed themselves because they must reappear in the next episode.

This is exactly what medieval morality plays attempted to do. Good was personified by God, Bad was personified by Satan, and the play showed that he or she who chose Satan was doomed to punishment and he or she who followed the ways of God was going to be rewarded in the afterlife.[13]

Romantic Melodrama. The other basic type of melodrama is *romantic melodrama*. This dramatic tactic tends to rely on abnormal characters to achieve laughter. An excellent illustration can be found in the comic strips that are syndicated in our daily newspapers. Like melodrama, these cartoons have static characters and portray a relatively simple moral universe that correlates with our own preconceived notions of right and wrong.

In *Bringing Up Father*, the first comic strip to achieve international fame, Jiggs and Maggie, the major characters, are virtually the same characters that they were in 1913 when the strip first appeared. Jiggs is an Irish immigrant who won the sweepstakes, but who, in spite of his wealth, likes nothing better than to spend a night with his buddies, drinking beer, eating corned beef and cabbage, and playing pinochle. Maggie, his ex-washerwoman wife, has higher ambitions and continually inflicts these on Jiggs by making him wear a tuxedo and attend the opera, for example. For many years, this comic strip has affirmed a popular notion that even though immigrants can be financially successful, they will never become culturally refined.

Another instance of romantic melodrama is *Blondie*, perhaps the most significant and influential comic strip in American history. Chic Young's lucid formula for the strip became the basis for hundreds of soap operas and situation comedies on radio and television and for numerous short stories in the popular press. More generally, Blondie and Dagwood have given rise to a full generation of myths about American domestic life. The formula is simple. Blondie, the wife and mother, is the boss of the house and holder of the purse strings. The men, on the other hand, with appropriate names like Dagwood Bumstead and Mr. Dithers, are sweet, bumbling, harmless jerks who have little or no common sense. The moral universe that is affirmed is one in which everybody has more sense than "Daddy," but "Daddy" is loveable, neverthe-

---

[13] Some cases of serious melodrama can be identified quickly. Others, however, are more difficult to classify because they masquerade or are mistaken for tragedy. In these plays

less. In the classic mass media comic melodramas that have relied on this formula, like "Father Knows Best," "Ozzie and Harriet," and "Danny Thomas," Daddy is sweet, innocent, and incompetent, and Mother really knows best.

And yet another example can be found in Al Capp's *Li'l Abner*, which is an extreme application of the "Chic Young Formula." Mammy Yokum is a hard-bitten woman who takes care of everybody; Li'l Abner is a living symbol of innocence, armed with candor and stupidity, who succumbs only to Daisy Mae, his semi-nude, perverse, but confident wife; Pappy Yokum is the personification of weakness and indecision, although good-natured; and Tiny is bumbling and being chased constantly by girls.

Of course, not all comic strips are romantic melodrama. Without much difficulty we could classify other series like *Little Orphan Annie, Steve Canyon, Terry and the Pirates, Mary Worth, Rex Morgan, M.D.,* and *Judge Parker*, as serious melodrama. Although these do not rely on abnormal characters to achieve laughter, they do have static personal roles that affirm the common morality.[14]

---

the major characters are villains and their evil can be rather attractive. But there is the same struggle between Good and Evil and Evil loses in the end. More specifically, merely because the main characters die at the end does not make the play a tragedy. Another characteristic of this type of melodrama that can confuse an unwary audience is the sordid nature of its topics. No matter how repugnant the subject matter, so long as the common morality is affirmed and not questioned, the play remains a melodrama. Some playwrights and directors prefer to be "relevant" and select plays with repugnant topics such as drugs, sadism, psychosis, and the like. The fact that the gangster Humphrey Bogart portrays is a neurotic alcoholic, however, does not mean that the film is necessarily a tragedy. We know that Bogart will be punished, that in spite of his sickness he is still a crook. This is not to suggest that such drama is somehow less worthy of esteem. Indeed, we can have exciting theater and still lack profundity of thought or insight into human personalities. We clarify these distinctions merely to keep us on our guard so that we will not apply the evaluative standards of tragedy to dramatic performances that are actually melodrama.

[14] Some of the "newer" comic strips often deviate from the melodramatic form. The characters still remain static and predictable, but they also question the moral order. Walt Kelley's *Pogo*, for instance, which first appeared in 1949, violently attacked Senator Joseph McCarthy in 1952 and severely censured President Lyndon Johnson in 1968. In others, virtue is not always rewarded and vice is not always punished. An example of this is Charles Schulz's *Peanuts*, in which Charlie Brown's faith in human nature is almost always cruelly deceived, and Lucy Van Pelt, whom Schulz has stated is a fascist (*Saturday Evening Post*, April 1954, p. 26), continues to get her way. The tension in *Peanuts* between the characters' personal roles as children (and hence "innocent and basically good" by our conventional wisdom) and the inherently mean games they play with one another, calls into question our clichés about human nature. *Peanuts* thus qualifies as genuine comedy—it "melts" our preconceptions and gently sets our minds afloat in uncharted realms—it makes us think apart from conventional moral rubrics. Cf. John Culhane, "Leapin' Lizards! What's Happening to the Comics?" *New York Times Magazine* (5 May 1974), 16 ff.

Farce

The major characteristic of *farce* is its violation of all dramatic conventions. Farce snickers or winks and tries to remind us that all the stage action we observe is simply spectacle; it argues that drama is a put-on. Instead of directing our attention to any one of the dramatic roles we have described, farce suggests that the whole series of concentric rings is an illusion. It exaggerates each of the roles to grotesque caricatures: The personal roles of the characters are almost, if not totally, unbelievable; their impersonal objectives are absurd; and the plots confront them with a series of incredible interpersonal situations. The realm of the poetic is the possible, and farce pushes the possible to its limits, and beyond.

When farce was introduced as a dramatic tactic in the late Middle Ages, it usually was performed as an interlude between other performances, as a kind of counterpoint to the poetic fiction, to remind the audience that the entire performance was not to be taken literally. Most farce has disappeared from modern theater (except for fraternity skits and various college lampoons). It has been replaced by film farce, because film is better able to stretch the limits of the credible to the point where it becomes in-credible.

Consider, for example, James Bond—a character who pushes the chivalric virtues of cleverness and athletic prowess so far as to make even Batman pale in comparison. Bond is indeed a deity for a technological age: He does everything so adeptly that we can only smirk—there is no way any human being could be so good; and so we momentarily set aside the virtues and ideals he personifies—we recognize them as simply ideals, and we smile at the prospect of a human pretending to exemplify them. For example, could anyone but Secret Agent 007 handle a beautiful Russian girl who has fallen so violently in love with his photograph that she defects to the West and vows to bring a cipher machine with her if Bond will come to Turkey to fetch her; or could anyone else but Bond possibly stop the maniacal, steel-pincered Dr. No from misdirecting United States missles or the avaricious, paranoiac Auric Goldfinger from seizing all the gold in Ft. Knox?

Or consider another farcical character, the coyote in the Roadrunner cartoons—who is really James Bond gone sour. Where James Bond gratifies us with his god-like (and thus humanly impossible) mastery of technology, the coyote offers a parody of the fallible human who is dependent on a constantly failing technology. In our lives we witness men walking on the moon even as our phone service fails and our electric toothbrushes shock us. Similarly, the coyote sets increasingly complex traps for the Roadrunner (the personification of sheer natural energy), only to have them invariably backfire and injure him. Like Bond, the coyote is a reminder to us that the whole theatrical enterprise is an illusion; and he does it by appearing to us in a melodramatic role drawn to grotesque proportions. He and Bond are both "beyond belief" in all their roles.

We have suggested that one way to distinguish various tactics in Theatrical games is to specify the roles on which spectators focus in each. We have demonstrated how the impersonal role is emphasized in tragedy, the social role in comedy, the personal role in melodrama, and how farce exaggerates all these. There is no doubt that these distinctions are too neat and tidy and that they are probably guilty of oversimplifying the complex nature of individual plays. Nevertheless, like all models, the classification should help us to understand some of the complexities of theatrical games and provide a framework for analysis of the experience of a particular dramatic performance.

We began this section by asking, "What does theater offer that is especially intriguing?" How would we answer that question now? Theater games are public performances that an audience can experience without necessarily actively participating. The audience does not enter the life space of a man on stage. Spectators do not jump onto the stage to stop the villain from tieing the heroine to the lumber mill saw or rush to administer first aid to the dying Madame Butterfly. Spectators do not, that is, let stage action motivate "real action."[15] What the audience *does* experience, if it *knowingly* shares the enactment with the actors, is aesthetic re-creation: The Theatrical game stirs the passions and inspires appreciation for and renewed involvement with the world.

But Theatrical games differ in their capacity to allow or disallow recreation. Our experiences with tragedy, comedy, and farce are unsettling. Each of these aesthetic games brings us nearer to some realization about man and his world:

TRAGEDY affirms the double-bind features of the universe we all inhabit.
COMEDY affirms the fact that men will be affected by their interactions with each other.

---

[15] The fact that most audiences intuitively make this distinction might possibly explain the temporary immobility of the audience in the Ford Theater immediately after Abraham Lincoln's assassination. Everyone was prepared to accept practically anything as "part of the play"; hence, it was a few moments before they realized that the shot and the scurrying in the balcony were not part of the play, but "real" events.

FARCE affirms the foolishness of convention; it mocks the rigidity that men impose on their world.

The experience of melodrama is less recreational. At its best it affirms what we already know and believe. At its worst it rehearses a superficial piety.

POETIC GAMES: ADVERTISING

In beginning our consideration of poetic recreation with a performing art such as theater, we entered upon our study through an art form with a rather strong recreational potential. Performing arts by their very nature have more recreational potential for an audience than do productive arts. In contrast, productive arts are somewhat less involving since the art object can exist independent of an audience; the fabricated work can persist in the physical world though never encountered by an audience, but a theatrical performance needs an audience to be realized.

Nevertheless, the productive arts can engage an audience and serve to provide in good measure that sensual restoration that is at the core of all Poetic communication games. Let us then continue our consideration of Poetic games by turning to one of the most popular recreational art forms in America today, commercial advertising.

If asked to illustrate an instance of the poetic in contemporary public life, most of us, even without reading the first part of this chapter, would probably cite some form of literature or music. There is, however, another poetic type that is even more common in our daily lives. Yet, perhaps because of this very profusion, we often neglect to see it as poetic. The variety of Poetic game that we allude to here is advertising. Commercial messages are everywhere: in newspapers and magazines, on billboards, on television and radio, in our mail boxes. It is true that the business executive who has a message created hopes most to persuade his audiences to change their beliefs about or conduct toward his product or corporation. His aim is to present a rhetorical message, to engage others in a Rhetoric game. Later we shall focus on this aspect of advertising. Now, however, we shall suggest that it is not only possible to regard advertising aesthetically, but that some ads are superb recreative entertainment.

This approach to advertising requires two important, although not unreasonable, concessions. First of all, to view advertising as a legitimate art form—as a message with aesthetic potential—requires that we

reevaluate the intellectual myth that advertisements are vapid and some-how beneath the interests of a sensitive educated individual. This reaction is based upon a limited definition of art, a definition that restricts "real art" to the galleries of museums and the pages of literary classics. Students of contemporary messages, however, must be willing to broaden this perspec-tive.[16] Surely we should still be sensitive to aesthetic intent as expressed in celebrated portraits and literature, but we should also recognize it in such diverse things as structural engineering, newspaper photography, haute couture and cuisine, jazz, preschool fingerpainting, and bread wrappers. Each of these, in its own way, can be considered as artistic or poetic—something whose aesthetic appeal can be appreciated regardless of its literal message.

Indeed, insofar as the messages created in a public arena serve to shape and reaffirm our passions by appealing to our sensuality, to that extent will they have an aesthetic facet. And further, as we earlier noted, insofar as it is the realm of the possible that is referred to by a message (that is, insofar as the message is understood as not having literal reference to the world), our interest will shift from the literal substance of that message toward the formal interrelations of the message components. And this appreciation of the form apart from the reference (which makes fiction possible in the first place) enables the audience to participate with the work of art whether it be music, an oil portrait, dramatic literature, poetry, or a commercial adver-tisement. It is in this sense that advertisements are poetic artifacts: They do engage us, appealing to our senses and our sensibilities, they are (as we shall shortly demonstrate) less literal than fictive, and they exhibit formal qualities that are capable of recreatively involving their audience in ways a classic sales pitch could not.

Furthermore, the fact that advertising is in the service of commerce should by no means limit its respectability. Indeed, it is typical that the most creative and imaginative talent of any given age will be hired to achieve material ends. Most of Handel's music, for example, was commis-sioned by his royal patrons for special occasions. When the great cathedrals were being constructed and the Church wanted certain religious principles glorified, artisans were hired. Once employed, the craftsmen released their creative energies on their particular assignments.

Dramatic literature, too, was frequently written for a price. In *Macbeth*, for example, Shakespeare praised the current monarch, King James I. But in spite of the fact that the play stresses the King's divine right and tradition

---

[16] Cf. S. A. Geyser, "What Do Americans Think of Advertising?" *Advertising Quarterly* 4 (1965):33–42.

has it that the King wrote Shakespeare a letter that possibly commanded him to write the play, we rarely regard *Macbeth* as political propaganda. We view it, instead, as a work of art that is to be evaluated for its own sake.

Even more vivid examples of sponsored art can be drawn from the list of British poet laureates. Men like Tennyson and Wordsworth were appointed for life as officers of the royal households. In return for their livelihood, they were expected to write poetry in celebration of court and national events.

It is not unusual, therefore, that we should find sponsored art in our own age. Many contemporary creative talents are attempting to manipulate symbols in a traditional fashion. Yet guided by the customary notions of artistic form and propriety, their objective is to highlight, amplify, or exemplify the good qualities of their sponsors. Musicians and lyricists are hired to write songs that will conform to a particular artist's established style; composers consent to create musical scores that will enhance the production of a film; photographers and portrait artists hope to capture their subjects' most flattering or engaging profiles; fashion designers and seamstresses hope to augment the desirable characteristics of their patrons' figures; architects are expected to express the spirit of the corporations whose buildings they design; and advertising agencies are approached by producers who want their products successfully presented to the buying public. Although these public artifacts are first inspired by someone other than their creators, there is no reason why we cannot evaluate each of them as poetic discourse—no reason why we cannot appreciate the song, the score, the portrait, the dress, the building, or the advertisement for its skillful expression and not its sponsor's aims.

To consider advertising as the most common form of public poetry in the twentieth century requires a second concession: We must acknowledge that poets and poetry as we traditionally know and study them are not really a part of the twentieth century. There are few contemporary poets who follow in the tradition of Wordsworth, Byron, Shelley, Keats, or Tennyson. Of course, it would be foolish to disregard such recent literary geniuses as Frost, Sandburg, Eliot, and cummings, to name a few. But these men are not the *public* men that poets once were. John Crowe Ransom, himself a poet, recalls how poets "used to be bards and patriots, priests and prophets, keepers of the public conscience, and, naturally, men of public importance."[17] How many poets fit this description today? Or, more specifically, how many contemporary poets could we actually name?

---

[17] J. C. Ransom, "Poets Without Laurels," *The World's Body* (New York: Charles Scribner's Sons, 1938).

This is not to suggest that poetry is a dead art in the twentieth century. Instead, what we are proposing is that it is necessary to redefine what is meant by poetic discourse today. Traditionally, poetry was a verbal art. In ancient, preliterate times it was an oral form beneficial to the transmission of information. The verbal tactics of rhythm and rhyme helped the speaker to be entertaining for his audiences and facilitated his memory as he recited. More recently we have come to know poetry as a written form. On the printed page we have become more sensitive to variations in rhythmic feet and lines and the subtleties of different rhyme schemes. All these poetic tactics are essentially verbal tactics.

In twentieth-century public discourse, however, there is an expansion of the range of materials and subsequently the flexibility afforded to the creative artist. He is no longer limited to the conventions of the written page or to his skill in using words. The contemporary poet can manipulate still or moving images that expand his resources for metaphor; he can utilize the actual sounds of animate or inanimate objects, which are potentially more vivid than the suggestive power of onomatopoeia; or he can rely on any combination of the verbal, the visual, and the auditory to express his aesthetic intentions. In other words, our expectations about the nature of contemporary poetry may have to change. We can no longer look for poetic works merely on the pages of books with titles like *Great American Poetry* or *Classic English Literature.* We must also be prepared to expect its appearance in aesthetic communications that do not rely on words as the chief means of expression. The best and most common examples of this type of poetry are found on television, radio, and billboards, and in magazines and newspapers in the service of commerce.

In spite of the fact that technological progress has provided the contemporary poet with a wider selection of poetic ingredients, many of the tactics he employs in producing his messages are essentially those which are also characteristic of traditional poetry. It is these basic similarities that enable us to continue to label the more diverse contemporary creative forms as "poetry." In the remainder of this section we shall mention four of these tactics as we exemplify the nature of advertising as a twentieth-century Poetic game.

Magazine and Newspaper Advertising

To begin our analysis we turn to advertisements that are taken from the pages of magazines and newspapers. It is easiest to start with this group of examples because they can be reproduced here in a way that approximates their original form. Of course, they rely on both visual and verbal symbols. Later we shall examine instances of radio advertising, which manipulate verbal-auditory combinations, and television commercials, verbal-visual-auditory combinations that exemplify contemporary sponsored poetry at its best.[18]

Emphasis on Expressive Form.   Both traditional poetry and commercial advertisements exhibit an extensive concern for aesthetic form. Although it is not necessary to demonstrate how this emphasis is characteristic of traditional poetry, we think it worthwhile to show how this is a tactic of the advertising game.

The most obvious example of aesthetic form is rhyme in the advertising jingle. Probably the most famous commercial jingle in our history was created late in the 1930's for Pepsi-Cola:

Pepsi-Cola hits the spot,
Twelve full ounces, that's a lot.
Twice as much for a nickel, too
Pepsi-Cola is the drink for you.

This extremely popular advertisement, which was still used as late as the mid-1950's, appeared on the printed page, was sung on radio, and even was played in jukeboxes. True, the simple and catchy verse is far from epic poetry but that hardly precludes it from being poetic. A Japanese Haiku is no less poetic than Homer's *Iliad*. Scale, size, and ambitious scope may not be the best criteria for judging the degree of success of poetic intent, as these examples show.

Commercial use of traditional poetic conventions is not limited, of course, to the rhyme and rhythm of verbal jingles and slogans. Many advertisers translate rhyme and rhythm into the qualities of visual composition; they replace tone and accent with physical shape and color. Consider, for example, the flowing visual rhythm and harmony in the Helena Rubenstein and Drambuie ads. In the portrait, notice how the artist has relied on graceful, soft lines and subtle shadows to accentuate the fragile femininity of the young woman. The almost total absence of straight lines lends a lyrical quality to the artist's expression. In the

---

[18] Before we start we should clarify two important assumptions. First, we are not suggesting that all advertisements are necessarily fine art or superb poetry. It is just as easy to find innumerable examples of artistically bad advertising as it is to find examples of inept poetry and prose. The samples we have selected to discuss here are not unique, but they are, of course, of better than average quality. Secondly, each of the advertisements we have chosen could possibly illustrate more than one of the four poetic techniques we will explore. We have used each ad only once, primarily because it is an exceptional model of a particular poetic device and because we want to generalize from a sufficiently large sample collection.

See also S. I. Hayakawa, "Poetry and Advertising," *ETC.* 19(1963):395.

I like fluffy blankets,
    boys with deep voices,
    the smell of any new season
    and my English instructor.
I like Mary Hopkin,
    horoscopes,
    old report cards,
    shelled pistachio nuts
    and Letters to the Editor.

I like moon craters,
    Swedish clogs,
    babies' tiny hands,
    long, burning looks
    and my English instructor.
I like wondering about Time Machines,
    the intelligence of dolphins,
    Mexican jumping beans
    and E.S.P.

I like antique dolls,
    houses with gables,
    Greta Garbo
    and boys with lopsided smiles.
    (I like my English instructor.)
I like aunts who remember birthdays,
    girls who are my height
    and dogs named "Pussycat."
I like thinking about things I like.
I like Heaven Sent.

I like perfume, cologne, dusting powder.
    Special gift sets to give people I'm fond of.
    Miniature solid perfume compacts.
    And those great, important-looking
    Heaven Sent Rings with solid perfume inside.

Heaven Sent

Helena Rubinstein

Evenings that memories are made of so often include DRAMBUIE
the cordial with the scotch whisky base

landscape, another artist has juxtaposed the curved bridge and its slightly blurred reflection over the hazy, but rigid lines of the buildings; his use of visual contrast emphasizes a romantic serenity that is complementary to urban sophistication. The traditional poetic qualities of these pictures are readily apparent.

Now, let us look at these illustrations again, only this time consider the advertising copy. In each case, the advertiser chose to emphasize the visual portion of the message, to express a quality of the sponsor's product with a visual image. Although the artist could have expressed himself verbally, he apparently preferred to capture the magazine reader's fleeting attention with a well-formed, interesting picture.

Emphasis on Connotation.   A second similarity between traditional poetry and twentieth-century advertising is that both emphasize connotation rather than denotation. Just as poems are not detailed descriptions of specific persons, places, objects, or events, commercials, too, are poetic fictions that rely on our emotional reactions. When, for example, Carl Sandburg says that "the fog comes on little cat feet," no one asks, except facetiously, how many feet are involved or how big they are. We recognize, instead, that he is alluding to the sense of grace and mystery that accompany a stealthy cat, any cat.

The connotative quality of a commercial message is often derived from its visual symbols. AT & T Long Lines, in this cozy family picture, is not making a comment about a real mother and daughter that a photographer happened to discover one sunny afternoon. We all know that models were selected and paid to depict this scene and expect no one to claim that the picture itself is a lie. The effectiveness of this advertisement relies, instead, on the emotional reaction we have to the pleasant warmth of family life.

Contemporary sponsored poetry relies on the connotative value of verbal symbols as well. Why, for example, did Miller High Life recommend itself as "the champagne of bottled beer"? Could its producers charge five dollars per bottle because of the claim on the label? Or, did an irate consumer have the right to request a refund of his purchase price because the beverage tasted like beer and not champagne? Poetic statements, we have argued, operate in the realm of the possible, not the probable or the absolute. The Miller Brewing Company was not asserting that its beer tasted like champagne. Instead it was hoping to suggest that Miller High Life was a beer that was "right" for festive occasions. We tend to associate champagne with happy celebrations and this was the connotation that the advertisement was attempting to evoke.

Exploitation of Ambiguity.   The third tactic that poetry and advertising share in common is that both of them exploit the ambiguity of symbols; they both rely on double meanings. When Sandburg alludes to the fog coming in "on little cat feet," for instance, does he mean that the

"…My flowers all blew away…"

Remember the gifts that pleased your mother most, when you were a little girl? The valentines made from paper doilies… the whatchamacallits made from clay.

And the bunch of dandelions you picked— even though the tops blew away, she didn't mind. You had given them to her.

Now that you're grown up and moved away from home, the gift that just might please her most, could be a Long Distance call from you.

Long Distance is the next best thing to being there.

fog comes in like a kitten, that the cat is little? Or, does he mean that the fog minces in, that the feet are little? The poet relies on the aesthetic pleasure his readers derive in moving between the two meanings.

Ironic ambiguity is also the essence of this poem by Emily Dickinson:

> *The Bustle in a House*
> *The Morning after Death*
> *Is solemnest of industries*
> *Enacted upon Earth—*
>
> *The Sweeping up the Heart*
> *And putting Love away*
> *We shall not want to use again*
> *Until Eternity.*
> *Emily Dickinson*[19]

In these two brief stanzas, the poet juxtaposes the meanings we have for two extremes—death and housekeeping.

Although twentieth-century commercial poets resort to less metaphysical topics, they often use ambiguity with equal effect. Poets rarely explicate all the subtleties of their verses for their readers; the J & B Scotch and Quaker Oats advertisements are obvious illustrations of this poetic technique.

Elevation of the Commonplace.[20]   The final tactic that traditional poetry and contemporary commercial messages employ in common is the attempt to invest everyday experience with significance, to take the commonplace and make it somehow special. Walt Whitman, an American romantic poet who followed in the tradition of Rousseau, Wordsworth, Shelley, and Emerson, is noted for his celebration of the commonplace and the trivial and for his incorporation of the ugly as he sought to invoke the immediacy of human experience. In the following poem entitled "A Noiseless Patient Spider," notice how he expands the spider's mundane perseverance to symbolize the steadfastness of the human soul:

---

[19] Thomas H. Johnson, ed., *The Complete Poems of Emily Dickinson* (Boston: Little, Brown and Company).

[20] Cf. A. Navasky, "Advertising is . . .", *New York Times Magazine* (20 November 1966), 52ff.

Hot nourishment in two speeds.

Namely, Fast and Instant.

When you have a little time to get yourself and your family going, there's Regular Quaker Oats.

But when you have no time, there's Instant Quaker Oats. Plop a packetful in a bowl. Add hot water. And quicker than you can say "fill'er up" you've got beautiful, steamy, cooked oatmeal.

And Quaker Oats, Regular or Instant, happens to be one of the most nutritious cereals you can fill a young body up with. (Or an old body. Or anybody.)

Because there's more protein in Quaker Oats than in any other whole grain cereal.

And protein is an essential body builder. It helps make kids grow. And keep grownups in good shape.

But Quaker Oats has other starter-uppers, too— B Vitamins and important minerals.

And it's got plenty of something else. Flavor. Quaker Instant comes in the original hearty, nutty, oat flavor. And in some pretty original new varieties too: Raisins & Spice, Apples & Cinnamon, Maple & Brown Sugar, and (believe it or not) Chocolate. All with the power you need to rev up on a cold winter's morning. So get out the Quaker Instant and . . . vvrrrrrrooooooooommmmm!

"Nothing is better for thee than me!!"

A noiseless, patient spider
I mark'd where on a little promontory it stood isolated,
Mark'd how to explore the vacant vast surrounding,
It launched forth filament, filament, filament, out of itself,
Ever unreeling them, ever tirelessly speeding them.

And you O my soul where you stand,
Surrounded, detached, in measureless oceans of space,
Ceaselessly musing, venturing, throwing, seeking the spheres to connect
*   them,*
Till the bridge you will need be formed, till the ductile anchor hold,
Till the gossamer thread you fling catch somewhere, O my soul.

Walt Whitman

Whitman is not unique. Poets typically begin with trivial objects or common acts (e.g., "Ah Sun-Flower," William Blake; "Mowing," Robert Frost; "Morning at the Window," T. S. Eliot; "To a Mouse," Robert Burns; "Meeting at Night," Robert Browning), and they use these to illustrate a deeper, hidden meaning or special significance.

Commercial poets of the twentieth century do essentially the same thing. They take common acts such as preparing a meal (Accent ad), washing the floor or the car, doing the weekly shopping or laundry, and going to work or to bed and invest them with feelings of domestic tranquility and happiness. They glorify routine personal hygiene with a sense of beauty and elegance. They focus on relatively ordinary events, like moving from one location to another (Allied Van Lines ad) or making a long distance phone call, and imbue them with dramatic tension or excitement. They take the necessary objects of personal apparel and link them with luxury or security and confidence (Pennyrich and Jockey ads). And this list is only the beginning. In each case the advertiser could simply have illustrated a picture of his product. But few commercial messages merely show their audience how the cake mix box, the typewriter, or the deodorant looks. They choose, instead, to transform the use of the product beyond the realm of everyday experience, to give it some special meaning or value.

The Poetic game of advertising encompasses tactics that enable the game to be re-creative for the spectators. The commercial message invites the spectators to bypass the dull restraints imposed by the form of the product and to celebrate life through the aesthetic form of the message itself. When advertisements celebrate a can of beer, or a tube of toothpaste, or a drain cleaner, they do not really celebrate the objects them-

In life the little things are so often the big things.

A wave, a smile, a kiss—these things announce and symbolize and preserve the bigger realities. So it is with Accent.

Accent wakes up the flavor nature puts in food. Accent doesn't put the flavor there—it brings it out.

Accent makes just about every plain and fancy dish you can prepare taste better.

Accent is no big deal. But it would appear to be a mighty big small deal.

When you add Accent, you know you're doing everything possible to make that dish the best possible.

A little Accent (like a little love) surely helps.

But Dad, they just elected me co-captain*

Seems like everybody in the family can come up with a better reason for staying than you have for moving . . .

And those reasons are the really important things you worry about when you have to move. What will it do to the kids? Will we like the new neighbors (and vice versa)? Schools? Doctors? Taxes?

To give you the time and courage to worry and explain about the important things, we go about our part of your move with an unobtrusive calm that's taken us forty years to master. We're gentle with the kids,

reassuring with wives, kind to fathers . . .

. . . and with furniture, so respectful you'd think we were still making payments on it.

When you have a brand new co-captain to move, call the Allied agent in your town. He's pretty fond of his family, too.

*Son, that news could make the new coach the happiest man in town. You don't leave your talent behind when you move.

ALLIED VAN LINES

We move families, not just furniture

selves. In most cases the products themselves are interchangeable: As we watch a man on a picnic relishing a can of beer, he could just as well be extolling his toothpaste, a drain cleaner, wax paper, or baked beans. The game of advertising-as-poetic is to enhance the product's worth by associating it with a fine art object. Should the ad extol the product's virtues in the process, that is all to the good, but as we hope to show in the section on Rhetoric games, there is no reason to believe that such persuasive efforts have any significant influence in selling the product. Only when we can recognize the aesthetic potentials in ads, rather than presuming a rhetorical potential that is largely absent, will we be in a position to understand the communicative experience of advertising.

the
Rich one
.... and
worth
    every
Penny....

Enjoy the rich excitement of comfort and beauty of a Penny-rich Bra. The Pennyrich Bra was designed for the richness of comfort, beauty, and performance. It trains — shapes — strengthens the bust. The unique patented design lifts and shapes the large bust — enhances the small bust without padding. The rich one and worth every penny because there is more to a woman than meets the eye.

Your underwear should do more than cover you up.

It should protect you. Protect you against strain. If it doesn't, you might as well wear a fig leaf.

You see, everyday actions like walking up stairs or lifting a golf bag, can place sudden strain on a man.

That's where Jockey* briefs come in. This brief firmly supports a man in everyday activities. At the same time, it's comfortable.

And its special design gives a man a feeling of security and confidence.

The Jockey brief is knit with soft absorbent cotton. Tailored precisely to fit perfectly, front and back. Its unique construction is the secret of its firm yet comfortable feel.

The Jockey Classic brief was invented 35 years ago. And over the years, a lot of people have attempted to copy our design.

But unsuccessfully.

Next time you buy briefs, remember a man needs our special kind of support. Be sure you get genuine Jockey brand. Look for the famous Jockey boy on the package.

The Jockey Classic brief. Still just $1.25.

Still a lot more for your money.

Radio and Television Advertising

Although it is difficult for us to illustrate broadcast advertising with the same precision that we can reproduce magazine and newspaper advertising, we can easily argue that radio and television commercials are twentieth-century poetic forms. Certainly, commercials can be tasteless, boring, and too loud; we are all aware of how justifiably fashionable it is to be contemptuous of them. But it is likewise true that many commercials are apt to be more appealing than the programs they interrupt.[21]

Imaginative radio advertising has come a long way since the innovative Pepsi Cola jingle of the 1930's (reprinted on p. 269). Today's programming is interspersed with commercial messages in the form of miniature dramas, parodies, clever montages of sound effects, and even 90-second songs composed to blend in with "Top 40" formats. Many advertising agencies, aware of this aesthetic growth in radio advertising, have started to submit their efforts to national competition. Since 1967, formal evaluation of commercials is no longer made solely in

---

[21] Thus it is that preschoolers, who are often bored with television shows, are enchanted by the commercial interludes.

terms of the sales receipts of the products, but in terms of their character as art objects as well.

As an illustration, consider the following one-minute radio commercial that advertising executives judged the outstanding single entry among national campaigns in the 1967 American Television and Radio Commercials Festival:

Music:	*Tympani Roll*
ANNOUNCER 1:	Announcing the 1966 Chun King!
Music:	*Rapid underscore, punctuating throughout as announcer speaks.*
ANNOUNCER 2:	(Over music.) Sleek . . . arrogant . . . A different breed of Chow Mein. You see it instantly in its bold new bean sprouts . . . Its crisp aggressive water chestnuts . . . Talk about extras! . . . You want bucket bamboo shoots? . . . Power onions? . . . You've got it mister in the 1966 Chun King Chow Mein. . . . Outside too!! You'll notice the revolutionary labels . . . More pick up in the two cans taped together. That's standard equipment on this baby!! . . . Look at the way she handles. . . . In the bottom can . . . where the action is . . . over 27 cubic inches of succulent Chun King Sauce loaded with high performance chicken . . . Step up . . . to the tuned Chow Mein! The 1966 Chun King! *Underscore punctuates and ducks out.*
ANNOUNCER 2:	Noodles optional . . .
Music button![22]	

The poetic qualities of this advertisement are readily discernible: The conventional rhythm is audibly punctuated with music; the power, excellence, and luxury of a new model automobile are connotatively attributed to the chow mein; there are ambiguous references to the standard equipment and extras of both automobiles and prepared chow mein; and the entire 60-second effort certainly invests the everyday can of chow mein with significance.

---

[22] Freberg Ltd. in *Best TV and Radio Commercials,* Volume Two, 1968, p. 134. International TV Study Foundation of the American TV Commercials Festival, Inc. Reprinted by permission of Freberg Ltd., Beverly Hills, California.

The most compelling examples of advertising as instances of Poetic public games are found in television. In fact, we could probably argue that television commercials have shown more aesthetic growth in the past ten years than any other art form in America. The hard sell, sock-it-to-'em advertisements that dominated the 1950's gave way to fun-filled commercials with high entertainment values in the 1960's. One of the more notable revolutionaries was the 1964 Alka Seltzer "No Matter What Shape Your Stomach's In." This innovative film showing nothing more than a quick succession of people's stomachs has become a Madison Avenue classic. Such changes were inevitable because advertising agencies were beginning to recruit top talent—famous screen and stage personalities, award-winning cameramen and fashion designers, highly respected directors—to highlight, amplify, and exemplify the good qualities of their products.[23] Today, the production costs of a one-minute commercial frequently exceed $50,000—about ten times more than a minute of standard television fare. Even so, more and more sponsors are willing to pay such prices because they realize that the average television viewer is becoming commercial-saturated and that creativity is necessary to gain viewers' attention.[24]

POETIC GAMES: MASS ENTERTAINMENT DREAM MACHINES

By far the most massive proportion of entertainment objects we encounter in modern life are those industrially produced messages intended for mass consumption, including girlie magazines, tabloid newspapers, the bulk of television and radio broadcasts, and most feature films and hit records. If we regard involvement in an experience as an important recreational factor in public communication games (an idea we first articulated in Chapter 9), then it suffices to note that (with rare exception) most mass entertainment games as they currently appear in our society are closer to impersonal ritual than to the Poetic games of advertising and theater that we have just considered.

---

[23] Cf. A. Rich, "The Melody Is the Message," *New York Times Magazine* (20 May 1971).

[24] According to the National Commission on the Causes and Prevention of Violence, the average American spends nearly 3,000 days watching television between his 2nd and 65th year—almost 9 years of his life. A similar survey (reported in "As We See It," *TV Guide* 19[4 September 1971]) suggests that the average American sees probably as many as 73,000 commercials a year.

Mass Entertainment and Re-Creation

In this respect, mass entertainment, in its focus on momentary escape and relaxation rather than re-creation and restoration, serves in the main to perpetuate the inauthentic and superficial in human communication. (The re-creative criterion is necessary for value judgment.) This does not make each and every television game show or situation comedy bad, any more than a candy bar is inherently bad; but neither do these communication activities qualify as recreational communication games merely because they are filled with the chatter of human sounds and an artificial laugh track. Most mass media fails as entertainment for the same reason that rituals do: The audience is left out of the game. Several bags of caramels may serve to stuff the consumer without providing proper nourishment. Just so, a glut of typical mass media "entertainment" messages may satiate consumers (or at the very least fatigue their eyes) without ever engaging their sensuality or revitalizing their capacity to experience their passions.[25]

We must at this point enter several disclaimers. First, our contention about the triviality that overwhelms the nation's airwaves and printing presses should not be taken as just another (rightly suspect) attack on mass media and/or the society within which it operates. Secondly, what we are going to argue about mass entertainment is not meant as an attack on mass production of poetic artifacts as such. The mere facts that such messages are mass produced and meant for huge audiences do not of themselves make for either bad or immoral art. We have already demonstrated that this is the case for advertising. The fact that mass entertainment is commercially sponsored or otherwise seeks a profit does not exclude the possibility that it will be innovative or recreational. Finally, we are not taking sides in that increasingly well-worn debate over the need for "public service" programming in the mass media. That debate has been unfortunately dominated by moralists more concerned with *how men ought to enjoy* than by thoughtful analysis of public messages as outgrowths of public communication institutions.

Television: Public Service or Pleasure?

Shall television, for example, become a public service communication medium? Some people think it should; they want it to be "educational"

---

[25] Quite literally, such amusement lacks a capacity to "inspire" us, that is, to make us more noble-minded, to renew us by enhancing our natural love of Being in the world apart from working at goal-directed tasks. See R. McKeon, *Thought, Action, and Passion* (Chicago: University of Chicago Press, 1954), pp. 30–53.

in the same sense that a museum is educational—presenting uplifting subjects like lectures and concerts of classical music, presentations in which the viewer will have to invest energy, patience, and time in the hope of thereby improving himself.

But those who control commercial television are pleasure-mongers, whether they know it or not. For them, television is not an extension of the museum but of the neighborhood pub. The local tavern is a total immediate-reward arena. People go there to unwind, to gossip, to laugh it up with friends; it is, in short, an intrinsically rewarding place where one might spend a cheerful evening and have nothing good to show for it the next day. Which model suits television? The intelligentsia favor the museum model (and hence idolize England's BBC), but in the United States most programs on the commercial networks are in fact designed to accompany a group of congenial beer drinkers, much as pretzels and peanuts are. And so it is with most mass entertainment: It is not necessarily escapist as much as it is intrinsically pleasurable and trivial (which is not to say that it is either unethical or tawdry).

Television: Popular Entertainment Lacking Sensual Involvement

In this regard, television has become the most appealing popular entertainment medium in history. It satisfies many needs in our age. For one thing, it is universally available. Because it can be broadcast directly into one's home, the individual need not seek it out. Unlike theater, which is clearly public entertainment (requiring that we "attend" it in the company of other men, that while in attendance we accept the gazes and the code of conduct of others as our own, and that we control our creature impulses), television is private entertainment. It is there when the viewer wants it and on his terms. How he watches, in what state of undress, for instance, is beyond public view. In the privacy of his home, the viewer may belch, scratch, snore, and gulp as he will.[26]

A second advantage of television is precisely that it requires no sensual involvement by the viewer since the shows are designed to demand minimal attention. Thus it is possible to eat lunch and "watch" TV, or to read a newspaper and "watch" TV, or to "watch" a show even

---

[26] Think of the continuing popularity of morning television "game" shows in this light. Whereas when seeing such shows in the company of others, the natural response of many people is to snicker, it is apparent that many of these same people, when they are free of the eyes of others, take some delight in these ritual enactments of human greed. Cf. W. Stephanson, *The Play Theory of Mass Communication* (Chicago: University of Chicago Press, 1967), pp. 45–65.

though we may wander in and out of the room where the set is located. In fact, the role of television in the modern home is as an electronic hearth. In premodern times the hearth was the core of the home; it was necessary to keep an eye on the hearth in order to see that the fire did not go out, that the meal did not burn, etc. Ordinarily this would be the task of the dimmest member of the family, a senile aunt or the youngest child. The same is true today in that we often assign the least able family member (be it senile elder or youngest child) the task of watching the set and calling us should anything of moment appear on the screen.

Indeed, there is no cost to television watching except time. And in our increasingly leisure-oriented society, time is cheap. Since many people lead increasingly aimless lives, they find it ever more important to expend time on structured activities such as television watching in order to keep their minds in an "idle" condition.

In this respect, it is no accident that watching television becomes a consumer ritual rather like attending church faithfully. Thus a typical exchange between two teen-age friends upon meeting might run as follows:

First Teen: See "The Brady Bunch" last night?

Second Teen: Yeah. Neat. And I picked up that new Alice Cooper record. Hear it?

First Teen: Sure.

Notice that in this exchange there is response, but no comment. Nor is comment expected. The questions are comparable to, "Did you go to Mass this morning?"—the ritual acknowledgments of a trend-conscious consumer society. Friends keep one another alerted to the latest symptoms of consumer piety. To respond is to affirm your membership in your appropriate peer group. A teen-ager who spent a week denying that he had met his group's norms (for example, by admitting that he had *not* seen last night's shows or bought the latest hit records) would likely be treated as a pariah; his friends simply would no longer have anything to say to him since he would not fit into the ceremony.

How, then, if television (and to a lesser degree other mass entertainment forms) so adequately fills these crucial needs in our lives, is it still possible to maintain that it is inadequate if not corrosive as recreation? For the same reason that the U.S. Surgeon General warns us that cigarettes, even though many derive pleasure from smoking them, are bad for one's health, for the same reason that nutritionists would brand a steady diet of nothing but chocolate as suicidal, mass entertainment messages *need not* be fatuous or shoddy merely because they are industrially produced (as we demonstrated with advertisements), but the plain fact is that they are. And because they are, they do not fulfill our needs for recreational play. We can *consume* them, but they are so produced as to make *participation with them* almost impossible. And when the opportunity for participation is lost, the prospects for aesthetic renewal also fall by the wayside.

Most mass entertainment messages fail as recreation because, as Abraham Kaplan has pointed out, they substitute industrial criteria for poetic ones.[27] All art removes the trivial and tangential from its portrayal of life, but in successful recreational messages the standards of selection (purity, relevance, harmony, significance, etc.) are intended to heighten the viewer's or listener's aesthetic experience and so rejuvenate his passions.

Mass Entertainment and Cost-Cutting

Most mass entertainment ignores these criteria in favor of such norms as are related to cost-cutting and corner-cutting. The primary criterion is: What will yield the largest financial return for the promoters? The mere fact that mass entertainment artifacts are produced by industrial means does not impose this criterion; the history of modern art is filled with magnificent efforts to prefabricate objects of excellent quality in large numbers (lithographs, for example). But invariably many imitators, seeking to get rich quick, have debased the art forms, using them as a cosmetic cover to sell shabby merchandise. Thus, the functionalism of Mies van der Rohe's architecture quickly became an excuse for realtors to blight the landscape with massive high-rise slums. Similarly, in any contest between quality and profits in mass entertainment, it is quality that is more often slighted.

Such cost-cutting leads at times to bizarre results. Some contemporary films insert a gratuitous scene with characters singing a song that is unrelated to the film except for a commercial tie-in that the film's backers have arranged with a record company to try to peddle the song (which will be released simultaneously with the film).[28] Animated cartoons, too,

---

[27] A. Kaplan, "The Aesthetics of the Popular Arts," *Journal of Aesthetics and Art Criticism* 24(Spring 1966):351–364.

[28] Recall the "Raindrops" song from *Butch Cassidy and the Sundance Kid.* See B. Davidson, "The Entertainer," *New York Times Magazine* (16 March 1975), 69; P. H. Daugherty, "A Bulova-Paramount Venture," *New York Times* (3 April 1975), 63.

are purchased in bulk for Saturday morning kiddie shows on the basis of low unit cost (so many reuseable chase film clips, so many episodes with a rabbit and a hippo) and with little apparent regard for dramatic features such as plot, characterization, or even technical quality. Sensuality is sacrificed for mass production.

Is it not curious, then, that we continue hour after hour to watch our favorite weekly TV shows even though one episode is virtually indistinguishable from the rest, that we insist on watching all the Bowry Boy films long after their novelty has worn off? In each of these cases we have the entire series already canned in our heads. We watch to reconfirm the formula and to "kill time."

Television Talk Shows

What are the effects on us as consumers of a steady diet of such "popcorn" mass entertainment as we have been considering in place of more nearly recreational poetic messages as theater and commercial advertising? Let us explore these consequences by considering as an illustration how the typical regular viewer encounters one such instance of the mass entertainment phenomenon, the highly popular television talk show. Jack Parr, Johnny Carson, Merv Griffin, Mike Douglas, and Dick Cavett all share in common in the development of a peculiar industrial artistic format: Public relations chitchat masquerading as salon conversation. In this arena Carson's "Tonight" show, though not the earliest of its type, has long been the paradigm others have imitated. There are two basic tactics for putting every show together:

1. Constantly refer to the regular features and guests on the show as "weird," "zany," and "wild" in order to give the illusion of novelty night after night;
2. Yet in contradiction to this, constantly repeat all the ingredients of the "pop-corn" formula to give the illusion of familiarity while continuing to celebrate a ritual that remains identical night after night.

Carson (who once emceed a daytime game show called "Who Do You Trust") has elevated these elements into a ritual that has kept him a major national figure for over a decade. The formula is perhaps most clearly detected during his opening monologue, which has in all these years relied on a single joke, repeated with variations several times every evening: that joke is the vacuous look of a jester (our vulnerable friend Johnny) who is failing in his stumbling efforts to make a buck by making us laugh.

Here is how it operates.[29] The comedy writers for the show employ a pegboard schedule of categories of stale jokes; these jokes are repeated on a regular basis:

1. Topical gags (weather, mugging, pollution).
2. Commonly despised and so uncontroversial institutions (Con Ed, AT&T, the local commuter railroad, commissary food).[30]
3. Old burlesque saws updated:
   a. NBC's meteorologist (jokes about weathermen).
   b. Ed McMahon's drinking (a vehicle to plug in "drunk" jokes).
   c. Doc Severenson's gaudy clothes ("boys in the band" jokes).
   d. Sunset Strip crazies (a variation on the Borscht Circuit line, "When I was a kid in the slums it was so bad . . . ").
   e. Old Jack Benny radio gags about California weirdos (originally referring to the LaBrea Tar Pits and Pismo Beach muscle boys, now referring to massage parlors, Taco Bell restaurants, and used car dealers).
4. Infrequent "political" jokes: Bob Hope style references to some idiosyncracy or physical feature of the politician (Agnew's golf, Nixon's nose) rather than to his political policies.

Were these gags taken in isolation, each would fall flat. And that is precisely the point: We nightly witness a repetition of a single unchanging ceremony; a poor struggling nice schnook tells weak jokes and fears the response of the audience. And apparently Americans' compassion wells up, or maybe we just recognize our own futile careers in his look of pain mingled with dread. But watch Carson's eyes. He has been telling his one joke so long now that even he is bored. More and more he is coming to rely on the cue card, more and more he rushes through the opening monologue, like a rural priest who has memorized the Latin prayers so thoroughly that he has forgotten what they say.

Although this single feature is the formula's "core," we can of course elaborate on it. The recipe for a typical talk show goes as follows:

---

[29] An increasing number of analyses are being offered of the talk show as a public address form and of its lack of poetic potential. Among the best of these studies are those by Chris Welles, "The Sociology of Dumb," *Esquire* (May 1970), pp. 102ff.; Peter Hellman, "What Makes David Frost Talk," *New York Times Magazine* (7 Dec 1969), 54ff.; Richard Schickel, "Performing Arts," *Harpers* (March 1970), 116, 120.

[30] Many of these institutions are located in cosmopolitan centers such as New York and Los Angeles and have no effect on the lives of the bulk of viewers who are mainly viewing from the Midwest and South. These viewers in particular seem to relish news from the Big City. They feel a bit less provincial for being let in on current metropolitan happenings (it's just like seeing the latest fashions). Also, paradoxically, hearing about all the horrors of life in the Big City, like ghost tales before bedtime, makes them shudder gratefully that they are home safe in bed in Indiana.

1. Monologue: Featuring a host with one of two prepackaged images:
   a. Daytime shows—an apple-pie sweet family person (Mike
      Douglas or Dinah Shore).
   b. Evening—mom's favorite mischievous little child-cum-
      twinkle (Carson, Cavett, Griffin, Smothers Brothers, or
      Bishop).
2. First guest: Preferably a "starlet" who comes on stage in a risqué
   dress intended to draw wolf-whistles from the audience and
   leers from the host. Like the host, the guest is plastic, having
   usually hired a gag writer to prepare several clever rejoinders to
   the host's prearranged straight lines. The whole exchange was
   worked out at a "preshow interview" where the starlet's manager worked out details with the show's representative.
3. Guest stars: Actually a sort of Sears catalog for rubes. In the old
   days farmers would cheer themselves of a winter's night by
   leafing through the Sears catalog looking at all the luxuries they
   could order from "back East." They do the same thing today,
   with the talk show serving as a kind of amateur hour for professional touts. Each guest is selling something: a recent film, a
   ghosted book, a guest spot upcoming at a state rodeo (Everyone
   knows that Doc will be guest marshall at the Des Moines Old
   Home Day, that Buddy Hackett has attached his name to a new
   parlor game)—these "guests" are in fact unlikely to engage in
   genuine conversation. They have come on the show to take
   advantage of free time for commercials in the guise of idle after-
   hours chatter. Thus the apparent cycle of guest-commercial-
   guest-commercial is actually an extended series of commercials.
   Evidence for this huckster element in the formula is that with
   rare exceptions, few hosts even bother any more with the pretense that they have read their guests' new books. And why
   should they? The ghosted book is itself as plastic as the show
   itself.
4. The "regulars": We are all familiar with the steadies, with Zsa
   Zsa and Rex and Tony and Truman and Phyllis and Joan. They,
   too, avoid real conversation, confining themselves to pre-
   scripted, innocuous super talk. What we are witnessing with this
   "celebs-after-hours" chitchat is a television version of the movie
   fan magazine. The conversation runs to strings of "inside show
   biz" anecdotes in which the regular relates his recent experiences ("while he was playing golf") with other famous people.
   Note that the regular is seldom a celebrity him/herself. A true
   celebrity is famous for some skill or achievement (such as George
   C. Scott for acting or Joe Namath for sports). Regulars are "per-

sonalities," famous only for being famous; their value to the show consists in their ability to drop names from the charmed circle without being sued by the celebrities mentioned.

There have been, of course, repeated attempts to change this basic talk show formula, most notably by Steve Allen, Dick Cavett, David Frost, and David Susskind; to date each of these has passed unmourned from the air after a few months or else lingered on, unwatched, like consumptive pensioners of the networks. The nation seems to have developed an increasing intolerance for ambiguity in its television, preferring the dull certainty of a bedtime ritual, however empty, to originality of any type.

Results of Plastic Mass Entertainment

The result of such recurrent plastic performances that are fabricated to be as unvarying, and as bland, as sliced sandwich bread is that the audience is left no room to participate or share in the event; it can only consume, never actively experience. Instead of rejuvenation we suffer a gradual aesthetic corrosion as the time we require for recuperation from the world is devoured by non-involving ritual. (Think of the stuffed but soggy feeling one often has after having spent six or more uninterrupted hours watching television shows; the feeling is rather comparable to the bloated sensation one might have upon eating a dozen hot dog rolls as a snack.) Our openness to reality gradually gives way to a simple recognition of conventional categories. We process data into the approved pigeonholes rather than in any way interact with the event. We are, in other words, not really amused by Johnny Carson or his jokes, but we do experience a low-level sensation of being "pleased with ourselves" for having the minimal wit to recognize that a punch line, albeit a weak one, has been delivered. This is the same sort of glee that overcame us, when, in the fourth grade, we knew the answer and waved our hands calling, "Me, teacher!" Such gratification as occurs is in no way related to a restoration of our sensual capacities but is rather similar to that derived from munching potato chips: It is no more re-creative or a gratifying communicative game than is reading highway markers out of boredom.[31]

A similar lack of participation exists in many other mass entertain-

---

[31] See H. Hardt, "The Dilemma of Mass Communication: An Existential Point of View," *Philosophy and Rhetoric* 3(Summer 1972):175–187; K. Giffin, "Social Alienation by Communication Denial," *Quarterly Journal of Speech* 56(December 1970):347–357.

ment media. In the typical grade-B film Western, for example, a cowboy in black hat and mustache rides into town while sinister music swells in the background; the menacing stranger reaches his destination, dismounts, and kicks a dog. These cues signal film viewers inwardly to acknowledge fear and loathing as the culturally appropriate response. But notice that such a constellation of images, having been so often repeated as to become hackneyed, can no longer of itself evoke the feelings themselves in the viewers, but only the recognition that such feelings are appropriate; the signals remain as labels for the category of the feeling, not stimuli for the feelings themselves. Similarly, American television audiences apparently need to hear "canned laughter" (fabricated laughter synthetically created on tapes at a console and ranging from electronic simulations of a titter all the way to a rollicking belly laugh) as part of most "comedy" shows in order to reassure themselves that they recognize the appropriate places to laugh and to assure themselves that what they are watching is indeed funny.

Additionally, because we are unable to actively (or actually) experience anything, too full a schedule of mass entertainment dulls our capacity to respond appreciatively in other circumstances; our poetic sensibilities atrophy into a set of conditioned responses. The steady television viewer who has become accustomed to not really feeling anything when watching entertainment shows comes to depend upon directions as to how to feel under any conditions. He or she is like a child who is ordered to "Be happy." Whereas initially his or her perceptual discrimination becomes dull through endless repetition of the same rituals, eventually it is emotions themselves that decay. One's emotions, however, are not subject in this fashion to arbitrary command; the child may smile for the camera, but the mere fact of the order tends to preclude spontaneous feeling. Just so, consumers of mass entertainment who succumb to having their emotions so directed eventually lose their capacity to have their emotions engaged under any circumstances; their emotional responses come more and more to resemble the soggy potato chips they munched as they watched the shows.

We can see a clear illustration of this corrosive impact in the rapid trivialization suffered in the recent movement for sexual equality. "Women's lib" made the fatal error of allowing some of its spokespersons to make their case on the television talk shows. Instead of concentrating on spreading their gospel throughout the land in local contexts, the women were suckered (partly in self-defense) into the nationwide talk-show formula and the movement was consequently reduced to a form of tag-team wrestling:

- Tonight: Norman Mailer versus Germaine Greer
- Tomorrow: David Susskind versus Kate Millet
- Next week: Hugh Hefner versus Bella Abzug *and* Betty Friedan
- Grand finale: Bobby Riggs versus Billie Jean King

What emerged was the undifferentiated pulp that emanates from all talk show appearances: Women with a serious purpose found themselves devoured in the ritual and processed into clown vaudeville. The issues (which were and remain legitimate topics) were lost in the apparel (that is, in the outer costume, the style of the participants), and the public was left believing that the burning question facing "Women's lib", as a movement was, "Should one wear Fruit of the Loom?"

While the general, long-term effect of steadily consuming plastic mass entertainment without adequate recourse to aesthetically recreative discourse is to deaden public sensibilities, we need to remind ourselves again that such inadequacy is not inherent in mass entertainment. As we have demonstrated, commercial advertising, where talents and efforts are lavished on producing messages of excellent quality, can engage an audience in genuinely Poetic games. The same is true of some recent children's television shows such as "Sesame Street," where care is taken to produce an aesthetically engaging message. But, in general, we must conclude that most mass media as they exist in America today remain simply as *broadcasters* in the original sense, spewing out over the landscape messages that bathe the consumer in indulgent clichés which, if they affect him or her at all, serve only to immunize him or her from both the outer world and his or her own immediate feelings.[32] They may fill empty time in our lives while we wait to die, but their inadequacy in fulfilling the recreational functions *expected of* entertainment is plain.

---

[32] The reader can confirm the rigidity of the talk show formula for himself by replicating a small experiment we ran concerning the guest list for the Carson show. Picking shows at random during the summer of 1974, we arrived at this profile for the typical guest who appeared:

1. Ordinarily four guests appeared.
2. One of the four was invariably a comic.
3. Another of the four sang or played a musical instrument.
4. The last guest of the evening was a curio of some type: an astronomer, a government bureaucrat, an animal curator from a zoo, or an old-time sports or jazz figure. This last guest, who offered the only real variety in the nightly guest list, seemed to be placed at the end of the show, after most viewers had fallen asleep, so that the variety would not disturb the formula.
5. The remaining guest for the evening was, in our sample, either the pretty girl we mentioned earlier or, in about one fourth of the cases, a celebrity such as Jack Palance.

In this chapter we have considered a sample of popular Poetic games, messages generated on behalf of auditors who seek, through their encounter with the aesthetic features of the message, to revitalize their sensibilities. We began by proposing that the traditional distinction between performing arts and productive arts remained of value precisely because it aided our understanding of the experiences of the audience as spectators to the aesthetic games.

THEATER invites us to achieve a heightened awareness of our everyday game-play performance through the histrionic impersonation that lies at its core. In causing us to affirm or question the conventions and roles we take for granted in our daily game play, it opens up to expression crevices of our passions that might otherwise lie cramped and unrecognized in our souls.

ADVERTISING seen in its poetic aspect is a productive art that enhances our sensibilities and expands our imaginative capacities as a by-product of its avowed function of celebrating or memorializing sponsors and their products. Advertisements incorporate many traditional poetic tactics in their efforts to charm and entertain, if not to seduce an audience into taking a given product to heart. Although we would not go so far as to claim that advertisers have any altruistic motives in so entertaining the audience, the generally high level of artistic talent employed frequently assures that advertising messages will exhibit elements of beauty that can only enrich and rejuvenate spectators who are engaged by them.

MASS ENTERTAINMENT includes a vast and diverse array of poetic messages, but on the whole they prove to be less recreational and more amusing than either theater or advertising. What passes for entertainment on television, for instance, tends to be so designed that revitalizing emotional participation is minimized on the part of the audience, and the spectator is left only with the option of consuming a product with limited emotional potential. In this regard, mass entertainment treats its audience as if an impersonal game were being played, with little regard for the auditor's self-image or topic-image or even the image of the message source. Unlike theater and advertising, that strive at times to offer the auditor aesthetic gratification, the vast bulk of mass entertainment seems to settle for customers who do not complain about the product. The product itself tends too often to empty chatter that is consumed by individuals who do not apply aesthetic or emotional discrimination to it.

11

Rhetoric Games: Publicity and Political Dialog

Rhetoric public games are those whose telos is consensus: The messages generated invite the participants to experience political intent.

We shall turn our consideration now to the second general category of public communication games, those that we have labeled *Rhetoric games.* We have already suggested that Rhetoric games alter the beliefs or conduct of men through persuasion. Before we examine some specific Rhetoric games, we should like to describe more precisely the characteristics that typify the rhetorical messages that the games generate and the features that distinguish our experience of Rhetoric games from our experience of other public communication games.

It is, of course, possible to recognize some degree of persuasive intent or persuasive consequence in virtually every public message. We could, for instance, view a simple road sign ("Hennepin Avenue Next Right") as "persuasive" insofar as it alters a driver's conduct by encouraging him to turn off the highway at the proper exit. Our interest in this chapter, however, is limited to those messages in which perceived persuasive intention or persuasive consequence is the *dominant* aspect.

Recall our earlier distinctions between Poetic, Rhetoric, and Dialectic public games. We suggested that situations in which absolute certainty is not a possibility—situations in which truth is necessarily only probable or contingent—are the situations that give rise to Rhetoric games. In such ambiguous circumstances, men play Rhetoric games in an effort to arrive at a common view of the problem before them and of the appropriate response to it. The telos of these games is consensus—collective agreement. Rhetoric games, therefore, are necessarily "political" activities, regardless of the topic under discussion, because they are attempts to bring disparate individuals together into a "community" of men who are united in sharing a common view. Conversely, we cannot play a Rhetoric game without becoming, at least for the duration of play, unified with a larger faction with whom we join in sharing the particular topic being discussed. Rhetoric games thus allow their players to enter the political realm by virtue of their "fraternal" quality. The recreational outlet offered to players of Rhetoric games is the opportunity to arrive at willful consensus on matters of common action.

We may approach a given Rhetoric game, then, as a communicative activity constituted by at least three elements: a *persuader* who is carrying on public business with an *audience* by means of a *message or series of messages*. The persuader's decision to enter the public arena with *this particular message* and an auditor's decision to attend to *this particular message* are both conscious choices. A given rhetorical message, therefore, has a two-directional, Janus-like, quality about it. It simultaneously reveals information about the choice(s) of the persuader and information about the preference(s) of the auditor(s). In our present capacity as observers and consumers of public communication games, therefore, we may, on one hand, look at *a rhetorical message as a reflection of the point of view of its creator,* and inquire about the options that are available to anyone who would want to unify an audience about the topic under discussion. When we choose this perspective, we ask how a persuader adapts and appeals to an audience in order to make his interpretation of reality attractive to them. Alternatively, we may as observers prefer to look at *a rhetorical message apart from its creator*—to consider how the message and its public *find* and *make* each other. From this perspective, we ask how and why groups of message-consuming individuals cluster around commercial, political, erotic, or supernatural images; why they deliberately and repeatedly seek out some particular message elements in preference to other available images that they *could* choose but do not. When we adopt this second perspective, our interest is to discover what dramatically appealing themes are manifested in the message that could engage the attention of individuals and unify them into a "public" for the interpretation of the reality that is offered by the message.[1]

FOUR RHETORIC GAMES

In Chapters 11 and 12 we shall draw upon both points of view as we consider four specific Rhetoric games that seem to span the spectrum of possibilities for human re-creation (see Chapter 9) and for willful influence: the rhetoric of the *marketplace* (where messages are employed in the service of commercial enterprises), the rhetoric of the *forum* (where messages are employed in the conduct of public affairs), the rhetoric of the *soul* (where messages are employed in the conduct of the various healing arts), and the rhetoric of the *sewer* (where messages are employed in the service of counterfeit political gratification). In each game we shall consider how the game and its tactics contribute to the recreative aim of maintaining the convivial[2] conditions that are so necessary for united political action by free men. First, however, let us begin with a few general observations that apply in some degree to most Rhetoric games.

THREE FACTORS IN RHETORIC GAMES

So far we have said that rhetorical messages are, by and large, assertive interpretations of reality that deal with matters whose resolution is probable or contingent rather than certain. To clarify further the nature of the experience of Rhetoric games, let us now add to this description by considering the role of three other factors that converge in Rhetoric games: (1) the pleasure/pain principle, (2) the potential for fraternal gratification, and (3) the influence of the communicator's presence.

---

[1] These two critical perspectives are by no means exhaustive of the range of options available to observers of rhetorical messages. For a discussion of the full spectrum of critical alternatives, see Chapter 13.

[2] We are using "convivial" here to refer to the sense of communion the individual must feel with community endeavor if he is to enter actively into public affairs. See R. McKeon, *Thought, Action, and Passion* (Chicago: University of Chicago Press, 1954), pp. 30–53.

The Pleasure/Pain Principle

The pleasure/pain principle is the one basic persuasive principle in which all Rhetoric games have their origin. Simply stated, this principle says that: *The human organism strives to achieve, possess, or become that which offers pleasure, happiness, or good; the organism also strives to avoid, reject, or destroy that which offers pain, unhappiness, or evil.*[3] This key observation about human behavior, which underlies all contemporary theories of rhetorical discourse, is obviously not esoteric. It merely suggests that if someone believes that a particular person, place, idea, or thing has certain good attributes, then he will try to emulate, possess, or be associated with it. And to the extent that he believes that there are bad attributes related to some other person, place, idea, or thing, he will try, instead, to avoid, if not to dispose of, it.

Rhetoric games use, follow, or take for granted this pleasure/pain principle; each game in one fashion or another conforms to the principle in the generation of messages for the audience. A player tries to link an assertion with all the good attributes he or she possibly can and to disassociate it from any potentially bad attributes.

A good example of the pleasure/pain principle in action is provided in Meredith Willson's hit musical comedy *The Music Man*. Obviously, *The Music Man* is essentially a poetic message, not a rhetorical one. The music and lyrics function within the context of a performance of the play primarily to entertain the audience, not to persuade or to instruct them. Early in the action of the play a con man, Professor Harold Hill, sets out to convince the citizens of River City that they ought to buy his product—musical instruments and band uniforms. So far as we know, no member of the play's audience ever went out and bought a single band instrument or uniform as a result of witnessing Harold Hill's pitch in *The Music Man*. However, our focus is not upon Willson's musical comedy and its audience, but upon the interaction between Harold Hill and *his* audience *within* the play. They are engaged in a Rhetoric game.

As the opening move in his rhetorical effort, Professor Hill interprets the existence of a pool hall in the town as fraught with danger, pointing out how it creates a situation filled with many evils.[4] In a long speech

---

[3] This psychological pronouncement is by no means "new": It was enunciated by the ancient Greeks, later affirmed by the Epicureans, and has been echoed more recently by the eighteenth-century utilitarian philosophers—notably Jeremy Bentham and David Hume.

[4] See the original cast recording of *The Music Man*, Capital Records, no. SW 990, side 1, band 3.

Professor Hill shows the town residents the negative features that attend a pool hall—alcohol, gambling, neglect of duties, cursing, and the like. He presumes that the citizens will dislike such evils and that they will want to disassociate their town from them.

His next move is to offer a proposal to alleviate the problem. He associates the presence of his product (band instruments and uniforms) in the town with pleasures that will counteract the sinfulness of the pool hall. The "Music Man" suggests that if the parents of River City were to adopt his proposal of a boys' band, not only would they be able to eliminate the conditions that had been corrupting their children, but they would also be able to provide an atmosphere conducive to good citizenship and fun for all.

It is unfortunate that the bads and goods are not always as easily distinguished as Harold Hill suggests. In many persuasive situations, a given characteristic can be either bad or good depending on the standard of evaluation that is chosen. For example, an increased federal budget can be bad for economic reasons but be good for humanitarian reasons. Or, one producer can brag that his product is re-usable while another can brag with equal enthusiasm that his is disposable. One product sells because it is "new and improved," while another is just as successful because it is "the old reliable." A luxury automobile can be bad because it is neither economical nor easy to park, while it can be good because it is roomier and holds the road. One cigarette sells because it is a silly "millimeter longer," another claims that it is "5 millimeters shorter," and yet another asserts, "It's not how long you make it."

In spite of these conflicting claims, we are still able to make some kind of decision and sometimes to be reasonably content with our choice. And in the right conditions, some of the choices we make may even be radically different from those that we have made in the past. The following formula has been used for nearly forty years as a way to elaborate the pleasure/pain principle and apply it to analyzing common patterns in Rhetoric game-play situations. Once again, we offer what is admittedly a simple formula for use as a general guide to rhetorical messages—not a set of exhaustive categories. It provides a handy rule of thumb for generating strategies in persuasion situations:[5]

1. Catch the attention of the audience.
2. Establish the need or describe the problem.

---

[5] Alan H. Monroe, *Principles and Types of Speech* (New York: Scott, Foresman and Company, 1939).

3. Propose a plan or solution to alleviate the problem.
4. Visualize the plan—illustrate how the good solution can eliminate the bad problem.
5. Call the audience to action.

Returning to *The Music Man* example, we can see all five discrete
steps in Harold Hill's message to the people of River City (in a real life
situation these five steps might comprise the stages of an extended
advertising campaign): He (1) calls attention to himself and to the pool
table. Then he (2) establishes a need by describing all the evils caused by
the presence of a pool hall in town. Next he (3) asserts that the
townspeople can avoid the evils they despise by organizing a boys' band
and buying his uniforms and instruments. He then (4) visualizes the
excitement and thrills of his proposals—the glittering trombones, rolling
drums, prancing horses, and flashy uniforms. He implies that not only
will the sins of the pool hall be erased, but that many good things will
accompany the band as well. Finally, Professor Hill (5) calls the community to action, saying in effect, "Here I am; buy my uniforms and instruments."

So far, we have seen that persuasive messages are all, in one form or
another, shaped by the pleasure/pain principle: They attempt to associate
the *communicator's* product or proposal with the *listeners'* notions of
happiness. At the same time, the messages seek to disassociate such
notions of happiness from those products or proposals that the communicator opposes. Most writers on the subject of rhetoric have felt that
these tactics of associating and disassociating were at the core of all
rhetorical messages. Indeed, most criticisms of Rhetoric games have
resembled our earlier remarks about the lack of nourishment provided by
ritual-like amusements; the claim is often made that such manipulative
communication, such "mere rhetoric," is an inferior activity that neither
gratifies personal recreative urges nor serves the needs of society.[6]

Such disparagement of Rhetoric games would be well founded were
rhetoric nothing *more* than a matter of manipulating people according to

---

[6] In one of the earliest of such critiques, Plato, in his dialog *Gorgias,* claims, especially in
a democracy, that the Rhetoric game is just so much spicy entertainment, bombast and
glitter, that persuaders seldom treat matters of substance (which would nourish in the
fashion of meat and vegetables), that Rhetoric players get too caught up in self-display of
their acrobatic adeptness at making connections like Professor Hill's, and so miss the
realm of serious ideas and of truth. Plato, *Gorgias,* 517; see also W. J. Oates, "Classical
Theories of Communication," in L. Bryson, ed., *The Communication of Ideas* (New York:
Cooper Square, 1964), pp. 27–36; R. W. Quimby, "The Growth of Plato's Perception of
Rhetoric," *Philosophy and Rhetoric* 7(Spring 1974): 71–79.

the pleasure/pain principle and the five-step formula provided by the motivated sequence. In that case, rhetorical messages would appeal only to our hedonistic impulses and fail to meet our needs for the companionship of others in willful action. And it is true that if we were to confine our analysis only to the messages produced in Rhetoric games (rather than considering the games themselves), we would be tempted to regard persuasive manipulation as the crux of rhetorical discourse.

But at its inception rhetoric was understood in a radically different way, as a means of publicly consummating good fellowship among free men. A look at its history to see how rhetoric was very early formulated into a tool for political action will help us to distinguish the recreative elements from the purely persuasive ones and will help us to clarify the revitalizing potentials from the formal structures of rhetorical messages.

Fraternal Gratification

Some of the earliest systematic accounts of the Rhetoric game were described by the ancient Greeks, who are said to have invented rhetoric during the course of the Trojan War. In the course of periodic war councils the participants became aware of several things. For one, in addition to coordinating battle tactics, the Greeks began to develop a sense of community (so much so that henceforth they were to see themselves and their blood relatives as being a distinct group—called the *Hellenes*, quite apart from other men who were now to be called *Barbarians*). For another thing, they became aware that they had evolved a new sort of game, just as difficult in its own way as physical combat—the game of public persuasion. Men who followed Achilles and other leaders did so as free men, without being forced (in contrast to Barbarians, who obeyed out of fear of their masters). Hellenes were influenced, not coerced; they followed leaders who were physically strong and brave, and clever in words.

Note here how the seeds of a public rhetorical tradition originally developed in contrast with that of Harold Hill's simple salesmanship. First, those taking part in the deliberations were peers; each man had a right to participate in the discussion, each had a degree of independence, and each was accorded a degree of respect appropriate to his authority. Secondly, the participants met as a deliberative body charged with making definite decisions. That is to say, they constituted a representative assembly charged with making choices in the name of all the Greek soldiers. Thirdly, their rhetorical activity focused on the future, for the deliberations were about what battle plan to adopt. In this, the Greeks had learned the secret essential to political power. For whereas in the past each Greek had acted alone to change the world, and was thus effective only in proportion to his isolated strength, the Greek warriors had found a way to act in common on the world, and this consensus of wills (as contrasted with mere physical strength) became the foundation for power. It was clear even then that the creation of power by the voluntary uniting of wills was a vastly significant force for confronting the world. This is to say that even the process of achieving agreement (or of arriving at a common decision) was a major force for influencing the shape of the future (which in human affairs is always contingent and thus open to human choice). Finally, the Greeks found that verbal interaction was a lot of fun. Not only did the system of planning work; many of the chiefs found that they enjoyed the deliberations of the morning as much as they relished the slaughter later in the day. Indeed, the whole mythos of distinguishing themselves from Barbarians centered upon the claim that as Greeks they had discovered how to achieve agreement and concerted political action by logos (words, reason) and no longer had to rely exclusively on threats or violence—they were, in other words, more "civilized" than their barbaric counterparts.

These four qualities of the original rhetorical activity—equality, willfulness, the power of consensus, and good fellowship—have formed the spine of all political rhetoric in Western democracies down to our day. Even the court trial, which is based on an evaluation of past events to determine guilt or innocence, is in fact a force for shaping the future (by declaring the accused guilty or innocent and then disposing of the victim's grievance by a legally established procedure).

We may characterize the experience of rhetoric as *fraternal*—the affection and attachment we feel in the presence of those whom we identify as members of our community. When they speak, we are not coerced to act but we are in-spired (filled with their "breath," their spirit) by qualities they manifest that we recognize as emblems of our kinship—signs of the commonality of our life space images that distinguish us a community among mankind. Where interpersonal communication games enable us to be touched by an individual more or less intimately, Rhetoric games enable us to experience more or less fully our fraternal participation in a community.[7]

---

[7] Aristotle, *Nichomachean Ethics*, 1159ᵇ30–35.

Presence

We have so far suggested that Rhetoric games in one degree or another rely upon the pleasure/pain principle and invite an engagement of the spirit of brotherly comradeship among those who play them. At this point we wish to explore one final feature of Rhetoric games that contributes to their recreational potential, and that is *presence*—the enchantment that may be produced by the speaker's immediate physical appearance and action before an audience. Admittedly, part of a speaker's capacity to persuade an audience arises from his or her ability to use threats and to make simple pragmatic or hedonistic appeals. No less significant a part of the speaker's power to influence an audience resides in his or her ability to charm them through the virtuosity of his or her performance. The Belgian philosopher Chaim Perelman has sought to restore this notion of "presence" to our thinking; he reaches for the root component of the experience this way:

> By the very fact of selecting certain elements and presenting them to the audience, their importance and pertinency to the discussion are implied. Indeed, such a choice endows these elements with a *presence*, which is an essential factor in argumentation and one that is far too much neglected in rationalistic conceptions of reasoning.
> . . . It is not enough indeed that a thing should exist for a person to feel its presence. . . . Accordingly one of the preoccupations of a speaker is to make present, by verbal magic alone, what is actually absent but what he considers important . . . or, by making them more present, to enhance the value of some of the elements of which one has actually been made conscious.[8]

The relation, just hinted at here, between consciousness and the speaker's ability to enchant his or her listeners is extremely subtle. Once again, we can best explore it by recourse to the original Rhetoric game.

As the Rhetoric game became more popular with the Greeks (after the Trojan War) there arose a profession of coaches and professional players of the game. Called *sophists* (literally "wise men"), they took as their domain the "mind" (in a special sense that we shall shortly explain). They claimed that in teaching a citizen to converse more persua-

---

[8] C. Perelman and L. Olbrechts-Tyteca, *The New Rhetoric: A Treatise on Argumentation*, trans. J. Wilkinson and P. Weaver (Notre Dame, Ind.: University of Notre Dame Press, 1969), pp. 116–117. See also T. Mader, "On Presence in Rhetoric," *College Composition and Communication* 24(December 1973): 375–381, for an excellent extension of the notion from language itself to the speaker's very appearance as an instrument of influence.

sively they were actually developing his keenness, his capacity to remain alert and aware in the company of his comrades. And because in the ancient world the words *conscious* and *conscience* were equivalent (if a man were *aware* of moral implications it was presumed that he would *obey* his moral instincts), sophists came to be seen as teachers of virtue as well as developers of alert thinking and discourse.

Because they traveled from town to town teaching their art, they observed that the ground rules for such things as proper dress, conversation, and polite manners were conventions that varied greatly from place to place. As they came to realize how arbitrary such habits were, they took on the appearance of "city slickers," who remained skeptical of local customs, yet were also too quick and alert to be bested in sharp conversation. So in some respects the sophist came to be viewed with resentment and suspicion that he had to overcome with a certain gracefulness and charm if the well-to-do residents were to agree to send him their sons for instruction.

The essence of the original Rhetoric game, then, was a virtuoso performance which of itself replenished its captivated listeners by the very charm of the performance. There was thus a seductive quality over and above the simple hedonistic association of pleasures and pains and fraternal gratification of free discourse. The audience was also renewed by the very presence of a clever speaker; they were enhanced through their contact with a man of excellence.

What was the character of this presence? What natural attractiveness were the sophists able to employ to captivate otherwise suspicious townsfolk in order to win them over, apart from any formal arguments other teachers may have offered in their own behalf? As best we can tell, it had less to do with clever speech than it did with the sophists' physical appearance. For the Greeks, the word *soma* (corpse, body) meant literally "skin and limbs" and *psyche* (soul, life) referred to "breath and motion." Thus, to be alive, to have presence in the world, was both to *appear* (skin) and to *be active* (limbs in motion); and what distinguished a sheer carcass from a living creature was this dual capacity to move in the world and to speak (act among men in a public setting).[9]

---

[9] See R. M. Pirsig, *Zen and the Art of Motorcycle Maintenance* (New York: Morrow, 1974), pp. 367–380; G. B. Kerford, "Sophists," *The Encyclopedia of Philosophy*, VII, pp. 494–496. There is ample evidence that the early Greeks recognized and appreciated this aspect of charm in the Rhetoric game. See also Pedro Lain Entralgo, *The Therapy of the Word in Classical Antiquity* (New Haven: Yale University Press, 1970), pp. 22–63; Oates, p. 32; Plato, *Euthydemus*, 289A–290A; Parmenides, Fragment No. 16; and Bruno Snell, *The Discovery of the Mind*, trans. T. G. Rosenmeyer (1953; New York: Harper and Row, 1960), pp. 5–19.

Presence was thus a matter of how the players of the Rhetoric game appeared in the world of their fellows, of how the citizen spectators were enchanted with the speakers so that they were *willingly* influenced by the speakers' advice in matters of public (political) concern. But to say that rhetoric involves appearances (or more precisely, presence), which would hardly be denied by a sophist, is not to say that it is a false or sham art as Plato and its other detractors have claimed.[10] It is only to contend that in democratic societies, where all men are presumed to share a fraternal equality, spectators to Rhetoric games are reinvigorated when a speaker can so charm them that they willingly reach out and join with him in some action, as much in appreciation of the game and his presence as for the goods or pleasures he associates with the proposals contained in his speech.

In summary, we may thus conclude that Rhetoric games fulfill their recreative function to the extent that they incorporate the three factors we have been considering. First, Rhetoric games employ the pleasure/pain principle to motivate an audience to willingly accept some proposals and to reject others. Secondly, Rhetoric games enable the audience to experience the fraternal gratifications that come when free men willingly join as equals to create consensus. Thirdly, the most exhilarating Rhetoric games will also enable the speakers to display their virtuosity by their very presence, to captivate the audience with the deftness of the persuasive performance itself. To the extent that a particular Rhetoric game does not recreate in this fashion, it will provide its audience with the experience of a ritual instead of renewal. We are now in a position to examine various Rhetoric games in an effort to discover what recreational value each contains because of the inclusion or absence of these three fundamental features.

Let us begin with a very popular Rhetoric game, the rhetoric of the marketplace, which relies almost exclusively on the pleasure/pain principle and which displays very little regard either for the audience's sense

---

[10] It is in these terms that one can understand the interesting "stage directions" Plato provides in his dialogs. For example, in the dialog *Protagoras* when he has Socrates meet the eminent sophist Protagoras, he describes Protagoras as moving gracefully around a room making grand gestures—and as he moves he is followed by a train of acolytes moving as a chorus line in imitation of him. Protagoras, regarded as a fine rhetorician, is demonstrating his graceful style (or appearance), and his students are seeking to develop a comparable coordination. Again, after Protagoras has delivered his famous speech explaining his art, Socrates remarks that, because he has sat quietly enchanted by Protagoras, his mind is numb, and it will take a moment of conversation to revive it. In this dialog, as in others, Plato has Socrates engage in discussion with the sophist and show that the "art" of rhetoric they teach is a mere art of appearances, lacking in any theoretical or formal substance.

of comradeship or for the rhetorical presence of the performance. In its most common form this game is known as Publicity.

RHETORIC OF THE MARKETPLACE: PUBLICITY

We have already suggested that one of the most prevalent Poetic games is advertising, yet it is apparent that corporations do not spend enormous sums just to create poetry. Few firms are prepared to spend $100,000 just to produce an attractive television commercial for one minute of entertainment. The sponsor's avowed purpose is rhetorical: He wishes to influence the public.

The five-step formula that we discussed earlier is a convenient way to understand in general terms how the persuasive strategy is commonly employed, not only when others try to sell us something, but when we have something to urge on others. However, there are important tactical variations in its application in different Rhetoric games. The first Rhetoric game we shall consider is *publicity*, in which the formula is severely compressed, and in which we as consuming public are given the smallest number of options for response to the message. In the contemporary commercial realm the space and time needed to present persuasive messages are so expensive that few advertisers can afford to present as complete a message as that of the "Music Man," Harold Hill (and, indeed, few consumers would likely devote the energy needed to hear out such a lengthy message). In addition, advertising is usually promoting competing brands of a particular product (be it cigarettes, laundry soap, hygiene spray, razor blades, or political candidates) that are qualitatively similar to their competitors. Publicity is thus a persuasive game employed to cope with these conditions.

The origins of publicity can perhaps tell us a good deal about its character. The word *publicity* itself derives from the Latin *publica* or "folk." The term probably originally referred to the spread of rumors or gossip among the commoners (as distinguished from the active citizens who took part in the discussions of the Roman forum). It gained currency at the end of the Middle Ages when individuals began to move about the countryside with less fear. At that time it became common for craftsmen and innkeepers to post signs outside their establishments to announce to travelers the availability of services. (Thus, a large wooden boot would indicate a cobbler.) This central function of announcement has remained with publicity to this day, as can be seen in the remarkable variety of posters, billboards, bus ads, road signs, and the like that are in toto the most common vehicles for advertising.

Of course as man's means of transportation evolved and increased in speed, the character of publicity also developed. In fact, as announcements from the eighteenth, nineteenth, and twentieth centuries indicate, the shift of the traveler from a pedestrian, who could stop and examine an ad at close range, to a rider in a horse drawn buggy, to the early auto, to our own age of high-speed turnpikes and plane travel have meant that publicity (and not just poster advertising) has increased in size, intensity, emphasis on form, and simplicity, all in the interest of simply catching the traveler's eye.

But with these stylistic developments, the essential *announcing* character of publicity has remained. For one thing, publicity has always functioned as a "broad-casting" form of address; it is intended for the public at large in distinction to such forms of address as telephones and mail, which are addressed to particular individuals. For another thing, publicity contains within itself no logical place for a response or feedback from a receiver of the message. As publicity consumers, we may not even have much choice about ignoring the message, as its effect on our awareness is often not even a conscious one, and we may respond more out of habit than from active interest. What is at stake with advertising, be it by sign or poster, is the hope that the consumer, taking notice, will purchase some product or service; but there is no expectation that the consumer will in any manner enter into a dialog or in any other way seek to modify the original message. Thirdly, publicity functions as fortuitous communication—by and large individuals "happen upon" it, and those individuals are in no way charged with making any significant public decision (as are the jurors in a trial or the members of a board of education). The receiver of publicity makes decisions that are in the main personal—concerning what purchases he may make to increase his creature comfort. Finally, the subject of publicity tends to be a product or service already in existence that the owner is seeking to distribute; publicity can thus be said to follow upon events—it brings to our notice that which *is* (be it a new brand of toothpaste or the decision of an oil company to act in an ecologically responsible way); any given publicity message is, for the most part, the end product of events rather than a significant shaper of those events. With these qualities in mind it may be easier to understand the persuasive character of most of the publicity we encounter.

Tactics of Publicity

Three tactics of publicity are: gaining and maintaining attention, arousing existing needs, and linking the product and the attribute through slogans.

Gaining and Maintaining Attention.   The first characteristic that distinguishes publicity from more traditional Rhetorical games is the greater priority given by publicity to gain and maintain attention; a publicity message is not *of itself* persuasive. If we know, for example, that the President is about to deliver a speech in which he plans to explain his new economic policy, we presume that he will not have to try to catch our attention with a corny joke. People who want to hear what the new Presidential policy is going to be will attend to him regardless of his introductory remarks. Those who are disinterested in the policy will likely avoid or ignore his speech from the start.

The opposite is true for most publicity—messages whose emphasis on attention is at times almost total. We need not elaborate the techniques that publicists employ to gain attention because we have already discussed them at length as the poetics of print and broadcast advertising. At this point it is enough to say that at one time or another every advertiser has challenged the limits of his creative imagination in order to find ways to bring his product to our attention. The Chanel No. 5 and Del Monte Peas ads suggest this diversity and illustrate the preeminence of attention-getting in the completed message. Notice how little is actually said about Chanel No. 5 perfume. This ad is publicity at its simplest: The purpose is to take a product already in existence and bring it to public attention.

Furthermore, when something *is* said, it is often insignificant. Does the "quiz" on peas serve any real educational purpose other than to bring the can of Del Monte Sweet Peas into focus?

Even better examples of publicity's emphasis on attention-getting are found in radio and television commercials. To combat the popular practices of leaving the room during commercial breaks or having the radio on merely as background noise, broadcast publicity is often louder and/or more creative than the regular programming. Although it is difficult to duplicate this 30-second radio spot with the charm and flair it deserves, it is still possible to see how it can grab our attention and yet accomplish little more than a favorable emotional response to the commercial and, perhaps, to Laura Scudder's Potato Chips:

Child: "I'm serious . . . I'm going."

Mother: "You can't run away from home on an empty stomach."

Child: "I'm not hungry."

Mother: "Let me fix a sandwich. You can take it with you."

Child: "Well, maybe I'll take some Laura Scudder's Potato Chips."

Mother: "We're all out. But I'm going to the market tomorrow.
    Can't you wait until then to run away?"

Child: "Mmmm . . . I wanna leave now."

Mother: "Well, goodbye."

Child: "Aren't you going to drive me?"[11]

---

[11] Doyle Dane Bernbach, in *Best TV and Radio Commercials*, W. Ross, ed. (New York: Hastings House, 1969), p. 137.

Can you see what's wrong with these peas?

They're below Del Monte Brand standards. Crowded and misshapen.
This indicates the peas are over mature, tough and starchy.

The more you know
about peas,
the better for Del Monte.

No effort is made to suggest that we need potato chips or that Laura Scudder's Potato Chips are even the best potato chips. But if we can remember the name of the product, if it has been adequately publicized, the ad is a success. In a market of hundreds of competing products, the Laura Scudder name must register. Thanks to publicity, brand consciousness is a significant feature of American life.

Arousing Existing Needs.   A second, corollary shift in emphasis is that, unlike traditional rhetorical forms, in publicity there is seldom any effort to demonstrate that a need actually does exist. Publicity messages do not try to convince consumers that there is a problem which must be solved. These messages assume that as the consumers of products we are the experts about our needs. The most any given advertisement can do is to *remind us that we already have a need*. If we happen to need a certain product, an advertisement can bring that need to our attention. If we do not have a need, then the advertisement will have no effect on us.

Consider, for example, a hypothetical billboard urging you to eat a particular brand of bread. Assume that a man sees this billboard as he drives home every day. If he happens to be driving home around 2:00 P.M., after lunch, he *may* notice the billboard. It might catch his attention because the figure is cute, the lettering is clever, or whatever. But the ad can have no other effect on him. It may momentarily distract his eyes from the road, but that is all.

If, on the other hand, he should notice this as he is driving home hungry at 5:00 P.M., the billboard might remind him that he is hungry or that he is out of bread at home and that he should stop at a supermarket. When he arrives at the market, he may buy this kind of bread or the sign might have reminded him that he needed to buy some other kind of bread or even some other product (jam, perhaps, or even green ribbon bows). And when he finally gets home, he may not even eat the bread but might satisfy his hunger with something else.

In other words, the sign has made no effort to prove to him that he needs bread, that bread will satisfy his hunger any more than any other product, or that this type of bread is somehow better than all other breads. All that billboard has done is to bring the product to his attention and remind him that if he in fact needs bread, he might try this brand.

Hundreds of magazines are filled with ads stressing pre-existent needs like the Christine Valmy Skin Care ad. We have all seen them, yet how many of us can honestly say that we have mailed in the coupons to request the special acne creams, muscle builders, tooth polishes, or hair restorers? Unless a reader already hopes to improve his or her complexion, sagging physique, yellowing teeth or baldness, he or she will not be affected by ads of this sort. They may be entertaining and catch our attention, but they will not be persuasive.

Although the Maidenform ad may catch the eye of its male audiences, does it persuade them to purchase Maidenform underwear? It might make them wish their wives had better figures or give them the idea to give underwear as a gift, but is it possible that the ad alone could

Ecology comes to SKIN CARE

INTRODUCING
CHRISTINE VALMY
Natural, Byogenic™ Face Treatment

A complete at-home skin care program for

ACNE

Pimples, Blemishes, Blackheads, even Cystic Acne

Here at last, a clean skin guarantee through ecology. A tested, 6-step home cleansing method for acne skin developed over the past 20 years by European skin care specialist Christine Valmy. Not a cover-up. . .not a medication, the all-new Valmy method has already helped thousands of acne sufferers to soothe, smooth and protect their skin with gentle deep cleansing. The secret is a proved all-natural approach through byogenic™ treatment.

SAY NO TO "ACNE DIETS", ABRASIVE SOAPS, RINSE-AWAY MASKS, COSTLY FAD TREATMENTS

It's a fact that air pollution, chemicals, drying soaps and other unnatural agents are deadly enemies of clear, glowing skin. The Valmy method approaches the task

of cleansing skin in today's environment with a totally unique idea. BYOGENIC skin care. The new, all-natural way to clean acne skin as no other chemical or artificial method can.

FIND OUT THE DO's AND DON'Ts OF DEEP PORE CLEANSING, MAINTAINING PROPER ACID MANTLE, VEGETALE SKIN TONING, SEBUM CONTROL, NATURE'S EMULSIFIERS, SKIN VITAMINS
and much more!

So many people are joining the move to hygienically-clean skin—THE BYOGENIC WAY—that Christine Valmy has prepared a documented FREE FACT KIT of byogenic information, illustrations, testimonials, case histories and more that fully explain her unique method of scientific

skin care. IT'S FREE. Never before has such informative material been made available to the general public.

TO GET YOUR COPY just clip and mail the coupon below and this information will be rushed to you right away. See how clean skin is possible—even for "hopeless" cases—with Christine Valmy's all-new breakthrough in skin care: BYOGENIC FACE TREATMENT.

NATURE LOVES YOUR SKIN. FIND OUT FREE HOW BYOGENIC™ SKIN CARE WORKS

Don't delay. This information is available only through Christine Valmy and has already helped thousands of acne sufferers across the country who had tried everything until ecology came to skin care. *We know we can help you.*

JUST RECEIVED!

Actual excerpts from unsolicited letters received from users of the unique Valmy byogenic method

". . .I am completely amazed with your treatment. My complexion is completely cleared and I just love it. . ." **B.G., Endicott, N.Y.**

". . .thank you for my 'new complexion'. . . it's a miracle! My skin hasn't looked so smooth and glowing since I was a child. . ." **J.M., Phoenix, Ariz.**

"I'm actually receiving compliments on my complexion, which hasn't been clear of acne for well over 10 years. . ."
L.H., El Paso, Texas
Names and addresses available on request.

". . .I have been using your method for only 10 days and my skin is better than it's been in 15 years. My husband and I are jumping with joy! Thank you. . ."
Mrs. G.M., Hawthorne, Calif.

". . .I could not believe that any method, be it scientific or not, had been developed to stop acne. . .Thank you again. . .My only regret is that I did not discover your method 10 years ago. . ."
A.Z., La Habra, Ca.

Ultra Salon Face Treatment in New York

When in New York visit our scientific skin care salon, and discover the new byogenic™ way to possess enchanting skin with Euro-

pean souplesse. Call (212) 581-9488 for a private consultation with your very own dermaspecialist. **Christine Valmy Salon, 157 W. 57th St., N.Y., N.Y. 10019**

CLIP & MAIL TODAY!

55

TO: Christine Valmy Skin Care
157 West 57th Street
New York, N.Y. 10019

© 1971, Christine Valmy Inc.

Yes, I want to learn how to attain clear skin the byogenic way. Please rush your FREE Fact Kit of information right away.

Name_____

Address_____

City_____

State_____ Zip_____

'Here's looking at you!'

SEA DREAM® COLLECTION BY maidenform

'Here's Looking at You!'™ demi-bra. Softly underwired. Shimmery, stretchy Antron† and Lycra† tricot. Plum Perfect, Red, Taupe, White. ABC, $6.50, D, $7.50. One-size-fits-all bikini, $3.

create a need in them for Maidenform products? Or, more fairly, what kinds of needs does the ad try to establish in its female audiences? Does it persuade the woman who has just purchased a lot of lingerie that she bought the wrong kind or that she needs more? Does it persuade the liberated female that she needs *any*? We would argue that it is more accurate to say that this example of publicity awakens a pre-existent, latent desire for bras and girdles and that it merely seeks to attract attention and to link desirable attributes with the name Maidenform.

The Curity Gauze Diaper ad is an attention-getting ad, even though more complicated, and is yet another good example of publicity. Is it able to sell diapers to anyone who has no use for them? Even if you have no contact with babies, does the ad convince you that you have a need for diapers anyway? It is true that the ad offers considerable proof for its claim that cloth diapers are more desirable than disposable diapers. But this claim is not to be confused with an attempt to establish an objective need for Curity diapers. This kind of proof is valuable only for people who already have such a need to make the decision between cloth and disposable diapers. In other words, the ad incorporates no attempt to sell diapers themselves; there is merely an effort to sell a certain type. As a matter of fact, it is possible for a concerned parent to read this ad, decide that cloth diapers are best, and then purchase some brand other than Curity.

Curity Diapers feel like fresh air and sunshine.

It's healthy to expose baby's tender bottom to air and sunlight. But unless you live on a South Sea island, your child can't go naked all the time. The best thing next to his birthday suit is a Curity Diaper.

That pure white cotton gauze is soft as a caress. Always feels light and airy, natural as a second skin. So absorbent, it keeps baby cozier between changes. And it gets even softer with wear.

Cloth diapers are more economical than disposables. You can recycle five dozen Curity Diapers, saving at least $234 in the 27 months the average child uses them. Then save them for your next baby, or give them to your sister or a friend. They're too good to throw away. Don't take our word for it - ask your mother! Kendall

CURITY ® gauze diapers

For the most part, publicity is competition for brand loyalty. As we mentioned earlier, brand consciousness is a significant feature of American life. Ads for cigarettes, alcoholic beverages, and automobiles are noteworthy examples. Little attempt is made to convince the audiences that they should smoke, drink, or ride in cars. Instead, the advertisements depend on audiences that already have an interest in smoking, drinking, or driving. The Early Times ad, for example, will not persuade a teetotaler to buy whisky, let alone Early Times. Similarly, shrewd automobile advertisers recognize that it is no longer necessary to convince potential buyers that cars are a desirable means of transportation; their major purpose is to publicize the appearance and name of a particular make of car. In other words, rather than asserting, "You need our *product*," these ads claim, "You need our *brand*."

Ads that publicize brand names appeal to a different type of need than those ads that publicize particular products. Up to this point, we have been focusing on *objective needs*. Needs of this type are for things we can point to—objects or activities for which we have referents in the real world. The ad for Joy perfume, for example, relies on an objective need for perfume; if a reader has been thinking about purchasing some perfume, the ad might catch her attention.

But we also have *subjective needs*. Subjective needs are internal; they do not exist in the real world. In this category are needs for such things as emotional security, self-esteem, higher social status, and sexual reassurance. Brand name publicity often relies on subjective needs like these. The ad for Joy appeals not only to a need for perfume, but also to a subjective need for lavish personal indulgence. Nevertheless, publicity here again only exploits whatever needs may exist; a given message seldom creates a subjective need.

Critics of advertising frequently assert that commercial messages make people buy things that they do not need. They claim that the "mad men" of Madison Avenue possess hidden powers that enable them to mold the minds of consumers. We would not deny that consumers often purchase items for which they have no objective need. But we would deny that the consumer was tricked, that the advertiser has some magic power. For instead of satisfying an objective need, the alleged unnecessary purchase sometimes satisfies the consumer's pre-existent subjective need.

Let us turn our attention toward advertisements for clothing. Most of these appeal to subjective needs. It is difficult to argue that someone satisfies an objective need when he or she spends $15,000 on an item from the current Yves St. Laurent collection. On the other hand, it is easier to argue that those who purchase high fashion originals or fre-

Our marriage will cause quite a stir.

THERE IS ONLY ONE JOY...
THE COSTLIEST PERFUME IN THE WORLD

quent only the "finest shops" buy more than a suit or a dress; they satisfy their subjective needs for self-respect, high social status, and so on. People who scoff at such an extravagant life style are not likely to make such purchases. Their needs for self-respect and social status, if any, will be satisfied in more modest ways. At the other extreme, there are those who will be more impressed by a recent purchase at a nearby Army surplus store or thrift shop. To the point: While everyone except the avowed nudist has the same objective need for some kind of protective clothing, each of us has different subjective needs that will influence what we buy and choose to wear. Examine the Nunn Bush ad and try to specify the kinds of subjective needs it seeks to satisfy.

Subjective needs influence more than the clothing we buy and wear.

The Cadillac advertisement, for example, appeals to one's taste for elegance; it invests the car with an aura of the "fine life." The ad is like a promise: If you purchase an Eldorado you can rest assured that you are an especially elegant person. There is probably no major objective difference between the Eldorado and the similarly high-priced, full-sized Oldsmobile 98. But notice how the ads for each appeal to different subjective needs. One reminds its readers that if they need reassurance of quality

Eldorado. For people with an instinctive taste for elegance.

A very special car for very special people. Eldorado by Cadillac. It looks to be exactly what it is—the world's most elegant personal car. And, with its 8.2 litre engine, it acts the part. Moreover, Eldorado is the only luxury car with front-wheel drive, variable-ratio power steering, and Automatic Level Control. In addition, you may now specify American-made, steel-belted radial tires (inset) for your Eldorado. Also available: a Dual Comfort front seat

and Track Master, Cadillac's skid-control braking system. As the classic coupe shown or as the only luxury convertible built in America, this is motoring at its finest. Maybe it's presumptuous to imply that any car can change your life-style. In the case of Eldorado, maybe not. Judge for yourself when you see your authorized Cadillac dealer and test-drive the Eldorado of your choice. Cadillac Motor Car Division

 Cadillac

Can a person under 30 appreciate the Oldsmobile Ninety-Eight?

Not likely. Their time will come, but not before they've really worked at it for awhile. Growing into the Ninety-Eight isn't something that happens overnight.

Living rooms on wheels.

Youth has always scoffed at the big cars, calling them, rolling palaces. Or living rooms on wheels. Sooner or later the scoffing stops and one begins to see what the Ninety-Eight is all about.

Everything is so comfortable inside, including the ride. To find out how rough the road is, you have to look. You're supported by 6 inches of contoured foam in the front seat, as you drive. Armrests and ashtrays surround you. Power steering and power brakes, with discs up front, are standard. The Ninety-Eight is indeed an elegant living room on a 127-inch wheelbase. In some ways, it's even more comfortable than your living room.

A whisper, not a whooosh.

Remember when you "cracked" the car window to get outside air and it always whooooshed inside? The Ninety-Eight has turned the whooosh to a whisper with a far better way of bringing in the air. And power ventilation circulates it continuously, whether the car is rolling up the miles or standing at a stoplight.

Working within the environment.

This year's Ninety-Eight 455 Rocket V-8 emits, on the average, 80% less hydrocarbons and 65% less carbon monoxide than engines of 10 years ago. So we can all breathe a little easier.

Within the Ninety-Eight itself, a long list of GM safety features is provided for your protection. Some, like the seat and shoulder belts, are visible; but many more, like the steel side-guard beams in the doors, are not.

A different kind of power.

When you were younger, a car that didn't lurch and rumble dramatically was devoid of power or status. The 1972 Ninety-Eight neither lurches nor rumbles; you can scarcely hear the engine from the driver's seat. Or feel the incredibly smooth automatic transmission at work. Yet, the Ninety-Eight performs better than anything you drove in your youth, and it does it in a quiet way, which is most satisfying now that your priorities are different.

A natural progression.

The Ninety-Eight is a car you're not likely to drive with the windows down, radio turned up and your elbow sticking out. There's an atmosphere of peace inside—a hospitality you can count on. Urging you to relax—and enjoy. And when you do, you'll find there's far more to a Ninety-Eight for you to enjoy.

OLDSMOBILE NINETY-EIGHT. QUITE A SUBSTANTIAL CAR.

and elegance, the Eldorado promises to be "the world's most elegant personal car." The other appeals to readers who feel insecure because their age excludes them from the cultural emphasis on youth. The ad promises that if one buys an Oldsmobile 98 he will demonstrate that he is older but wiser.

If necessary, we could comprise an extensive collection of advertisements that appeal to subjective needs. But the purpose of this discussion is not to supply such an exhaustive analysis. Our brief concern with subjective needs serves merely to elaborate the second distinguishing feature of publicity: *publicity does not create needs in its audiences; it exploits the needs* (objective or subjective) *that audiences already have.* Publicity is not in and of itself a persuasive enterprise.

Linking through Slogans. The third and final feature distinguishing publicity from other Rhetorical games involves the tactics used to link the product (X) and attribute (Y) in the consumer's mind. Most Rhetoric games, such as those commonly played in political arenas[12] try to *prove* the connection of X to Y, and thereby to raise or lower the consumer's degree of belief in the linkage. To do this, three sorts of linkages (commonly called "proofs" although they are actually psychologically bonding agents) are ordinarily conjointly employed: logical connectors, emotional connectors, and ethical connectors. *Logical* proofs include both logical inferences and evidence such as statistics or examples. *Emotional* proofs include appeals to love, hate, loyalty, envy, and greed among others. *Ethical* proofs include the influential presence of the source or his supporters (such as well-known, competent, trusted,

---

[12] One of the most interesting changes to occur in recent American public affairs has been the ever increasing intrusion of publicity tactics into political games and the consequent decline in the use of proving tactics in political dialog as advertising agencies, who are unskilled in its use, come more and more to dominate political discourse. Thus it is easy to understand why reputable scholars would describe modern political campaigning tactics as follows:

> The attempt is to show the candidate as possessing a view of the world which corresponds with that of the potential voters. Information relative to the candidate's stand on issues is interpreted as evidence of the kind of man the candidate is in respect to his potential electors, *not as proof of his qualifications to hold . . . office* per se. Just as the buyer of a television-advertised product is induced to purchase on the basis of the necessity to have or maintain a certain self-image, so the potential elector is encouraged *to vote for himself*—that is, the candidate closest to his own self-image. [Italics added.] (J. H. McBath and W. R. Fisher, "Persuasion in Presidential Campaign Communication," *Quarterly Journal of Speech* 55[February 1969]: 18.)

As J. McGinnis (*The Selling of the President, 1968* [New York: Trident, 1969]) has argued that when candidates are packaged as if they were corn flakes, we tend to consider less the extent to which we believe their assertions than we estimate how easy they are to swallow. What we swallow or ingest, is, after all, soon to become a part of us.

and/or well-liked people) who make known their agreement with the proposition under discussion. No matter what combinations of proof are used, however, they are functioning to link X and Y closer together in the public's minds.

Although, as we shall shortly illustrate, most publicity does not use proving as a linking strategy, we can at this point draw upon a few ads that do, so that you will have the tactic in mind when we consider it in relation to political Rhetoric games. The Pitney Bowes ad, for instance, is a sample of logical proofs used to persuade the reader as to the worth of a postage meter. The ad seeks to connect X (postage meters) and Y (preferable to stamps). To help raise the reader's esteem for meters over ordinary stamps, the ad offers a number of logical proofs: Meters operate any hour of the day or night; they save secretarial time; they enable the user to process letters and packages easily and quickly; metered mail is precancelled and therefore quicker.

In contrast, one ad for aspirin combines logical and ethical proof. The sponsor, seeking to refute two popular assertions (that any non-prescription pain reliever is satisfactory and that all USP-standards aspirin are alike) relies on the ethical credibility of the AMA for the layman by citing the AMA Council on Drugs to support its own claims.

But most commercial advertising does not in fact seek to increase believability. Instead of trying to change opinions (as to who is the best candidate, or which is the best law to pass, or what type of pain reliever can best counter a headache) the game we are calling Publicity seeks instead (with a few exceptions of the sort we haved noted above) to take a product or policy already in existence and bring it more vividly to the public attention. Publicity messages are found on billboards; posters; ads on buses, subway trains, and taxis; neon road signs; television; radio spots; and the like. These messages act not so much to prove as to announce: "Welcome to Centerville, City of Opportunity"; "Read the *Times*"; "Bill's Bar and Grill"; "Grandma Gus Makes Crisp Pickles"; "5 miles to Sam's Truck Stop." In none of these instances is the linkage between X and Y either fused or detached; rather, it is merely asserted.

Consequently, the proving strategy is not ordinarily employed in the Publicity game. A far more common strategy is the slogan strategy, which relies on behavioral laws of conditioning to create a minimal associative connection between product X and attribute Y. Advertisers who rely on publicity use two tactical devices to create and strengthen these associational bonds.[13] One means to establish and/or strengthen

---

[13] Whether and to what extent these tactics actually accomplish any persuasive aim is a matter that need not concern us here.

You can't buy postage that costs less.
But you can buy postage that's worth more.

It costs 8 cents to mail a first-class letter. Whether you happen to be General Electric or Sarge's Delicatessen.

You can't get a better price.

But you *can* get a better deal.

The trick is to meter all your mail instead of using stamps.

A stamp doesn't do much more than provide carfare for your letters and packages. Metered mail, on the other hand, works a lot harder.

Case in point. When your stamps run out, your secretary has to run out. A trip to the Post Office and back can take 20 minutes or more. When you're paying a girl $3.60 an hour, those 20 minutes are costing you $1.20. Or enough postage to mail 15 letters.

A Pitney Bowes postage meter can hold enough postage to make you forget what the inside of the Post Office looks like. And hold it safely, because the postage doesn't exist until you print it your-self. In any denomination. At any hour of the day or night.

Not only can our postage meter save your secretary time, it can save your mail time. Stamped mail goes through a number of steps on its way through the Post Office. But our postage meter eliminates some of these steps by dating, cancelling and postmarking your mail at the same time that it prints the postage. Metered mail is shortcut mail, often getting to its destination faster than stamped mail.

There's a morale factor connected with metered mail, too. No secretary likes to lick stamps and envelope flaps, not even the most devoted one. With a Pitney Bowes Touchmatic Postage Meter, tap, tap, tap, she touches a few buttons and the job is done. The letters and packages go out looking neater and more business-like, too.

You don't have to be a big company to get the big benefits of metered mail.

One third of the users of our postage meters spend less than a dollar a day on postage.

When you use a Pitney Bowes postage meter instead of stamps, you're not exactly being a pioneer. Almost half the mail in the country is metered. You're not the only one who wants more for his money.

For information, write Pitney Bowes, 1269 Pacific Street, Stamford, Conn., 06904, or call any one of our 190 offices throughout the U.S. and Canada.

 **Pitney Bowes**
POSTAGE METERS

Mailing Equipment, Copiers, Counters and Imprinters, Addresser-Printers. Labeling and Marking Systems.

the association between product and attribute is the law of *contiguity*. The law states that the closer in space and/or time a product and attribute are presented, the greater the probability that the consumer will associate the two. A second means of strengthening associations is through the law of *repetition*. This law states that the more often a product is associated with an attribute, the stronger will be the association between the two. This is why advertisers repeat in a saturation program a given piece of publicity. What we have in publicity, then, is the utilization of laws by which any potential attribute can become associated with any potential product by simple exposure. These associational tactics are then encapsulated by advertisers as the product's slogan. Few of us can recall the statistical evidence that would justify our purchase of Ultra Brite, but many of us can probably remember the catchy, hummable slogan chosen to register the product's name fast and often: "Ultra Brite . . . gives your mouth . . . sex appeal."

All that is required to discuss the characteristics of this or any slogan is to summarize the features we have already attributed to publicity. By this we mean that if a slogan represents a *telescoping of the persuasion process*—if it is going to *link X and Y by sheer association, without proof*—it must both attract attention and focus on the consumer's needs. These, we remind, are the distinguishing marks of publicity.

But no matter how often a slogan is repeated, its success still depends on the pre-existent needs of a consumer. One can blithely repeat "Winston tastes good like a cigarette should" or "When you're out of Schlitz, you're out of beer" or "Fly the friendly skies of United" or "Things go better with Coca-Cola," but unless he needs a cigarette, a beer, a plane, or a drink, each slogan will have no effect. In order for the slogan "Ultra Brite gives your mouth sex appeal" to have any real persuasive effect—in order for it to sell Ultra Brite toothpaste—the audience must (1) have a need for toothpaste, (2) have a positive regard for sex appeal, and (3) remember the alleged link between Ultra Brite and sex appeal. Lacking a presence of its own, the ad must seek an auditor who *needs* to be sold; of itself the ad usually lacks the potential to charm or to recreate the listener.

In summary, we claim that the rhetorical dimension of advertising more closely approximates publicity's focus on proofs. We suggest this classification because advertising tends to emphasize three things:

1. Gaining and maintaining attention
2. Arousing existing needs
3. Associational linking through slogans

An abbreviated Rhetoric game like publicity is no doubt necessary in a noisy, commercial society such as ours. It is especially valuable for those sponsors whose sole aim is to make audiences aware of products or events; in this instance publicity is an ideal form. But publicity is clearly unsuited when the game called for is more complex. A speaker who insisted on calling attention to his product, or a candidate who continued to campaign on his own behalf, in front of an already hostile audience, would seriously risk further irritating his listeners rather than persuading them if he relied solely on publicity tactics. Similarly, speakers who want to argue for a change in existing attitudes cannot hope to accomplish their persuasive goals by merely repeating slogans; such tactics will only create confusion in the public's mind. In such circumstances a more complex Rhetoric game needs to be played, a game that does more than celebrate a product (or candidate, or idea) in ceremonial fashion. What is needed is an involving, revitalizing Rhetoric game that recognizes that the spectator is more than a hedonistic consumer. One such game is Political Dialog, a Rhetoric game that now seems to be enjoying a revival of popularity in America after several decades of eclipse by political affairs that imitated the Publicity game.

RHETORIC OF THE FORUM: POLITICAL DIALOG

We shall turn now from persuasion in the service of commerce to consider rhetoric in its original sense—persuasion employed in the conduct of public affairs. In this day and age of advance men, special interest lobbies, weekly opinion polls, and zoning regulations, we are accustomed to think of politics as a mystical, at times squalid, business that goes on in smoke-filled rooms at City Hall. But to confuse the "paraphernalia of officialdom"[14] with the actual game of politics is like mistaking football pads for the game of football itself. If we understand the political game in terms of its root experience—the formation and expenditure of power—then we can lay aside momentarily such banal aspects as parking tickets and sewer legislation, and even such obvious rule violations as corruption, gerrymandering, and bought judgeships, in order to get a clearer picture of the game itself. A few years of municipal corruption, after all, are no more unusual than a football game in which both teams are guilty of many fouls. The fact that particular plays of the game violate the rules does not change the essential nature of the game.

With this in mind, recall our earlier discussion of the Rhetoric game as developed in ancient Greece. There the leadership councils of the

---

[14] H. Arendt, *Between Past and Future* (New York: The Viking Press, 1968), p. 3.

Trojan War proved to be an excellent way to mobilize community consensus. Following that war, the system was carried back to the Greek city-states where it became a treasured means for enlisting civic cooperation in the handling of municipal affairs. No sooner had the Greeks formulated the Rhetoric game, however, than they began the debate over how it should be played. Almost from the start, there were wide differences of opinion concerning the aptness of the ground rules and the best tactics for the game. In the next few pages, we wish to consider four of the most influential and persistent responses in Western thought to the question of the proper role of communication in the conduct of civic affairs and of the appropriate tactics for those who would enter the political arena to engage in the Rhetoric game.

Specifically we shall explore: (1) the *Empirical* ideal of Aristotle, who studied and described the political communication tactics he saw actually being used in the polis (the Greek city-state); (2) the *Investigative* ideal of Cicero, who suggested tactics that civil servants could employ both to find the arguments they would need to resolve public controversies intelligently and to explain their decisions in ways that would encourage popular support for their administrative decisions; (3) the *Therapeutic* ideal of Plato, who distrusted democratic institutions entirely and argued that those few leaders of the state who have the truth should use the tactics of propaganda to manipulate the innocent masses so they would behave in ways that were best for their collective well-being; and (4) the *Participatory* ideal of Arendt, who locates the very essence of being human in the realm of political activity and who therefore sees speech (the disclosure of self in the public realm) as the fundamental tactic by which men and women weave a common social fabric and each defines and maintains his or her position in that fabric.

Empirical Tactics

Perhaps the most popular approach to the political game in modern-day America is the one advocated by behavioral scientists such as Harold Lasswell, Daniel Bell, Seymour Lipset, and B. F. Skinner and the bulk of management-oriented social reformers. Echoing the seventeenth-century philosopher Spinoza and the Utilitarian Jeremy Bentham, they hold that man has no innate nature, no inherent goodness or evil, only more or less efficient structures for group living. For them, the job of the political game is to adjust public institutions to provide for some optimal conditions that will encourage general satisfaction.[15] Tacticians who adopt this dispassionate, "value-free" attitude toward the political game tend also to see rhetoric as an amoral instrument rather like a surgeon's tools: A surgeon may use his art morally to save lives or immorally to kill someone, but in each instance he employs some tools. In the same way, rhetoric can be used for moral ends (as in "educating" the public to accept enlightened reforms, such as fluoridation of water supplies, use of seat belts, needed trade tariffs) or it can be used immorally (misleading the public through "propaganda" so that the public votes for corrupt candidates, opposes civil rights legislation, favors inopportune changes in the law). But the tools of communication are themselves neutral. Morality enters in when we try to assess the communicators' intents, either selfish or in the community's best interests. Likewise, the use of public opinion polls is viewed from this empirical perspective as just one more tool the political players can use to ascertain community opinion as part of a complex process of operating a government in a technological age.

The originator of this empirical approach to political activity was the Greek philosopher, Aristotle. He was the first to see that human communication was a *process* that helped sustain the operation of the polis, and his technique of analysis, the conjectural method (systematically gathering information on the behavioral manifestations of power utilization based on his direct observations, his experiences, and the verified records of the past) was the first truly empirical method for studying rhetorical messages as used in the politics game.[16] His contribution as a scientist was to provide a dispassionate "theoretical" taxonomy of how public messages enabled political institutions to accomplish the ends of a stable polis.

By and large modern empirical approaches to politics echo Aristotle in their efforts to service political machinery, to examine it dispassionately, to offer the rulers advice on how to adjust or repair it when it does not seem to be working as well (efficiently, productively, quietly) as it might. In his day Aristotle (in his seminal work, *The Rhetoric*) discussed how messages served to facilitate the operation of key social institutions such as the courts, the assemblies, and the ceremonial rituals. For him rhetorical messages were rather like the physiology of various public

---

[15] See D. Germino, *Beyond Ideology* (New York: Harper & Row, 1967), pp. 190–206.

[16] Note that the empirical method of analysis relies mainly on observation. Several modern behavioral methods rely on experimentation—interposing the experimenter into his observations with an aim to altering the political game as well as observing it.

institutions, and he sought to investigate what sorts of messages one might find in stable political bodies. Aristotle's heirs do much the same thing today, with their studies of organizational communication in corporate and bureaucratic institutions, of the place of propaganda as part of collective bargaining or diplomatic negotiation, and the efficacy of public opinion campaigns in swaying voter sentiment on particular issues. In the case of Aristotle and his modern counterparts there is always an implicit recognition that politics is a matter for professional brokers who mediate among pressure groups, but who must secure at least acceptance by an anonymous public that is for the most part apathetic if not rather ignorant of the complexities of running a modern corporate system. That sounds harsh, but for those of an empirical persuasion, "that's the way things are." They prefer not to think about how the political game ought to be played; instead they confine their analysis to clarifying the effectiveness of particular rhetorical strategies in facilitating or obstructing various political aims. This detached view of the political technician seeks to understand discourse as a component in the dynamics by which political institutions are sustained.

Investigative Tactics

An alternative understanding of political rhetoric was first offered by the Roman lawyer Cicero, who saw the aim of public discourse as not merely maintaining political stability but also of establishing the fame of those public-spirited citizens whose virtuosity and articulateness in the forum would ensure their immortality.[17] As an experienced participant in Roman public affairs, Cicero believed that having to make and discuss political decisions in the midst of social controversy sharpened our ability to think critically and brought out the nobler (civic minded) side of our nature. His practitioner-oriented view of clear thinking in the forum has come down to us embodied in such political superstars as Daniel Webster, William Jennings Bryan, Winston Churchill, and Charles De-Gaulle.[18]

It has often been noted that the Romans were a practical people, more given to engineering than to pure mathematics, interested more in

---

[17] Cicero, "Scipio's Dream" in *On the Commonwealth*, trans. G. H. Sabine and S. B. Smith (Columbus: Ohio State University Press, 1929), pp. 256–268.

[18] See Lewis J. Edinger, "Where Are the Political Superstars?" *Political Science Quarterly* 89(June 1974):249–268.

administration than philosophy.[19] It was just this pragmatic bent that influenced Cicero's notion of political rhetoric and, through the tradition he established, many of the foremost statesmen of Western civilization. To transform rhetoric from the leisure pastime of free and equal men into a form more suitable for Roman temperament (with its traditional suspicion of all things intellectual) Cicero had to make major revisions in the character of the game. For one thing, he had to give it a vocational objective. As the foremost lawyer of antiquity, Cicero saw clearly that skill in the Rhetoric game was a valuable asset not only for his own profession, but also for the general career of public administrator.[20]

In the first century B.C. a series of successful wars and generous peace treaties had made Rome master of a vast territory encompassing a wide variety of peoples and cultures. Where previous empires had followed a simple and brutal policy respecting conquered peoples, Rome did not so much conquer others as it annexed them (the Roman word for "law" is *lux*, which literally means "coupling" or "connection," hence procedures for relating formally) and established a formal structure of relations.

As this governmental system expanded and became ever more complex it became clear that capable administrators were needed to govern wisely. What was needed was a corps of diplomat-lawyers who could think clearly, communicate effectively, and rule through the respect of foreign peoples rather than through their fear. From these needs, Cicero reconstituted rhetoric as a tactic of critical thinking and authoritative discourse used by leaders to maintain the respect of varied populations.

The first of these features—a discipline concerned with rational analysis of public issues—can be understood today as the sort of prelegal training in development of evidence and argument typical of men such

---

[19] The Roman poet Horace may have caught this aspect of his people best in his invidious comparison of Greek and Roman:

> Greece had a genius, Greece had eloquence,
> For her ambition and her end was fame.
> Our Roman youth is diligently taught
> The deep mysterious art of growing rich,
> And the first words that children learn to speak
> Are of the value of the names of coin;
> Can a penurious wretch, that with his milk
> Hath suck'd the basest dregs of usury,
> Pretend to generous and heroic thoughts?
> And can rust and avarice write lasting lines?

(*Dramatic Technique*, 323–332).

[20] See Cicero, *De Oratore*, for a comprehensive justification of the game on these grounds.

as Ralph Nader, Robert MacNamara, and Admiral Hyman Rickover: The need was to train men to think systematically about pressing and often emotional issues, to be able to employ effectively the subtleties of litigation and negotiation, to avoid fallacious reasoning, to be able to weigh analytically the appeals and advice of all sorts of petitioners, to arrive at sound decisions on matters of policy in the absence of ready advice from Rome itself, and then to implement their policies in clear and forceful language to secure the cooperation of the subjects without having to resort to force.[21]

Thus, Cicero foresaw the rise of a public corps of civil supervisors, and he shifted the emphasis in the study of rhetoric from matters of presence to those of "invention" (or procedures for thinking public controversies through in a systematic manner by careful reckoning of consequences—not likely to lead to original thinking, but then originality was mistrusted by Rome; what was sought, and achieved, was a competent, rational, thorough calculator).

The second objective was to develop leaders who could rule through the weight of their authority and their appeals to their subjects' civic nature rather than with an army at hand to terrify the populace. Here again, Cicero made crucial changes in the Greek notions of rhetoric. Where for the Greeks, public discourse was addressed to one's peers and to fellow citizens, all of whom had an equal voice in the decisions of the polis, Cicero had to consider hierarchical communication between leaders and publics. So he devised the sort of rhetoric suited for a benevolent army, where the flow of messages is both down the line (in the form of orders and memos and commands) and up the line (entreaties and prayers, etc.). The Roman administrator was no petty tyrant (at least in theory; there were obviously abuses): He was not expected to merely send out edicts (at least if he expected to control with a minimal armed force for protection). It is in this Roman sense that we must understand authority: It is not the threat of punishment or violence, but the willing subordination to a leader because there is some common respect of ruler and ruled for a set of legal parameters.

A large part of the dignity and respect that the administrators established was due to their rhetorical training in the elements of "ethos" or the character a man reveals in his public communications and in the development of a memorable style capable of inspiring a populace; the

---

[21] It must be recalled that it would have been both uncivilized and impossible to control such an enormous empire through simple violence. The incredible success of the nineteenth-century British in maintaining a worldwide empire using just such a cadre of professional administrators is modern confirmation of Rome's wisdom on this matter.

Romans developed this quality of noble character revealed in discourse and incorporated it as a key goal of their educational curricula.[22]

Cicero's influence on the rhetorical-educational system was so great that his ideas are reflected in education to this day. For one thing, the notion of a liberal arts curriculum to train a well-rounded person is an outgrowth of his conception of *humanitas;* the Ciceronian ideal of a tolerant, self-controlled, rational, politically active, urbane person who understands Nature and cooperates to make the established republican social order function required a person educated in a broad range of knowledge.[23] To assure that such a person was trained, Cicero described the categories of necessary knowledge (the quadrivium—mathematics, music, astronomy, and history) and thus laid the foundation for what was to become the collegiate "core" areas of humanities, sciences, and social sciences that all students in American colleges must study.

Cicero also contended that the well-equipped leader needed to be capable of eloquence, and so he should study the trivium (grammar, logic, rhetoric). Have you ever wondered why most state education systems require twelve years of English composition, and then colleges top that off with more required English courses and perhaps some foreign language requirements? It is because Cicero felt that skillful expression was an essential attribute in the character of the educated person, and the weight of his authority persists, often unacknowledged to our day. Again, the prevalence of law schools, schools of business administration, social work, and political science departments that have professional or vocational focus is an outgrowth of the Ciceronian effort to transform Greek theoretical studies into a form more palatable to Roman vocational interests. Roman education valued shrewdness rather than theoretical wisdom.

Cicero's influence is finally felt in our respect for the professor in the classroom. Whereas in Greece the teacher-student relationship was intimate and personal, in Rome it became an opportunity to rehearse the student in respect and for him to gradually assume the position of equal

---

[22] It is worth noting that the heart of Roman education was self-respect and concomitant respect for those for whom an official was responsible—*virtu et dignitas* (character and dignity)—even the Roman slave system was nowhere so inhumane as our own American slave system. Even a slave, though he was low on the hierarchy, had rights that were respected according to his station. Thus, it was possible for a shopkeeper who went bankrupt to sell himself into slavery much as he might today accept employment in a large corporation.

[23] For us the humane man is compassionate over another's suffering. This sentiment clouds Cicero's original notion of a rational, open-minded person committed to uphold justice for all by maintaining an open forum where all were free to discuss "public business" (re-public).

to the teacher—from whence he could step into the world and assume the mantle of authority in the Rhetoric game with some degree of gracefulness. It is only in our own day that the Roman distance between teacher and student is coming into question, along with these other Ciceronian educational notions designed to provide administrative training for a cadre of skilled public managers. That these educational concepts have lasted a full 2000 years past Cicero himself and 1000 years past the last vestiges of the Roman Empire attests to the popularity of the republican variation of the Rhetoric game. The game itself continues to be played in those hierarchical societies where power is conferred with office (as it was in Rome) rather than being freely volunteered as was the democratic practice of Athens.

Therapeutic Tactics

The third fundamental approach to political rhetoric is one most popular in a society where a sect of priests, experts, zealots, or philosophers gains a monopoly of knowledge and seeks to change the forum into a closed arena for their own exclusive use. This version of the game was first proposed by Plato, who opposed Greek democratic practices and sought to make rhetoric into an instrument for the social control of the unenlightened masses; his was the first coherent theory of propaganda. His heirs exist today in the governments of all totalitarian and corporate institutions that presume that power is the exclusive property of those in executive positions and that all other members of the institution (be it an industrial firm or a nation) must have their interests looked after by those who "know what is best."

Plato's antidemocratic rhetoric is stated most cogently in his dialog *Phaedrus*. There he describes the young student, Phaedrus, meeting the philosopher, Socrates, and in a burst of enthusiasm urging Socrates to walk with him into the countryside and hear him practice a speech he is preparing to deliver as homework to the Sophist Lysias. Socrates lets himself be drawn to a quiet romantic place beside a stream, and there Phaedrus delivers a speech on the nature of love. To Phaedrus' disappointment, Socrates is not impressed by the speech. After a brief exchange on the nature of effective speaking, Socrates offers his own, technically better, speech, on the same topic. After further discussion Socrates consents to deliver yet another, even more profound speech. Through this dialog, perhaps one of the most subtle pieces of prose in history, Plato reveals his conception of the ideal Rhetoric game.

His major contention is that Rhetoric players should be limited to those who "know the truth." Note here at the outset that Plato rejects the Greek commitment to communication among peers; Plato is advocating the "experts only" notion that rhetoric is the exclusive domain of those who have some special knowledge. Rhetoric is to be employed to inform, uplift, or otherwise educate the masses who are not expert. Nowhere in this scheme is there an opportunity for the ruled or the uninformed to communicate with the rulers as there is in the Roman hierarchical scheme.[24]

But the notion of a man "knowing the truth" is deeper than simply an elitist conception that some men reason better than others. It requires that we understand a bit of how Plato viewed the character of public life as he knew it in Athens. He offers us that view in his allegory of the cave in the *Republic* (514–521). There he depicts a cavern that bears a startling resemblance to a modern movie theater. He asks us to imagine all the inhabitants of a community having spent their entire lives seated (indeed chained, by their limbs and necks, so they can neither move nor turn their heads to speak to anyone) and watching the images being reflected from a screen. In this condition of living death (Homer's word for the underworld of afterlife is a combination of shadow images, so bodies that can neither move nor speak, i.e., lack soul, are oddly enough "the dead who live") they remain narcoticized, and they come to believe that the distorted images on the screen are reality. (These images are placed on the screens by the "image makers," the poets and rhetorician-politicians.) Plato then asks, what would happen if one man were somehow freed of his chains and were forced to stand up and turn around? We can imagine the effect that occurs when someone stands up in the middle of a film: He notices all the ashen-gray faces of the audience, staring silently ahead like so many mute zombies; he also feels an unsteadiness as he stumbles up the aisle. Most important for Plato, although such a man has never seen reality, he becomes aware that the images on the screen are not reality. Plato goes on to describe the freed man's arduous struggle up the aisle (comparable to a genuine education

---

[24] We might note in passing that, surprising as it may seem, our contemporary system of "mass media broadcasting" in which messages are literally cast broadly out to the public with no formal provision for public response is an ideal Platonic system of communication for it destroys the possibility for interaction. This approach to public communication, in which an elite bombards the public with advertising, political campaigns, or propaganda, has become the standard in all "mass" communications since the French Revolution. One is provoked to ask what extent technology has developed in its present form in response to political and philosophical ambitions rather than as a free and undirected curiosity.

in mathematical ideals)—as he bursts finally out of the cave-theater he will enter the realm of reality (philosophy), and, in his dizziness at being flooded by bright sunlight, he will realize how far removed the images of the cave are from truth.[25]

This then is the man who knows the truth—the philosopher-expert who has come to recognize the eternal and unchanging forms of knowledge (cognitions) as real and the clichés and conventional images (opinions) held in common by the living dead (who do not in fact communicate with one another) of the polis, the common mass who share as equals in their illusory ignorance, whose idle chatter fails to communicate ideas.

It is at this point that the philosopher, as a moral man with humanitarian instincts, finds it necessary to return to the cave in an effort to *en-lighten* the masses; he enters the cave in a political act, to tell the others about reality. But of course upon re-entry from the bright sunlight into the cave's darkness, he gets dizzy yet a third time. The people see him stumbling down the aisle ranting in a weird way about the higher truth. The audience will at first be confused and startled by this odd sight, they then may become amused, perhaps in the same way that a movie audience is by a drunk struggling down the aisle; then they will become irritated because the disturbance is distracting them from the show. As the philosopher continues his ranting and approaches nearer, the audience may become fearful, as though he were a madman who might do them harm. And if the philosopher yet persists in trying to arouse the people, they will become enraged, and, if they can in any way reach him, will seize and kill him.

Thus Plato envisages the philosopher employing rhetoric as a means of bringing the ignorant masses to the higher realms of truth without himself falling prey to them. He must communicate with them, but he must do so artfully lest his ideas so enrage them that they destroy him as the Athenians, in their ignorance and fear, had destroyed Socrates.

We can appreciate why Plato would have taken the position he did; what interests us here, however, is the fact that from his time to this day, virtually all dictatorships or elitist political groups have employed Plato's rationale: All have claimed that they *know* the eternal truth, all have claimed to know what is good for society, all have treated the masses with the fearful contempt we reserve for the ignorant. In this sense, then,

---

[25] Five to be exact: (1) if the sun represents the direct light of truth, the objects outside the cave can be seen or understood with the (2) reflected light of the sun. In its turn, (3) a film (or shadow to stay closer to Plato's words) contains images or representations of objects; but a film must be projected using (4) artificial light, and, within the cave, that artificial light must be (5) reflected off a wall before it is seen by the captive audience.

we can understand how it is that the Platonic notion of rhetoric is therapeutic—it is designed for conditions where a knowledgeable expert claims to be in communication with individuals who are handicapped by a lack of knowledge and who are living in conditions which they, in their misguided ignorance, see as good. And so from his day to ours, all autocratic institutions, the Catholic Inquisition, Fascist and totalitarian political groups, various militant extremists, corporate organizations controlled by a managerial elite, psychiatric and medical asylums—any organization that is controlled by a group of superior experts who claim to be ruling for the benefit of those incapable of self-government—have relied upon Plato's theory of rhetoric to justify their measures of propaganda, coercion, censorship, even torture. After all, if as a moral man you happen to know what is the highest good for others, why let them wallow in sin and error? Why not seek to "correct" them?

Given this basic principle of who may practice Rhetoric, what is the

art the philosopher will employ? Plato suggests that when the philosopher enters the cave, he should begin by learning the nature of one man's soul, finding out what motivates him, what he fears, what vanities or ambitions govern him. Plato then advises the philosopher to find out how to adapt the truth to that one man, to play upon his needs, desires, fears, and motivations, in order to get that one man to behave correctly.[26] Having come to dominate this one soul, the philosopher would move on to another soul and say or do whatever was necessary to get that second person to behave correctly. And so it would go, with the philosopher-rhetorician gradually learning to manipulate all men's souls through artful persuasion to meet his vision of the common good. In this effort to gain obedience through motivational manipulation, Plato differs markedly from Cicero, who would have the orator obtain the willing cooperation of his public by inspiring them and setting an admirable example of reasonableness. Note also that it does not matter to Plato either what the philosopher's motivations are (only true believers would appreciate his humanitarian instincts—the others, being ignorant fools, would only laugh, or worse) or whether the philosopher imparts any truth to them (Plato, unlike the Sophists, argued that most men are incapable of grasping the truth even if it is offered them). All that matters is that all men come to abide by the true dogma, that the members of society all reach norms of proper behavior suited to a well functioning state (where artisans produce, policemen regulate automatically, and all fill their proper custodial social roles). At that point, says Plato (foreshadowing Marx), there will be no more need for Rhetoric, so the philosopher-king's propaganda apparatus will wither away and all that will remain will be a society of contented folk automatically doing the correct thing in accordance with ideal laws of justice and otherwise amusing themselves with hobbies.[27]

Participation Tactics

Most closely resembling the original Greek version of the Rhetoric game are those believers in "participatory democracy" typified best by John Adams and in our own day by the political philosopher Hannah Arendt. Herself a student of both Heidegger and Karl Jaspers, Arendt's thinking on the character and place of Rhetoric in our lives (to which we have

---

[26] Note that there is no need for the man to understand or comprehend. All that matters is that he behave correctly.

[27] Bear in mind, however, that Plato realizes the historical impossibility of ever achieving this ideal condition; he writes in irony, an attitude that seems to have been lost on Marx.

referred throughout these pages) is a complex amalgam and extension of both these philosophers, most particularly in seeing thought as an outgrowth of the "loving combat" that is authentic communication. As communication is the foundation of the philosophical enterprise, so is speech (or the disclosure of self in the public realm) the foundation of political intercourse.

Arendt's theory entails the rejection of several rubrics of American political science.[28] For one, she regards our popular notion of government by the consent of the governed as an elitist ideology that blurs government *by* the people with government by "professionals" who occasionally get the passive approval *of* the people; Arendt holds that genuine politics consists, not in submission to orders but in common participation in public activities. In this regard, speech is the specifically human form of action because speech reveals the individuality of the participant in the arena marked out for human inter-action. She is thus best known as the republican theorist of "participatory democracy."

But Arendt's work is more subtle than simple polemic agitation for more civic participation in political affairs. She also rejects the American political scientist's most sacred authority, Thomas Hobbes. Hobbes felt that the primary political emotion was fear, that because in a State of Nature (or literally a lawless society) life is (in his famous phrase) "nasty, brutish and short," men must have logically (if not historically) created political institutions out of fear of each other. Hence it follows that they would give government the primary task of assuring the survival and physical protection of each man in his place. Government is, therefore, given a license to kill the individual if it chooses. In this sense, Hobbes presumed that we could set our fears somewhat to rest if we gave all sanction for killing to the Leviathan (the sovereign); in that circumstance, we would have only one person to fear. "Authority" becomes, for the Hobbesian, the power of the government to do violence to members of the civil population. On its face (largely because the Founding Fathers were influenced by Hobbes' thinking) these notions seem cogent to Americans: Doesn't the government force us to obey laws by the threat of punishment? Can't the government compel us to serve in the armed forces and thus risk death? And in addition to these prerogatives do we not become especially upset when we feel that the government is not fulfilling its obligation to maintain "law and order" in public places, to prevent the streets from becoming a "jungle"?

Arendt counters this assumption; she claims that men come to-

---

[28] See M. Conovan, *The Political Thought of Hannah Arendt* (New York: Harcourt Brace Jovanovich, 1974).

gether, not out of fear, but because they only thrive as humans in the company of others. Social institutions are erected so that men will have arenas in which to display their virtuosity. Thus, the walls of the city are not meant to offer protection from the ravages of Nature but from the loneliness that men must endure who live alone in Nature. Political commerce is thus a liberating element that men use to escape the solitude of beasts—as creatures of display we have a human need to perform actions in the company of others, so we establish arenas (public institutions) that invite performances:

> Performing artists—dancers, play-actors, musicians, and the like— need an audience to show their virtuosity, just as acting men need the presence of others before whom they can appear; both need a publically organized space for their "work," and both depend upon others for the performance itself. Such a space of appearances is not to be taken for granted wherever men live together in a community. . . . [It is] a kind of theater where freedom [can] appear.[29]

This presumption that it is the ham in mankind that is best serviced by political affairs means that politics is indissolubly bound up with speech activity. In contrast to such traditional public activities as political campaigns and office holding (which are limited to a small number) we should look to all arenas where the widest array of people do more than listen silently to "leaders"—where they interact (by which Arendt means to reveal themselves in the public light as well as listen actively to such human disclosure). Carried to its logical extreme, Arendt is even prepared to reject the secret ballot because it isolates the citizen alone in the ballot booth, when he should be more human in his role as a juror, thinking and expressing himself in the presence of his peers. She is further prepared to reject bureaucratic rule as the worst form of tyranny (because, where a dictatorship is at least government by one person, bureaucracy is government by none) and to applaud student uprisings for their recognition of this natural impulse to perform in the company of others:

> . . . it turned out that acting is fun; this generation discovered what the eighteenth century had called "public Happiness," which means that when man takes part in public life he opens up for himself a dimension of human experience that otherwise remains closed to him and that in some way constitutes a part of complete happiness.[30]

---

[29] H. Arendt, *Between Past and Future*, p. 154.

[30] H. Arendt, "Thoughts On Politics And Revolution," *New York Review of Books* (22 April 1971), 8.

If Arendt is right about the fundamental desire for virtuosity and display as the motivation for political action, then student rejection of lectures makes a great deal of sense. In spite of many studies that show that students learn more by lecture than by seminars, most students insist that they prefer the small seminar; indeed, students prefer a bull session in a coffee shop to any structured situation with a teacher in charge. The reason is not hard to find in Arendt's schema: What they do not enjoy in the lecture is their role as passive consumers (while the professor hugely enjoys the opportunity to display himself before a captive audience). They would rather learn nothing if in return they had the opportunity to reveal themselves to their peers. The cycles of student rioting also make sense: A riot is the one arena that no self-respecting administrator would try to co-opt and lead—whereas college officials have long since taken over other extracurricular activities such as sports, theater, debate, etc. "in the interests of the students" (and thereby upstaged the students and taken the fun out of the activities).

It is clear that, contrary to the negative position of Hobbes, who sees men associating out of common fear, yet always harboring a kind of loathing for public life, Arendt sees public interaction as the greatest *fun* (indeed, as she rightly points out,[31] in a city where one had any personal pleasure he wished, the predominant emotion would be boredom). She illustrates her contention by citing John Adams, who saw that democracy as practiced in colonial New England was successful for precisely this reason—that people attended to their civic business, not out of any lofty sense of obligation (for all duties are burdens), but because in a society where people were scattered on farms, working long arduous days, with no diversion such as television, the opportunity to come into town and bicker over taxes, legalities, and other public matters, was a pleasure. Adams noted the somber efforts of the French revolutionaries to impose obligations of citizenship, and he sniffed his contempt: "They think they shall have an American Revolution, yet they have not one American among them."[32]

So Arendt sees public Rhetoric games as:

1. An exercise in freedom; the extension of one's existential self into the public arena (which has been marked out for just this purpose, in the same way that a space is cleared to enable the acrobat who defies Nature to amaze us with the dexterity and control of his body). In speech we fulfill a natural yearning for the companionship of others.

---

[31] H. Arendt, *Men in Dark Times* (New York: Harcourt, Brace and World, 1955), p. 234.
[32] H. Arendt, *On Revolution* (New York: Viking Press, 1963), p. 116.

2. The reification of thought; the opportunity to "object-ify" and give social significance to ideas that would dissolve without ever appearing in the world if we left them unarticulated (lacking linguistic formulation) inside ourselves.
3. The fulfillment of the natural human instinct to reveal oneself to others, to earn their admiration, and so to surpass beasts (who live only to survive and reproduce). In this regard, as she rightly points out, anyone who did not at least desire the appreciation of others (no matter how small the arena), would be pathological.[33]
4. Finally, a contribution to the social process. Speech enables its participants to develop a sense of community: Through our many communications with each other we weave the strong fraternal social fabric that is our "common" sense—while as individuals we retain our place *in* the social fabric through our verbal contributions and our acceptance of the verbal gifts of others.

When we approach the rhetoric of the forum, whether as players or as spectators, the first question we must ask is "What is the nature of the game?" Each of the four theorists we have examined has a different idea of the function that political dialog serves, or ought to serve, in society. Each, therefore, advocates a different order of tactics as appropriate for participants in the political Rhetoric game.

ARISTOTLE, the scientist of communication, looked on politics as the means by which social institutions function. Rhetoric, for him, was the leisure pastime of free and equal men, and he described the set of tactics for the game which, he observed empirically, helped to sustain the operation of the city-state.

CICERO, the Roman lawyer, viewed politics as the vehicle by which public institutions were administered. Rhetoric, for him, was a means for thinking clearly and speaking authoritatively in the midst of social controversy in order to inspire the respect and cooperation of various publics. Accordingly, Cicero outlined a set of tactics for the game based upon the model of administrative efficiency—tactics to sharpen the players' critical thinking ability, develop their capacity to make decisions in the public interest, and enable them to communicate effectively from their positions in the administrative hierarchy.

PLATO, who divorced rhetoric from democratic institutions, saw

---

[33] It is interesting in this regard, also, that the role of administrator in most bureaucracies involves precisely training oneself not to reveal oneself publicly—to leave no traces among men or documents.

politics as a totalitarian exercise in social control in which the rulers, who possess the truth, should manipulate the behavior of the naïve masses. Plato advocated a set of tactics for the game grounded in a therapeutic conception of rhetorical discourse. He believed that rulers should employ propaganda, instead of violence, to keep the populace under control and to get them to behave in accord with the dictates of "truth," which they could not be expected to understand.

ARENDT, whose perspective is more personal, sees politics as enabling players in the public arena to fulfill their innate human urge to be active in the company of others, and to receive the recognition that is due them as contributors to the affairs of men. Accordingly, Arendt advocates participation in the public arena as the primary tactic through which men can exercise their freedom, interact with their fellows, express themselves, and become part of a community.

12

Rhetoric Games: Healing and Pornography

Rhetoric public games are those whose telos is consensus: The messages generated invite the participants to experience political intent.

By now it should be clear that although all public recreation is concerned to some extent with enhanced pleasure and the alleviation of pain, those public communication games we call Rhetoric games are uniquely concerned with the experience of political consensus. In a mass society, every individual is surrounded by other distinct individuals among whom he or she must move and with whom he or she must come to terms. The individual who willfully participates in Rhetoric games experiences "common sense" (that is, a reality shared in common with others). In shirking the loneliness that continually threatens isolated persons, Rhetoric players create or maintain fraternal cohesion among those who share some identity such as self-interest, social class, or ideology. Thus unified, the individuals achieve freedom to act in their own behalf with their peers in common political enterprises.

But within every social institution almost every member at one time or another, for a variety of reasons, may be excluded or forced to withdraw from the common activity. For almost everyone there is a point at which he or she is unable or unwilling to derive satisfaction from the ordinary fraternal games of the group. This is no problem with respect to voluntary alliances such as country clubs, from which the member may choose to resign. Nor is it necessarily damaging to those who choose to withdraw by retreating into themselves (such as philosophers) or into a religious sect insulated from common sense (assuming that the society at large practices religious toleration). But it is a problem for those who unwittingly "lose their way" or otherwise go astray from common sense reality. For these "lost souls,"[1] who cannot or do not experience political consensus, many societies establish a special set of persuasive "healing" games. Playing one of these games restores the individual's capacity to act conventionally in arenas whose "common sense" eludes him. The games free the individual from the anguish that loss of human contact is presumed to inflict. In the next section of this chapter we shall consider a number of these re-creative "healing" games.

RHETORIC OF THE SOUL: HEALING

We turn now from persuasion in the conduct of public affairs to consider how rhetoric is employed in the conduct of the various healing arts. At this point you may well wonder whether we are using "healing" in some special sense, and whether a rhetoric of healing is just a specialized game for doctors more than for ordinary communicators. After all, most of us do not like to think of ourselves as "sick," and if we are, we go to see a medical healer who deals with facts and natural processes—not to some Rhetoric game that "operates where truth is uncertain or contingent." In short, how can healing be called a Rhetoric game, and how does any such game involve the average communicator? In what sense can we be critics of "healing"?

First, we hope to show that the world of physical healing is not so remote as some might hope from the other uncertainties of living. Without going into a detailed investigation, we can take note of a great deal of recent research that suggests how difficult it is to distinguish the healing process, be it in the physical or mental realm, from persuasion.[2] In any case, perhaps we can gain considerable insight into all kinds of "heal-

---

[1] The term *soul* is deliberately chosen in distinction to "mind" and "body." It refers to those body-bound springs of passion in sentient creatures which, though they are distinct from simple cognitive processes of the mind, are nevertheless experienced as insubstantial. Their most common manifestation is emotion. The best psychological description of the soul is found in Aristotle's seminal work, *De Anima* (*On the Soul*), especially 403ª5–414ª.

[2] See R. D. Laing, *The Politics of Experience* (New York: Pantheon, 1967); R. D. Laing and D. G. Cooper, *Reason and Violence* (New York: Pantheon, 1971); J. D. Frank, *Persuasion and Healing* (New York: Schocken, 1961); S. M. Jourard, *The Transparent Self* (New York: Van Nostrand, 1971); E. F. Torrey, *The Mind Game: Witch Doctors and Psychiatrists* (New York: Emerson Hall, 1972), among others.

ing" operations if we explore the ideas that persuasion is a sometimes neglected and often underrated facet of the curing process and, beyond this, that almost all ordinary individuals find themselves at least occasionally subjected to somebody's efforts to restore them to "health" of some kind. Whether the healing props used are splints and medications or ads and pamphlets, whenever the "healer" enters into contact with a "sufferer" in an effort to liberate the sufferer from an affliction (to "make him *feel* like a new man") what ensues is a rhetorical transformation (which may have physical characteristics) in which the sufferer is restored to the companionship of his fellows.

A recent news report may help to dispel some of the mystery from what we are talking about here. The federal government in 1972 awarded a training grant to the Rough Rock (Arizona) Demonstration School to develop a formal program for training Navajo Medicine Men. According to the Navajo director of the program:

> . . . Navajo doctors are completely different from white anglo doctors. Some white man's hospitals don't cure the Navajos. They treat the illness, not the person. After an operation, a Navajo often goes to his medicine man to be purified. . . . You go to a hospital and maybe once a day the doctor comes around and he stays there, maybe five minutes. He talks a little bit but he asks you questions. Once in a while they give you a little medicine, but just a little bit of it. About the only thing they do is to put something in your mouth and see how hot you are. The rest of the time you just lie there but the medicine men help you all the time—they give you lots of medicine and they sing all night. They do lots of things all over your body. Every bit of your body is treated.[3]

It should be further noted that the training program for new medicine men presumes that the Navajo curing rituals are so complex that the medicine men will have to specialize:

> To graduate from the Rough Rock school, the trainees must perform one complete ceremony to perfection. If the medicine man commits an error, the Navajos believe, he could do the patient serious harm.[4]

How scandalous! Could the government actually enter into such a fraudulent program? Have members of the government taken leave of their senses? Some may ask what witchcraft has to do with medicine. What indeed! We shall attempt to show that a loose but persistent thread connects all the healing arts—witchcraft, psychotherapy, brainwashing, religious revivals, transcendental meditation, the sensitivity movement, and, yes, medicine. That unifying thread is the use of persuasion as a significant and necessary (though not a sufficient) component in the healing ritual.

By means of healing games, almost any member of a society who is temporarily "lost" may be invited to return to the fold, and, in this sense, we must all be concerned with what healing games may seem to have in common.

We have already generally defined persuasion as the use of messages to change the certitude with which auditors hold beliefs on contingent

---

[3] J. N. Wilford, *New York Times* (7 July 1972), 33.
[4] Ibid.

matters. We seldom think of persuasion in relation to healing because we presume that certain facets of our lives (our emotions, various somatic processes, our "native intelligence") are beyond our personal control. And since we intuit that we always assent to be persuaded, it seems to be a contradiction in terms to think of someone voluntarily becoming fearful, or stupid, or healthy.[5]

For the moment let us accept the following as a rough definition of "health": *the capacity of the organism* (in this case the human) *to adapt to the changing conditions in which he finds himself* (so that the bird that is unable to fly South when the snows come is liable to freeze or starve to death). From this it follows that the initial step in the process of remaining healthy will be the will and the capacity to adapt, to remain on genial terms with one's world.[6]

In order to retain this capacity to adapt, the healthy human displays two qualities: (1) he recognizes reality (for the most part he does not deny his common sense—his images of circumstances parallel the facts); and (2) he constantly checks his perceptions by comparing them with those around him. This confirmation of images and perceptions by comparison with others is what we shall mean by "group identity."[7]

We identify with two classes of people, peers and superiors. Peers include those whose experiences are presumably similar to ours, while superiors (or authority figures) are those whose experiences give them a somewhat "better" perspective in a given case than our own. Thus, if you were to consider purchasing a foreign automobile, you might first seek out a friend who had bought the model to see if he was satisfied, the assumption being that his driving habits would be similar to your

---

[5] Lest we become ensnared in issues of determinism and free will, let it be appreciated that we are not here seeking to deny factuality—a broken bone is broken and is not illusory. However, to the extent that spontaneity and unpredictability remain as features of human behavior, then it must be recognized that men are agents of their own destinies to a greater extent than they themselves sometimes acknowledge. (Cf. B. Vogt, "The Metaphysics of Human Liberty in Duns Scotus," *Proceedings of the 16th Annual Meeting of the American Catholic Phil. Assoc.*, vol. 16, 1940, pp. 27–37. See also H. D. Duncan, "The Search for a Social Theory of Communication," in F. E. X. Dance, *Human Communication Theory* (New York: Holt, Rinehart and Winston, 1967), p. 252 and H. Arendt, "Thinking and Moral Considerations," *Social Research* 38(Fall 1971):417–440.) We are here suggesting, not that the past can be undone (one cannot will that a bone not have been broken, any more than one can promise to have done something), but that the course of the future is continually shaped by human consent (will) or lack of consent (nil), and this in matters of health respecting the interaction of curing no less than other matters of public concern.

[6] For most animals, whose lives are dominated by biological necessity, adaptation means submission to physical realities. But man is a social creature; civilization frees him of some biological laws in order that he submit to social circumstance. See M. Conovan, *The Political Thought of Hannah Arendt* (New York: Harcourt Brace Jovanovich, 1974), pp. 55–62; A. Portmann, *Animal Camouflage* (Ann Arbor: University of Michigan Press, 1959).

[7] See H. Jonas, *The Phenomenon of Life* (New York: Harper & Row, 1966), p. 135.

own. But in addition to getting the opinions of a peer, you might also ask a mechanical engineer or the local garage mechanic for their opinions; here we would have two authorities on the subject of autos who might have some expert opinions that would be of value. So under ordinary conditions we tend to affirm that reality remains stable by checking our expectations against our perceptions, those of our peers, and those of various authorities.

What then happens to the healthy individual confronted with a sudden change in his environment? Imagine this absurd situation: You wake up one morning, walk to the nearest bus stop, and discover that the road and bus stop are gone and have been replaced overnight with an airport. What feelings might you have? Confusion? Fear? A sense of disorientation? And what might you do? You would probably engage in some sense confirmation moves, not all of them helpful: Check your bearings to see that you had not lost your way, look at your watch, check your date book. But in this odd situation where your own images are so clearly at variance with the facts, you would more likely seek out peers for help—perhaps there are other bewildered people waiting for a bus in the middle of the runway. Or you might seek out authorities—surely a policeman or a street cleaner would know what became of the road, or maybe a pilot on one of the planes could be of help. Your goal in all these fumbling efforts would be to seek further information that would allay your confusion ("Yes, something does seem to be odd this morning") and perhaps involve some minor adjustment in your beliefs. ("Oh, didn't you read about the plan to replace the road? It was in all the papers.")

We could contrast this *healthy* behavior with deviant behavior,[8] in which the individual, unable to initiate the adaptive and information gathering processes, engages instead in behaviors that simply aggravate his inadequate adjustment to a changed situation. The widening gulf between himself and his environment only serves to increase his anxiety as he finds himself increasingly unable to play the ordinary games that comprise daily life.

Two factors are related to this inability to adapt. First, the gap between our expectations and the facts of the world may simply prove too substantial to bridge by minor modifications. Most Americans are not so surprised to hear of a Mafia leader being gunned down in the streets; such incidents fit the common perceptions of how lawless men live and die. But in 1963 the idea that a United States President could be

---

[8] Keep in mind that our paradigm applies to either physical or mental illness; although we recognize that the notion of "mental illness" is sometimes a political label we apply to those whose thoughts are deviant, and in these cases our paradigm is tautological.

gunned down in the streets for no reason was preposterous—so much so that the assassination of John Kennedy was traumatic for most Americans. During the four days in which events connected with the assassination and burial were televised the great majority of Americans suffered such physical illnesses as nausea, sleeplessness, and headaches. Another natural outcome of events that were literally "senseless" (which is to say, beyond common sense) was that many Americans developed an intense belief in the possibility that the killing was not happenstance, that it was part of some larger political conspiracy—for a political plot would make sense and would therefore relieve the intense anxiety that has built up and never been adequately exorcised.

A second source of ill health is the sudden drastic loss of confirmation by those peers and superiors on whom we rely. Should you, for example, chance upon your very closest friends laughing at you, and if they should inform you that they really all detested you, you would be shaken by the sudden loss of group support. You might naturally feel a mixture of depression and anger, and perhaps you might snap back at them concerning their hypocrisy, which would confirm for them that you are crabby and only make you feel more left out.[9]

Either of these conditions creates an intense stress between the individual and the environment, and that stress can in its turn lead to such overpowering anxieties as to immobilize the individual and prevent him from making efforts to adjust to the changed conditions (or perhaps it could spur him to maladaptive behavior that might only worsen the conditions; witness Jack Ruby's unfortunate reaction to John Kennedy's assassination).

The disoriented seek an explanation that will restore congruence between the world and their understanding of it. Just as the terminal cancer patient travels around the world seeking a miracle cure, just as the man with the atrophied heart hopes for a miracle transplant, just as the Israelites hoped for a Moses to lead them out of Egypt, the oppressed hope for restoration by a non-conventional event. They hope for a miracle—a positive event that could in no conventional way be predicted. The healer, then, for any group will be he who has the capacity to work miracles.

When one turns to a miracle worker, he allows the healer's sheer presence to act directly on his sensibilities; he allows the healer to be successful in the awe-full and magical acts of healing. The awe-fullness of these acts is rooted in the belief that the healer cures that which the

---

[9] Which feeling of being left out is what is meant by "alienation." Cf. K. Giffin, "Social Alienation by Communication Denial," *Quarterly Journal of Speech* 56(December 1970): 347–357.

sufferer fails to understand. The healer is, in a word, a man of "excellence," whose ability to enchant is taken to entail magical powers. (Our respect for the doctor is of this order, though his "excellence" stems from knowing arcane lore).[10]

Under these conditions, the "healer" may be defined as *a person licensed by society* (through apprenticeship, diploma, ritual investiture of knowledge, or whatever means the society accepts) *to lead the sufferer in personal or group activities* (crusade, rain dance, operation, medication, burning at the stake, or whatever) *which the society believes will offer relief from suffering, offer a return to the companionship of community activities, and provide an arena for miracles to be performed.* The healer, then, is a midwife—he does not so much cause a cure as he mediates symbolically between the sufferer and society, or between the sufferer and whatever scientific/supernatural forces are involved in the cure. What is necessary to understand is that the healer has been *appointed* by society to have a sincere and compassionate concern for the patient's suffering, welfare, and recovery. But as to title, that will depend upon the kind of social myths suitable for the society. The healer may thus be a witchdoctor, evangelist, brainwasher, therapist, psychiatrist, medical doctor, or guru—the title is less important than that the society and the patient have *faith* in the reliability of both the healer's *presence* and the healing institution. That faith in and of itself is not enough, but it is an absolutely essential precondition of a successful cure.[11]

In many ways we could say that the relationship between the healer and the sufferer is an interpersonal one and that the interaction between them is not unlike the interaction that characterizes any other interpersonal relationship. At the same time, all the public values of society are involved in the relationship; the public values of any of us who are witnesses are involved, and so are the public values of individual healers and sufferers. The healing relationship is a clear instance of the borderline situation that we alluded to in the middle of Chapter 9: The healer and the sufferer may be engaged in interpersonal communication, but each is also acting as a representative of a larger community. The healer is enacting a role prescribed by society—he has the designated authority to engage in certain socially approved activities intended to restore the

[10] See P. L. Entralgo, *The Therapy of the Word in Classical Antiquity* trans. L. J. Rather and J. M. Sharp (New Haven: Yale University Press, 1970), pp. 11–31.

[11] S. M. Jourard, *The Transparent Self*, pp. 84–85: "Psychotherapists, physicians, quacks, and witch-doctors all can attest that confidence of the patient in the 'powers' of the healer must be inspired if the healing rituals are to work. They do not hesitate to use all manner of symbols that in many instances serve as conditional stimuli evoking the faith response, which truly does the healing."

sufferer to the community. The sufferer is also representing the public. First, he agrees that he *is* sick, that because he does not meet societal norms, he is unable to play the usual games. He accepts the socially approved norms and recognizes his own deviance: If his peer group values clear articulation, the fact that he lisps makes him uncomfortable; if his group values good facial tone, he is self-conscious of his wrinkles; if his group praises running speed, he is annoyed by his club foot; if his group values a well-functioning heart, he is distraught that his electrocardiogram suggests malfunction; if his group prefers that he be possessed by only one demon, the fact that he is possessed by more than one may drive him to frenzy. The sufferer continues to act as a societal representative by seeking out a socially approved healer (speech pathologist, plastic surgeon, orthopedic surgeon, heart specialist, priest) and participating in the proper healing games (speech therapy, face lift, orthopedic surgery, open heart surgery, exorcism). Then, just by participating in the approved healing process, the sufferer receives public support ("You sound horrible. Did you see a doctor?" "Good . . . What did he say?" "Okay, now you get to bed and take those pills.").

For us, then, to understand *the Rhetoric of healing* is to understand *the public process of persuasion in which a "sick" person has faith in the ability of his "healer" to change his condition to one of "health" and thereby enable the disabled sufferer to re-enter the realm of his peers as a more fit player.*

Using this rather simple paradigm, let us consider how the vast range of human healing institutions are similar in their basic mode of action. We shall start by turning to primitive magic and review the witch doctor's role in the healing process. Before doing that, however, let us emphasize that we use the label *primitive* merely to designate a way of life that is not technologically advanced. In no way are we suggesting that we choose to start our analysis with this healing practice because it is any less efficient or valuable for the people who resort to it. We start here rather because this form of healing is perhaps most removed from our everyday experience, and in describing it we can readily focus on the importance of persuasion. It is easy to see "magic" in the lives of others. Afterwards, we should be prepared to see the rhetorical elements that are more directly part of our contemporary American healing institutions.

Primitive Magic

Although it is difficult to generalize about illness in primitive society, it is probably accurate to say that inherent to the category (why we label it *primitive* in the first place) are classifications of disease that bear no resemblance to those of Western medicine. Whereas Western medicine tends to distinguish between mental and physical illness, between illness of the spirit and illness of the body, between healers of the soul and healers of the body, "primitive" medicine tends to blur such distinctions. More specifically, a so-called natural, physical ailment (vomiting, blindness, broken bones) may be directly attributed to a supernatural cause (an evil spirit, an ancestral ghost, a curse, an offended deity). To cure the natural ailment, which is merely a symptom, one usually must confront the supernatural cause.

Since an illness can and often does therefore involve the whole person, not merely "half" of him, we must bear in mind what a terrifying prospect it is. In medically advanced societies physical illness has become, in many instances, a delightful escape from the humdrum of work. It is an opportunity to shed ordinary responsibilities while possibly collecting medical insurance, to indulge in childish behavior and assorted irritations, to vegetate at home—watching daytime television without feeling guilty, to allow relatives to feed and pamper us, or even in a few lucky cases to get an expenses paid trip to a restful vacation spot for recuperation.

But a member of a primitive community is not so fortunate. Physical ailments are often attributed to someone's violation of some taboo or the consequences of someone's animosity; they are symptomatic of a greater personal or interpersonal failing. A serious illness can spell disaster for both the ill person and his family. The nature of the illness can humiliate the family personally and can be economically disastrous as the family is forced to care for the ill one while continuing to try to keep the family solvent. And the terror can be compounded in some of our urban ghettos, where the prospect of municipal hospital care is almost as frightening as the illness.[12] Illness can, in a word, cause distress and immobilizing fear to spread through the entire family.

Under such conditions, it is understandable why an ill person would turn to someone who has demonstrated his power with the supernatural. The witch-doctor, medicine man, shaman, or sorcerer is seen as having the ability to name the supernatural cause and to lead the sick through the appropriate healing rituals. Through a personal mystic experience, apprenticeship, and/or inheritance, the witch doctor has acquired a power to influence or control the supernatural, to trespass the rules that govern mortals without risking injury to himself or the sufferer.

---

[12] The person who is suspect of Western medicine—the germ theory of disease, doctors who must look things up in books, and unfamiliar diagnostic instruments and tests—goes to such a hospital, if at all, only when all other healing techniques have failed. A hospital is seen as a place to die.

William Madsen spent considerable time studying the healing practices of Mexican-Americans in the Lower Rio Grande Valley in South
Texas. In discussing the techniques of the curandero, the best-known
type of Mexican-American healer, Madsen illustrates how the curandero
mediates between the sufferer, his family, and the supernatural:

> The most common techniques of curing practices by the general
> curandero are: "cleaning" the patient's body with a handful of
> medicinal herbs and an unbroken egg to draw out the contamina-
> tion which is causing the illness; administering herb teas; reciting
> prayers; and making offerings of flowers and candles to God or the
> saints. The cleansing ("limpia") ritual is used to treat espanto,
> susto, evil eye, and some kinds of bewitchment.
>
> The curandero's procedure may be illustrated by a typical treat-
> ment for espanto. The patient suffering from this disease must be
> taken immediately to a curandero or witch doctor who is skilled in
> treating espanto. The diagnosis is based on the patient's pulse beat.
> The patient lies on a dirt floor while the curandero outlines his
> figure in the earth with a knife. After the sick person rises, the
> curandero scoops up the dirt from the marks of the outline, mixes it
> with water, and gives the mixture to his patient to drink. Next he
> drinks an herb tea made with a few sprigs of pennyroyal ("poleo")
> boiled in water. Finally, the curandero cleans his patient with a
> handful of herbs including pennyroyal and rosemary ("romero").
> Through the treatment the curandero recites the Lord's Prayer and
> chants Hail Marys. This treatment must be performed daily for nine
> days or repeated three times a day for three days. During this
> period, it is the duty of the patient's family to urge the offending
> ghost to return to purgatory and seek eventual rest. God is asked to
> reclaim the ghost from this world. Prayers are accompanied by
> offerings and vigil lights placed on the home altar. The family tries
> to obtain a photograph of the man whose ghost is causing the
> illness. If they succeed, the picture is sprinkled with fresh flowers
> dipped in holy water every day during the period of treatment. A
> much simpler cure for fright from natural causes involves cleaning
> the patient with an unbroken egg and giving him herb teas.[13]

If nothing else, participation in rituals such as these are a dramatic
break in the usual routine of the sufferer and his family. Moreover, as
the chief object of the ritual, the sufferer's feelings of self-esteem are

---

[13] William Madsen, mimeographed report, "Society and Health in the Lower Grande
Valley, A Guide for Medical and Welfare Workers Among the Mexican-Americans,"
sponsored by the Hogg Foundation for Mental Health, Austin, Texas, August, 1961, pp.
28–29.

heightened and as the members of his family perform their parts or watch attentively, the sick person is reintegrated with the group.[14]

But our concern here is not to question the effectiveness of such curing institutions.[15] Rather we hope to show in what senses they employ rhetoric (in this case faith in the healer's power and presence as communicated by symbolic rituals) as a significant part of their service. Just as important as a witch doctor's power to declare a garden fertile, is his power to declare the sufferer's illness at an end. The witch doctor's claim that an evil demon has been exorcised will often be enough to give relief, causing the patient and his family to feel better, which in turn makes all members of the family function more effectively in the belief that they have enlisted a powerful ally on their side. This renewed confidence makes everyone feel better still, and so a cycle develops.[16]

Doesn't the fact that he sometimes fails to effect a cure damage the witch doctor's credibility? Apparently not. When a witch doctor declares that a sufferer's soul is forever lost or that his illness is beyond cure, the survivors are comforted in knowing that it was not the witch doctor's fault that the patient died; as far as they are concerned, "He did everything that was possible."

What we are trying to suggest in our discussion of the rhetoric of primitive magic is perhaps best summarized by the noted French anthropologist, Prof. Claude Levi-Strauss:

> That the mythology of the shaman does not correspond to objective reality does not matter. The patient believes in it and belongs to a society that believes in it. The protecting spirits, the evil spirits, the supernatural monsters and magical monsters are elements of a coherent system which are the basis of the natives' concept of the universe. The patient accepts them, or rather she has never doubted them. What she does not accept are the incomprehensible and arbitrary pains which represent an element foreign to her system but which the shaman, by invoking the myth, will replace in a whole in which everything has its proper place.[17]

We can thus see the rhetorical function served by such sorcery. In

---

[14] See, J. D. Frank, *Persuasion and Healing*, pp. 49–53.

[15] Indeed, in recent years our own American Medical Association has grudgingly formed committees to study the seeming effectiveness of herbal home remedies used by "primitives," to say nothing of acupuncture.

[16] See W. Madsen and C. Madsen, *A Guide to Mexican Witchcraft* (Mexico: Minutiae Mexicana, 1972), pp. 26–52.

[17] C. Levi-Strauss, *Anthropologie Structural* (Paris: Librarie Plon, 1958), p. 217, quoted in J. D. Frank, p. 50.

opening otherwise unthinkable passages back to normal life, the shaman, invoking the authority of the supernatural, lends his presence and the sufferer's faith to the restorative task of persuading both sufferer and community of the sufferer's well-being.

Brainwashing

The term *brainwashing* originated after the Korean War to describe the techniques of persuasion and indoctrination employed by Chinese Communists with American prisoners of war.[18] The American public was unprepared for the sorry record of its soldiers: Of some 7,200 Americans captured by the enemy in Korea, fully one-third collaborated—ranging from momentary opportunism (assisting Communist guards in return for better food, informing on comrades) through writing anti-American propaganda and on to agreeing to spy for the Communists once released (75), some even refusing to return to the United States (21). Even more shocking was the 38 percent of United States POWs who died in captivity, not from mistreatment by the enemy, but for the most part due to the callousness of their peers—wounded men had their food stolen or were even tossed into the cold to freeze to death by other prisoners. Of all American prisoners it could only be said that 13 percent resisted the enemy totally.

These figures contrast vividly with the 1,000 British soldiers captured: 65 percent did nothing that in any way resembled collaboration, while the bulk of the 4 percent who complied with Communist wishes had been sympathetic to Communist causes even before they left England. Even more stark a comparison is drawn with the Turkish troops—of 230 who were captured, not a single one collaborated; although half the Turks who were captured were wounded prior to capture, not a single Turk died in captivity.

Even granting that England and Turkey had volunteered elite troops to the war effort, whereas the bulk of American soldiers were draftees, the American record was so dismal, even in comparison to past wars (for example, no Americans escaped from a Communist prison camp, whereas several had managed to do so in the Second World War), that the United States Army launched an investigation. That study revealed that the Chinese had, in the belief that Americans are "sick" with the

---

[18] All data in this section are taken from J. A. C. Brown, *Techniques of Persuasion* (Baltimore: Pelican, 1965), pp. 255–264. Copyright 1963 the Estate of J. A. C. Brown. Adapted by permission of Penguin Books Ltd.

illness of Capitalism, induced pathological symptoms in many prisoners, and then had "healed" them into, if not Communist advocates, then at least pliant accomplices. Their procedures are very revealing of the character of pathology for here we have an instance where the Chinese presumed the POW's were ill to begin with and sought to "restore" them to normal Communist games.

The first aim was to induce a state of total anxiety (comparable to the terror experienced by the ill in a primitive society) by shattering the orderly relation between the prisoner and his social environment. One ploy was to so harass the prisoner and fatigue him (by sudden random awakening at night, for example, or hours of forced calesthenics) that he could no longer control his body or perceptions. Another was to sow distrust among the prisoners, breaking up friendships, periodically isolating prisoners from each other, removing emotionally mature prisoners from contact with less stable prisoners to prevent prisoners from reassuring or supporting one another.[19] A third tactic was to subject prisoners to public humiliation, depriving them of any privacy (a most important feature of our culture, where a normal part of upbringing is to give children separate bedrooms and to put doors on all rooms to ensure privacy) by observing them constantly—even in the latrines, and in general "mortifying" them (treating them as if they were dead carcasses).[20] A fourth tactic was repeated "educational" sessions in which prisoners were required to memorize various Communist tracts as a preparation to "correcting" their thinking. Related to these education sessions were periodic confessional sessions in which prisoners were forced to criticize one another publicly in terms of their mutual failure to achieve the objectives of a happy Communist character. This last seems silly unless one appreciates that men who have been harassed for many months may eventually become more vulnerable to such criticism by peers—at least coming to resent those who comply and publicly

---

[19] The effect of these forms of sensory and social deprivation on both physical and emotional well-being have by now been extensively studied. See G. Palonzi-Horvath, *The Undefeated* (Boston: Little, Brown, 1959).

[20] In this regard we should not be prepared to brand this sort of treatment inhumane unless we are equally prepared to condemn a great deal of institutional care in America. It would seem to be no accident that such humanitarian institutions as facilities for the mentally retarded, children's summer camps, school physical education programs, hospitals, and army basic training programs should all violate customary personal integrity (by exchanging clothing for common ill-fitting garb, removal of such personal effects as billfolds, forcing all inmates to get a uniform haircut, etc.) in virtually the same manner as the Communists did. Might this initial dehumanization and de-personalization in some fashion contribute to the institution's healing capacity? The issue is not at all clear-cut, public protestations against such custodial care to the contrary. See E. Goffman, *Asylums* (Garden City: Anchor, 1961).

humiliate others—so that the criticism that begins as a lark is gradually taken more seriously and further separates the men from potential peer support.

There was, finally, a complex interrogation process involving a questioner who obviously had a sincere concern for the prisoner's welfare and, in addition, saw the prisoner as ill and in need of salvation through party doctrine; the interrogator saw himself as a kind of priest or therapist whose duty was to lead the deviant toward the insight and rehabilitation offered by Communism. During the questioning, the Communist would sometimes decide that the prisoner needed to undergo torture as part of his education, but he did not relish the inflicting of pain except on humanitarian grounds (much as do our psychotherapists who practice behavior modification by using electric shocks or "chemical castration" to extinguish certain conduct).[21] Also during the questioning, the interrogator would relentlessly insist on the prisoner's "guilt" but would give no clues as to the crime—demanding instead that the prisoner have "insight" (and in the process participate in determining his own guilt).

To clarify the tactics underlying this type of rhetoric, let us focus on a particular case in point.[22] In the post World War II years, a Dr. Vincent was a practicing physician in Shanghai. Unexpectedly one evening, he was arrested by five armed Chinese policemen and charged with "crimes against the state." Dr. Vincent began that night a three-and-one-half-year indoctrination program which passed through four phases. We offer his case here both as an example of the technique used in the rhetoric of the soul and because the phases of this particular case parallel so closely the phases of spiritual conversion to which we shall turn shortly.

Phase I lasted only about three days. It was designed to induce in Dr. Vincent feelings of guilt. The rationale here is obvious. If the patient can be persuaded that he is guilty, then he is vulnerable to acts and beliefs that could purge him of his guilt. In Dr. Vincent's case, three tactics were employed to induce guilt. First, social pressure in the form of intensive interrogation and extreme isolation in the form of a windowless 8 x 12 cell were used to create anxiety. Second, all semblances of order were systematically removed from his life. He would be fed randomly, awakened and summoned for questioning at odd times, and

---

[21] That such tactics have become institutionalized in prisons and hospitals has been amply documented. For example, see J. Nordheimer, "Experts Feel Miss Hearst May Have Undergone Brainwashing," *New York Times* (28 May 1974), 30.

[22] An extended analysis of this example may be found in J. A. C. Brown's *Techniques of Persuasion*, pp. 271–282.

never allowed to sleep a regular interval. In this way, the awe-fullness of chaos was systematically imposed on Dr. Vincent's life-style.[23] Third, he was stripped of all human dignity. He was forced to eat with his hands, drink from the floor, and reside in his own excrement. Here are Dr. Vincent's comments on the effects of this first phase:

> Not all the time—but moments—you think they are right. "I did this, I am a criminal." If you doubt, you keep it to yourself. Because if you admit the doubt you will be "struggled" [harassed by other prisoners] and lose the progress you have made.[24]

Once guilt has been established in the patient, he must be provided a means of cleansing *himself* of the guilt. This sacrificial stage defines Phase II of the process. In Dr. Vincent's case, an originally composed confession was the means of sacrifice. This confession, which took two months to secure, was taken by his interrogators to be the first real sign of rehabilitation. Two common tactics were employed to obtain the confession. First, modeled directly upon the behavioral notion of negative reinforcement, threat was used to induce compliance. If he did not compose the confession, he would be tortured and threatened with death. Simultaneously, this threat tactic would be juxtaposed with its behavioral opposite, positive reinforcement or promise. From this perspective, if he confessed, he was promised better treatment, a more cordial social life, in other words, acceptance into the realm of everyday activities. As before, these two tactics were used in no set pattern. They varied randomly to continue the social disorganization and thereby increase the need for compliance. Of this second phase, Dr. Vincent notes:

> You are obliged to stand with chains on your ankles and holding your hands behind your back. . . . You eat as a dog does with your mouth and teeth. You arrange the cup and bowl with your nose to try and absorb broth twice a day. . . . They continuously tell you that, if you confess all, you will be treated better. . . .
>
> [Eventually], you do whatever they want. You don't pay any more attention to your life or to your handcuffed arms. You can't distinguish right from left. You just wonder when you will be shot—and begin to hope for the end of all this.[25]

---

[23] See E. Ziskind and T. Augsber, "Hallucinations in Sensory Deprivation—Method or Madness?" *Science* 137(1962):992–993.

[24] Robert J. Lifton, Quoted in J. A. C. Brown, p. 276.

[25] Robert J. Lifton, Quoted in J. A. C. Brown, p. 272 and p. 273.

After securing an acceptable confession (one which is criticized by other prisoners concerning its "authenticity"), the longest and most involved phase begins. This third redemption stage lasted for over three years. There were two tactics employed. The first might be called extensive sensitivity session with both interrogators and other prisoners. Typically, these sessions would begin by the group considering a "statement" that summarized past Western insults against China and argued that Dr. Vincent, say, "under the guise of medicine" had been nothing more than a lifelong spy, an agent of the Imperialist forces. When his defenses were found to be erroneous, Dr. Vincent was requested by the group to "re-examine himself" and seek the causes for his reactionary tendencies. Thus, each discussion, beginning at an intellectual level, soon became a personal analysis and evaluation. The second tactic under this phase involved scapegoating. Throughout, Capitalism was suggested as the ultimate cause of any discomfort Dr. Vincent was experiencing. After this three-year ordeal, these were Dr. Vincent's thoughts:

> In the cell, twelve hours a day, you talk and talk—you have to take part—you must discuss yourself, criticize, inspect yourself, denounce your thought. Little by little you start to admit something, and look to yourself, only using the "people's judgment."[26]

The final Phase is salvation. Once Phase III is really over, the patient is rehabilitated by definition and once more ready to enter Communist society. If he has been saved, as his interrogators hope, he will not only enter society in the "proper" state of mind, but he will be a passionate spokesman for the party because he has "re-created" that ideology in himself over a three-year period. Not only will he understand its intellectual ramifications, but, more important, he will have those intellectual points forever enmeshed in his soul. Or so goes the argument. Of this, Dr. Vincent concludes:

> You begin to believe all this, *but it is a special kind of belief.* You are not absolutely convinced, but you accept it—in order to avoid trouble—because every time you don't agree, trouble starts again.[27]

Notice again that the Communists were not interested in forcing counterfeit confessions—they wanted genuine ("heart-felt") confessions

---

[26] Robert J. Lifton, Quoted in J. A. C. Brown, p. 275.
[27] Robert J. Lifton, Quoted in J. A. C. Brown, p. 276.

as part of a conversion process, because they honestly believed they were being humanitarian in offering the American the opportunity for rehabilitation. Nor is this dogmatism so strange. Were you to walk down the hall of an American mental hospital and be approached by an inmate who informed you that he was a victim of a plot, that he was not crazy but was being kept prisoner against his will, you might well take his odd behavior as further confirmation of his madness; if walking down the hall of a prison, you heard a prisoner whisper to you that he was innocent and would you please aid him in escaping, you would again likely take this as evidence of his criminality. Likewise, the Communist interrogator took protestations as evidence of recalcitrance, and he spotted efforts at false confessions as cases of malingering—he was interested in genuine insight only.

Under such unstable conditions, some prisoners who lacked strong convictions and confidence in themselves did on occasion come to rely upon the interrogator, since he was the only seemingly reliable figure in their environment. Because he displayed a heartfelt compassion for the prisoner's well-being, the interrogator in some cases became an authority figure (that is, a person with the magical powers to cope with the situation), and as the prisoner came to rely on him to maintain contact with common sense reality, he also began to have faith that Communism was indeed a salvation. The prisoner thus gradually began to adapt to the frame of Communist ideology, in some cases to the point of voluntarily defecting to the enemy (that is, joining wholeheartedly in enemy games).

It is still difficult for most of us to understand the place of this kind of rhetoric in our society. Perhaps Dr. Robert Lifton located it best when he said:

> Some people considered [thought reform] a relentless means of undermining the human personality; others saw it as a profoundly "moral"—even religious—attempt to instil new ethics into the Chinese people. Both of these views was [sic] partly correct, and yet each, insofar as it ignored the other, was greatly misleading. For it was the combination of *external force or coercion* with an appeal to *inner enthusiasm through evangelistic exhortation* which gave thought reform its emotional scope and power.[28]

While Americans and Westerners generally remain skeptical of applying this kind of rhetoric directly to motivate individuals' conduct of

---

[28] Robert J. Lifton, Quoted in J. A. C. Brown, p. 270.

public affairs (since we value our political "rugged individualism"), we nevertheless come very close to easy acceptance of those Rhetoric games in other areas such as medicine.

American Medicine

We have already shown that faith in restoration of the deviant to the human community is greatly reliant on the set of metaphysical myths the society accepts regarding how men relate to their natural environment. In primitive societies that tie is often through the mediation of super-natural spirits, while in Communist nations, it is determined by party ideology. In America it has been the case that our scientific-industrial outlook on the physical world for the past three centuries has caused us to unconsciously perceive ourselves as rather machine-like. Think, after all, of how we commonly talk about our bodies. When in need of an operation we speak of "checking the old ticker," "getting our gears in order," or "going in for a tune-up." We imagine the brain to be a miniaturized computer. While driving cross country we eat lunch, not so much for pleasure as to "gas up." A recent radical slogan asked everyone to "turn on, tune in, drop out" as though we were all radios. A mentally deranged person "has a screw loose."

If we do indeed think about the world in such a mechanical way that we talk of ourselves in mechanical terms, then it follows that whenever we have some sort of "breakdown" or malfunctioning, we should call upon a high grade mechanic to do the repair work. And this turns out to be the case—our doctors seem to model themselves on our appliance and auto mechanics in a number of important ways. We will see this mechanical emphasis most markedly in the rhetoric that accompanies the healing process.[29]

This is not to deny the seriousness of the American medical profession. Malfunction is an awe-full condition; disorientation is chaotic. The power we invest in our doctors over the resolution of this confusion is

---

[29] William A. Nolen, the "best-seller" surgeon, implies this connection in the following advice:

> There's no simple, surefire formula for choosing a doctor; but then, neither is there one for choosing a lawyer, a hairdresser or a mechanic. You ask around, and you take your chances. I'm at the mercy of the guy who tells me I need a $300 valve job—whatever that is—on my car. He's at my mercy when I tell him he needs a $300 operation on his gallbladder.
>   I find out all I can about the mechanic and then hope and trust that he's as capable and honest as he's cracked up to be. He has to put the same kind of faith in me.

W. A. Nolen, "Examining Your Doctor," McCall's (October 1972), 22.

real, not trivial; "the men who cut and patch and sew the human heart inspire awe even among cynics, precisely because they are working at the beating heart of life."[30] Our claim is merely that a mechanical aspect flourishes in the rhetoric that accompanies the American medical process.

For one thing, where the shaman, operating out of the frame of supernatural power, may employ incantations and blessings and touching of wounds with sacred objects, the medical doctor employs vastly different symbols of authority—a lab coat, stethoscope, medical prescriptions (to which we shall return shortly), and various "scientific" tools for diagnosis and repair work. It is important to realize that, in addition to assisting the doctor in his examination, they all serve to reassure the patient that he is being treated by someone with a scientific, dispassionate set of values. And as Kenneth Burke has noted, "even when the apparatus can't restore a man's health, it can help him die well."[31]

The use of medication is a special category in the persuasive process. Imagine that you went to a doctor and told him you had the sniffles, a headache, and a weak feeling, and he responded: "You have just been hexed by a demon who has been making the rounds; there is little to do but go home and rest in bed for a few days until he leaves town. My bill is $20." You doubtless would not be satisfied; you might even refuse to pay your bill under such circumstances. But suppose you went to the same doctor, described the same symptoms, and he responded: "You are just infected by a virus that has been making the rounds; go home and rest in bed for a few days. Here is a prescription for a brand new, very powerful antibiotic medication; take it every six hours for three days, and you should be all right. That will be $20 for the visit, $15 for the medication, please." Now here is a fine doctor, worth every cent he charges. Notice the two elements that have changed—the doctor has employed a scientific vocabulary (virus for demon); and he has given you an amulet—medication that carries the authority of the scientific world; you are grateful for the power he has given you in the little bottle.

Now doctors are no fools: They know that patients will not be satisfied with the simple advice to go home and rest (especially if they are paying $20 to get the advice). The patient needs a manifestation of the doctor's concern and of his scientific presence so the doctor very often prescribes a "placebo"—"fake" medication, sugar pills dressed up

---

[30] Keith R. Johnson, review of *Hearts*, by Thomas Thompson, *Time* (5 October 1971), 96.

[31] K. Burke, *Grammar of Motives and A Rhetoric of Motives* (Cleveland: World Publishing Company, 1962), p. 696.

in scientific labels or miniscule amounts of some active, but inappropriate ingredient. We have no sure statistics on the amount of placebos prescribed in America. Probably because the use of one kind of placebo, prescribed by clinicians to determine the efficacy of a medicine, is unknown to both the patient *and* the physician.[32] What is most intriguing

---

[32] Incidently, it is in these so-called double-blind situations that the placebo is most effective.

about placebos, however, is that their effects are not illusory: Not only do we *feel* better just because a medicine is prescribed, but in many instances placebos actually seem to "cure" illnesses.

The rhetorical effects of placebos are recorded in the history of medicine. One medical historian commented, "The history of medical treatment, although concordant with scientific progress in general, is at the same time incredible."[33] His catalogue of medicinal substances includes chameleon blood, the oil of skinned puppy, the saliva of a fasting man, and moss scraped from the skull of a victim of a violent death.[34] Despite the use of what seem bizarre substances, people believed that these were appropriate substances and were "healed" and physicians continued to be useful and highly respected members of society.

We do not mean to suggest that people who are cured by placebos were never really ill, or that they are necessarily stupid or highly suggestible. Even today, placebos are officially credited with marked physiological effects—both favorable and unfavorable. One out of every three suffering patients, for example, has intense pain cut at least in half by a placebo.[35] Some placebos even effect change in the patient greater than would normally be attributed to potent substances.[36] Alternatively, the administration of a placebo can effect a toxic reaction—nausea, drowsiness, diarrhea, and hearing loss.[37]

Instead, we are suggesting, along with Jourard, that "the physiological effect of drugs . . . accounts only for *part* of the total variance in healing and that perhaps a greater proportion, maybe all, can be accounted for by the attitude toward, and faith in, treatment manifested by or inspired in the patient."[38]

In addition to the display of symbols of authority and the prescribing of medication, the doctor engages in one further practice that aligns his rhetoric with the industrial cultural values so many of us trust; he displays a workshop mentality in his reliance upon hospitals, profes-

---

"Placebos indentified as such by the patients or the doctors don't work well," according to Frederick J. Evans ("The Power of a Sugar Pill," *Psychology Today* [April 1974], 59).

[33] A. K. Shapiro, "The Placebo Effect in the History of Medical Treatment: Implications for Psychiatry," *American Journal of Psychiatry* 116(October 1959):299.

[34] Ibid.

[35] Frederick Evans, "The Power of a Sugar Pill," 55–59.

[36] S. Wolf, "Effects of Suggestion and Conditioning on the Action of Chemical Agents in Human Subjects—the Pharmacology of Placebos," *Journal of Clinical Investigation* 29(1950):100–109; J. D. Frank, *Persuasion and Healing*, pp. 65–74; *New England Journal of Medicine* (31 August 1967).

[37] S. Wolf and R. Pinsky, "Effects of Placebo Administration and Occurrence of Toxic Reactions," *Journal of American Medical Association* 155(1954):339–341.

[38] S. Jourard, *The Transparent Self*, p. 79.

sional buildings, and asylums—repair places—which signals that, as his counterparts in the auto and television trades, the complex appliances he repairs need to be brought into a specialized workshop for adequate repairs. If we stop for a moment to consider the essential personality traits of an ideal medical repairman, we find that they are astonishingly close to those of any other repairman. We would like our doctor (as opposed, for example, to an actor or lawyer) to be polite, formal, pleasant. Technical competence should dominate other aspects of his personality; competence is paramount to all else. Should the doctor be friendly, that would be a gratuitous bonus: More important, we expect our doctor to investigate thoroughly, unsqueamishly, and unintrusively whatever matters of medical fact are necessary. We demand that his craftsman's intelligence proceed systematically, efficiently, parsimoniously, economically, and in orderly fashion.[39]

This was not always the case, of course. A century ago, all tradesmen made the rounds of a neighborhood. The peddler brought his tools to the house and sharpened knives or fixed a broken chair; and doctors too made house calls. With the coming of mass production and factory warranties, however, repairmen began to insist that a broken appliance be brought to a shop, signed for, and left in their care until it was ready to be returned to the owner. Following suit, doctors came to rely more and more on hospital complexes.[40] Today, if your auto needs a repair, you drive it to a garage, turn it over to a receptionist with a clipboard and white coat, perhaps sneak a glimpse of a huge repair area with work spaces designated for various mechanical specialists (each man has his tools on a separate bench with his name emblazoned on the wall) and special heavy duty equipment for wheel alignments and the like. But if you wish to wait for your auto, you must do so in a small reception room filled with old *National Geographics* and plastic sofas in mock Danish not-so-modern or early-motel. You recover your auto when a notice comes to the front desk telling you what the bill is.

In like manner, should you need to enter a medical clinic, you are treated like the auto. You are met as you enter by a nurse with clipboard and white coat who takes all your personal belongings, checks your medical coverage, hands you a receipt and some ill-fitting garb that is clearly not meant for you (often it is a too-short nightgown opened up the back to deny you the least sense of privacy)—you are transformed into a non-person. Some parts of the clinic consist of a row of examina-

---

[39] D. Bakan, "Psychotherapist: Healer or Repairman?" *Merrill-Palmer Quarterly of Behavior and Development* 8(1962):129.

[40] See Erving Goffman, *Asylums,* pp. 321–386.

tion rooms where each doctor has his name on the door and his tools inside. The heavy duty equipment (X-rays and lab equipment) is shared in common at the same place in the clinic where the wheel alignment equipment would be in the garage. In place of a spare parts department, most clinics have a pharmacy; in place of an oil change, there are blood banks and transfusions; in place of a used car lot, there are donors for kidneys and corneas. But clinics have the same waiting rooms as garages, decorated with the same furniture and magazines.

Is this all purely coincidental, or may there be rhetorical elements here, assuring the patient that he will be treated as a proper non-person, that he will receive the same expert care his television set would if it were broken? As we stated earlier, to understand the rhetoric of healing is to understand the public process of persuasion in which a "sufferer" has faith in the ability of his "healer" to change his condition to one of "health" and so restore to him his privileges of entry to fraternal games.[41]

Perhaps it is easy enough to see how our society has managed to put its physical health concerns into the pattern of the healer/sufferer Rhetoric games. But does the rhetoric of physical healing apply to the rest of our society—its social problems, values, and norms? We propose to show some of the ways that American medical practices have strongly influenced how our society handles the relationships between "normal" people and others.

Psychotherapy

Perhaps nowhere is the rhetoric of healing so clearly illustrated as in the vast "mental health" industry that today dominates such a large share of our collective compassion for those we regard as "less fortunate than ourselves" (or, in plainer words, those unable to play our favorite communal games). It must be understood that until this century our society did not define its norms in terms of "mental health," and very few people were regarded as mentally deranged. There were madhouses in the nineteenth century, but they were mainly populated with those who suffered from syphilitic brain deterioration, and so they were more properly quarantine centers. There were of course individuals whom we would today describe as psychotic, but they were treated through the legal system, sometimes as religious heretics or political deviants, sometimes (as in the case of the mentally retarded) allowed to wander

---

[41] See I. Illich, *Tools for Conviviality* (New York: Harper & Row, 1973).

harmlessly about the town performing simple tasks in return for their keep or tended by members of their families. They can be found characterized in plays of the period as "the fool."

Be that as it may, twentieth-century societies have developed large bureaucratic apparatuses for dealing with those whose behavior deviates from publicly acceptable norms. What is most interesting for our purposes is that aside from the sheerly custodial aspects of the mental health profession (keeping records on the neurotic, the aged, the orphaned, and the retarded, housing them, controlling them through tranquilizers, and training them in simple vocational skills), whatever "healing" is performed is primarily verbal. Let us consider a typical instance of a mental health game, the one called therapy. To play therapy you need at least two players (unless you are playing group therapy)—one called the *therapist* and the other called the *client*. How can you tell one from the other? Not necessarily by their overt behavior or their uniforms; society just designates the healer as "therapist," and the other person as "client."[42]

The therapy game is played in the following fashion: The client is designated by society as being "poorly adjusted" or "not able to function in conventional society," which is to say, his game play rocks the boat.[43] He and the therapist engage in repeated verbal exchanges during which the client tries to achieve "insights" into his behavior (just as does the prisoner in the Communist prison) such that he eventually changes his behavior. That is how the game is played. Notice that there is a presumption that the therapist does not change; should the therapist in the course of play somehow become more like the patient, both would lose the game. In fact, what occurs during therapy is a phenomenon known as "convergence"[44]: The game is declared over whenever the therapist says it is. And how does he know when to call a halt? When the client's attitudes and/or behaviors shift (or seem to him to shift) to become more "normal," i.e., more like those of the therapist. Thus, if a patient were to go to a Freudian analyst to play therapy, he would likely soon begin to

---

[42] Actually, it is fairly easy to spot the client. He is the "insane" one, by which we mean someone who insists on playing different games than we do. When we are all ready to play swimming, he comes with a tennis racket; when we want to play swingers, he plays sounding. The insane is a deviant who often: (1) is more conscious than the conventional man, and (2) insists on telling everyone what he perceives. We ordinary mortals, in our fear at his bizarre behavior, call him *crazy* so we can dismiss his messages. See T. Szasz, *Ideology and Insanity: The Manufacture of Madness* (New York: Harper & Row, 1971).

[43] See C. Reich, *The Greening of America* (New York: Bantam, 1971), p. 147, for a sketch of mental-emotional norms for modern technocratic America.

[44] See H. B. Pepinsky and T. O. Karst, "Convergence: A Contribution to the Working Through Process," *American Psychologist* 19(May 1964):333–338.

dream in Freudian symbols, even if he had not previously. And if he went to a Rogerian therapist, he might soon begin to talk using Rogerian jargon. If and when such manifestations occurred, they would in all likelihood be taken by the therapist as "evidences of progress" toward a cure.

We can thus see that as a study in Rhetoric, what happens is the opposite of what we might expect. Instead of the therapist giving aid or advice to the patient, it is the patient who does the persuading; he tries to persuade the therapist (and perhaps himself) that he is mentally sound. And he does this by coming to speak of the world in the terms used by the therapist. This game has recently been subjected to severe criticism by Thomas Szasz, among others. Szasz, who calls mental illness a form of psychiatric propaganda, basically feels that the game is unfairly weighted in favor of the therapist. He argues that the therapist resembles the exposer of witches in the Middle Ages in that neither the therapist nor Torquemada can do any wrong. For the patient, or the accused witch, either admission or denial serves as confirmation of guilt:

Therapist: "You are filled with rage."

Client: "On the contrary, I feel very calm."

Therapist: "That feeling is just your defense; you can't bear to face your rage."

And just as the witchmonger was under considerable pressure to display his skill by identifying symptoms of demonology, so is the therapist judged by his skill in diagnosing neuroses:

First Matron: "Dr. Frood is just wonderful; he noticed me doodling with a pencil and commented at once on its evidence of my penis envy."

Second Matron: "Oh, yes! My sister was telling him of a dream she had about putting on her cosmetics and he spotted *her* penis envy in her inability to put her lipstick on properly."

But these matters are of interest to us here only insofar as they reveal the rhetorical features of the healing game: The patient's anxiety is decreased by the knowledge that he can persuade a respected and trusted therapist that he, the patient, understands what is wrong.[45] As we have men-

---

[45] See E. F. Torrey, *The Mind Game—Witchdoctors and Psychiatrists*, pp. 15–33, for a more elaborate discussion of the "naming process" which he labels "The Principle of Rum-

tioned previously, in other contexts, the legitimacy of this interaction as a game is better left to those concerned with political and legal matters.[46] For our present purposes, it is enough to note that these patterns for classifying people as "sick" or "abnormal" are a matter of concern to every member of society.

Revivalism

For most Americans the industrial myth still holds promise; they have faith that science will protect them and in whatever mysterious ways see to their welfare. But a growing number of Americans have been disappointed by science, having either been cast aside by the industrial economy or having glimpsed the limits to the promise. The first group have fallen back upon traditional religion for faith and the second group have cast about for post-industrial spiritualistic faith. The first group consists mostly of the rural elderly whereas the latter is younger and college educated. The first have traditionally relied on evangelical religion for healing, while the second have developed a variety of transcendental food fads and communal rituals to assist in their healing. The first enjoy country and western music while the second tend toward rock. Let us consider each group in turn, realizing as we do that the two groups share a distrust of science as a means of salvation, although their rituals differ in superficial details.[47]

To whom does religious revival appeal as a means of restoring health? We can summarize the group by saying they are those who have been excluded from the glitter of modern industrial myths. They tend to be older, to live isolated, lonely lives, and to have been repeatedly insulted by the prevailing industrial culture. Often they are those who have been failed by science. Typically they suffer chronic illnesses that cannot be cured by doctors. (An old man goes to an M.D. and says, "Doctor, I feel a pain in my back." The doctor responds, "I don't see anything on my X-ray; the pain is all in your head." "No. Doctor," responds the old man, "I feel the pain in my back, not my head." "I'm sorry," says the M.D., "my X-ray shows that there is no real pain in your back.") Most important, having been brought up with a deep fundamen-

---

pelstiltskin" and which he considers "one of the most important components of all forms of psychotherapy."

[46] The legal ramifications of this issue are documented by W. K. Stevens, "Psychiatrists Debate Private Rights and Public Saftey," *New York Times* (13 May 1974), 22.

[47] W. G. McLaughlin, "Pietism and the American Character," *American Quarterly* 17(Summer 1965):163–186.

talist religious belief in a supernatural deity who punishes those who fail to live a religious life, these people are now confronted with both chronic illnesses and the awareness that they have been left behind by economic forces in spite of their constant personal efforts to work hard and live honest lives. Clearly, their rejection by society must seem some sort of divine punishment for their sins, even though they do not today subscribe to any formal religion (and perhaps for that very reason are they suffering pains as well as alienation).[48]

These people, for whom the industrial-scientific myths hold no promise, often fall back upon the revivalist's myths (which have a long and honorable tradition in America).[49] The roots of revivalism are the pietistic and egalitarian principles that were brought to the American colonies during the eighteenth century by such radical sects as the Baptists and Methodists to compete with the decaying and institution-based Puritans. The established Puritan church practiced a policy of exclusion even as it claimed that those who were not members would be damned in the afterlife. As settlers began to move into Connecticut and New York and later into Kentucky, they were more and more isolated for long periods of time under conditions of great uncertainty and anxiety (fear of Indian attacks and plague being two of the more obvious causes); it was certainly no help to know that theologians were adding to their headaches by claiming that despite all their best efforts in this difficult life, all who were not members of the elect were doomed to go to Hell in the next.

Into this situation came preachers with radical religions, claiming with St. Paul that one could *experience* salvation (i.e., God's Grace) and not have to rely on membership in an elite organization, and that, furthermore, since each man was potentially able to achieve redemption directly with God, all men were essentially equal in the eyes of God, social status notwithstanding. It is no wonder that with a message such as this, charismatic preachers such as George Whitefield and later Albert Finney had backwoods-people flocking to hear them. And so developed

[48] D. Ungurait compiled the following demographic data on the make-up of the audience for an Oral Roberts Crusade in Madison, Wisconsin, 17–26 June 1960: 3.5 percent Catholics, 24.5 percent Lutherans, 11.3 percent Methodists, 31.1 percent Pentecostals, 3.9 percent Baptists, 6.4 percent no affiliation; average age—48; rural population—67 percent; female—67.8 percent; average education—9th grade; income—54.7 percent under $2,000. "A Preliminary Study of an Oral Roberts Crusade, 1960," unpublished M.A. Thesis (Madison: University of Wisconsin, 1960).

[49] For representative studies of this tradition with special reference to the rhetorical features we are considering, see C. W. Ferguson, *Organizing to Beat the Devil* (New York: Doubleday, 1971); D. R. Heisey, "On Entering the Kingdom: Birth or Nurture," in D. Holland, ed., *Preaching in American History* (New York: Abingdon Press, 1969), pp. 150–167.

the frontier revival, where thousands of the faithful (that is, people who wanted to believe and had great respect for the preacher's powers) traveled long distances to gather for several days in "camp meetings" (given transportation hardships, it was necessary to camp—no convention facilities). These were very dramatic gatherings, devoted to prayer in the company of the faithful. One can imagine the excitement and stimulation as simple rural folk who had lived virtually alone, struggling with a relentless and forbidding Nature for months or years on end, were suddenly surrounded with like-minded peers all of whom had such faith in the preacher that they had endured an arduous journey to be in his presence. And the preacher himself was a man who, whether his message was the horrors of damnation (Jonathan Edwards) or the joys of salvation (Whitefield), was skilled in stimulating emotional energies over a period of a few days (keep in mind that these men had to develop techniques that would channel their listeners' potent but unchanneled emotions into religious fervor in a short period of time, since once the revival was over, the participants would separate into their isolated lives—all confirmation had to occur in the camp meeting).

These dramatic meetings, replete with prayers, sermons, and entreaties to sinners (that is, "lost sheep who had strayed from God's fold") to seek God's grace, operating with the pressure of both peers and the charismatic presence of the preacher, often had a cathartic impact on many of the participants. Their anxieties (from all sources of their lives) would well up and be experienced in a gush of emotion as a renewal. Feelings that had to be contained on the frontier could afford to be released, and this release, with its concomitant sudden elation, was taken to be the experience of contacting God (comparable to the "beautiful moment" that occurs in an encounter group where, under peer and trainer stress, someone breaks down and cries). This pietistic tradition of personal responsibility for one's moral well-being and egalitarianism based on a shared emotional experience gave those who had been so saved a certain superiority and pity toward those stray lambs who hadn't been so fortunate as to have shared the renewal experience. It also invested preachers who could induce these cathartic experiences with tremendous authority; they were known for their ability to perform miracles.

The revivalist, whether he is preaching in a huge, filled coliseum or over television develops a message that: (1) makes his listeners aware of his presence as a man of God (who, for example, has the power to employ TV); (2) makes his listeners aware of the many others (peers) who have faith (the listener is not alone; in this circle his religious beliefs are not mocked; he can afford to express them); and (3) seeks to transform self-pity into fraternal regard by getting the listeners to pray for one another.[50] In this way the preacher enables some of the listeners to experience redemption and some may even have remissions of their illnesses.

Perhaps our discussion of the rhetoric of revivalism can be best summarized by the following excerpt taken from a report of Kathryn Kuhlman's visit to Minneapolis, Minnesota, in 1973:

> A young girl, wearing a brace, came on stage in tears. She took the brace off, held it over her head. The audience cheered, the big auditorium organ crashed into life. Kathryn Kuhlman put her arms around the girl.
>
> "This is God," she cried, "this is the power of God."
>
> The girl said she had polio as a baby and had worn the brace since. Her leg was deformed. Ms. Kuhlman told her to walk around the stage. The girl, still sobbing, obeyed.
>
> "Don't cry, honey," she told the girl. "Dear Jesus, I give You praise . . . the power of God has gone through this body." The girl swooned, and as she was being helped, Ms. Kuhlman turned. "There is somebody behind me with migraine headaches who was just cured," she said. "The spirit of Jesus is healing."
>
> Two men standing in front of the stage embraced. "Praise the Lord," one said. "Yes, praise the Lord," the other replied. All over the audience, hands were in the air, raised toward God, eyes were shut, prayers were being whispered.
>
> In a hallway outside the main auditorium, an old lady with a cane was stopping everyone to tell her news.
>
> "I spent a fortune on operations," she said. "I have two crushed vertebrae. I've been in agony for years. But here today that woman cured me, praise God, I'm healed." And she twirled the cane in the air and skipped a few steps. A woman, walking by, reached out to touch the cane. "God bless you, sister," she said to the old woman. "Praise the Lord."
>
> Two other women walked out a door to the street.
>
> "What a quack," one said. "She couldn't cure a hangnail. All she's after is the money."
>
> If appearances were any indication, the scoffers were in the minority. More than 65 buses had brought people from as far away as Canada to see and hear the faith healer, and only a few people left, despite the heat.[51]

---

[50] By shifting attention away from his own worries, the listener immediately begins to feel better; he also improves his own self esteem—if his prayers can benefit someone else, then he is himself not a total cipher.

[51] Reported by Zeke Wigglesworth, *The Minneapolis Star* (4 June 1973), 7A.

This incident aptly summarizes the manner in which the revival serves as a vehicle for restoring communal sensibility even as it heals the sufferer who would otherwise be excluded because of his or her affliction.

Sensitivity and Encounter Groups

If pietism was the Romantic source of the revival, then other Romantic elements of the eighteenth and nineteenth centuries gave rise to the other major anti-mechanistic healing movement operative today in America: the general counter-culture trend toward the use of organic foods, "Jesus" sects, T-group and sensitivity sessions, communal living, and "camp" followings of various gurus and mystics. Except for a pagan denial of a formal deity, there is a great deal of similarity in the root myths of revivalism and the sensitivity movement, for both are Romantic and fundamentalistic at base.[52]

As Christianity collapsed as a motivating force in eighteenth-century Europe men turned to a new divinity—Nature—as a replacement. Nature was a suitable alternative because it was not of man's creation but was itself the source of creation. It had the added advantage of being unlike formal religion (which was arid and stuffy): It was above all sensual.[53]

It was Rousseau as well as anyone who, exiled at Lake Geneva from the affairs of men, had first become aware of the role of scenery in abandoning one's self to sheer sensation. For hours at a time he would sit enraptured watching reflections upon the smooth water, and gradually allow the stream of his consciousness to merge with the reflections as he immersed himself in the experience. Through this exploration of more direct modes of knowing than logical inference he claimed to renew himself.

These Romantic components—sensual (not to say sexual) experience, adoration of Nature (and through it, by extension, the "natural" and authentic), and an admixture of pietism (the belief in the personal experience of redemption outside of formal religious institutions), but without the keystone of God, combined in the nineteenth century in American Romanticism in such projects as adult education (Chautauqua)

---

[52] T. Ogden, "The New Pietism," *Journal of Humanistic Psychology* 12(Spring 1972); C. Brinton, "Romanticism," *Encyclopedia of Philosophy*, VII, 206–209.

[53] See E. M. Collins, Jr., "The Rhetoric of Sensation Challenges the Rhetoric of the Intellect: An Eighteenth Century Controversy" in D. Holland, ed., *Preaching in American History* (New York: Abingdon Press, 1969), pp. 98–117.

and city parks (for the spiritual renewal of industrial man—a Nature museum).

From this common Romantic source has come the desire of those younger members of society who lack a fundamentalist religious upbringing, but who nevertheless find the mechanism of contemporary science and reason to be lacking in sufficient spiritualism, to turn to the alternatives mentioned. Perhaps the most phenomenal social event of our age was the Woodstock rock festival. In a natural setting, despite heat, lack of food, water, and even reasonable sanitation provisions, reactions of the participants were unanimous: "Wow!" "Uplifting" . . . "Unreal." There are literally hundreds of accounts that likened the Woodstock experience to a massive *familial* gathering: It was as if the half million people there were participating in the actual birth of a culture and were celebrating, symbolically, the joys of delivery. Comments on the privilege of just "being there" are particularly significant. For *being* there is apparently what really *was* there: conviviality.

We can take as another simple illustration of this cultural recycling, the national trend to encounter groups.[54] Like its Romantic counterpart of revivalism, its two main themes are either fear of damnation (Schutz, Perls) and/or the joys of salvation (Rogers). But where the revivalist has, ever since the days of Jonathan Edwards, placed the burden for emotional scars upon a man's moral relationship to God, the sensitivity trainer has, with most Freudians, placed it upon a man's family upbringing. And where the evangelist enlists God's authority, the trainer calls upon psychology.

Aside from these sectarian differences, however, the overriding aspects are similar. There remains the pietistic opposition to establishment orthodoxy (for sensitivity, it is often the educational establishment that is attacked), a moral fervor and ethical preoccupation with purification and personal renewal, restoration of fraternal respect for one's fellows, invocation of procedures and activities intended to renew the pleasures

---

[54] We are by now engulfed by an evermore extensive list of surveys, both scientific and journalistic, of the encounter group as a convivial gathering intended to restore fraternal gratification for those who feel cut off from such relationships in their lives. We are not in a position to assess, as so many others have done, the success or failure of such groups to achieve their aims. Our only purpose is to set them in a conceptual context that will relate them to other recreational communication games. For further treatment of the sensitivity group/encounter group phenomenon, see J. Howard, *Please Touch* (New York: McGraw-Hill, 1970); D. G. Appley and A. E. Winder, *T-Groups and Therapy Groups in a Changing Society* (San Francisco: Jossey-Bass, 1973); A. Burton, ed., *Encounter* (San Francisco: Jossey-Bass, 1970); K. W. Back, *Beyond Words* (New York: Russell Sage Foundation, 1972); L. N. Solomon and B. Berzon, eds., *New Perspectives on Encounter Groups* (San Francisco: Jossey-Bass, 1972).

one derives from the company of others, the intensification of group experience in hopes of having a direct contact with divine (or authentic) experience (this coupled with the counterpoint of escape from social interaction through exercises in spiritual solitude), and, finally, a sanctimonious pity and sense of superiority over those "lost lambs" of whatever social or economic stations who have not had the luck to have been saved.

The other collective forms we have mentioned—fondness for Eastern religions, cultic fascination with the recuperative powers of organic food, communal life—also partake of the same historical trend that rejects our prevailing materialism in favor of a "Natural" or Romantic spiritual regeneration.[55] In fact, in their preoccupation with sensual re-creation we might be justified in regarding the periodic emergence of such collective movements as the health food fad of the 1920's, and its robust offspring, the organic food fad, as primarily poetic in character. Since we are here concerned with their persuasive force as procedures for cleansing the soul and restoring the individual to a collective social harmony, we should categorize them by their rhetorical aspect.

In these cases, as in those of the old woman who is "saved and cured" at a religious revival, our attitude should be less one of skepticism or contempt for superstition than it should be one of compassionate understanding of how the persuasive process works upon the soul. Those who feel secure with an industrial-medical myth will likely be cured (for the most part) by medical doctors. Those who reject that myth will develop curing procedures more appropriate to the myths they hold in common with the particular community from which they feel momentarily isolated. In some instances (as in Torquemada's day), curing may demand burning at the stake, in others, electric shock therapy in a mental asylum, or rededication to religious principles at a revival, or "re-education" in a political prisoner camp, or joining with other like-minded peers in whatever collective institution is a suitable political vehicle for the age and society. In all these instances the student of human communication will not look with less respect upon the medical doctor-therapist, but with somewhat more understanding and affection for his forefather, Torquemada.

Let us pause to reflect again on the differences among the various

---

[55] The first American pure food advocate was in the early ninteenth century. Sylvester Graham, best known today as the creator of the Graham cracker, who, because he opposed such industrially processed foodstuffs as mill ground flour and commercially processed meat, was regarded by all, except his loyal college-age following, as a madman and a threat to the peaceful pursuit of commercial gain.

public communication games that invite their players to experience will-ful common action. Some of these Rhetoric games directly facilitate active participation in civic affairs (telling us, for example, what to buy or how to engage in public dialogue). Others, like those we have just examined, are more remedial. They literally re-habilitate or re-create their partici-pants; they heal those who have somehow lost touch with common sense reality and in so doing prepare them once again to act in concert with their fellows.

The final Rhetoric game that we shall consider is one which is played by those members of a society who sense that they are excluded from participation in civic affairs and who (for whatever reason) accept their isolated state. Rather than accepting any need to play a healing game in order to seek readmission to the civic arena, however, such players are attracted to a different order of persuasion game—one which implicitly confirms their enforced passivity and impotence but which offers in compensation a species of counterfeit political gratification, similar in some respects to the counterfeit aesthetic recreation afforded by certain mass media amusements.

RHETORIC OF THE SEWER: PORNOGRAPHY

We turn now to consider the Rhetoric game that is played in such lonely arenas as the X-rated theatre and the adult bookshop, and that generates those bizarre communicative artifacts that are dismissed, if not de-nounced, as "pornography." Despite the fact that we now have explicitly erotic films, public readings of avowedly obscene poetry, federal research into the "effects" of pornography on readers and viewers,[56] and literary explorations of the genre by a number of admired critics, there has been little, if any, thoughtful consideration of the Rhetoric game of pornography—little consideration, that is, of how pornographic dis-course and a given public interact. We would suggest, however, that in some respects it is as a Rhetoric game that pornography is most interest-ing, and most informative, to an observer of human communicative behavior.

Our concern with these messages will be partly with questions of how they find their appeal in large, perhaps unrecognized, segments of

---

[56] See the Technical Reports of the Commission on Obscenity and Pornography (Washington, D.C.: U.S. Government Printing Office, 1970).

the public. But we will also be concerned with how some of these "pornographic" patterns of appeal may serve as possible indicators of alienation that should be confronted more directly.

For a variety of reasons, we shall not begin with an in-formed particular of obscene material as the point of departure for our discussion. We are not intending by this omission to be coy. It is just that the arguments we wish to make are not readily illustrated by isolated snippets of erotica. We seek to interpret the significance of a pornographic work "taken as a whole."[57] Therefore, let us attempt to suggest more specifically what we mean when we use the term *pornography* in this discussion.

We shall be concerned with what is often called "hard core pornography," rather than with merely erotic or bawdy literature. Admittedly, the distinction is sometimes difficult to draw. As examples of such bawdy literature—and *not*, in our terms, *pornography*—consider the tales of Chaucer, Rabelais, or Boccacio, or the films of the Marx Brothers. These messages are robust, often sexually explicit and/or sensual, but they are not ordinarily sexually stimulating. Their focus is only incidentally upon profane acts. More central to bawdy fiction is the creature exuberance that lurks beneath the surface of polite manners and often erupts with embarrassing consequences. Bawdy literature displays the lucid innocence of the child; its impulse is mainly boisterous. Hard core pornography has, as we hope to show, more serious implications.

Most examinations of pornographic discourse follow one of two alternative approaches. Literary critics are prone to interpret erotica from the creator's perspective, considering the author's intentions, motivations, or tactics for exploiting his or her audience. In contrast, psychological commentary usually explores the receiver's perspective, asking either what behavioral changes are elicited by contact with erotic artifacts or how the individual reader gratifies his or her immediate personal needs through the consumption of obscene materials. Asking about the artistic intentions of the creator of pornography, or about the immediate effects of such discourse upon an audience, however, is not the same thing as considering the appeal of pornography for those who regularly and repeatedly seek out pornography for themselves.

We would suggest that the appeal of pornography for its public[58] can

---

[57] The classic Supreme Court definition of obscenity invokes this same unitary standard: "Whether to the average person, applying contemporary community standards, the dominant theme of the material *taken as a whole.* . . ." E. Kronhausen and K. Kronhausen, *Pornography and the Law*, rev. ed. (New York: Ballantine Books, 1964), p. 167. [Italics added.]

[58] We do not mean to suggest by this phrase that pornography is something that only "they"

best be explained if we view pornography from the perspective of a Rhetoric game. That is, if we view it as an implicit invitation by the creator of the message for his audience to join in putting a common pattern on imaginary events in terms of the pleasures and pains those images afford, we are in a position to ask what vision of the world is projected by pornographic messages and to speculate upon the fraternal kinship that is awakened in the members of a public who are drawn to collect around and consume a particular pornographic message.[59]

If, as the Greeks knew and as Arendt reminds us, man's natural condition is to seek the company of friends, of arenas where he can actively participate in influencing public affairs and can seek an audience, what happens when he is denied these opportunities, when, for whatever reasons, he is not allowed active involvement in public life? Where such is the case, we might expect he who was not content with personal games would seek out or be attracted to a different type of public game, one which on one hand enabled him to deal with his enforced passivity and impotence, and on the other functioned as a substitute for the freedom he felt lacking. These Rhetoric games are played in back alleys, dingy theaters, and tawdry bookshops. For these games comprise those curious messages to which we hesitate to accord public recognition. These are the Rhetoric games we call *pornography*.

At its core, the consumption of pornography by a given audience offers, we shall contend, a surrogate for the freedom experienced in Rhetoric games. As such, it comes into being at the point where some of the spirit of freedom that pervades a community seems to be fading; and at the point where a large public finds itself unable to enjoy the fruits of public rhetoric by openly consummating its sense of good fellowship among free people. As an individual comes to renounce an intolerable world, he simultaneously seeks the comfort and obscurity of an interior landscape, a "phantasy realm" free of external coercion. But in spite of his efforts to flee such coercion, the public realities will intrude upon and ultimately inform the pornographic artifacts that begin to attract him and other similarly deprived members of his community.

The plausibility of our contention is confirmed by the term "pornography" itself. Pornography is named by joining two Greek words:

---

consume while "we" never do. As with the other games discussed in this book, most of us play the pornography game at one time or another. However, just as it is possible to make inferences about those who habitually play only Polite Greeting, for example, or Turn Off, so too we can consider what needs are gratified for habitual consumers of pornography by examining the nature of the game itself.

[59] An earlier version of the material to follow appeared in L. W. Rosenfield, "Politics and Pornography," *Quarterly Journal of Speech* 60(December 1973):413–422.

harlot-writing. This root has several often overlooked residual meanings. It can refer to writing *about* harlots, and this is how it is commonly employed. But in addition it may refer to *what* harlots wrote, to the wall scribbles we today call *grafitti*. So in this secondary sense pornography is something very public indeed: It denotes those anonymous, vile statements to which one cannot attach a source.

But in a third sense of the term, the harlot must by nature be anonymous. In classical oratory the speaker "appeared" and was given to his listeners; he thus "made his mark" on the community (for the Ancients had a single-minded interest in "displaying" themselves in the company of their comrades and thereby achieving a kind of immortality in the realm of human affairs),[60] whereas the prostitute was literally anonymous. The harlot was condemned to the realm of "private" matters in the body politic, and for the Greeks and Romans such matters were so banal as to mark their pursuit as undignified (and thus unspeakable).

So in its original senses "pornography" calls to mind discourse created by, for, and about the disenfranchised, those who were consigned to mortality with no opportunity to attain the glory that goes with appearance, recognition, and influence in community affairs. In this sense, pornography became the social fabric of the disenfranchised. For those who were thus deprived of rhetorical companionship it became the only viable communication game through which some measure of public citizenship could be experienced.

Understood in these terms, we can propose that most modern commentators on the subject may have matters reversed with the allegation that society inhibits our sexual instincts and causes us to turn to political and aesthetic outlets in order that we may fantasize our sexual longings in a code drawn from the images of daily life. For our purposes, we can just as well account for the domain of pornographic discourse in terms of game participation. When we are denied access to political activities we turn to fantasy games, and perhaps most often to those which most directly seem to represent rhetorical potency, sex fantasies. If readers are especially fond of tales of women objectified and abused under particular circumstances, we might ask ourselves to what extent those readers imagine themselves victimized under comparable conditions in their own daily lives. For it may well be that the popularity of a given theme

---

[60] Psychological support for this interpretation can be found in W. J. Gadpaille, "Grafitti: Its Psychodynamic Significance," *Sexual Behavior* (November 1969), 46, who observes that, "Even those with the crudest sensibilities would not write grafitti on their own bathroom walls," and contends further that grafitti is motivated in part by the desire to gain "a certain pitiful immortality."

in sexual literature is a public indication of society cramping our needs for social intercourse with our fellows, causing us to sublimate those political desires into sexual fantasies.

Accordingly it could prove more instructive to draw our understanding from Jean Genet than from literary or psychoanalytic interpretations when examining pornography.[61] Himself author of several pieces that might qualify as "documentary pornography" on the theme of official brutality (*The Thief's Journal; Our Lady of the Flowers*), Genet has caught the elusive connection between sexual fantasy and political impotence in his play, *The Balcony*, which depicts bordello clients using sexual encounters to express power lusts even as a corrupt society collapses in revolutionary upheaval:

> *Bishop*:   So long as we were in a room in a brothel, we belonged to our own fantasies. But once having exposed them, having named them, having proclaimed them, we're now tied up with human beings, tied to you, and forced to go on with this adventure according to the laws of visibility.
>
> *Chief of Police*:   You have no power. I alone. . . .
>
> *Bishop*:   Then we shall go back to our rooms and there continue the quest of an absolute dignity. We ought never to have left them. For we were content there, and it was you who came and dragged us away. For ours was a happy state. And absolutely safe. In peace, in comfort, behind shutters, behind padded curtains, protected by a police force that protects brothels, we were able to be a general, judge and bishop to the point of perfection and to the point of rapture! You tore us brutally from that delicious, untroubled state.[62]

Pornography seen in this light is clearly a rhetorical event. It exerts an impact on the feelings, imagination, motives, and even the physiology of the recipient. And it is a desperate political act as well; it finds its audience among those furtive souls whose power-less-ness consists of their being denied the companionship of others.[63]

---

[61] For instance, the conventional observation that repeated exposure to pornography leads to diminished sexual activity is entirely too superficial apart from Genet. Empirical investigation has in fact shown that an individual's rate of sexual activity over an extended period remains fairly stable. Exposure to erotic stimuli can thus influence the specific time in which such activity occurs, but it does not alter the overall rate. We feel this is further evidence for looking to political rather than psychological factors controlling preferences for erotic stimuli. See J. Mann, S. Starr, and J. Sidman, "Sex Films and the Married Couple," paper presented to the Fourth National Sex Institute of A.A.S.E.C. (St. Louis, April 1971).

[62] J. Genet, *The Balcony*, trans. S. Frechtman (New York: Grove Press, 1958), 79–80.

[63] Once again it is Arendt, echoing Aristotle who has shown to what extent power is a phenomenon that must be held in common:

This formulation helps us to understand the seedy nature of pornographic theaters and book stalls: They are populated with more than their share of our culture's harlots—those lonely, despised, nameless old men whom our economic system has rejected and doomed to an anonymous living death in cheap hotels. Pornography appeals to those who feel in some degree incomplete for their lack of comradeship and participation in the human affairs that shape their destinies. But it is by no means the merely economically disadvantaged individual who is the main consumer of pornography. It seems to be precisely the person in whom the "spirit of freedom" has been choked off, who feels himself most lonely in his daily "respectable" surroundings, who typically purchases (and this needs to be distinguished from the activity of habituating the pornoshop) such materials: "The average purchasers are middle-aged married men in their 40's who are financially well off and have several children."[64] It is singularly appropriate that pornographic literature finds its culmination in masturbation, a symbolic gesture of impotence.

Nor should we be surprised by the revulsion ordinarily felt by members of "responsible society" at the thought of exposure to pornography. In its fury, pornography often attacks fundamental cultural values on the most violent symbolic ground, by reversing the social designations of sacred and profane. It was entirely in order for Mr. Nixon, as perhaps the last spokesman for .conventional morality, to resolutely op-

---

Power corresponds to the human ability not just to act but to act in concert. Power is never the property of an individual; it belongs to a group and remains in existence only so long as the group keeps together. When we say of somebody that he is "in power" we actually refer to his being empowered by a certain number of people to act in their name. The moment the group, from which the power originated to begin with (*potestas in populo,* without a people or group there is no power), disappears, "his power" also vanishes. (H. Arendt, *On Violence* (New York: Harcourt Brace Jovanovich, 1970), pp. 44.

In consequence, it comes as no surprise to note the recurrence in pornographic literature of acts of extreme cruelty, invariably acted out in remote and secluded places, regions in which the victim is shut off from the eyes of men and thus deprived of any possibility for joint political action:

In a castle, surrounded by high walls and silence, the victim of cruelty is in a situation from which he is powerless to escape, and into which no help for him could come. Cruelty is becoming not so much a matter of pain as a matter of an imbalance of power, an imbalance created and maintained by isolation. (Philip P. Hallie, "Models, Burglary, and Philosophy," *Philosophy and Rhetoric,* [Fall 1971]: 221–222.) See also S. Marcus, *The Other Victorians* (New York: Basic Books, 1964), p. 268; D. Stafford-Clark, "Forward" to G. Freeman, *The Undergrowth of Literature* (New York: Dell, 1967), pp. xxi–xxiii.

[64] Personal communication from Dr. S. Starr, Chief of the Family Study Unit of the Palo Alto V.A. Hospital and one of the investigators in the preparation of the Commission on Obscenity and Pornography's technical reports. Volume IV of those reports provides detailed market studies of customers for pornography. The market studies are perhaps best understood in light of Phillip Slater's seminal critique of contemporary suburban ideals in his *The Pursuit of Loneliness* (Boston: Beacon Press, 1971).

pose the slightest endorsement for "public exposure" of pornographic "filth." As he rightly intuited, the appearance of pornography simultaneously embodies a shrill cry of a victim and the ultimate rejection of the prevailing community. And what is rhetorically more significant, it probably attracts a like-minded audience. As S.D.S. slogans of the last decade would seem to testify, shouted obscenities are less a "loss of reason" in the sense of being irrational than they are magnets for frustrated rage.[65] And if this is so, we would do well to hear them as symptoms of alarm instead of dismissing them as signs of delayed puberty.

Our intention is not to offer extensive empirical support for the hypotheses generated here, though empirical confirmation is by no means hard to come by. Witness the argumentative strategy employed by the Russian literary establishment in response to the recent publication in the West of the underground Russian pornographic novel, *Moscow Nights*. The book was denounced, as have been earlier instances of Russian pornography, as a forgery in *Literaturnava Gazeta*. Yet in a most revealing remark the Novosti press agency claimed: "It is plain that the author of this book is a deeply amoral person, who hates his people and the land which nourishes him."[66]

Pornography's rhetorical character may also account for the common observation that decaying civilizations (that is, those in which the public arenas are corrupted, the games no longer fair) typically increase their output of such decadent literature, while societies in the throes of political revolution become exceptionally puritanical in their habits. As the public domain shrinks and men are increasingly confined to undignified games, we could expect the rise of certain prurient themes reflecting their anxieties, while those ages of political turmoil when all men have at least potential entry to *res publica* would experience a concomitant decline in erotica.

Let us illustrate what we have in mind. William Faulkner's potboiler, *Sanctuary*, deals with a popular erotic theme—the rape and ultimate prostitution of a Southern debutante by Popeye, a hunch-backed homosexual tramp. It is not hard to read this episode as an allegory concerning the suffering that decadent Southern aristocracy endures at the hands of illiterate rednecks who have "seized" power. But might we not extend such

---

[65] See Karl Jaspers, *Nietzsche and Christianity*, trans. E. B. Ashton (Chicago: Regnery, 1961) p. 30.

[66] Cited in *New York Times* (6 February 1972), 9. For further insight into the place of pornography in a society where ordinary political games are outlawed, see Peter Sadecky, *Octobriana and the Russian Underground* (New York: Harper & Row, 1971).

analyses to uncover the hidden appeal of other themes in drug store erotica? Why, for instance, would anyone develop a taste for stories involving the violent rape of innocent virgins and suburban housewives by gangs of black thugs? Might the reader of a decade ago have felt threatened by the rising militancy of American blacks? Might he have used these stories to articulate his fears (he replacing the virgin) in an effort to master his terror? What kinds of persons found Popeye's attack in the corn crib so fascinating that they lingered over the passage, sought out similar scenes in other literature, and returned time and again in their most private moments to the images Faulkner's words provoked? Which readers of *Sanctuary* found instead Temple's degradation in the Memphis brothel or Popeye's impotent whinnying to be the most secretly gratifying? If we can explore the rhetorical impact of "good" literature, we can as well ask the same questions of less aesthetic but equally explosive works as *Back Seat Love, Lash of Lust, The Flesh Mob, Passage to Pleasure*, and *A Star Is Made*. Is it mere accident, for example, that Victorian England seems to have favored erotica that highlighted caste differences (country maids, upperclass prodigals, chimney sweeps) and humiliations of "social posture" (flagellation, betrayal of innocence)?

Again, what are we to make of the recent spate of stories depicting Hell's Angels engaged in violence (again acted out primarily upon virgins)? Let us propose that the real-life significance of motorcycle gangs lies in their communictive function as masquers. Their mode of dress is so similar, one to the other, that it must be seen as a uniform: bedecked with chains, mirror sunglasses, profane insignia (usually Nazi swastikas), grimy with filth, slovenly, outfitted mainly in studded black leather and denim—they personify the popular stereotype of the "pig." Pig? Notice the clownish aspect inherent in the costume: Motorcycle police wear black leather and reflecting sunglasses and assorted paramilitary patches and equipment. And a significant portion of society's wretched look upon the police as "pigs." It thus becomes eminently plausible for some of those despised individuals to don clown costumes that demonstrate how policemen appear in the world. In short, the Hell's Angels costume and behavior represent a parody of the police tactics we all witnessed on television these past few years and have had reported to us by civil rights activists for over a decade.

Romantic enchantment with bike violence erotica by a segment of the public could, therefore, very well reflect an effort to overcome terror of police brutality. The obligatory gang rape scene in such books represents, in its turn, an infantile fantasy of abuse the reader-victim fears he might suffer at the hands of swaggering bullies acting as agents of the law. Recall, after all, the nationally broadcast 1968 Democratic National Convention, showing massed police beating young civilians *with night sticks*. Recall also that the ritual sacrifice at Altamont rock festival was by Hell's Angels acting as "enforcers of order" in a grotesque caricature of ordinary police riot control. Are we prepared to dismiss the profound impact of such incidents upon members of the public merely because we were disgusted rather than terrified by the events? We should alert ourselves to indications that individuals are articulating their political fears in their literature rather than decrying their literary taste.

Nowhere is our contention that pornographic involvement is the province of those denied recreational access to political Rhetoric games more strikingly evident, however, than in the works of America's most famous living pornographer, Henry Miller. Miller stands to his art as Sockless Jerry Simpson stood to politics: He is an arch clown. One need not be a Marxist to recognize threaded throughout Miller's novels a decisive rejection of exploitative social institutions. But his rejection is coupled with a reluctance to overthrow those very institutions that victimize him.

> Combating the "system" is nonsense. There is only one aim in life and that is to live it. In America it has become impossible . . . to live one's own life; consequently the poets and artists tend to move to the fringes of society. Wherever there are individuals says Miller (like Thoreau) there are new frontiers. The American way of life has become illusory; we lead the lives of prisoners while we boast about free speech, free press, and free religion, none of which we actually do enjoy in full. . . . The only thing for enslaved men to do is to move out to the edge. . . .[67]

Rather than struggle or resent his fate, Miller cheerfully submits, and thereby achieves a measure of freedom within bondage:

> The book [*Tropic of Cancer*] is sustained on its own axis by the pure flux and rotation of events. Just as there is no central point, so also there is no question of heroism or of struggle since there is no question of will, but only an obedience to flow.[68]

The theme is echoed through Miller's other popular novels, *Tropic of Capricorn* and *The Rosy Crucifixion*: Conventional institutions enslave the creative spirit; render unto them the absolute minimum necessary to

---

[67] Karl Shapiro, "Introduction" to H. Miller, *Tropic of Cancer* (New York: Grove Press, 1961), p. xxii.

[68] Anais Nin, "Preface" to *Tropic of Cancer*, p. xxxii.

ensure your continued security in their dependence, but celebrate their decadence by refusing to take them seriously.

Virtually all the blue scenes in these novels are what we would today regard as "healthy" heterosexual encounters—any traces of either homosexuality or sadism are lacking. What is present is a pervasive mood of promiscuity: Miller's main characters are unfaithful; they "sleep around." The political spine to the stories suggests Miller's reluctant dependence upon the two coercive, demeaning, exploitative institutions that dominate his banal existence: the corporate monopoly (symbolized by the Cosmodemonic Telegraph Company—referred to in moments of gaity as Cosmococcis—in whose nominal employ the central character ekes out a boring living) and domesticity (seen most clearly in his wife Maud—a stupid, unfeeling, overbearing bitch—and echoed in an endless string of girlfriends).

Miller repays both institutions in kind. As a telegraph messenger, his "hero" is an unreliable loafer, given to white-collar filching, confirming the management's expectations that he is an ungrateful, lazy wastrel. Yet he needs the company for his miserable livelihood just as it needs him to confirm its contempt for workers. This symbiotic relationship parallels the one with his wife. Although he needs her for daily necessities (i.e., room and board), he abuses her at every opportunity, debauching her when necessary to quench their common lusts but always refusing to gratify her main desire—maintenance of the proper appearances of respectability. Both Maud and Cosmodemonic are devoid of spiritual qualities or imagination; only the tramp author has authentic sensual impulses. And yet, because they own him, wife and company can exact their price from him.

Miller is redeemed from despair only because he responds to his enslavement with a sense of humor, a determination to live to its fullest the banality and irresponsibility that limits his life. His behavior parodies the free enterprise huckster—he spends his days and nights shrewdly "taking suckers" (bedding dumb broads, begging pennies from his friends, avoiding work, cheating on his wife) and thereby acting out his passive revolt against respectable institutions. But in all this he is able to retain his freedom of action only at the cost of his dignity—a cost, Miller seems to be saying, the artist must be prepared to pay with no regrets if he is to transcend the pedestrian expectations that oppress him.

Although this is not the place to do so, we could pursue this critical approach, using political Rhetoric games, by exploring in detail the complex pattern that ties political impotence to an individual's taste for certain varieties of pornography. Those who may choose to do so will need to re-examine De Sade's feudal allegories, in which Enlightenment values are turned upon themselves, as well as such relatively taboo topics as the sorts of "pious pornography" preferred by women. In these and numberless more common (though often less readable) instances of erotica the sort of political analysis we have proposed will demonstrate that the literature is not meant for potential rapists but for those who see themselves victimized by various social institutions and forces.

Final evidence for our claim can be found in the cinematic techniques employed in current pornography films. What we have in these films is ultimate intimacy expressed by politically suppressed people. We see in these films the ultimate effect of political suppression on the "human-ness" of mankind. The actors and actresses in these films are indeed automatons; they go through their mechanical rituals in much the same way as one inserts bolts into auto differentials on a corporate assembly line. This mechanical effect is reinforced by film editors who dwell for up to five minutes on an extreme close-up of a penis entering and withdrawing from a vagina. The cinematic effect upon most people is complete anonymity and ultimate boredom; that is the point. From our perspective, political disenfranchisement leads to mechanization and ritualistic non-involvement in the most intimate human activity.

Although we have not spelled out in complete detail the relation here asserted, the consequences of coming to terms with that relation should be evident.[69] Far from merely reflecting the personal vision of an isolated poet (though in exceptional cases such as De Sade or Miller it may do that as well) or the idiosyncratic taste of isolated sexually deviant readers, pornography can be understood as well as socially scorned but nevertheless "public" address. In these terms we can argue that a public's taste in pornography serves as a sensitive monitor of Freedom's fortunes at a given time and place in history. It is thus not sufficient to define a single entity as "pornography," nor to measure the sheer quantitative bulk of erotic discourse. Rather, qualitative predilections and changes in preferences should be studied extensively and dispassionately. For changes in either the quantity or quality of favored erotica could well signal men's altered perceptions of their political fields of action, of their range of participation in their own public affairs.

---

[69] Recently, for instance, several writers have begun coming to grips with the relatively taboo topic of women as a potential public for erotica. It is just this sort of careful analysis of the appeal particular images hold for particular publics that has until now been lacking in discussions of pornography as a communicative form. See Germaine Greer, *The Female Eunuch* (New York: McGraw-Hill, 1971), pp. 178–185; Lois Gould, "Pornography for Women," *New York Times Magazine* (2 March 1975), 10ff.

We have tried in these two chapters on Rhetoric to consider some of the main Rhetoric games played out in public arenas, those games whose telos is to awaken a sense of agreement or "common sense" among men in their capacity as political creatures. We have examined these games with an eye to determining to what extent various Rhetoric games either facilitate or inhibit what have traditionally been regarded as the primary rhetorical qualities of the persuasion experience: a recognition of pleasures and pains as motivating factors in behavior, a desire among Rhetoric players for a fraternal sense of inclusion in a public, and a sense of the presence of the speaker, of political virtuosity on display in the rhetorical performance.

MARKETPLACE RHETORIC (publicity) is a modern Rhetoric game whose sole focus is on manipulating the pleasure/pain principle to enhance the appeal of a sponsor's product. This game can be amusing, or even entertaining; since it calls on its audience only to consume and not to act in concert with a spirit of comradeship, its persuasive gratification is limited.

FORUM RHETORIC (political discourse) is the most elaborate and, for its participants, the most gratifying of the Rhetoric games we have examined. Although in some of its modern variations it is coming to resemble industrially produced publicity rather than the sort of live public performance that traditionally has given men a sense of contributing to the well-being of their community, it nevertheless comes the nearest, even today, to offering a more extended notion of happiness than more limited persuasion games.

SOUL RHETORIC (healing) employs the pleasure/pain principle and the authoritative presence of a healer in a game whose aim is to bring back to the community the lonely individual who seems to have strayed from the path of common sense and, being unable to find his way back, suffers certain physical symptoms. This restoration to the companionship of one's fellows may require medical tactics, but it is clearly a rhetorical process.

SEWER RHETORIC (pornography) is a game resorted to by individuals who have either strayed too far from the community or who have no desire to return to the common sense companionship. Though some consumers of pornography may be respectable members of a community, in a real sense they all form themselves into a public of outlaws insofar as they remain locked in lonely isolation from the fraternal gratification or the public happiness or the satisfaction that active performance in the company of comrades can bring. It seems to be a historical fact that in those societies where the rhetoric of the forum has been reduced to empty ritual, or where it is suppressed entirely, pornography develops as a substitute for those who would otherwise be fans of political games.

13

Dialectic
Games

Dialectic games are those whose telos is intellectual understanding: The messages generated invite the participants to experience philosophical intent.

I n Chapter 11, we noted how Rhetoric games attempt to engage the will and exploit the persuader's presence to gain assent to the propositions that are advanced. We come now to our final general category of public communication games, Dialectic. With Dialectic games we move out of the realm of the immediately familiar into activities that are more thoroughly intellectual. Dialectic games try to release the will, to remove the influence of a persuader's presence, and permit the "facts themselves" to force the mind's agreement. In its early Greek formulation, Dialectic was a game in which people who were fond of one another joined together in a sort of conversational "loving combat" to examine a serious topic and to sharpen their mental faculties by stimulating one another's minds.[1] Thus, it is not accident that the Socratic dialogs and the setting for several Ciceronian writings depict close friends meeting together to engage in civilized inquiry.[2]

---

[1] R. Hall, "Dialectic," *Encyclopedia of Philosophy* (New York: Macmillan, 1967), II, pp. 385–389.

[2] Indeed, the acme of this type of inspired conversation is depicted in Plato's *Symposium* (literally "drinking together") in which a number of comrades gather for dinner, drinking, and a lively discussion concerning the nature of love.

The modern counterpart of the original Dialectic game that first comes to mind is the TGIF (Thank God It's Friday) session, in which close acquaintances gather at week's end to share a beer, relax, review the week, and in general engage in good conversation. But there is a crucial difference between the two activities. The mental exhilaration of the TGIF encounter stems from the fraternal experience, from the comfort afforded when those in fundamental agreement confirm rhetorically their "common sense" of those affairs of the day that they celebrate in conversation ("the boss is an ogre," "taxes are too high," "the bar maid is cute"). By contrast, Dialectic, as originally played, entailed the *withdrawal* from common sense that came when a fresh mind (a student) encountered a wise one (the sage) and both were freed from the affairs of the day, from the political realm of rhetorical influence, and from the very thought patterns to which a particular community of men had become accustomed.[3] In so liberating themselves, the players entered a state of serene *contemplation of what is*—a state in which conventional assumptions about the world were brought into question and commonly disregarded facets of existence became meaningful.

To gain a sense of the differences between a TGIF discussion and the ancients' conception of the Dialectic game, consider Richard Robinson's description of the ground rules for the game as it was exemplified in Plato's earlier dialogs:

> The partners in this enterprise were not identical in function. The one led and the other followed (for essentially dialectic was a conversation between precisely two persons at a time; any third was, for the time, merely a listener). The leader questioned and the follower answered; for the conversation was always predominantly question-and-answer. The question was usually a request for judgment on a given proposition, requiring the answer yes or no. . . . The answerer was expected to say what he himself really thought, and nothing else. . . . On the other hand . . . consistency was required. The answerer's opinions must agree with each other. . . . When . . . a conflict arose between consistency and "what I really think," consistency won the day, and the answerer had to abandon one of his opinions, whichever he chose. . . . There should be complete agreement between the speakers. . . . If the answerer declines to assent the leader . . . must reinstate agreement either by abandoning the proposition, or by going back and obtaining the answerer's assent by showing that the proposition follows from

[3] M. Conovan, *The Political Thought of Hannah Arendt* (New York: Harcourt Brace Jovanovich, 1974) p. 111; F. Nietzsche, *Joyful Wisdom*, trans. T. Common (New York: Ungar, 1960), p. 110.

others to which he assents. The answerer must always answer. . . .
It is essential to the method to put every suggested proposition into
one of two categories, accepted or rejected. . . . Neither party may
accept a proposition from anyone else, however near or great. The
only authority is what seems true to us two here and now.[4]

This deliberate renunciation of common sense, this momentary
forgetfulness of the world of men, has a number of extra-ordinary con-
comitants. For one, withdrawal not only ignores what the group or
community ordinarily takes to be the "reality" of everyday life ("Is the
boss really an ogre?", "By what standard would one say that taxes are too
high or that the waitress is cute?"), but it also causes the dialecticians to
appear to be "absent-minded" (the players' minds are "elsewhere" insofar as the players are oblivious to their scene-images and their entire
attention is fastened on formulating meaningful abstractions about their
topic-image). Thus dialecticians appear somehow foolish in their disregard of their comrades, their seeming refusal—while playing the Dialectic game—to play Polite Conversation Among Friends and cheerfully
agree with what each other says, or encourage the others to join in
discussion.[5] They choose instead to examine each proposition critically,
and if necessary to allow what they once took as "realities" to dissolve
into mere semblances.

This perception of the dialectician as both devoted to abstractions and
lacking in the common sense of a clever man is reinforced by a third feature:
The original Dialectic game disengages the participants' wills. The game
does not, as Rhetoric, provide pragmatic solutions to practical problems; it
has no utilitarian aim and can only be played for the pleasure of the
intellectual activity itself. The results of Dialectic are in no way profitable.[6]
The Rhetoric game involves mental activities in which means and ends are
calculated and decisions made as to how to accomplish projects in the world
(see Chapter 11). But Dialectic as played in the ancient world caused men to
withdraw from the world and to *stop* calculating in favor of sheer thinking.[7]

---

[4] Richard Robinson, *Plato's Earlier Dialectic* (Ithaca: Cornell University Press, 1941), pp.
81–83.

[5] Plato, *Theaetetus,* 174–175.

[6] Were this refusal to succumb to the means-ends system of cognition not already evident,
it could be demonstrated by the dialectician's natural propensity to re-think seemingly
settled ideas, to constantly undo what has previously been done, to refuse to come to rest
content with what has been thought on a matter. There is indeed a congenital antagonism
that political men—whose impulse is toward willful consensus and decisive action—often
feel toward "egghead intellectuals" whose pleasure seems to come from endless examination and talk, with little concern for action.

[7] K. Jaspers, *The Future of Mankind,* trans. E. B. Ashton (Chicago: University of Chicago
Press, 1961), pp. 209–210; F. Nietzsche, *Joyful Wisdom,* I, 3.

But Socrates discovered an even more curious variation on the Dialectic game. Pushing the notion of withdrawal from common sense yet a step further, he found that sheer solitude opened up the possibility for *reflection*, the continuation of intellectual communication that takes place when one carries on an internal conversation with *oneself*. For when the entire Dialectic game is internalized it carries all the conditions for mental activity a step beyond the intimacy of student and sage: The withdrawal from the world of men is more complete, the rejection of common sense can become more radical, and, indeed, mental phenomena can become even more completely "desensualized" when one can consider ideas with one's self, in solitude. This variation of Dialectic (which is what Plato, Descartes, Spinoza, Kant, and Hegel, all referred to as "pure reason" or some similar term) makes thinking a completely intrapersonal activity with virtually none of the distractions or temptations offered by human affairs. In such a state it proves possible for the thinker to lose himself all the more completely in that state of serene contemplation that the Greeks called *theoria* and whose rough equivalent in our own day would be meditation.

It soon became apparent to the ancients that those who were most skillful in dialectical exchanges (men such as Protagoras, Socrates, and Zeno), those whose paradoxes challenged common sense, were in some strange way intellectually "stronger" than others, not in the sense of being bullies and forcing their opinions, but in just this sense of "loving" conversation, of being sufficiently committed to excellence of thought that they repudiated, however gently, spurious remarks.[8]

In all likelihood it was from this recognition of intellectual strength and tranquility that the discipline of argument and the rules of logic (or the ground rules for rational inquiry) emerged. But notice that this capacity originally attached itself to an individual, to a sage renowned for his ability to stir fresh thoughts in the minds of others by his very presence. Socrates compares his gift—which we might today describe as "heuristic dialectic," the ability to inspire original insights in others—to the art of being a midwife:

> The triumph of my art is in thoroughly examining whether the thought which the mind of the young man brings forth is a false idol or a noble and true birth. . . . The god compels me to be a midwife . . . and therefore, *I am not myself at all wise*, nor have I anything to show which is the invention or birth of my own soul, *but those who converse with me profit.*[9]

---

[8] See Nietzsche, *Twilight of the Idols,* trans. R. J. Hollingdale (Middlesex: Penguin, 1968), 29–34 on Socrates as a criminal in this respect. See also Wayne Brockriede, "Arguers as Lovers," *Philosophy and Rhetoric* 5(Winter 1972):1–11.

[9] Plato, *Theaetetus,* 150.

Insofar as such heuristic dialectic contains any "message" at all apart from love for the players, it is Christ's "Follow *me*," to be inspired by admiration for a life of noble thoughts *as lived*.[10]

With the coming of the Catholic Church as an institution a change in emphasis occurred and the Dialectic game began to shift away from loving, thoughtful conversation by a sage with a student (since admiration for a sage other than Christ was considered pagan) and toward a more specialized game—Didactic, the pursuit of an immutable Truth that will stand apart from the men who utter it. And as men came to seek unalterable Truth through intellect, they began to use the products of such mental activity in a new communication game, one which, unlike the original Dialectic, did not so much inspire the listener to free thought as it overwhelmed his mind and caused him to submit to the ideas presented through the sheer weight and rigor of their inference. Thus the development of mental and academic "disciplines."[11] Hence, we can see evolving, as early as the second century A.D., an interest in a discourse game whose intent is less and less to stimulate the mind and more and more to still the doubts of the faithful and the naïve. This game replaces the sage of an earlier day (whose wisdom inspired in his partner an urge to emulate) with an "expert" (one whose influence resides in his possession of arcane knowledge),[12] who transmits a pre-determined message to less qualified listeners. Thus does the dialog of the original Dialectic game give way to rational monologue—or "lecture."

In other words, as the urge to love one's fellow conversationalist was eliminated from its primary place in theology and discourse, untrammeled thought was replaced by the desire to eliminate doubt by absorbing Knowledge. The consequences for the game of Dialectic had emerged quite early. By the thirteenth century the writings of the great theologian Saint Thomas Aquinas clearly reflect the subordination of all traces of curiosity or "thought-ful-ness" to the tyranny of sheer inference. Coherence ("does everything fit together neatly?") became the criterion of cognition. Technical and specialized communication (messages to instruct, as Cicero would call them) became ever more prominent in theological and secular matters. Dialecticians sought to exclude from

---

[10] K. Jaspers, *The Future of Mankind*, p. 188; F. Nietzsche, *Joyful Wisdom*, 351; H. Arendt, *Between Past and Future* (New York: Viking Press, 1968), pp. 247–248.

[11] See R. D. Sider, *Ancient Rhetoric and the Art of Tertullian* (New York: Oxford University Press, 1971); I. Kant, *Critique of Pure Reason*, B. 367.

[12] J. C. Lehman, "Preface to a Reconciliation of Ethics, Rhetoric, and Persuasion" (paper delivered at Speech Communication Association Doctoral Seminar, University of Iowa, Iowa City, March 1974).

their peculiar games all facets of *human* interplay other than rigorous reasoning. Thus there developed ever more reclusive, systematic methods of generating knowledge that could then be distributed by qualified experts to less knowledgeable laymen. Dialectic as the activity of *performing philosophical inquiry* yielded to Didacticism as the activity of *producing and reporting philosophical findings*. The loving combat of Dialectic gave way to the respectful attention of the amateur for the pronouncements of the expert.

It is therefore in their didactic form that most Dialectic games are played in our contemporary world. This is not to say that only didactic discourse exists today, but it is to suggest that only didactic forms are accorded formal academic recognition in our times as legitimate forms of inquiry, whereas more heuristic, less rigorous discourse is often dismissed as "mere speculation" in much the way an umpire might declare a foul in a football game.

Even in their most didactic form, however, dialectical messages represent attempts to reason through reality's structure, to objectify, interpret, and make meaningful statements about reality. In the rest of this chapter, we shall examine three of the most persistent Dialectic games: Science (which seeks to make meaningful statements about natural phenomena); Criticism (which seeks to make meaningful statements about human creations); and History (which seeks to make meaningful statements about the human past). In view of the admittedly rather didactic tone of our own introduction, perhaps we ought to emphasize that our purpose in examining these games is *not* to "expose" or "debunk" those who play them. Instead, our aim is to clarify the rules, tactics, and customs that regulate the play of these games in order that we may increase our appreciation of the discourse that they generate, and in order to assess their capacity to restore or enhance our potential for thought.

Dialectic games, we have emphasized here, seek to disengage the will, to negate the influence of any persuader's sheer presence, and allow the facts themselves to coerce the mind's assent. It follows, then, that the most important step toward increasing our appreciation of the messages generated by Dialectic games is to understand how each game conceives of "facts" and how each game's players discover and make use of the facts that are relevant to the game. It is these aspects of Science, Criticism, and History that we shall seek to highlight as we examine each game below.

DIALECTIC/DIDACTIC GAMES: SCIENCE

If we view Science as a communication game in which careful reasoning overshadows all other features in importance, then it is necessary to understand that scientific discourse operates as three levels: experiential data, theoretical propositions, and mathematical models.

The Level of Experiential Data

In its simplest form, science can be understood as a communication game, played between the scientist and Mother Nature.[13] The game resembles the children's game of Twenty Questions: with the single proviso that the scientist is always in the position of trying to guess what Mother Nature has in mind. Now Nature is a special kind of adversary—not malicious, not attempting to hide anything, and certainly not inclined to cheat (so far as we thus far can tell), but extremely reluctant and crafty about revealing herself. So the scientist, if he is to expose any of her features, must put questions in such a way that Nature will reveal as much of herself in responding to each question as possible. And if this all sounds somewhat lascivious, it should—at its best science operating at the level of experiential data is a kind of seduction.

The object of the game is for the scientist to develop a dialog such that Nature discloses as much of the "truth" about herself as possible. In these terms, the process of experimentation can be seen as a way of putting questions to Nature so the replies will be meaningful and reliable rather than capricious. Most children who play Twenty Questions soon learn that they use up their allotted questions futilely if they ask such things as "Are you thinking of a soda can?" "Are you thinking of a loaf of bread?" It is far better to put questions, at least in the early stages, that will divide the domain of possibilities more effectively (such as, "Are you thinking of a living thing?"). Hence, in the Science game, we have found that the "scientific method" (or the rules for how to perform proper experiments) consists in fact of rules agreed upon by the best scientists of a given discipline[14] as to how best to play the game. It follows that the particular experiment that may be performed is equivalent to the scientist's question, his effort to communicate with Nature by momentarily interrupting her in her natural processes. The experimental

---

[13] J. L. Aranguren, *Human Communication* (New York: McGraw Hill, 1967), pp. 142–145.

[14] Cf. S. Toulmin, *Human Understanding* (Princeton University Press, 1972), Vol I.

results then represent Nature's reply to the question. We can see why scientists are so concerned with correct methodology in experiments; they wish to be assured that the questions have been put to Nature in a sufficiently careful way that Nature has been unable to respond evasively.[15]

But to play such a question-and-answer game requires that the scientist make a number of unprovable assumptions about reality. The first of these is that sense data somehow offer an accurate reading on reality, that "truth" is ultimately open to the senses (rather than, say, the glands), that our observations (or experimental results) are in a serious way "real." The biochemist *could*, for example, posit that cancer is caused by invisible and undetectable demons, but for him to do so would place him outside the arena in which scientists have agreed to play their game. A demon is by definition beyond ordinary observation; however, a virus (which resembles a demon in many respects) is by definition an observable entity and so "real" (if not always seen) for the Science game. A demon is thus a foul ball in the Science game. Similarly, scientists do not deny the existence of God, but they do refuse to talk of him as an entity during their working hours. Since we are unable to determine God's size, odor, color, shape, or location, he is "nonsensical." God too is a foul ball in Science and so God's revelations are excluded from the realm of scientific "truth." Thus, the scientist considers as "real" only those entities that are revealed to his senses.[16]

The second and related assumption made by the scientist has to do with the vocabulary. The scientist, in discoursing about Nature, uses only those words that meet the test of either the Pragmatic Maxim or Operationalism.

The Pragmatic Maxim. This principle[17] states in its most extreme form that our concept of anything is merely the sum total of its sensible effects on us; that is, there is virtually no meaning (except tautological

---

[15] R. Carnap, "Testability and Meaning," *Philosophy of Science* 3(1936):419–471.

[16] In a broader historical context, this raises several interesting problems; for instance, the discovery of X-rays at the end of the nineteenth century called into doubt man's senses as a viable means of detecting reality. In a very real way, such discoveries have led to a loss of nerve or at the very least, man's confidence in his ability to know Nature—we may even suggest that today, loss of confidence in our "common sense" has led to a condition where any "non-sense" has a legitimate claim on our minds because the non-sense revealed by X-rays has proven to be more real than the truth offered by common sense. Nor does the problem stop here. As Susanne K. Langer argues (*Philosophy in a New Key* [New York: Mentor, 1951], p. 29) even our sense data are symbolic translations of physical events.

[17] After C. S. Peirce.

statements such as "All circles are round") apart from our common sense observations. For example, the word *hard* is in this scheme defined by the results of tests in which various substances are used to make scratches. Thus, because steel can scratch wood but wood cannot scratch steel, we say that steel is the harder substance, and since diamonds can scratch steel, we say that diamond is the hardest of the three substances. Following this line of thought, the word *hard* is reduced to a short-hand notation for "the effects of scratching as perceived."[18]

Operationalism.   Related to the Pragmatic Maxim, but different in one vital respect, is the much abused notion of Operationalism. This concept was first articulated by the physicist Percy Bridgman in 1927 as the result of a controversy that had divided the scientific community for a number of years.[19] Some scientists, seeking to discover the properties of electrons, had weighed atoms and by this route arrived at a certain description. Other scientists, however, had approached the problem of determining the electron's property by measuring the atom's velocity (by measuring the scratches atoms made when they collided with photosensitive paper); their descriptions of the electron were markedly different, in fact, incompatible with those asserted by the first scientific group. Bridgman was able to demonstrate that the contradictory descriptions arrived at by the two camps were due, not to error, but to the fact that they had performed completely different measuring operations in the process of observing. Hence, he arrived at his notion of Operationalism: The meaning of a scientific term is the sum of the measuring operations used to specify that term's properties. Note here the emphasis is on the testing procedures employed (the character of the scientist's laboratory intervention with Nature), rather than on the resultant observations derived from the testing as in the Pragmatic Maxim.[20]

Verifiability.   When we combine these complementary notions, we derive the overriding standard by which to assess the use of scientific vocabulary: the principle of verifiability.[21] Scientists, insofar as they play the game of Science, are obligated to use a vocabulary made up of "public terms." That is, the language of Science must refer to observations that any ordinary observer could replicate (find verifiable) under specified condi-

---

[18] Cf. R. vonMises, *Positivism* (New York: Braziller, 1956); A. J. Ayer, *Language, Truth and Logic* (New York: Dover, 1946).

[19] P. W. Bridgman, *The Logic of Modern Physics* (New York: Macmillan, 1927).

[20] G. Schlesinger, "Operationalism," *Encyclopedia of Philosophy*, V, p. 545.

[21] M. Black, *The Labyrinth of Language* (New York: Mentor, 1968), pp. 177–185.

tions; i.e., scientific language is restricted to objects and events that persist such that they can be perceived by several people—they must have a "publicity factor," or as the philosopher Stephen Toulmin puts it: "Each of us thinks his own thoughts; our concepts we share with our fellow-men. . . . The language in which our beliefs are articulated is public property."[22] The vocabulary of Science cannot refer to subjective sensation, private language, connotations, or idiosyncratic revelations that might be limited to the user. The language of Science is not allowed to carry covert associations as poetic discourse does. Scientific truth is what the common man could ultimately confirm with his own sense organs if he so wished. The meaning of terms in Science must be readily susceptible to fairly common and durable experiential sense-confirmations. If a given term has no perceivable meaning (as is common with mystical language such as the Hindu mantras), it is declared to be nonsensical and ruled meaningless in the context of scientific communication, just as the foul ball is illegitimate as a hit in baseball.[23]

The Level of Theoretical Propositions

Few scientists are sheer empiricists; that is, the scientist is usually not content to collect and record observations as ends in themselves (although that is an honorable vocation in the general scientific enterprise). Rather, in the ideal case (ideal, because it seldom happens with such simplicity and logical elegance) the scientist who has made any observations eventually extrapolates from his collected measurements some statements in which he attempts to draw generalizations about how and why Nature behaves as it does. These abstracted statements, known as hypotheses, constitute a set of assertions, each of which claims that some general underlying causal, correlational, or generic pattern holds among elements in the sense world. In other words, the scientist makes a logical leap in which he induces from his collected observations a set of generalized theoretical statements that he claims can be held to govern the entire class of events, including those members of the class not yet observed.

Having stated what he believes to be a general account, he will then test the rightness of his hypothesis by seeking further observations to see if the theoretical statement does indeed hold for instances not previously observed. In other words, where the criterion of adequacy for

---

[22] S. Toulmin, *Human Understanding*, p. 35.

[23] Cf. D. Harrah, *Communication: A Logical Model* (Cambridge: M.I.T. Press, 1963).

scientific vocabulary is its verifiability, the criterion for theoretical statements is their predictive capacity, their ability to enable us to foretell
Nature's replies to questions we ask in the future but in comparable
circumstances. However, the scientist's hypothesis is not a prediction
about the future in the same way that a fortune teller forecasts what is
not yet, *ex nihil*. The scientist's "prediction" is actually that *the past will
recur;* i.e., his observations have been so powerful and thorough that,
presuming Nature does not change its character radically and no un-
toward factors such as miracles interfere with the steady course of events,
under such circumstances his previous observations will characterize
observations not yet made.[24]

As an illustration, let us imagine that the aged astronomer, Professor
Quackenfuss of Miasma University should tomorrow come to a startling
conclusion, that on the basis of his previous observations and calculations, it is Mars, not the moon, that is made of cheese. How would
Quackenfuss' colleagues greet this scientific hypothesis? While as humans they might choose to avoid him at the Faculty Club and might even
remark behind his back on his senility, as scientists they would have to
be a bit more tolerant. Presuming that Prof. Quackenfuss has reasoned
from genuine observations, some of them might propose a test of his
hypothesis—say, a rocket would be launched to the planet containing
some mice. When the rocket landed, radio and television reports would
determine if the mice rushed out of the ship, went into paroxysms of joy,
and began nibbling at the surface of the planet. If they did, we would
have evidence to confirm Prof. Quackenfuss' hypothesis; if, on the other
hand, they remained apathetically aboard the rocket and continued to
munch their K-rations, we would have observable evidence to dis-
confirm the theory.

An almost identical situation arose early in the United States space
program. An eminent cosmologist, Professor Thomas Gold of the Cornell
University astrophysical center, using telemetry measurements derived
from rockets that had approached the moon, as well as from telescopic and
radio signals, hypothesized that the surface of the moon might not be a
crust as is the surface of Earth, but it could as well be a thick layer of
dust, such that if a manned ship landed on the moon it might sink in as

---

[24] Cf. S. J. Macksoud, *Other Illusions* (privately printed: Binghamton, N.Y.: Vail Ballou,
1973), p. 14. In *The Structure of Scientific Revolutions* (Chicago: University of Chicago
Press, 1962), p. 24, Thomas Kuhn's discussion of "normal science" and "shared
paradigms" concurs with this position: "No part of the aim of normal science is to call
forth new sorts of phenomena; indeed those that will not fit the box are often not seen at
all. . . . Instead, normal-scientific research is directed to the articulation of those
phenomena and theories that the paradigm already supplies."

if in quicksand. Another group of scientists at the Jet Propulsion Lab of C.I.T., using the same data, theorized that the moon's surface was a rocky crust. To resolve the difference (and to prepare for a safe manned landing), an experiment was agreed upon: An unmanned rocket with a small shovel-like device would land very gently on the moon, stick its shovel into the surface, and weigh the density of the dirt thus picked up. The experiment when performed showed that the moon's surface was not dust.

What is most intriguing about this outcome for our purposes is that the result was announced by Professor Gold himself, who was in fact delighted to find that his theoretical statement was disconfirmed, and who lost none of his eminence for having received a "no" answer from Nature—he had done his job as scientist by developing and properly testing a plausible hypothesis. That further observations did not confirm the theoretical statement in no way diminished his reputation.

In sum, the steps necessary to establish statements at the level of scientific theory are these:

1. Make verifiable observations (encounter an object's sensible properties and operationalize the experience so that others may share it)
2. Generalize
3. Predict
4. Verify by further testing and observation

It should be clear that when scientists talk of running experiments they are actually discussing the final stage in the sequence of determining accurate theoretical statements. The specialized study of "experimental design" concerns the proper phrasing of the scientist's questions to Nature in this final stage. The study of statistics for experimentation is the study of the inferences by which the scientist can confirm or disconfirm his theory. Data analysis is, in its turn, the formal means by which the scientist decodes Nature's responses. But all these scientific methodologies are developed primarily for assisting the scientific dialog at this fourth stage of theory articulation.

This heavy concern for methodological purity in the final stages of theory development brings us to a crucial issue that plagues scientists who concentrate on the last stage: What is to be the actual purpose of an experimental test in relation to the hypothesis? On this issue, "the sciences" have divided into "legitimate" and "quasi" sciences. Virtually all those sciences that are today regarded as "genuine" by the intellectual community (such as molecular biology, geophysics, high energy physics, genetics—many of these being disciplines that have made enormous contributions to our knowledge in less than three decades) are all marked by a commitment to what is often called "strong inference"[25] in this final stage of establishing the hypotheses. The quasi-sciences, on the other hand (such as psychology, sociology, political science, economics, and the like—all of which have been in existence as formal disciplines for some one to two centuries, and all of which are also characterized by the tendency to be still debunking the same general issues that they were examining at their founding, few resolutions having ever been achieved), seldom employ strong inference as a standard part of their experimental procedures.[26]

What is strong inference that it can so clearly divide those scientific studies that seem to make rapid intellectual progress from those that perennially debate the same issues? Very simply, strong inference is a procedure intended to maximize the possibility that the scientific experiment will *disprove* a hypothesis; quasi-sciences usually employ experimental tactics in such fashion that hypotheses are *confirmed*.

The steps in strong inference as a procedure in the verification stage of scientific analysis are as follows:

1. Scientists faced with a mass of observations will try to generalize a number of equally plausible but different hypotheses to account for their observations. (Thus, Professor Gold's suggestion that the moon could as well have a surface of dust based on man's knowledge at that point was in fact a contribution to the first step in strong inference.)
2. The scientists will then agree on one or more "crucial" experiments—tests whose outcomes could be said to decisively eliminate at least one of the reasonable alternative hypotheses from consideration. (In the dust versus crust controversy, Gold's group and the JPL group were able to agree on the rocket-cum-shovel test: Had the rocket and shovel sunk out of view upon landing there would have been reason to dis-confirm the hypothesis that the moon has a solid surface.)
3. Scientists carry out the crucial experiment(s), seeking "clean" results that leave no room for equivocation as to which hypothesis is to be eliminated. (The rocket experiment provided

---

[25] J. C. Platt, "Strong Inference," *Science* (October 1964), 347–352.

[26] The term *quasi-science* is used here in preference to other common references such as "would-be discipline" and "pseudo-concept." See S. Toulmin, *Human Understanding*, pp. 378–394; Benedetto Croce, *Logic as the Science of the Pure Concept*, trans. D. Ainslie (London: Macmillan, 1917), pp. 179–180, 338–339.

clear disproof of Gold's proposal when the shovel measured a surface density of the moon similar to that of the Earth.)

4. Scientists repeat this procedure in a recycling fashion, each time eliminating plausible hypotheses (that is, equally reasonable alternatives, given the observations at hand), until only one hypothesis is left.

Thus, the focus of strong inference is on disproving—any conclusion that is not simultaneously an exclusion is seen as obscure and in need of further examination. A scientist whose alternative hypothesis was disproven by this method loses no stature among his peers; but a scientist who neglected to generate a likely alternative for consideration before he began his experiments would suffer in their eyes. For the aim in this sort of scientific reasoning is not to reject all hypotheses, but only to design experiments that offer a clear opportunity for such rejection if Nature is of such a mind.

It is not at all clear why the quasi-sciences have not adopted the practice of using strong inference in their experiments,[27] but it is a brute

---

[27] One obvious *result* of this failure is clear enough, however: That is, competing schools in the quasi-sciences often far more reflect prevailing political preoccupations and, indeed, allow their modes of inference to be dominated by political biases, than anyone would like to admit. Professors Caplan and Nelson (H. Caplan and S. D. Nelson, "On Being Useful," *American Psychologist* [March 1973], 199–211) are very suggestive on this point:

> Why does one kind of poverty concern us, and another does not? Why do we constantly study the poor rather than the nonpoor in order to understand the origins of poverty? Why do we study nonachievement among minority group members as undesirable behavior but do not study exaggerated profit motive among "successful" businessmen as a form of deviance? Why do we study the use of marijuana as a "drug problem," but not federal government involvement in the drugging of "minimal brain dysfunction" (MBD) children in our grammar schools?

They also argue rather convincingly that the bulk of psychologists devote most of their energies to isolating and defining populations of "deviants" who are then implicitly "blamed" for their own unhappiness:

> If the causes of delinquency, for example, are defined in *person-centered* terms (e.g., inability to delay gratification, or incomplete sexual identity), then it would be logical to initiate *person change* treatment techniques and intervention strategies to deal with the problem. Such treatment would take the form of counseling or other person change effort to "reach" the delinquent. . . . Or if it seemed that . . . impediments at the root of such "antisocial" behavior were too deeply ingrained or not amenable to routine help . . . it would follow that coercive external control techniques (e.g., confinement or possibly medical solutions) could be instituted."

The political significance of research that implicitly puts the blame upon people in difficult situations for their own predicament would be obvious, as should the approach more common to sociology—that of placing the blame for people's unhappiness in given circumstances upon the society that tolerates the circumstances. In either case, the unexamined assumptions move the investigation out of the realm of science and shift it unannounced into the political backyard. The problem with such behaviorism (as distinct from the empirical study of man) is not that it is in error, but that if acted on by unthinking men, it could come to be true. At that point human action would be eliminated in favor of sterile behavior, bereft of any experience but that of ideological conformity.

fact of history that, with few exceptions, they have not. Instead, the ordinary experimental psychologist, say, designs a test by which he can *confirm* his favorite hypothesis, instead of seeking ways of refuting it. Hence, quasi-scientists seldom design "crucial" experiments that will give clear grounds for rejecting one of a set of equally compelling possible explanations.

Virtually every issue of an experimental journal in the social sciences carries reports of experiments, all of which have a happy ending in which the pet theory of the experimenter was confirmed (sometimes with minor qualifications or emendations to account for observations that contradicted the theory).[28]

The problem with the quasi-science approach is that theories that are open only to confirmation are not theories at all. A theory of this sort never excludes anything, and it never runs the risk of rejection, so we never have a way of telling for sure if it is wrong. Such theories that predict everything in fact predict nothing, for the supporter can always explain away seemingly contradictory results. The theory then becomes simply a verbal or quantitative incantation repeated over and over by the experimenter and his followers.

Worse still, the quasi-Science game places scientists with different views into a posture of competing with each other rather than in alliance with each other in a common endeavor to understand Nature. The result is to drain the energies of participants in quasi-sciences in endless personal struggles to establish the predominance of one's favorite hypothesis over the statements of rivals.

The Level of Mathematical Models

In the Utopian world of ideal science, there would come a time when the number of highly predictive and secure theoretical statements had accumulated to the point where they needed to be sorted out and arranged—governed, as it were, by some higher abstraction.[29] At that

---

[28] For further treatment of this topic, see Q. McNemar, "At Random: Sense and Nonsense," *American Psychologist* 15(1960):295–300, and Richard Weaver's description of how social science writing is marred by "pedantic empiricism" in *The Ethics of Rhetoric* (Chicago: Henry Regnery, 1968), pp. 191–195.

[29] Of course, the actual history of scientific endeavor shows that the procedure is not nearly so systematic—but we are here concerned with the logical relations of various levels of scientific abstraction to each other. Those who wish to explore the actual process further would do well to read T. Kuhn, *The Structure of Scientific Revolutions* (Chicago: University of Chicago Press, 1970).

point, a scientist, such as Copernicus (in astronomy) or Einstein (in physics), would seek to specify a set of propositions that would make explicit (or transform) the underlying logical premises of the science. And where the criterion for empirical data is its verifiability and for theoretical assertions their predictive capacity, the criterion of propositions at the level of the model is their logical consistency. Thus, the scientist (such as the theoretical nuclear physicist), operating at this level, seeks to root out possible logical contradictions among propositions. If he exposes a contradiction, for example, between two hypotheses, it will be necessary to recheck data or in some other manner seek to reconcile the contradiction. Thus, scientists ultimately came to choose the Copernican model of astronomy over that of Ptolemy, not because either was more "right," but because the model offered by Copernicus provided certain extra-empirical (one is tempted to say "aesthetic") advantages such as "elegance," ease of computation, and power respecting the solution of some measurement problems.

The model, then, is an effort to specify the formal preconditions that make a domain of theoretical propositions intelligible; the model is a kind of syntax that makes the generation of theoretical sentences possible. Two sorts of statements will be found to comprise the model, according to T. Kuhn, one of our foremost commentators on the subject.

Evidentiary Rules.   For example, in solving a jigsaw puzzle, we know that the general task is to "make a picture." But we are governed in our effort by implicit conditions such as—all the pieces in the box must be used; the plain sides should be turned down; the pieces must interlock; one cannot "force" the pieces (by such methods as trimming) to link up; when the puzzle is finished neither extra pieces nor holes may remain. In the same fashion, scientific models often specify the form and character of correct evidence or inference in a discipline. They are rule-restrictions that define the range of permissible inferences.[30]

The Key Exemplar of the Discipline.   Other writers have contended that the central instance or exemplar of human communications is the homeostatic organism (balance theories) or the growth and flowering of a plant (humanistic psychology). The paradigm case in any discipline is the perspective from which the scientist unconsciously marks his examination of any other instance he may observe and interpret. Like the North Pole for

---

[30] T. Kuhn, *The Structure of Scientific Revolutions,* pp. 38–39.

the maritime navigator, the paradigm enables the discipline to orient itself as it confronts the murky frontiers of its contacts with Nature. In this sense, we might imagine that those who lay out the exemplars, and indeed all who work to clarify or change the models underlying a science, function much as cartographers do in designing maps for navigators.[31]

What can we say about science insofar as it functions as a type of Didactic game? The overriding consideration is that it is a language stripped as bare as possible of poetic and rhetorical qualities; it is a language geared almost totally to description and explanation. Poetic language, after all, strives to be as pleasing, beautiful, expressive, and/or harmonious as possible; Poetic games are those that invite their spectators to expand their aesthetic awareness of the world. Scientific games deliberately avoid these attributes, lest the audience be enchanted and carried along by some faculty of mind other than sheer reason. A scientific report is structured to correspond to the tactics of scientific reasoning: survey of previous research on the subject at hand/statement of hypotheses being tested/description of techniques and instruments used in observation/results of the experiment/ analysis of the data/discussion of the significance of the experiment for theory.[32] Thus the formality of a Scientific game tends to make for dull reading to the layman who is not as thrilled or motivated by the game's rigorous reasoning as are other scientists.[33]

Nor is there any overt effort to retain the rhetorical quality of language. Players of Rhetoric games try to interpret reality to make it fit a predetermined set of ideas; Rhetoric games invite their audience to share in the exhilaration of belief in the ideas. In contrast, Scientific games at least allege that fact and reason speak for themselves. They invite an audience to comprehend the appearance of things. In playing the game the scientist adjusts his hypothesis to fit the facts of his observations. That Scientific games approach but do not always attain the didactic purity they seek is no reflection on those who play the games, but rather is comment on our inability to make human discourse function solely to meet our desires, no matter how hard we will it.

---

[31] T. Kuhn, *Structure*, p. 175.

[32] Cf. W. Sacksteder, "Kinds of Theoretical Communication," *International Philosophical Quarterly* 4(1964):110–121.

[33] Some scientists who recount their efforts are capable of fine prose, as evidenced by a recent best-selling story of the search for the DNA molecular code—but that was really a study in the history of science rather than a report of scientific findings.

DIALECTIC/DIDACTIC GAMES: CRITICISM

One of the most common forms of present-day Didactic games is criticism—those communicative games played by academicians, intellectuals, and social commentators of all sorts who seek to assess the goodness, worth, beauty, significance, or morality of things. To understand the general game they play, we propose to examine criticism in terms of three guiding questions: What is a critic? What is the logic of his act? What types of critical tactics does he employ? Answers to these questions should provide us with insight into this type of didacticism.

The Critic as Spectator at Other People's Games

Whenever the word *critic* comes up in conversation, a variety of images is liable to come to mind. Some think of the book reviewer or the drama critic for a newspaper. Others, who equate "critic" with "carper," are reminded of a sour, negative individual who cannot be pleased. Still others may imagine that "speech" or "literary" critics are intellectual historians of public events. Clearly, common usage has made the term so vague as to be practically meaningless.

One way to sharpen our understanding of "critic" is to ascertain what actions we may ordinarily expect of one who is fulfilling the office of critic. To guide us, let us exemplify all the human events and artifacts discussed by critics by focusing on those events we commonly call *athletic*. In the main the critic closely resembles a special kind of "spectator" at athletic events. It is easy enough to understand that some sporting events are not only played but are observed by persons we call *spectators*. If these spectators are genuine fans, they do more than purchase tickets of admission so that they may be near the action. Among the characteristics of genuine fans is their interest in contemplating and discussing and evaluating the events they observe. That is, the role of spectator is not passive. It entails reflection and communication about the event witnessed (see Chapters 9 and 10). Consider, for example, the "Monday Morning Quarterback" clubs for football and winter "Hot Stove" meetings for baseball. In both cases, spectators-as-communicators gather together and derive a certain satisfaction from debunking and praising the maneuvers executed in recent football or baseball games. Both the fan and the critic share a mutual interest in observing and discussing the games they witness.

A second similarity between sports fans and critics is an appreciation for the execution of the event being observed. The involvement of some fans is limited to the practical dimension of the event. Their concern is whether a team accomplishes what it sets out to do—whether it wins or loses. They are interested in each aspect of the event only to the extent that it contributes to the final score. True enthusiasts, however, take more from the event than an outcome. Regardless of the final score, these fans delight in seeing a video tape replay of the game they witnessed in person several hours before. For these fans, the event has a structure, a coherence, an experiential dimension that surpasses its pragmatic elements: One can still appreciate the uncaught pass, the double-faulted serve, the form of the last-place runner. It is this shared appreciation of how things are executed regardless of what end they accomplish that further distinguishes true fans and critics.

A third factor that unites the critic and the spectator is that both gain an intensified satisfaction from the heightened appreciation of an event's execution. That is, it is possible to be trained to observe events with ever increasing pleasure.[34] The football fan, who recognizes that an array of tactics is being used to "set up" the opposition for one particular play, can derive greater satisfaction than the fan who only knows the formal rules. In other words, the more you know about the game and the principles on which the game is played, the more you can appreciate it and the more satisfaction you can derive even from a bad instance of the game.

A final commonality follows from the notion of heightened appreciation. Some spectators, because of especially fine training and/or acute sensitivity, attain the status of "experts." In the athletic sphere such persons are often hired to act as sportscasters and sportswriters, and in other realms they may be called upon to review books, plays, and the like. Their title of "critic" is not derived so much from the fact that they are appointed or paid to perform these tasks as it is from their exceptional understanding of the events they are asked to assess. They make judgments of appreciation or explanation in the way that the ordinary fan could not.

How, then, do we answer the question "What is a critic?"

1. A critic is a certain type of spectator who reflects and communicates his or her reflections on human artifacts or performances.

---

[34] I. Kant, "First Introduction" to *The Critique of Judgement*, 226–232.

2. A critic is a person who appreciates the artifacts and performances for their own sake; he or she is not concerned merely
   with pragmatic questions.
3. A critic is a person whose increased knowledge of the artifacts
   and events he or she observes heightens his or her appreciation
   of them.

Accordingly, when we say that an individual assumes a "critical posture" we are saying that he or she possesses a *capacity to act as an expert
commentator:* He or she has the capacity to understand the execution of
objects or events and thereby achieve a heightened appreciation of them
and the capacity to function as a commentator on the objects or events so
experienced.

The Critical Act

This list, no doubt, has a familiar ring. Throughout this book we have
been encouraging our readers to join us in assuming just such a "critical
posture." But this posture alone does not make one a critic. The simple
capacity to render commentary is not yet "criticism." The expert-
spectator who relishes the event he or she observes but does not relate
his or her appreciation to others is not a critic. Criticism normally refers
to the critic's verbal commentary on the event he observes. Criticism is
therefore a special type of communication game that results when an
expert-spectator makes comments about the event in question.

An initial way to understand this game is to distinguish it from
other games that we would not call criticism. To make this distinction,
let us consider an instance of criticism and attempt to deduce its properties. The following is critic Herbert Wichelns' response to a speech
delivered by General Douglas MacArthur to a Joint Session of Congress
(and, through direct broadcast, to the nation) on 19 April 1951.

> Demosthenes had the problem, too: how much to spell out, how
> formal and explicit to make his proposals. At times Demosthenes
> judged it best not to "make a motion," but merely to offer comment
> and advice at large. MacArthur made a similar choice. In the main
> he chose not to debate, in the sense of formulating proposals and
> defending them in full. Instead he indicated the heads for debate,
> leaving no doubt as to the direction of his policy. Definite propos-
> als were few, and sharply limited to Formosa and Korea. Support-
> ing reasons were very sparingly given, and sometimes confined to

bare assertions (as on the extent of China's present military commitment and Russia's probable course). But the call for a harder and more aggressive policy is plain from the beginning ("no greater expression of defeatism"). The chief support for that policy is neither logical argument nor emotional appeal, but the self-portrait of the speaker as conveyed by the speech.

It is an arresting portrait. Certain colors are of course mandatory. The speaker respects Congress and the power of this nation for good in the world. He is free from partisanship or personal rancor. He sympathizes with the South Koreans and with his embattled troops. He prefers victory to appeasement. He seeks only his country's good. He hates war, has long hated it. If these strokes are conventional, they take little time, except for the last, on which the speaker feels he must defend himself.

More subtle characterizing strokes are found in the "brief insight into the surrounding area" which form a good half of the speech. Here the General swiftly surveys the nature of the revolution in Asia, the island-frontier concept and Formosa's place in the island-chain, the imperialistic character of the Chinese communities, the regeneration of Japan under his auspices, the outlook for the Philippines, and the present government of Formosa. All this before reaching Korea. Most of these passages have no argumentative force. But all together they set up for us the image of a leader of global vision, comprehending in his gaze nations, races, and continents. The tone is firmest on Japan ("I know of no nation more serene, orderly and industrious"), least sure on the Philippines, but always positive.

Rarely indeed have the American people heard a speech so strong in the tone of personal authority. "While I was not consulted . . . that decision . . . proved a sound one." "Their last words to me"—it is the Korean people with whom the General has been talking. "My soldiers." The conduct of "your fighting sons" receives a sentence. A paragraph follows on the General's labors and anxieties on their behalf. The pace at which the thought moves, too, is proconsular; this is no fireside chat. Illustration and amplification are sparingly used; the consciously simple vocabulary of the home-grown politician is rejected. The housewife who "understood every word" was mistaken; she missed on *epicenter* and *recrudescence* and some others. But having by the fanfare been jarred into full attention, she understood quite well both the main proposition of the speech—a harder policy—and the main support offered—the picture of a masterful man of unique experience and global outlook, wearing authority as to the manner born.[35]

---

[35] F. W. Haberman, "General MacArthur's Speech: A Symposium of Critical Comment," *Quarterly Journal of Speech* 37(October 1951):328–329.

One feature this example displays is that it contains a *verdict*. Wichelns provides an evaluative judgment of a public event. Not all assertive discourse contains this judgmental dimension. Scientific reports, for instance, display an exploratory impulse rather than an evaluative one. This is not to imply that critical verdicts are final assessments. Wilchelns is careful to avoid judging MacArthur's speech as unequivocally good or bad. He invites us to accept his judgment on how the speech was executed (what made it work as it did). In Wichelns' judgment the speech called for a harder policy and this call was supported by the speaker's self-portrait. Thus, Wichelns presents us with a settled, though not necessarily final or definitive, judgment as to the speech's worth. In this sense, criticism eventuates in, or at least has as its ultimate objective, evaluation.

A second feature that is embodied in criticism is *reasons functioning to justify the verdict*. If we examine Wichelns' essay more closely, we discover that the bulk of the discourse comprises such reasons. Notice, for example, Wichelns' assertion that MacArthur's main form of proof was his own self-portrait. This statement is supported by three reasons: first, that it was an arresting portrait, employing both "mandatory colors" and "subtle . . . strokes"; second, that the speech is otherwise lacking in argument and abounding in assertion; and, third, that the speech was couched in the language of personal authority. From these reasons, Wichelns is able to conclude that the speech offered "the picture of a masterful man of unique and global outlook" as support for MacArthur's claims.

A final feature that underlies the critical act is that like the reasons used in a court of law, the *reasons offered will themselves compare ideals* (laws or models of artistic excellence) *and the particulars* (facts as observed in the event being assessed or the case being considered).[36] The "closer" the events being assessed approach the norm or canons of excellence, the more likely the critic will be to render a positive verdict. By contrast, the wider the deviation of a given artifact or performance from the ideal, the more likely the evaluations will be negative. Indeed, the critic's talent consists precisely in his capacity to move sensitively between general principles and particular observations.[37]

Contrast this reasoning with the sorts of reasoning common to other Didactic games. In syllogistic logic, for instance, the conclusion of a chain of inference is somehow demanded by the premises. Thus:

1. If it is the case that all men are mortal,

---

[36] I. Kant, *Critique of Practical Reason*, p. 71.

[37] I. Kant, "First Introduction," *The Critique of Judgment*, pp. 211–217.

2. And if it is the case that Socrates is a man,
3. Then it follows, *of necessity*, that Socrates is mortal.

There is no choice for the reasoner; having accepted the premises, his mind is driven to accept the conclusion of a valid syllogism.

Critical reasoning is quite another matter. In criticism the reasons support the conclusion that the critic draws, but the conclusions do not follow inevitably from the reasons. The proposition, "I read the novel *Tom Jones* last week" can support the conclusion, "I think *Tom Jones* is a good book." But the same reason ("I read the novel *Tom Jones* last week") can also support the verdict, "I think *Tom Jones* is a bad book." The critical verdict *needs* reasons in support (composed, as we have said, of norms and observations juxtaposed), but those reasons serve to *justify* or support the verdict, whatever it might be, not to guarantee it as the inevitable conclusion.

A similar contrast can be recognized between scientific reasoning and criticism. To claim, for instance, that "I was sick *because* of what I ate" is different from "It is a lovely painting *because* of its harmony." The one is a causal statement; the other a determination of goodness ("lovely") as justified by certain aesthetic precepts ("harmony").

Observe how Wichelns illustrates the forensic reasoning pattern that characterizes criticism. He opens his essay by distinguishing between speeches that offer advice and those that join a debate. He thereby establishes the norm. He then spends the remainder of his first paragraph drawing attention to those facts about the speech that place it in the category of speeches of advice. In his next paragraph Wichelns formulates the principle that some remarks are mandatory on this kind of occasion and then observes the extent to which MacArthur met those demands. In his third paragraph the critic implies that some rhetorical tactics reveal a proconsular image and then presents facts that enable him to ascribe such an image to MacArthur. The forensic pattern is evident throughout Wichelns' essay. Wichelns' verdict is implicit in his analysis: To the extent that meeting these three criteria make for a satisfactory speech, the verdict is positive; to the extent that other, unmentioned criteria were not met, the speech leaves something to be desired.

Critical Strategies

Bearing in mind the nature of the critical posture and the logical structure of critical inference, we turn to the tactics that critics use. It is a commonplace that different critics with roughly the same credentials often reach opposite or at least contradictory verdicts regarding the same event's worth. To understand this seeming paradox, we need to know that the critics were probably not employing the same tactics. They were, in other words, looking at the same event from different perspectives or foci. In the remainder of this section, we will discuss the tactics that critics employ and attempt to specify how the conclusions critics reach are determined primarily by the particular tactics they use in playing the criticism game.

We propose that four variables are relevant: the source of the object or event to be evaluated (S), the object or event itself as a public message (M), the environment or social context in which the object was created or the event occurred (E), including the historical background and the im-

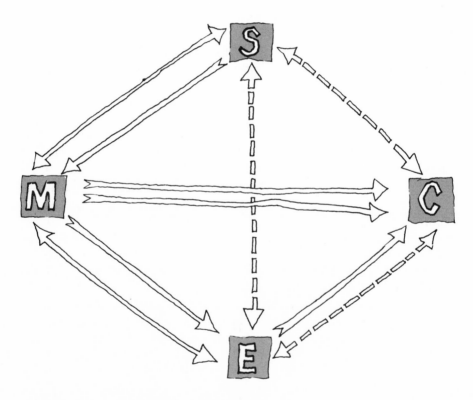

○ All tactics involve message.
○ Dotted-line combinations are not direct parts of critical tactic.

mediate audience, and the critic (C). Obviously, in a thorough interpretation of an artifact or performance, all four variables are relevant. But equally obvious from past critical practice is the fact that such all-encompassing analyses will be rare if not impossible for the single critic. We will concentrate, therefore, on six strategic combinations of these four features, strategies that we believe typify the way most criticism is played today.

In narrowing our focus, we are restricting our attention to that subset of criticism that concerns human communication. Thus, all the critical tactics we are about to consider will include the message (M) variable. It should be noted, however, that many genres of criticism can be generated from these variables. For example, we might identify sociology as that which takes an ES (the environment and the source of the event to be evaluated) focus.

The MC Strategy.   The MC (message, critic) combination is used by the introspectionist; it seeks to gauge the critic's personal response to the aesthetic object.[38] This perspective rests on the premise that communication is essentially a personal, unique event—a private transaction between message and receiver that can never be known to a third party. The critic is simply one more receiver of the message, albeit more sensitive than the typical untrained receiver.

If one accepts this notion that critical interpretation is so uniquely personal, it follows that no critical judgment is more than a justification of the critic's own state of mind as he responds to the aesthetic object. Subsequently, one's faith in the critic's explication and overall taste constitutes at least as important a means of support for the verdicts offered as do the critic's stated reasons. It is even possible to imagine that the primary function served by reasons submitted by a critic playing the MC critical game is to demonstrate to an audience his competence as a critic, to "exhibit his credentials" to make authoritative judgments.

MC criticism may account for the propensity of prominent critics to set forth lists of their favorite books or the best plays or speeches of all time. Having achieved eminence, they need no longer justify their selections, but are allowed to telescope or even abort their arguments in favor of short explications of why a particular book, play, or novel pleased them personally.

---

[38] This cryptic account is obviously not the entire story. The critic is not privileged simply to report his pleasure and/or pain on confronting the object or event. He is in some manner obligated to explain how and why the work *justifies* his particular response. It is also important to note that contemporary literary critics who claim to focus entirely on the work itself are in fact often employing the MC paradigm.

The next three strategies are related to each other in their denial of an introspectionist stance and in their advocacy of greater detachment and objectivity.

The SM Strategy. The SM (source, message) play of the criticism game concentrates on understanding the message as an expression of its creator. Most often the critic attempts to trace out the creative process by which the source externalized and structured the feelings, thoughts, and experiences contained within himself. The strategy may be further refined into two tactics. In one, the critic makes inferences *from* the source's life *to* explain the message in question (S——→ M). In the other, the critic makes inferences *from* the message *to* the psychological forces that must have been present within the source (S ←——M). This latter tactic is often used by neo-Freudian critics who consider messages as psychoanalytic data from which to reconstruct past histories of patients.

The ME Strategy. The ME (message, environment) strategy also embodies two major tactics. In one instance (M ←——E), "environment" is interpreted broadly (as by historians and literary critics) to encompass the age and the civilization in which the message originated. The historian of ideas attempts to set the historical background in which the particular work or clusters of works were produced, showing how the messages are themselves a reflection of the era. This option finds its rationale in the assumption that to the extent that an aesthetic event can be considered typical of its age it will provide valuable insight into the intellectual and social trends of that age.

The second optional tactic of this strategy (M——→ E) interprets "environment" in a more prescribed sense, referring to the specific audience to which the message was addressed. Players choosing this tactic consider the "functional" relationship that existed between the message and its receivers. They seek to determine how the receivers used the messages presented to them. The assumption underlying this option is that whatever the source's intention, the receiver attends to a message in a manner that fulfills his own personal needs. Thus, an old man may attend a July Fourth celebration, not prepared to be persuaded or inspired to increased patriotism, but simply because the ceremonial oratory reminds him of the speeches he heard on similar occasions in his youth. In cases like these, the ME critic might concern himself with determining expectations of the audience as well as the extent to which those expectations were fulfilled by the message.

The SME Strategy. The final impersonal strategy, SME (source, message, environment) assumes a pragmatic stance. Essentially, this way to play criticism treats a message as an effort to influence an audience and ventures to assess the artistic skill of the source in achieving his persuasive goals with his audience.

Because the critic takes for granted the Janus-like quality of public address, revealing simultaneously the communicator and the social environment to which he seeks to adapt himself, the SME critic emphasizes in his study the mediating nature of the message in moving (or failing to move) the audience toward the source's vision of how the demands of the occasion ought to be met and resolved.

These last three strategies—SM, ME, and SME—comprise a set because they share one quality that distinguishes them from the introspectionist reports of the MC game. This shared quality is a stress on impersonal, verifiable critical statements. By placing the expert-spectator outside of the critical equation, each method attempts to make criticism an objective report of what actually "is," a judicious, unbiased account of properties that inhere in the communicative event itself. In so doing, they imply that the critic should strive to produce an analysis of the essential nature of the phenomenon apart from any idiosyncrasies in his personal responses. In this sense, these three strategies comprise the most "detached" perspectives a critic can take.

The last two strategies we shall mention—SMC and MEC—are used by critics whose focus is human communication. Together these strategies reject the cleavage between the introspective and the impersonal ways to play the public game of criticism and seek to restore some heuristic elements to the Didactic game. Justification for these strategies stems from the recognition by contemporary science that the very act of observation interferes with, and so alters, the event being observed and thereby makes truly detached observation impossible. The distortion can never be overcome by more precise observations or measurements, but can only be acknowledged by specifying a degree of looseness and uncertainty in one's formulations.

A less scientific but perhaps more comprehensible way of explaining the basis for these two strategies is to hearken back to the ancient notion of *aletheia*, the un-hiddenness of things, by which they radiated or dis-closed their essence to the eyes of the mind.[39] Where the "objective" critics seek to establish distance on their subject of investigation, both the SMC and the MEC critics allow themselves to be momentarily

---

[39] This concept was re-established in our own day by Heidegger, who explained how if we did not regard ourselves as bounded objects, we could imagine ourselves as a cloud that "regions" with other cloud-entities. M. Heidegger, *Discourse on Thinking*, trans. J. Anderson and E. Freund (New York: Harper & Row, 1966), pp. 58–90. See also William Barrett, *What Is Existentialism?* (New York: Grove Press, 1964), pp. 138–140.

"overwhelmed" or "regioned" by the sheer radiance of the message—
they seek to appreciate it, to affirm its existence (which is by no means
the same thing as merely praising the message; to have gratitude for the
illumination offered by the "standing forth" of a given message is to
real-ize it for what it is, *as* it is). This celebration of the message (and its
relation to either the source or the environment) is not subjectivity (in
the sense of turning inward), but a real-ization, a reaching out to "shake
hands" with concretized reality, a joyful accommodation at the affirmation of life illuminated in the particular.

As applied to the critical act, such a position holds that criticism is
inevitably the product of the critic's encounter with the event, that the
locus of criticism is neither critic nor ontic events but the critic's intrusion
upon the event. It is from this existential overlapping of critic and event
that the event's presence is disclosed to the critic. Our final two
strategies suit the critic who accepts the elusive and inevitable relationship between critic and the events he seeks to assess.

The SMC Strategy. The critic who uses the SMC (source, message,
critic) strategy believes that he can apprehend an artistic intention radiat-
ing from a work of art; and the aesthetic experience, be it to speech or
symphony, is the experiencing and expressing of that intention. Artistic
intention is precisely the way in which the event unfolds itself to the
critic as he confronts it. The critic acknowledges the event's presence as he
observes it.

There are clues in messages that will be actualized when the message is encountered by the critic. It becomes the critic's task to investigate that cooperation of elements and ratios in the message that gave rise
to his apprehension of the art object-as-experienced. In other words,
source, message, and critic momentarily coalesce as the elements of the
aesthetic event unite into a semblance and move toward a terminal
condition. The critic's objective is to explicate that experience and the
communicative factors that contribute to or retard the transaction. The
critic seeks to determine the nature of the demands made by the event
upon him as beholder of the event; he is concerned with the nature of
the "regioning" that unites critic and event.[40]

The source enters the equation because it is posited that the source's
choice(s) in creating the message may provide a key to understanding
the presence emanating from the message. The critic assumes that the
source, by virtue of his close connection with the message, is something

---

[40] For a distinction between the aesthetic experience and the critic's ultimate interpretation,
see H. Osborne, "The Elucidation of Aesthetic Experience," *Journal of Aesthetics and Art
Criticism* 23(Fall 1964):145–152.

of an authority on the event; he often possesses special knowledge about the event that adds depth to the critic's own interpretation. Hence discovering these sources of knowledge can aid the critic in understanding and expressing an event's essence.

Consider, for example, Martin Luther King's "I Have a Dream" speech delivered at the climax of the march on Washington in August 1963. Few people know that this address was extremely well prepared and rehearsed—up to a certain point. The final minutes of that address, beginning with the initial statement "I have a dream," vibrated with spontaneity. This appeared to be King releasing himself to the electricity of the moment. Information as to whether or not this segment was indeed spontaneous could aid the SMC critic in heightening his own understanding of that peculiarly moving final segment. It is a key to understanding the compelling disclosure provided by the end of that speech.

Notice that the SMC strategy does not obligate the critic to accept the source's personal conception of his creation; the purpose of uncovering the spontaneity surrounding King's final lines is not to understand King, but rather to help unravel the parameters within which the event occurred. We seek to discover the source's point of view, his frame of mind, on the assumption that the symptoms of artistic and intellectual choice made by the source may lend depth to our own appreciation of the message.

The MEC Strategy. Like the SMC strategy, the MEC (message, environment, critic) combination rests on a conception of the critical act as an encounter with a semblance. It too recognizes the importance of an event's disclosure to the critic, of the demands made by the work upon the recipient of the message. The primary distinction between the two strategies is that MEC emphasizes the event as an act, a performance that is only fully consummated in that instant when message is apprehended by receiver. Just as a play is not theatre until it is being performed for an audience, so the artifact (script) *becomes* a message, acquires presence, when it is performed in a public arena or forum. The MEC critic, then, focuses his attention not upon the moment of *creation*, but rather upon the moment of *apprehension*.

One consequence of this shift in emphasis is that the MEC critic is less concerned with the source's influence on the message than the SMC critic. As the French symbolist Paul Valery has contended:

> *There is no true meaning to a text*—no author's authority. Whatever he may have *wanted to say* he has written what he has written. Once published, a text is like an apparatus that anyone may use as

he will and according to his ability: it is not certain that the one who constructed it can use it better than another.[41]

There are other differences between the SMC and MEC strategies. Whereas the SMC focus concentrates on the presence an event has on *an* auditor, the critic, the MEC focus concentrates on the presence the *performance* of an event has upon the auditors who originally experienced it. For example, the SMC critic might seek to assess the enduring worth of medieval morality plays, taking account of their original cast as inculcators of religious faith, while the MEC critic might distinguish between the presence of a morality play for an audience in medieval times and the presence of that play as performed today. Constrained thus by context, the MEC critic is more particularistic with the critic acting as a kind of surrogate for the audience he projects into the communicative event.

We have approached the didacticism of criticism in terms of three generating questions. We can capsulize our answers as follows:

1. *What is a critic?* A critic is an expert spectator with a heightened appreciation of human communicative events and an ability to express that interpretation in the form of critical discourse.
2. *What is the logic of the critical act?* Critical inference requires a comparison of observations and norms of excellence. The termination of this examination is a verdict, justified by reasons.
3. *What tactics are available to critics?* If we schematize an instance of public communication encountered by the critic, we intuitively recognize four variables:

   The source(s) or creator(s) of the message—S
   The message itself—M
   The context or environment in which the message is received —E
   The critic himself—C

Most critics of human communication events pursue one of the following strategic combinations of these variables:

MC: Personalized introspection
SM: Objective inferences about the source from the message or about the message from the source
ME: Objective inferences about the environment from an analysis of the message or about a message's capacity to fulfill the expectations of a particular audience

---

[41] Paul Valery, *The Art of Poetry* (New York: Pantheon, 1958), p. 152.

SME: Objective, practical assessment of the effects of a particular source's message on a specific audience

SMC: The critic's experience of the message is guided by the source's intent

MEC: The critic's experience of the message is guided by the context in which the message was performed

DIALECTIC/DIDACTIC GAMES: HISTORY AS CREATIVE PLAYTHING

Historiography, the *doing* of history, is a Didactic game that seems, like cribbage, to have fallen upon lean times. In an age that flirts with Future Shock, *historia rerum gestarum* (the account of past facts), if not memory itself, is being called into question in those rare moments it is not being happily ignored. If the game entails the discovery and interpretation of facts (or in this case, traces of the past)[42] with a view to resolving doubt in favor of certainty, then no matter how we may differ as to the tactics for synthesizing or interpreting them, factual data will be presupposed as the key units of historiography.[43] This reliance upon factuality as a means to ascertaining truth[44] can be found among three of the more common historiographical tactics for threading data together coherently.[45]

Sequence

We are all familiar with the first tactic, *sequence*, the straightforward historical narrative[46] in which the message tells a tale in the form of a

[42] C. L. Becker, *Everyman His Own Historian* (New York: Appleton-Century-Crofts, 1935), p. 231; K. C. Hill, *Interpreting Literature* (Chicago: University of Chicago Press, 1966), pp. 38–47. Hill, especially, offers a valuable distinction:

Traces of the past are the fundamental form of evidence, for traces include not only physical remains, like ruins and monuments, but what is basic to all history, memory; even verbal accounts of the past are themselves traces. Nevertheless, we may roughly divide historical evidence into two kinds: accounts of the past, and traces of the past.

[43] Cf. R. G. Collingwood, *The Idea of History* (London: Oxford, 1946), p. 124; G. Gentile, "The Transcending of Time in History," in R. Kiblansky and H. J. Paton, eds., *Philosophy and History* (New York: Harper, 1963), pp. 94–95; L. B. Cebik, "Colligation and the Writing of History," *The Monist* 53(January 1969):40–57.

[44] Cf. G. Leibniz, *Monadology*, 33; A. C. Danto, "The Historical Individual," in W. H. Dray, ed., *Philosophical Analysis and History* (New York: Harper & Row, 1966), p. 265. Danto's summation of the matter is apt: "By *historical sentence* I shall mean: a sentence which states some fact about the past."

[45] Cf. H. White, "The Structures of Historical Narrative," *Clio* I(1972):5–20; A. W. Levi, *Humanism and Politics* (Bloomington: Indiana University Press, 1969), pp. 160–203.

[46] Cf. W. B. Gallie, "The Historical Understanding," *History and Theory* 3(1963):149–202.

plot, seeking to reveal how it all came to pass ("it" being the exploration of Quebec, or the dreary chronical of the Thirty Years War or some other investigation of historical events). This essentially classical notion of history (classical because it originates with Herodotus and Thucydides) acts with a view to preserving in our collective memory the great deeds of a civilization's heroes in a manner that is otherwise the province of poets and myth makers—it is often the stuff of legends of heroic men and deeds, letting the legends serve as roots or inspiration for the present.[47]

Thematic Analysis

A second historiographical tactic, *thematic* analysis, is typified by such historians as Alexis de Tocqueville, Charles Beard, Lewis Hacker, and William A. Williams. The thematic tactic functions to elaborate a theme (the structure and ramifications of democratic principles in the case of de Tocqueville, of the imperialistic urge for Williams) in one society. In this thematic category of writing (which is similar to Hegel's "Reflective pragmatic" history)[48] might be contained those works of history as Ida Tarbell's study of the Standard Oil Company that advance an argument, seeking in the process of such "scientific" analysis to penetrate surface appearances of events in order to arrange facts as evidence of an underlying (hypothesized) cause(s) (Adam Smith called it the "hidden hand" of history) that shape(s) the data given to our senses. The thematic historian acts on the facts given him as surface appearances with his reproductive imagination, shaping them to fit his motif[49] in an effort to verify the operation of a historical force acting behind the backs of particular men and events.

Impressionistic Mode

A third tactic for doing history is the *impressionistic* mode, which consists of sheer detail collected under convenient rubrics. This tactic is typified by Jacob Burckhardt's *Culture of the Renaissance in Italy*, in which Burckhardt collects innumerable instances of one phenomenon—

G. Hegel described this tactic as "original history." See his *Reason in History*, trans. R. S. Hartman (1837; New York: Liberal Arts Press, 1953), p. 3.

[47] E. Barker, *Church, State, and Education* (1930; Ann Arbor, University of Michigan, 1957), p. 199; H. M. Pachter, "Defining an Event," *Social Research* 41(Fall 1974): 453–454; Levi, *Humanism and Politics*, pp. 169–179.

[48] G. Hegel, *Reason in History*, 7–8.

[49] Cf. Kant, *Anthropology*, 28; Levi, *Humanism and Politics*, pp. 179–190.

individualism in fifteenth- and sixteenth-century Italy—classifies them under headings such as the state, religion, and culture, and offers them to us raw for our inspection:

> The "point" of the story is . . . that there existed an age of peculiarly intense individualism. . . . It manifested itself in all aspects of society and culture; it resulted in the creation of objects of lasting beauty and interests; and it has now ended. Take it or leave it.
>   . . . The meaning of Burckhardt's "story" is the meaning of all Ironic elegies: this once was, but is no more.[50]

This example is especially interesting because it pinpoints a credence that historians of all persuasions share to some degree in their reliance on facts (whatever their tactical use of those facts) for truth: the ancient notion of *alethaeia*—after the fashion of EMC and SMC critics discussed earlier—that particulars (objects, events) are just what they appear to be for one who only looks, that factual data can "speak to us" by dis-closing or unveiling the truth they contain and thus dispel both error and deception.[51] It is only for us to reach out to the reality that is thus offered to our contemplation and grasp it serenely in its ground. In the ancient world, the facts in a given matter were considered to be held in common; they were seldom in dispute.[52] What mattered for the historian was how the facts that were held in common by all men might be ordered.[53] It is clear that Burckhardt's impressionistic tactic represents the extreme acknowledgment of this radiance in facts themselves (self-evident truth), this *aletheia* by which particular facts (in this, of their own accord, in more scientific historiography, through the intervention of the historian) dis-close reality to those whose goodwill (the goodwill of all in society in supporting this truth) permits them to see, appreciate, and articulate with the eyes of the mind.

We are now in a position to understand why the history game has lost its vitality. It is simply that the game's keystone, our faith in the

---

[50] H. White, *Clio*, op cit., 10–11. Another eminent practicioner of this method of analysis is Professor Harry Caplan. See his "Memoria: Treasure-House of Eloquence," *Of Eloquence* (Ithaca: Cornell University Press, 1970), pp. 196–246.

[51] Cf. H. Jonas, *The Phenomenon of Life*, pp. 147–176; H. M. Pachter, "Defining an Event," pp. 459–462; C. S. Peirce, *Values in a Universe of Chance*, P. P. Wiener, ed. (Garden City: Doubleday, 1958), p. 165.

[52] Historians of all stripes thus share with the ancients a recognition of the uniqueness of specific objects and events. In spite of variations in inferential stratagems, all historians acknowledge the centrality of factuality in their accounts. No description of one sea battle will ever fully suffice to explain any other sea battle. And it is in this sense that facts remain fundamental to the historiographic enterprise and so can never be replaced with such patterns of necessity as Hegelian "reason."

[53] Cf. M. Heidegger, *Introduction to Metaphysics*, 98–114.

ultimate truth of all witnessed factuality, has been eroded to the point that we treat all facts too cynically to take the history game seriously any more.

The past century has revealed modern man torn in two contradictory directions respecting factuality's place in his thinking: He has come to exalt and idolize facts at the same time that his increasing distrust of his own senses has caused him to shut himself off from their radiance. Caught in this contradiction, he has generated ever more data even as he has increasingly disregarded it.[54] That we have, on the one hand, achieved a veritable idolatry of facts is not hard to demonstrate. Virtually any governmental report of the last three decades in America can be shown to be short on any form of inference and incredibly bottom-heavy with data, as though its authors believed that laying on the sheer bulk of disconnected information would substitute exhaustiveness for thought. The Warren Commission report on the John Kennedy assassination attests to this as well as any: a tome of 912 pages contain 25,000 FBI interviews and an additional 1,500-odd Secret Service interviews with over 500 witnesses. Eleven elephantine volumes contain additional thousands of photographs of 3,154 exhibits ranging from coats to "sample punch-marks made by Cecil McWatter's punch" (he being the conductor on the bus that the assassin hopped aboard in the course of his attempted escape).[55] This encyclopedic barrage of detail (reaching such lengths as a deposition from someone who once happened to sit next to the assassin Oswald in a restaurant because that was the only seat available) attests to the extremes sheer knowledge collection and mass distribution of data can reach in the Didactic game. But in any case, such massiveness has in no way minimized the doubt of those who persist in believing that those terrible events in Dallas were due to some conspiracy. The accumulation of undifferentiated bulk, no matter how enormous, has even called the report itself into question.

Why is it that we distrust facts? Why can the facts no longer speak to us, a silence they have maintained for over a century now? It was Nietzsche who first explicitly recognized the decisive end of human faith in empiricism: "Once we abolish the 'true' [supersensual] world, the 'apparent' [sensual] one collapses and nothing makes sense anymore."[56] What Nietzsche recognized was that discoveries beginning in 1870 (of

[54] Barker, *Church, State, and Education*, p. 198.

[55] An excellent examination along these lines is offered by Dwight Macdonald in his "A Critique of the Warren Report," *Esquire* 63(March 1965):59ff. from which the illustrative data offered here were drawn.

[56] F. Nietzche, *Twilight of the Idols*, p. 41. Oddly enough, the seeds of suspicion concerning factual truth were sown at the beginning of the scientific age. See R. Descartes, *Meditations*, 1.

radiation) and culminating in 1895 (X-ray machines) ended man's reliance on his senses[57] and so signalled the death of "common sense"
(that reality by which the community of mankind shared the world—
factuality—upon whose validity all could agree). Henceforth "non-sense"
took precedence. Because my sense of the world has been undermined
by the likes of X-rays (Do I exist or am I merely a mad dance of electrons?), my sense was no more worth-while than any madman's (that
is to say, worth-less).

The resulting problematic nature of historiography's reliance on empirical data is strikingly evident in the following historical incidents.
In the summer of 1971, when Daniel Ellsberg released the "Pentagon
Papers" to the press, several notable figures, including former Vice-
President Hubert Humphrey and then-presidential foreign affairs ad-
visor Henry Kissinger, claimed they had never heard of the collection
prior to its press publication. Both men's denials seem to be controverted
by the facts on the public record. Any reader of the *New York Times*, for
example, would have read the announcement several years prior that the
Defense Department was beginning comprehensive historical study of
American involvement in Viet Nam; one would expect a Vice-President
to have had at least this casual awareness of the project. Of course, later
in 1971 Kissinger was shown to have been the recipient of one of the
original copies of the Pentagon Papers, so his denial that he had known
of their existence (which is not the same as denying he had read them
or was familiar with their content) wears a bit thin. Yet neither man was
ever publicly called to account for the seeming contradiction in his
denials. Somehow we have come to live in a world in which factuality
can be denied with impunity by men in high position,[58] when past facts
can be erased in favor of more comfortable "data" by those powerful
enough to command the very facts to conform to their mental visions of
how events *should* have been.[59]

Such captiousness with facts, such audacity to declare the past itself
"inoperative" (which is to say quite literally, "no longer working obe-
diently to the ends I wish to accomplish and so of no profit to me") as
casually as one would change a merchandise display is itself instructive.
We are not dealing here with anything so simple as partisan or ideological interpretation of raw information[60] nor the sentimentalizing of mem-

---

[57] Unlike the microscope and telescope, which extended man's normal vision, X-ray
machines called vision itself into question by revealing a reality not open to mere human
sense.

[58] See H. Arendt, *Between Past and Future*, pp. 227–264.

[59] Conovan, *The Political Thought of Hannah Arendt*, p. 104; Jonas, *The Phenomenon of Life*, p.
101.

[60] Paul H. Weaver, "The New Journalism and the Old," *The Public Interest*, no. 35(Spring
1974):68–71.

ory[61] by those who allow their feelings to impose an idiosyncratic order on the course of events, nor even the exploitation of a naïve/indolent press by opportunistic public relations flacks who are prepared to lie in order to promote collective non-awareness.[62] No, we are instead confronted in modern times with the relegation of memory itself to the mental pantry along with dreams, hallucinations, and other such unreliable fantasies as are currently denied legitimacy in the rational enterprise.

In such circumstances, investigations to determine the facts become a decorative art like calligraphy; for the very foundation of belief that made the reconstruction of past events a proper means to resolve doubt and to achieve some degree of dialectical certainty is itself open to doubt. As Nietzsche had foreseen, the collapse of our respect for the supersensual world also annihilated our faith in the sensual as well.[63] Where before, meaningfulness resided in the testimony of factuality and so granted a *prima facie* validity to particulars, man alienated from his own world was left with empty categories of "values" that could be twisted this way and that because they were de-prived of any grounding in necessity but "object-ivity" (the sheer surface appearance of things without the radiance). In other words, men were left with only their own internal responses to guide their constant efforts at reconciliation with the world. But in what posture are we left when "all values are relative" (i.e., when our perceptions bear a suspicious resemblance to phantasms and our moral sensibility is reduced to a jumble of arbitrary abstractions that has reference only to non-sense)? In such a world, what matters is the fabrication of data consonant with whatever non-sense the fabricator prefers, no nonsense having any special call on any community of men.

Perhaps we can illustrate the problem we face with a nonpartisan example of the fabricated quality that attends what we otherwise think of as raw factuality—the news presented to us over the wire services and on hourly news broadcasts. "The news" is well named, and in its original sense it is clearly a re-creational force. It claims to offer us continually fresh reports on an ever re-newed world in which men persist in initiating unexpected actions. To be up on the latest news is more than mere curiosity seeking, however; it suggests our own need to understand and remain in contact with an ever changing world created by and for men. And so the news gathering-and-disseminating industry serves the important function of providing us with facts beyond our immediate ap-

---

[61] The phrase is H. Arendt's. See her *Rachel Varnhagen: The Life of a Jewish Woman*, trans. R. Winston and C. Winston (1967; New York: Harcourt Brace Jovanovich, 1974), p. 11.

[62] Paul De Man, "Nietzsche's Theory of Rhetoric," *Symposium* 28(Spring 1974):40.

[63] H. Arendt, "Thinking and Moral Considerations," *Social Research* 38(Fall 1971):417–437.

prehension in order that such raw material can enable us to think about and understand our world. More important for our concern with the historiographic game, "the news" is history in the raw insofar as it represents our manner of bearing witness to those facts that will become the future historian's basis for understanding our times when "now" has been turned into "then" by the passing of time. We would therefore expect news events in particular to glow with the sort of radiance that would enable the historian to read them as the symptoms that distinguish "our times" from the ordinary social cycle of events.[64] We rely on the news to testify to significance; but in an era when factuality stands mute, the news often sounds like just so much meaningless chatter, and with good reason.

It should be apparent at once that the hourly bulletins, the nightly television news, and even whole weeks of newspapers only faintly pertain to the "newness" of the world. Even disregarding the ever-increasing number of "human interest features" (hourly reports, for example, on the whale at the aquarium that is expecting a baby), very little that is newsworthy from the perspective of understanding (whether factual or otherwise) is actually reported, and what *is* reported is often not newsworthy in this literal sense. Thus, the local paper covers in microscopic detail the efforts of one neighborhood to protect an old elm tree from street repair crews, while blissfully ignoring the massive consequences of allowing the city to be quartered by intersecting federal highways.

Of course there are exceptions to this inversion of sameness and news: Important diplomatic negotiations and congressional hearings are noted, municipal problems are investigated; but the vast majority of events and issues touching our lives significantly, such as the determination of oil import quotas, are ordinarily mentioned only in passing, if at all. To investigate or prepare a news report on the status of such quotas requires extensive research with government agencies. It takes commitments of time, care, and expense that news bureaus are seldom willing to make.[65] They find it far easier to fill up allotted air time with hourly reports of spectacular auto accidents in Paraguay and the birth of a baby

---

[64] A similar regard for news items is displayed by Maurice Merleau-Ponty. See his *Signs*, trans. R. C. McCleary (Evanston: Northwestern University Press, 1964), pp. 311–313.

[65] In recent years there has been one notable exception to this general rule, the superb investigative reporting of the staff of the *Washington Post* that eventually laid bare the Watergate political scandal for public scrutiny. The matter of oil import quotas has also received some consideration, though on a far lesser scale than Watergate, in connection with growing national awareness of an oil energy shortage. But in the scale of factors that influence our life and times, such matters as oil quotas continue to be barely visible in proportion to their significance.

whale in a local aquarium. The wire services make their profit by guaran-teeing the local radio station a commodity—enough news to fill five minutes of hourly broadcast time, and they try to do so at the lowest possible cost. That their offerings lack substance is seldom of concern to either the wire service or their station clients as long as the air time is filled.

What *is* reported? Primarily banal disasters: ecological/meteorological (earthquakes in Canada, tennis-ball-size hailstones in Arkansas), biolog-ical (twenty-five people murdered in Wisconsin, the birth of yet another deformed baby, train wreck in France), and civil (big crime, big trial, big strike, civil disorders, political squabbles, international disputes, bank-ruptcies), bizarre incidents that divert us but seldom signal a change or a newness that will invigorate our action in the world.[66] What genuine recreational news is provided (elections, congressional hearings, or votes) is ordinarily limited to intimations of political exposé (X is trying to ruin Y's career) not unlike that of celebrity magazines.[67]

Granting that this not-so-extensive list includes a massive number of trivial possibilities, there may yet be days when not enough such ordi-nary incidents that fit the list occur. However, since broadcasters must fill their news time come what may, it is sometimes necessary to generate a news report to fill air time and give the illusion that the public is being kept up to date on unusual events. You can write your own news report for such occasions; just rearrange the following cliché phrases into any random order, plug in whatever names or geographic places come to mind, and your work is done:

> . . . And now the news behind the news! Bloody fighting continues
> in . . . where after a night of horror, bands of . . . youths still roam
> the streets. Senator . . . lashed out angrily at his opposite number
> [can you picture the good Senator, bullwhip in hand?] on a special
> watchdog committee which indirectly accused Red China [now we
> have someone peeping around a corner with malice aforethought]
> of. . . . For a report on the iffy . . . situation, we turn to roving
> correspondent . . . who comes to you direct from the powder keg.
> . . . Negotiations remain deadlocked . . . as stepped up aid . . .
> staged a rally . . . and demonstrators shouted their support . . . as

---

[66] See David M. Berg, "Rhetoric, Reality, and Mass Media," *Quarterly Journal of Speech* 58(October 1972):260–262.

[67] Even in the Watergate episode the same thrust was apparent, although its implications were more profound. Withal, the initial public scorn toward the media for the Watergate revelations shows how disconcerting a departure real *news* can be when injected into the newscast ritual. For a careful study of the long-range impact of genuinely newsworthy media presentations, see F. C. Arterton, "The Impact of Watergate on Children's At-titudes Toward Political Authority," *Political Science Quarterly* 89(June 1974):269–288.

drastic economic measures were decreed. . . . And now the latest on the . . . story: Casualties were described as light as a jeering rock-throwing mob wrecked death and destruction. A joint communique described the dicussions as frank and honest [have the discussions ever been described as hypocritical and dishonest?]; the mood here in . . . the unsettled . . . situation exploded again; two teen-agers were slightly maimed while. . . . They were rushed to . . . by . . . in whose custody they were placed. . . . In a sharp verbal slap at . . ., Mr. . . . said the meeting would deal with a broad range of problems.

The result of this standardization of the news is a stereotyped message, comparable in the domain of news, to formula situation comedies in the poetic realm, an oversimplified class of endlessly repeated ritual events. Like so many bottles of ketchup, each indistinguishable from the rest, the news broadcasts come off an assembly line. They have been stripped of their individuality and left as a generic category. We cannot respond to the quality of a particular news broadcast or an individual episode of a situation comedy on television any more than we can prefer one bottle of ketchup to others of the same brand; we have here not individual specimens but a general category, united by a predetermined formula. And we listen repeatedly to the formula (yes, bands of . . . youths always roam the streets; yes, the world is filled with powder keg locations, some of which explode on occasion) for reassurance that the world "out there" remains as we know it. Chatter has eroded the news. Yet this predictably sensational gossip is oddly comforting. As long as far-off places are known to be filled with catastrophes, *homo faber* (man-the-worker) can rest content with his own mean but uneventful daily life. Our daily dose of other people's grief reminds one and all that there are advantages to dullness.

Nowhere is the ossification of news into mass entertainment more evident than in efforts by tabloid dailies (which include a spectrum of the press from the counterculture underground to the snobbish *New York Review of Books*) to sustain the muckraking tradition of "investigative journalism." Despite stylistic variations,[68] all tabloids share an allegiance to the same basic formula (in a sort of "Pulitzer paralysis"):

---

[68] The tabloid style, which, like makeup too liberally applied, lends an innocent-grotesque ambience to the most dreadful and platitudinous events. All fat ladies are "curvacious," short ones are "petite," ugly ones are "vivacious"; dark-haired females are "raven-tressed." Men, too, especially if they are involved in illegal activities either as victim or perpetrators, get the same pancake treatment. Shopkeepers thus become "business executives," and bookies are "sportsmen." This euphemistic impulse hearkens back to the Victorian age, when breasts were "bosoms," legs (be they human or piano) were "limbs," and all appendages—on furniture or humans—were liable to be covered by several yards of heavy brocade.

1. Political gossip (Gasp! What won't they hide next?)
2. Sexual exploitation (Gasp! What won't they display next?)[69]
3. Political exposé, requiring the journalist to account for any public figure's conduct in terms of one or more of three "acceptable" motivations:
   a. Personal animosity (LBJ hated RFK; Rocky hated JVL)
   b. Personal ambition (X is power hungry; he covets Y's job)
   c. Special interest pressures or obligations (Z is a tool of the auto interests, R of the old folks' lobby)

On the rare occasion when a public figure emerges who simply cannot be squeezed into the formula (such as Eugene McCarthy in 1968 and 1972), he is dismissed as a fluke, a Quixotic "human interest" aberration.

Additional elements of the formula have been developed to suit television journalism. The key terms are:

1. Fair time. If you devote five minutes to a black militant, you must also allot five minutes to a white bigot. This helps avoid the charge that you are politically biased.
2. In-depth. To demonstrate that television is just as sober as printed journalism, stage a few interviews with "spokesmen" for assorted causes, i.e., men sitting in leather chairs. It matters not if the interview is pointless; what matters is the event and the chairs.
3. Immediacy. Load a hand-held camera with old grainy film, take it out on the street, and try to get extreme close-up telephoto lens pictures of a notorious personality while shaking the camera. The resultant blurred film will give the impression of mobs of people jostling the cameraman as he tries to get documentary coverage of live and exciting events.

This sort of news reporting, where factuality is forced to conform to formula is nothing more than ritual—it cannot recreate our understanding because it is incapable of renewing our interest in an ever fresh human world. How then to separate factuality from fiction? There is no longer a way.[70] In Chapter 10 we discussed the distinction between fabrication (an activity that eventuates in an artifact that is detached from its creator) and performance (an activity in which the event is co-equal with the artist's action and which consequently requires an audience

---

[69] The *New York Review of Books* maintains its snob posture by confining this second feature of the formula to its classified ads.

[70] Cf. Carl Becker, "Detachment and the Writing of History," *Atlantic Monthly* 126(October 1910):524–536.

before which the artist can appear and display his or her skill). This distinction is complicated with the coming of film, videotape, Xerox, data banks, and the like. We no longer rediscover the past, we replay it. All factuality of action has been replaced by fabrication; all events and performances are now susceptible to becoming fabrications, behind which the creator can hide. To take a simple example: What chance is there today that some character seeking notoriety could appear on a television show and quite literally "display" himself (engage in the activity of removing his clothes)? Quite obviously, none. Most shows are videotaped for the specific purpose of removing "offensive" or "nonentertaining" segments; all spontaneity is edited out of the event. From this editorial control it is but a short step to bypassing even a semblance of spontaneity and to rehearsing every segment, fabricating a videotape that meets the approval of all the creators (editors, camerapersons, directors, sponsors).

But if modern technology makes such fabrication possible in the entertainment realm, why not as well in the political realm, which is, according to Arendt, a set of performing arts like football? Why risk the unforseen with open debate? Why not "stage" debates, arrange the "newsrelease" to fit strategic needs, project "winning images" (instead of risking votes by acting in a public realm where the audience might detect unsavory elements in the unedited performance)? Why not just manage the entire game of politics in the same fashion that wrestling "exhibitions" are managed to give the audience an exciting evening but assure in advance that the performers will not stray from the prearranged script? Thus is factuality destroyed and replaced with scenarios.[71] Consequently it is possible for Kissinger to deny the Pentagon Papers and others with power over the news fabricators to deny or propound whatever non-sense suits their fancy or immediate political convenience. Any contradictions need only be declared "inoperative."

Three Substitutes for Factuality

But with factuality thus destroyed, historiography too goes by the boards and modern man is left with only three alternatives: (1) pure mathematical inference (which is a flight from whatever reality remains beyond our skin, since it is not only devoid of facts, but of images as well).[72] (2)

---

[71] See H. Arendt, "Lying in Politics: Reflections on the Pentagon Papers," *New York Review of Books* 17(18 November 1971):30.

[72] Cf. S. K. Langer, *Philosophy in a New Key* (Cambridge: Harvard University Press, 1957), p. 28.

Thinking by topic, or conventional categories (typical of most bureaucrats)—otherwise known as "mail-room mentality." The technician learns a set of pigeonhole classifications by which he can process incoming fragments of data. He then shatters reality as he confronts it and drops the slivers into the proper discrete slots. This not only gives him the illusion that his information processing is thinking, but it also immobilizes him, since his topical categories need bear no coherent relationship to each other; he is unable to assemble data as a basis for action. Thus, you often hear a specialist say something like, "Well we need to gather political, economic, religious, educational . . . data before we act." What he is actually doing is displaying his pigeonhole category system. The gathering of such atomized data is in its turn a surrogate for action.[73] (3) Calculation—typical of students and others who feel themselves oppressed. Compute the most expedient (cheapest, fastest, safest) means to achieve certain conventional goals (a college degree, money, marriage, a new stereo). Calculation quickly reduces itself to alertness to rhetorical assessment of power relations in the world, since the most expedient means to any goal is to align yourself with powerful allies and to avoid antagonizing them.[74] It is clear that if factual truth happens to oppose a politically powerful group's profit or motive, it would be in your best interest not to remind them of it, since you stand to gain nothing by merely uttering the truth,[75] whereas you stand to provoke hostility from those powerful groups seeking to fabricate their own non-factual or "non-sensical" reality at the moment. Hence, the most expedient thing to do in a non-factual world is to find an ally in a powerful Don, allow him to project whatever hallucinations he wishes on the world,[76] and then fabricate whatever data match and neatly support that powerful man's (or group's) megalomania. Once factuality is no longer thought to disclose or reveal reality, it makes sense to mass produce whatever reality contents us, and so our history begins to take on more and more a resemblance to our dreams.

The foregoing analysis is not meant as a melancholy political polemic, but an examination of historiography's fate in our times. To the extent that our analysis is correct, we can suggest that the game of

[73] See L. Rosenfield, "The Experience of Criticism," *Quarterly Journal of Speech* 60(December 1974):489–496.

[74] Cf. T. Hobbes, *Leviathan*, part 21.

[75] We are confining ourselves for the sake of argument to simple factual truths such as the fact that our official body counts of the "enemy" in Viet Nam were rather exaggerated.

[76] Such fantasies were called *Potemkin Villages* when they made their first appearance on earth during the reign of Catherine the Great in Tsarist Russia. See M. Klonsky, *Fabulous Ego: Absolute Power in History* (New York: Quadrangle, 1974).

historiography as we have known it (the disclosure of the past as it radiated from past facts and was confirmed by historians) will come to an end, and the past will itself become a simple archive to be ransacked for mythic patterns—devoid of factual basis—that tickle the poet's fancy. For once facts are emptied of their radiance (apparent accuracy), the past becomes literally meaning-less, and historiography goes the way of two-handed bezique.

Here we have explored some of the more common Dialectic games played in modern times, games that serve to engage the intellect in order that we may renew our capacity to think. Where in the ancient world these games served in the main to enable players to achieve a contemplative tranquility, in our own time Didactic games serve more as public spectator games in which the audience develops some degree of mental rigor or otherwise acquires knowledge. Typical Didactic games include:

SCIENCE is a game of observation and inference by which man seeks to intervene with Nature in order to expose to understanding the mechanisms of natural process. But insofar as it is not simple curiosity that is the game's telos, but rather the need to *confirm* one's beliefs to public satisfaction, and insofar as the scientist seeks to open all his activities to public inspection, his game-play serves to inform or enlighten his audience.

CRITICISM is a game in which the critic employs his faculty for judgment to comment on assorted objects and events in order to heighten the appreciation of an audience composed of those who share a certain enthusiasm for those objects and events. The various critical strategies all serve to enlarge the awareness of members of the critic's audience concerning the significance of the objects and events under discussion.

HISTORIOGRAPHY is a game that seeks to extract meaning from facts about the past. It is slipping in popularity insofar as modern man becomes disillusioned in the perceptual faith by which he traditionally assumed that facts were a primary means for coming to know reality. Our contemporary ability to manufacture facts has drained the history and news games of their restorative potential in the realm of intellect.

14

Conclusion:
The Answer in
the Back of
the Book

F or those of you who have worked your way patiently along with us through these many pages, we would like to remind you once more of the perspective on human communication we have sought to provide throughout this book. We have assumed that only within a constellation of thoughtfulness, carefulness, and good humor is man's communication distinctive from that of animals' or machines'. And to the extent that we ourselves have remained faithful to that constellation in examining communication activities Jasper's words will be especially meaningful:

> . . . In this world where reliable factual community vanishes and men are increasingly torn from their historic roots, in these nations that unwittingly betray their own traditions—men can meet and join in reason, love, and truth. They can prepare the ground for the incalculable flowering of new worlds. Nietzsche's word, "Truth begins when there are two," is borne out by every community of individuals, especially under totalitarianism, but no less in free countries, where life may become a life of "total conventions." Here is the lastingly possible human substance, the most vigorous, the most reliable. All freedom lies in the individual. What shall happen freely cannot be shifted to events or institutions or causal

and contextual relations open to sociological analysis. Freedom dwells in depths that make all those relations look superficial. It can issue only from the individual, from many individuals who transcend outward communal forms and really meet one another in man-to-man communication.[1]

With Jaspers, we have proposed for your consideration a frankly moralistic interpretation of communication events, one that presupposes that not all chatter merits the name "communication," but only those free engagements that manifest and encourage man's potentialities as a thoughtful, careful, good-humored creature.[2]

Though at times our interpretations may have seemed either idiosyncratic or excessively biased, as indeed we warned you in Chapter 2 they might, our intent has not been to be either deliberately scandalous or merely novel. Rather, in line with Jaspers' injunction that freedom transcends all ideological or methodological commitments, we have attempted to open up for you, our patient reader, the implications that follow when the game-play model is taken to heart as a viable paradigm of human communication. In Chapter 2 we suggested that if you took what we offered seriously, then in places you would as a reader perhaps experience some discomfort with our interpretations of some communicative situations with which you are already familiar. That discomfort you felt is the freedom to which Jaspers refers when he contends that "All freedom lies in the individual." For even though we have given throughout this book the appearance of reasonableness in our analyses, your discomfort, your impatience, and, indeed, your pleasure or satisfaction with our material are all symptomatic of your free and sovereign scrutiny of a set of attitudes that have not as yet been made explicit (as perhaps they can never be made entirely explicit). Let us now, therefore, try to bring to the surface some implicit assumptions that are inherent in the game-play model as a possible aid to you in determining if your adherence to or rejection of these principles may perhaps be the source of some of your earlier reactions.

The game-play model disregards hierarchy. In a game all human actions are treated with equal seriousness; there is no innate standard of superiority for some players over others, be it brains, brawn, credentials, beauty, or achievement. As we have described it, the therapist's communication is intimately tied to that of the patient, and it is hard to

---

[1] Karl Jaspers, *The Future of Mankind* (Chicago: University of Chicago Press, 1961), p. 223. Copyright © 1961.

[2] Richard Weaver, *The Ethics of Rhetoric* (Chicago: Regnery Press, 1953), pp. 19–20.

isolate the jailer from the jailed, the medical doctor from the witch doctor. Players in communication games are no more separable (though of course they are distinguishable) than is the offense from the defense in a ball game.

Would-be political radicals are often at first attracted to this model because it seems to entail a rejection of the prevailing allocation of power. But such an understanding misses the essential point that viewing communication as game-play does not favor *either* criminal or judge insofar as their interaction is seen as symbiotic. The political militant is often less interested in altering institutions than he is in rotating the dominant personnel (think of the dictatorship of the proletariat), but the game-play model contains no such impulse. Nor does it offer comfort for advocates of institutional reform since its natural response to events is appreciation (and hence tolerance) for the human reality those events display.[3]

The game-play model largely disregards institutions themselves. Its focus is neither the stadium nor the rules but the game as played. Today such topics as "organizational communication" and "appropriate communication roles" are popular subjects for academic discussion. But our scheme regards participation in transitory "gatherings" as more revealing than blueprints or codes of etiquette for correct behavior in corporate systems of any type. People who strive to behave correctly in their circumstances, who constantly take their cues for conduct from their social environment rather than from the ongoing relationship between themselves and another tend to drift into ever more impersonal games. In this drift they become more susceptible to the twin occupational hazards of modern communication: an incapacity for action and a crippled sense of humanity. ("I'm sorry, your time is up; there's nothing I can do; I just work here.")

Such an impersonal mentality restricts action to calculable means-ends relations and so sacrifices the spontaneity that is the most crucial facet of action in the company of others. When calculation comes to substitute for action, the gratifications of freedom are replaced with the security of means-end relationships.[4] Yet the game-play model, far from questioning the validity of this limitation, accepts institutional constraints as a given that presents dilemmas to the communicative participants. What matters in a world in which men feel compelled to

---

[3] A. W. Gouldner, *The Coming Crisis in Western Sociology* (New York: Avon, 1970), p. 379.

[4] On the conflict between free volition and impersonal calculation see John Duns Scotus, *Philosophical Writings*, trans. A. Wolter (New York: Library of Liberal Arts, 1962), pp. 57–64.

pursue sometimes ungratifying goals within social institutions not of their choice are the crevices in the system, the momentary events wherein humanity sometimes creeps through despite company regulations.

In its focus on the here-and-now of communicative interplay, the game-model avoids both the melancholy of nostalgia and the disquiet of hoped for reform. It is only natural that someone who holds to humanistic principles will at times feel a certain impatience with those "mindless" social rituals that restrict the range of creative action. Yet an appreciation for what *is,* no matter how imperfect that which is may be, imparts a degree of tranquility that would be absent if the model were a suitable basis for institutional reform.[5] To concentrate exclusively on the present is to presume that human institutions remain largely impervious to enduring human reform. Yet if such an attitude smacks at times of conservatism, it also injects a sense of peacefulness into one's perspective. To believe that the present is thoroughly revealing is to believe also that both past and future will for the most part resemble the present in spite of human volition or good intentions. Neither the effort to reestablish a distant idealized past nor the tensions that accompany hope or fear for the anticipated future need interfere with the serene pleasure that comes of making sense of what does in fact already exist in the realm of communicative engagements. It is in this profound sense that we have offered here an apolitical model of communication.

The game-play model demands a persistent aesthetic detachment from those objects and behaviors conventionally (i.e., *custom-arily) prized.* Time and again in this book we have made disparaging remarks ("mere sentiment") about those behaviors. This detachment is also an inherent feature of the model. Insofar as game-play advocates anything, it invites one to *enjoy* appearances, to take incongruity to heart, to appreciate the superficial and corrupt, to affirm the moment-by-moment absurdities that abound in lives limited more and more by "correct" procedures.[6] Rather than modify or dissolve the rules that govern life, our model seeks to revitalize life as lived. But to eschew partisan reforms of all types is by no means the same as succumbing to authority or threadbare institutions. There is no greater denial of claims to respect than laughter. Thus,

---

[5] Perhaps no one understood the significance for maintaining a state of absolute decorum in confronting matters with political overtones as the great sixteenth-century humanist Erasmus: "What he wanted was the intellectual and spiritual freedom of the unattached, and so the story of his wandering is one of an obstinate and resolute search for independence." A. W. Levi, *Humanism and Politics* (Bloomington, Ind.: Indiana University Press, 1969), p. 39.

[6] A. W. Gouldner, *The Coming Crisis*, p. 384.

the relegation of comfortable behaviors to the scrap heaps of "senti-ment" or "custom" is a fundamental denial of institutions' right to intrude on the individual's emotions. Wit comes into our play as a precipitate of reason mocking sham experience.

We live in an age when most people live in terror of solitude—they are often willing to strike a bad bargain with the world in order to overcome isolation. Such individuals sometimes trade sovereignty over their own feelings in order to find companionship in the common dis-play of like emotions. Thus we are confronted with the emotional payoff in mass events such as football crowds, rock festivals, and other pageant-ry. As modern totalitarian leaders so well understand, the spectacle of masses marching to a single beat becomes a substitute for friendship. And although it is a poor replacement, such sentimentality (which clearly is both the antithesis of thinking and a counterfeit of passion) will be in increasing demand by those who lack gratifying human contact. And so films like *Love Story* (and its earlier version, the opera *La Boheme*) enable masses of emotionally destitute people to share-a-cry. How does this leave the student of game-play? Perhaps in not much better cir-cumstances; contempt for sentimentality is its own kind of rehearsal. It demands that one committed to celebration of the authentic reconcile himself to a life of relative solitude in order to maintain his tactical freedom and to avoid becoming addicted to the ersatz dial-a-tear offer-ings served up by cynics and fools.[7]

Game-play holds people in greater regard than any institutions, causes, or principles. As we mentioned at the outset of this book, we are not speaking of an undifferentiated devotion to "People" as an abstraction. An individual could no more love all the elves and hearth gods of earlier days: Some were cute, some were malicious, and some were frankly tricky little devils; nevertheless they were all fascinating, just as human beings are. And people remain so when compared with such careless salvations as sentiment, bureaucracy, or undivided loyalty to any hierarchy. All these latter alternatives are what Francis Bacon so acutely called *idols*.[8] Game-play theory holds that whether these idols are customary, ideological, or induced by submission to some superior force, they are false idols insofar as they are mindlessly accepted for the sake of convention or appearance or habit.

The game-play approach thus appeals to "winners" in life's games.

---

[7] A. W. Gouldner, *The Coming Crisis*, p. 387.

[8] As Karl Wallace rightly indicates in *Francis Bacon on Communication and Rhetoric* (Chapel Hill, N. C.: University of North Carolina Press, 1943), pp. 100–105, such idols involve cognitive errors of interpretation made by minds whose fallibility is a result of corruption.

"Winners" (those who are confident that they can outwit the system) are winners because they recognize that they are losers (they can in no way beat the system). This skeptical attitude toward reform of course denies the exhilaration of momentarily beating the system and instituting some minor improvement; but then it also removes the sting of losing—the disappointment of seeing one's hard efforts undermined by stupidity, greed, fatigue, frivolity, and all the naughty little stratagems that make mankind so interesting. It is only winners who can face the reality that they are fated to be losers. Losers are those who so fear to lose that they must pretend that they are winners.[9] This denial of any element of faith whatsoever—even in human charm—drains both the excitement of victory and the shame of defeat from those who have largely agreed with our interpretations. What remains for them is only the freedom that springs from a passionate commitment to keep playing the games in spite of their absurdities and their reminders of our mortality.

What, then, do we, the authors, feel we have offered to those of you who have followed what we have had to say with understanding, approval, and, at times, even relish? We believe we have provided at least a temporary fix on human communication, a reckoning that is suitable for an age that exalts appearances devoid of their ground. The game-player says, "Very well, if it is to be appearance alone that counts, rather than virtue or merit, then let us explore appearance with a vengeance, but always with an eye to genuine gratification." All superficiality thus becomes serious and, in its turn, a source of humor.

And so in the end our critical understanding turns upon itself and encourages us to think of man as the animal who laughs:

> . . . In comedy ambiguity, doubt, difference, and all forms of social disorganization are exposed, not cloaked. . . . In comedy we confront openly many things we must hide and repress when we are "serious."[10]

The moral implications afforded by this general perspective have been neatly expressed by Henri Bergson:

> And we shall experience [the comic] most strongly when we are

---

[9] See A. W. Gouldner, *The Coming Crisis*, p. 385. The Greeks had something like this equation in mind when they warned against too much hubris.

[10] Hugh D. Duncan, *Communication and Social Order* (New York: Bedminster Press, 1962), p. 437.

shown the soul tantalized by the needs of the body: on the one hand the moral personality with its intelligently varied energy, and, on the other, the stupidly monotonous body, perpetually obstructing everything with its machine-like obstinacy. The more paltry and uniformly repeated these claims of the body, the more striking will be the result. . . . Any incident is comic that calls our attention to the surface in a person, when it is the moral side that is concerned. . . . We laugh every time a person gives us the impression of being a thing. . . . The comic is that side of a person which reveals his likeness to a thing, that aspect of human events which, through its peculiar inelasticity, conveys the impression of pure mechanism, of automatism, of movement without life.[11]

Our effort in these pages has been to distinguish in the realm of human communication between those elements of the mechanical and thoughtless and the suppleness characteristic of living action. To a certain extent all the fashions of the day, be they in garment styles or communication games, are laughable. But our laughter is provoked out of enchantment with creatures who would encase themselves in ill-fitting costumes.

Those who insist on squeezing into such garb constrict their very existence, sometimes allowing the shell of appearances to suffocate the life within. So our observations at times leave us with the vision of fossils in motion—shapes, forms, and procedures whose sum total is less than the marvelous human creature. Yet, on occasion, one or another of the creatures we have studied violates all laws of behavior and transforms the fossil into a vehicle: He becomes a clown, and in the sheer exuberance of his human nature he is overcome, not with death, but with a spirit of frolic.[12] As if by inspiration he pays special heed to the surface of his surroundings, recognizing with penetrating innocence the difference between illusion and reality. And as we suggested at the beginning of this book it is just this playful spirit of recognition that we sought to share with you, our reader.

---

[11] H. Bergson, "Laughter," in R. W. Corrigen, ed., *Comedy: Meaning and Form* (New York: Chandler, 1965), p. 476.

[12] See G. Santayana, "The Comic Mask," in P. Lauter, ed., *Theories of Comedy* (Garden City: Anchor, 1964), p. 414.

Index

AASEC, 382n
Abbot, D., 48n
Abrahams, R., 149n
Abrahamson, M., 103n
Abrams, R., 117n
Abzug, B., 293
Accessibility, 73–74, 77, 216–217, 219
Acupuncture, 356n
Adams, J., 338, 341
Advertising as Poetic game: and aesthetic intent, 264, 266, 267, 277, 280, 294; elevation of the commonplace, 274–281; emphasis on connotation, 272; emphasis on expressive form, 269–272; exploitation of ambiguity, 272–274; as legitimate art form, 264–266, 269n, 294; and persuasive intent, 264, 280, 294, 308, 310; as sponsored art form, 266–267, 294; and traditional poetry, 267–268, 294
Advertising as Rhetoric game. *See* Publicity
Aesthetic intent, 229–231, 245, 253, 263, 266, 277
Affirmation, 229, 231–232, 238, 245, 247, 250, 253, 263–264, 294; not a necessary conclusion, 232
Agnew, S., 289
Agriculture, 225n
Ainslie, D., 404
Alathaeia, 419, 425
Albee, E., *American Dream, The*, 258; *Who's Afraid of Virginia Woolf?*, 189
Alger, H., 41n
Allen, S., 291
Altamont rock festival, 386
Ambrestor, R., 48n
American Medical Association, 356n; Council on Drugs, 324
American Medicine, 348, 352, 363–368; placebo, 364–366; workshop mentality, 363–364, 366–368. *See also* Healing.
American Pow's, 357, 358
American Revolution, 341
American Television and Radio Commercials Festival, 282
Amusement: defined, 248, 294; and Rhetoric games, 302; and thought, care, and good humor, 248
Anderson, J., 419n
Anticipation, 239
Appearance, 306, 307
Appley, D., 376n
Approaching game, 216, 221, 227; defined, 81–82, 85, 87, 213; how players evaluate, 85–86. *See also* Love, Personal Conversation Among Friends, Polite Conversation, Polite Greeting, Protocol.
Aquinas, St. Thomas, 395
Aranguren, J., 29n, 398n
Arena, 223–225, 227; defined, 223; borderline situations, 225–226; motives for interacting in, 226–227, 228, 339–340, 380

Arendt, H., 380; and Participatory ideal of Political Dialog, 338–342; *Between Past and Future*, 238n, 327n, 340, 395n, 427; "Lying in Politics: Reflections on the Pentagon Papers," 433n; *Men in Dark Times*, 224n, 341n; *On Revolution*, 341n; *On Violence*, 382–383n; *Rachel Varnhagen: The Life of a Jewish Woman*, 427n; "Thinking and Moral Considerations," 349n, 428n; "Thoughts On Politics and Revolution," 340n
Aristotle, 382n; and Empirical ideal of Political Dialog, 328–330, 342; *De Anima*, 346n; *Nicomachean Ethics*, 180n, 185n, 248n, 304n; *Politics*, 248n; *Rhetoric*, 329
Army Code of Conduct, 204n
Army surplus, 319
Arnold, C., 216n
Arterton, F., 430n
Ashton, E., 384n
Assertion, 234–235, 299
Association for Its Own Sake, 239–240
Attention: involuntary, 87; non-voluntary, 87; voluntary, 87
Augsber, T., 360n
Augustine, St., 182–183
Austen, J., 113n, 114
Austin, J., 207n
Avalon, F., 178

Back, K., 376n
Bacon, F., 441n
Bakan, D., 367n
Baptist Church, 372
Barbarians, 303
Barker, E.: translation of Aristotle's *Politics*, 248n; *Church, State, and Education*, 423n, 425n
Barnlund, D., 117n
Barrett, W., *Irrational Man*, 14n; *What is Existentialism?*, 419n
Baseball, 401, 409
Batman, 258, 259, 262
Bayne, R., 74n
Beard, C., 424
Beavin, J., 188n
Becker, C., 423n
Beisecker, T., 166n
Bell, D., 328
Benedict, R., 180n
Bentham, J., 300n, 328
Berg, D., 430
Bergson, H., 442, 443n
Berloquin, P., 29n
Berne, D., 117n
Berne, E., 29, 37n; *Games People Play*, 117n; *Sex and Human Loving*, 80n; *Structure and Dynamics of Organizations and Groups*, 118n; *What Do You Say After You Say Hello?*, 39n, 73n

Bernstein, B., 108–109n
Berzon, B., 376n
Bezique, two-handed, 435
Black, M., 400n
Blake, W., 277
Boas, G., 176n
Boccacio, 379
"Body," 346n
Bormann, E., 140n
Borscht Circuit, 289
Bowery Boys, 288
Boxing, 40
Brainwashing, 348, 352, 357–363; phases, 359–362; tactics, 358–359. *See also* Healing
Bridge, 41–42
Bridgman, P., 400n
British soldiers, 357
Brockriede, W., 394
Brown, J., 357n, 359n, 360n, 361n, 362n
Brown, R., 200n
Browning, R., 277
Bryan, W., 330
Bryson, L., 302n
Buber, M., 9n, 250n
Burckhardt, J., 424, 425
Burke, K., 48n, 364
Burns, R., 277
Burton, A., 376n
Burton, R., 250
Byron, Lord, 267

Campbell, P., 249n
Camp meetings, 373
Canaanites, 224n
Canada, 374, 430
Canned laughter, 292
Capitalism, 358, 361
Caplan, H., "On Being Useful," 405n; "Memoria: Treasure House of Eloquence," 424n
Capp, A., 261
Careful (Carefulness), 67, 437, 438; defined, 13–16; and amusement, 248
Carnap, R., 399n
Carson, J., 288, 289, 290, 291, 293n
Catherine the Great, 434n
Catholic Church, 372n, 395
Catholic Inquisition, 337
Cavett, D., 288, 290, 291
Cebik, L., 423n
Chapman, A., 128n, 166n
Charismatic preachers, 372
Chase, M., 256
Chaucer, G., 379
Chautauqua, 375
Chess, 41
China: 361, 412; Communists, 357, 358, 359, 361, 362; Red China, 430
Churchill, W., 330
Cicero, 228, 391; and Investigative Ideal of Political Dialog, 330–334; *De Oratore*, 331n; *On The Commonwealth*, 330n
"Civilized" societies, 224n
Classic English Literature, 268
Collingwood, R., 423n
Collins, E., 375n
Comedy, 254; defined, 255–256, 257, 263; and laughter, 255; and social role, 256, 263; and tragedy, 255
Commedia dell'arte, 48, 49
Commission on Obscenity and Pornography, 378
Commitment, 74–75, 77, 218–219
Common, T., 392n
Common sense, 345, 346, 349, 351, 362; in the Ancient world, 425
Communism, 359, 362, 363
Community, 234, 298, 303, 304, 340–341, 352, 380

Conovan, M., 339n, 349n, 392n, 427n
Conscience, 306
Consensus, 234–235, 238, 298, 307, 345
Contiguity, law of, 325
Conville, R., 255n
Conviviality, 299, 376; and encounter groups, 376n
Cooke, B., 106n
Cooper, D., 346n
Copernicus, 407
Cornell University, 402
Corrigen, R., 443n
Counter-culture, 375
Courtney, C., 41n
Coward, N., 256–257
Crew, 40
Cribbage, 422
Criticism: defined, 435; critic defined, 410, 411; critical act defined, 411–415; MC strategy, 416–417, 422; ME strategy, 417–418, 422; MEC strategy, 421–422; reasons and verdicts in, 413; and scientific reasoning, 415; SM strategy, 417, 422, SMC strategy, 419–420, 422; SME strategy, 418, 422
Croce, B., 404n
Culhane, J., 261n
Culture, 225n
Curandero, 355
Customs: defined, 43, 46–47. *See also* Rules, Tactics.
Czikszentmihalyi, M., 36n

Dance, F., 349n
Danto, A., 423n
Daugherty, P., 287n
Davidson, B., 287n
Defense Department, 427
De Gaulle, C., 330
DeMan, Paul, 427n
Democratic National Convention (1968), 385
Demosthenes, 411
De Sade, Marquis, 388
Descartes, R., 394, 426n
Des Moines Old Home Day, 290
de Tocqueville, A., 424
Deutsch, M., 162n
Dialectic games: defined, 236–237, 238, 391–396; and argumentation, 394; as *contemplation of what is*, 392–393; dialectical messages defined, 228, 236, 238, 396; and Didactic, 395; and independent truth, 395; as loving combat, 391, 394; originated by Greeks, 391–393; participants' withdrawal from "common sense," 392–393; as *performing* philosophical activity, 396; Plato's *dialogues*, 392; and Poetic messages, 248–249n; and Polite Conversation Among Friends, 393; as *producing and reporting* philosophical findings, 396. *See also* Criticism, Historiography, Science.
Dickinson, E., 274
Didactic games, 395. *See also* Dialectic games.
Distancing game, 216, 221, 227; defined, 81–82, 85, 87, 213; how players evaluate, 85–86. *See also* Intensity, Put Down, Put Off, Termination, Turn Off.
DNA, 408n
Dollard, J., 166n
Douglas, M., 288, 290
Dray, W., 423n
Duncan, H., "Simmel's Image of Society," 75n; *Communication and Social Order*, 204n, 442n; "The Search for a Social Theory of Communication," 349n
Duns Scotus, J., 439n

Edinger, L., 330n
Edwards, J., 373, 376
Egalitarianism, 373

Ehninger, D., 202n
Ehrmann, J., 42n
Einstein, A., 407
Eliot, T., 267; *The Cocktail Party*, 138, 142n, 144n, 150n, 151n, 155, 157n, 160n; "Morning at the Window," 277
Ellsberg, D., 427
Emblems of solidarity, 240
Emerson, R., 274
Emotional distance, 217, 222, 227
Emotional proofs, 323
Empathy, 14–15
Enemy, 161–164
England, 357
Entralgo, P., 306n, 352n
Epicureans, 300n
Erasmus, D., 440n
Escape: and Theater, 249; and Mass Entertainment, 284, 285
Espanto, 355
Ethical proofs, 323–324
Ethos, 332
Evans, F., 366n
Evans, W., 247

Fabrication and performance, 432–433
Faculty psychology, 238n
Farce, 254; defined, 262, 263, 264; and film, 262
Fascist political groups, 337
Faulkner, W., 384, 385
FBI, 426
Feldman, S., 93n
Ferguson, C., 372n
Festinger, L., 75n
Finney, C., 372
Fisher, W., 323n
Football, 30–38, 43–45, 327, 396, 409, 433
Ford, M., 200n
Formal Conversation games: backstage, 118–119; onstage, 119–121; vestibule, 118. *See also* Polite Conversation, Put Off.
Formality-Intimacy continuum, 210, 213, 216, 219–221, 227, 241, 247; defined, 72–73, 78, 87, 213
Formosa, 411, 412
France, 430
Frank, J., 346n, 356n, 366n
Freberg, S., 282
Frechtman, S., 382n
Freeman, G., 383n
French Revolution, 335n, 341
Frentz, T., 13, 216, 218, 219, 221
Freud, S., 48n, 73n, 80n, 369, 376, 417
Freund, E., 419n
Friedan, B., 293
Friedman, M., 250n
Friedman, P., 185n
Fromm, E., 179n
Frontier revival, 372–373
Frost, D., 291
Frost, R., 267, 277
Frye, N., 254n

Gadpaille, W., 381n
Gallie, W., 36n, 423n
Game: metaphor for human communication, 28–31, 47, 66–67; frivolous activity, 28; competitive battle, 29; hypocritical activity, 29; limited moral universe, 39–40, 42; perspective for spectators of human communication, 47; good and bad communication games, 85–86; participation games, 223; assumptions of game-play model, 438–443
Gap: intrapersonal, 57, 58; interpersonal, 57–58, 59, 72, 160–161, 195, 196, 216; intentional signals, 58; unintentional cues, 58; physical distance between individuals, 72, 117; emotional distance

between individuals, 72–73, 87. *See also* Accessibility, Commitment, Reciprocity, Spontaneity.
Gathering: defined, 222–223; borderline situations, 225–226, 227, 352
Genet, J., *The Balcony*, 382; *Our Lady of the Flowers*, 382; *The Thief's Journal*, 382
Gentile, G., 423n
Germino, D., 329n
Geyser, S., 266n
Giffin, K., 291n, 351n
Girlie magazines, 283
Goffman, E., 84n, 97, 99; *Asylums*, 358n, 367n; *Behavior in Public Places*, 93n, 95n, 96n, 97n, 99n, 107n; *Encounters*, 145n, 202n; "On Face Work," 45n; *Presentation of Self in Everyday Life*, 118n; *Relations in Public*, 93n, 120n
Gold, T., 402
Gomorrah, 224n
Good Humor, 67, 437, 438; defined, 17–19; and thoughtfulness, 19–21; and carefulness, 21–22; and amusement, 248
Gouldner, A., 74n, 439, 440, 441
Graffiti, 381
Graham, H., 212n
Graham, S., 377n
Greek tragedy, 254–255
Greer, G., 292, 388n
Griffin, M., 288, 290
Grotowski, J., 250n
Group identity, 349–350
Gullahorn, J., 117n
Gurr, T., 212n

Haberman, F., 412n
Hacker, L., 424
Haiku, 269
Hall, E., 106n, 181n
Hallie, P., 383n
Handel, G., 266
Hardt, H., 291n
Harland, C., 117n
Harrah, D., 400n
Hartman, R., 423n
Hayakawa, S., 269n
Hayes, L., 13, 216, 218, 219, 221
Healing: defined, 353, 368; *health* defined, 349–350; *ill-health* defined, 350, 354; *healer* defined, 351, 352, 354; behavior modification, 359; exorcism, 353; face lift, 353; healer's demonstration of authority, 352, 356, 364; healer's presence, 351, 352, 356; healer/sufferer relationship, 352–353, 355, 369–370; and interpersonal communication, 352; mental illness, 350n, 354, 368, 370; open heart surgery, 353; orthopedic surgery, 353; patient as non-person, 358n, 367, 368; persuasion research, 346; physical illness, 350n, 354; speech therapy, 353; sufferer's faith in healing process, 352, 356, 363, 366, 377; transcendental meditation, 348, 352. *See also* American Medicine, Brainwashing, Primitive Magic, Psychotherapy, Revivalism, Sensitivity and Encounter Groups.
Hegel, G., 394; *Reason in History*, 423n, 424, 425n
Heidegger, M., 338; *Discourse on Thinking*, 14n, 419n; *Introduction to Metaphysics*, 11, 425; *What Is Called Thinking?*, 13n, 45n
Heisey, D., 372n
Hell, 372
Hellenes, 303
Hellman, P., 289n
Hell's Angels, 385, 386
Heretics, 368
Herodotus, 423
Hewett, W., 41n
"Hidden hand of history," 424

Hill, K., 423n
Historia rerum gestarum, 422
Historiography: defined, 435; sequence, 423; thematic analysis, 424; impressionistic mode, 424–425; demise of the fact, 425–428; fabricated factuality and the news, 428–435; recreation and the news, 428, 430; the news formula, 430; tabloid formula, 431–432; tabloid style, 431n; three substitutes for factuality, 433–434
Hit records, 283, 287
Hobbes, T., 339, 341, 434n
Holland, D., 372n, 375n
Hollingdale, R., 394n
Holt, R., 50n
Homer, 269, 335
Homo faber, 431
Horace, 331n
Hot Stove meetings, 409
Howard, J., 376n
Howes, R., 33n
Hubris, 442n
Humanitas, 333
Hume, D., 300n
Humor. *See* Good Humor
Humphrey, H., 427
Hunt, E., 33n
Hupo-krisis, 56n
Hymes, D., 200n

Ik, 209n
Illich, I., 368n
Images: defined, 50, 58; scene-image, 50–51, 58; self-image, 51, 58; other-image, 51–53, 58; topic-image, 53–55, 58; persona, 55–56, 58; life space, 56; influence of gathering on, 222–223; influence of arena on, 224–225. *See also* Interpersonal relationship image.
Impersonal games: and Polite Greeting, 202. *See also* Protocol, Termination.
Informal Conversation games. *See* Personal Conversation Among Friends, Put Down.
Ingram, H., 234n
Insanity, 369n
Institution, 224n
Intellectual understanding, 236–237, 238
Intensity, 173; defined, 184–185, 213; placating, 185–186; tyranny, 188–195; and Termination, 210n
Interpersonal games: and Rhetoric games, 304
Interpersonal relationship image, 71–73, 77, 87; accessibility, 73–74, 77; commitment, 74–75, 77; reciprocity, 74, 77; spontaneity, 76, 77; before communicative encounters, 78–79, 85, 216; during communicative encounters, 79–80, 85; after communicative encounters, 81, 82–85, 216, 221. *See also* Approaching games, Distancing games.
Intimate games. *See* Love, Intensity.
Invention, 332
Israelites, 224n, 351

Jackson, D., 188n
James Bond, 262–263
Jandt, F., 163n
Jaspers, K., 338; *The Future of Mankind*, 10n, 393n, 395n, 437, 438n; *Nietzsche and Christianity*, 384n
"Jesus" sects, 375
Johnson, K., 364n
Johnson, L., 53, 261n
Johnson, T., 274
Jonas, H., 349, 425n, 427
Jourard, S., 76n, 77n, 346n, 352n, 366n
JVL, 432

Kabuki Theater, 48
Kant, I., 394; *Anthropology*, 424; *The Critique of Judgment*, 410n; *The Critique of Pure Reason*, 395n
Kaplan, A., 287
Karst, T., 369n

Keats, J., 267
Kelly, W., 261n
Kennedy, J., 350, 351, 426
Kerford, G., 306n
Kiblansky, R., 423
Kiesler, S., 77n
King, B., 293
King, M., 420
Kissinger, H., 427, 433
Klonsky, M., 434n
Kochman, T., 105n, 106n, 149n, 204n
Koestler, A., 9n
Kohl, H., 105n
Korea, 357, 411, 412
Korean war, 357
Kronhausen, E., 379n
Kronhausen, K., 379n
Kuhlman, K., 374
Kuhn, T., 402, 406n, 407

La Boheme, 441
Labov, W., 204n
Ladd, J., 44n
Laing, R., 56n, 346n
Langer, S., 238n, 399n, 433n
Larrabee, E., 247n, 250n
Lasswell, H., 328
Lauter, P., 443n
LBJ, 432
Lee, A., 56n
Lehman, J., 395n
Leibniz, G., 423n
Lenneberg, E., 70n
Leonard, H., 53n
Levi, A., 423n, 424n, 440n
Leviathan, 339
Levi-Strauss, C., 356
Lewis, D., 44n
Life space, 56, 71, 216; intrapersonal gap, 57, 58; interpersonal gap, 57–58, 59. *See also* Images.
Lifton, R., 360n, 361n, 362
Limited opportunity: in games, 41n
Lipset, S., 328
Literaturnava Gazeta, 384
Logical proofs, 323
Logos, 304
Love, 173; defined, 176–184, 196, 213; and Personal Conversation Among Friends, 178, 180
Lower Rio Grande Valley, 355
Lutheran Church, 372n
Lux (law), 331

MacArthur, D., 411, 413, 415
McCarthy, E., 432
McCarthy, J., 261n
McCleary, R., 429n
Macdonald, D., 426n
McGinnis, J., 323n
McKeon, R., 238n, 284n, 299n
Macksoud, S., 402n
McLaughlin, W., 371n
McLuhan, M., 46n
McMahon, E., 289
McNemar, Q., 406n
McWatter, C., 426
Mader, T., 50n, 305n
Mad houses, 368
Madsen, C., 356n
Madsen, W., 355, 356n
Mafia, 350
Mailer, N., 292
Malinowski, B., 115
Man: at his best, 7–24; masculine emphasis of English language, 12; as rat, 49; as thermostat, 49; as plant, 49; as actor, 50; as animal who laughs, 442

Manfull, L., 250n
Mann, J., 382n
Marcus, S., 383n
Mars, 402
Marx Brothers, 379
Marx, K., 48n, 338, 386
Maslow, A., 180n
Massage parlors, 289
Mass Entertainment Dream Machines: and advertis-
    ing, 283, 294; and public service, 284, 285; and
    mass production, 284, 287, 288; availability,
    285; attention demanded, 285; and Theater,
    285, 294; cost, 286, 287; spectator involvement,
    286–287, 291, 293, 294; television talk shows,
    288–291; and conventional categories, 291; and
    deadened public sensibilities, 292–293, 294
Masturbation, 383
Medieval morality plays, 259–260
Melodrama, 254; defined, 257–259, 263, 264; and
    Tragedy, 257, 260–261n; and Comedy, 257; and
    personal role, 257, 258–259, 261, 263; and affir-
    mation, 258; serious melodrama, 259–260
Merleau-Ponty, M., 429n
Methodist Church, 372
Metz, C., 70n
Middle Ages, 370
Miller, A., *Death of a Salesman*, 232, 254, 255, 258
Miller, G., 70n
Miller, H., 388; themes of novels, 386–387; *The Rosy
    Crucifixion*, 386; *Tropic of Cancer*, 386; *Tropic of
    Capricorn*, 386
Millet, K., 293
Milner, C., 164n, 165n
Milner, R., 164n, 165n
"Mind," 346n
Miracle, 351
Mischel, T., 33n
Moliere, *The Misanthrope*, 256
Monday Morning Quarterback Clubs, 409
Monroe, A., 301n
Montagu, A., 182n
Moon, 402
Moore, M., 258–259
Moscow Nights, 384
Moses, 351
Munro, D., 21n

Namath, J., 290
National Commission on the Causes and Prevention
    of Violence, 283n
National Geographic Magazine, 367
Navasky, A., 274
Nazi swastikas, 385
NBC, 289
Nelson, S., 405n
New York (New York), 289n, 372
New York Review of Books, 431
New York Times, 427
Nietzsche, F., 427–428, 437, 438; *Joyful Wisdom*, 178–
    179n, 182n, 392, 393n, 395n; *Twilight of the Idols*,
    394, 426
Nin, A., 386
Nixon, R., 289, 383
Nolen, W., 363n
Non-being, 205, 209
Non-person, 119, 139, 151, 200–202, 205, 206, 208,
    209, 210; and healing process, 358n, 367, 368
Nordheimer, J., 359n
Nous, 32n
Novosti press agency, 384

Oates, W., 302n, 306n
Objective needs, 317
Ogden, T., 375n
Olbrechts-Tyteca, L., 305n
O'Neill, G., 75n, 76n, 180n
O'Neill, N., 75n, 76n, 180n

Ong, W., 182n
Operationalism, 400
Organic food fad, 375, 377
Osborne, H., 420n
Oswald, L., 426

Pachter, H., 423n, 425n
Paidia, 248n
Palo Alto V.A. Hospital, 383n
Palonzi-Horvath, G., 358n
Paraguay, 429
Paraphernalia of officialdom, 327
Park, R., 55n
Parmenides, 306n
Parr, J., 288
Passage to Pleasure, 385
Passion plays, 249n
Paton, H., 423n
Paul, St., 372
Peirce, C., 399n, 425n
Penis envy, 370
Pentagon Papers, 427, 433
Pentecostal Church, 372
Pepinsky, H., 369n
Perelman, C., 305
Performance and fabrication, 432–433
Perls, F., 376
Personal Conversation Among Friends: defined,
    139–140, 154, 171, 213; arabesque, 142–144, 153;
    cheerleading, 150–151, 153; committee meet-
    ing, 145n; courting (duet; two-handed Personal
    Conversation Among Friends), 151–154; di-
    plomacy, 150, 153; flooding out, 145–146, 153;
    presto, 144–145, 153; shared silence, 151, 153;
    sounding, 146–150, 153; and Love, 153–154,
    178, 180; and Polite Conversation, 140–141,
    151, 154–155; and Put Off, 149
Persuasive intent, 297, 348
Phatic communion, 115
Philippines, 412
Philistines, 224n
Phillips, R., 70n
Phillipson, H., 56n
Philosophical intent, 236–237
Physical distance, 217, 222, 227
Physis, 32
Pietism, 373, 375
Pinsky, R., 366n
Pinter, H., 232
Pirsig, R., 306n
Pismo Beach, 289
Plato, 236, 393n, 394; and Therapeutic ideal of Political
    Dialog, 334–338; *Euthydemus*, 306n; *Gorgias*,
    302n; *Phaedrus*, 334; *Protagoras*, 307; *Republic*,
    335; *Symposium*, 392; *Thaetetus*, 393n, 394n
Platt, J., 404n
Play: as perspective for participants in human com-
    munication, 47; as metaphor for human com-
    munication, 48–50, 66–67
Poetic games, 237; defined, 229–234, 238, 245; re-
    newal, 247, 248, 263, 287; performing arts, 246,
    248, 263, 264, 294; productive arts, 246, 248,
    264, 294; action oriented, 246; fabrication
    oriented, 246; effects of lack of, 247; poetic mes-
    sages defined, 228, 236, 238, 294; and possible
    truth, 233–234, 235, 253, 262, 264; and Dialectic
    games, 248–249n; and Rhetoric games, 248–
    249n. *See also* Advertising as Poetic game, Mass
    Entertainment Dream Machines, Theater.
Poker, 42
Polite Conversation: defined, 114, 126, 134, 213;
    aficionado, 121, 126; gender signalling, 123,
    125; obligatory incantation, 121–123, 126; pre-
    courting (flirtation), 123–125; swinging, 123–
    126; and Dialectic games, 393; and Personal
    Conversation Among Friends, 140–141, 151,
    154–155; and Polite Greeting, 114, 117, 126

Polite Greeting: defined, 90, 99, 111, 213; played by casual acquaintances, 90–94, 99, 111; played by strangers, 94–99, 111; and Impersonal games, 202; and Polite Conversation, 114, 117, 126; and Protocol, 206

Political Dialog: Empirical ideal (Aristotle), 328–330, 342; Investigative ideal (Cicero), 328, 330–334, 342; Participatory ideal (Arendt), 328, 338–342, 343; Therapeutic ideal (Plato), 328, 334–338, 342–343; and proving tactics, 323n; root experience, 327

Political intent, 234–235, 345

Pornography: defined, 379, 380–381; artistic intention, 379; average purchasers, 383; and "common sense," 380; effects researched, 378, 379; film techniques, 388; and game participation, 381; graffiti, 381; passivity and impotence, 380, 383; and pleasure/pain principle, 380; R. Nixon on, 383–384; Russian, 384; substitute for freedom, 380–384, 386, 387–388

Portmann, A., 349n

Post, E., 96n

Potemkin villages, 434n

Powell, J., 117n

Pragmatic maxim, 339–400

Prather, H., 74n

Presence, 326, 332, 351, 352, 356; defined, 305, 306, 307; of the preacher, 373

Prial, F., 110n

Primitive magic, 353–357; and germ theory of disease, 354n; limpia ritual, 355; Navajo training program, 348; tactics of Mexican-American curanderos, 355; witch doctor's credibility, 356. See also Healing.

Protagoras, 394

Protocol: defined, 205, 206–208, 212, 213; and Polite Greeting, 206; and Turn Off, 206

Psyche, 306

Psychodrama, 249n

Psychotherapy, 348, 352, 368–371; "convergence" in psychotherapy, 369; psychotherapist client relationship, 369–370. See also Healing.

Ptolemy, 407

Publica, 308

Public institutions, 224

Publicity: defined, 307–308; announcing character, 308–309, 324; arousing existing needs, 313–323, 326; associational linking through slogans, 323–326, 327; and brand consciousness, 312, 313, 316, 317; "broad-casting," 309, 335n; contiguity as linking tactic, 325; and five-step formula, 308; follows upon events, 309, 324; fortuitous communication, 309; gaining and maintaining attention, 310–312, 313, 316, 324, 326; "hidden persuasion," 317; in Middle Ages, 308; objective needs, 313–317, 319; origins, 308; and personal decisions, 309; and presence, 326; and public decisions, 309; and recreation, 326; repetition as linking tactic, 325; and Rhetoric games, 310, 326–327; and rumor, 308; stylistic developments, 309; subjective needs, 317–323; and transportation, 309

Public-minded, 224

Public opinion polls, 329

Puritan Church, 372

Put Down: defined, 139–140, 161–164, 171, 213; hassling, 163–164, 166–170; hustling, 154n, 163, 164–166, 170n; and Love, 170n; and Put Off, 128, 161, 162, 169; and Turn Off, 161, 162

Put Off: defined, 114, 127–129, 134, 213; ambiguity, 130–132; distraction, 129–130; jabber, 133–134; silence, 132–133; and Personal Conversation Among Friends, 149; and Put Down, 128, 161, 162, 169; and Turn Off, 114, 128

Quadrivium, 333

Quimby, R., 302n

Rabelais, 379

Ransom, J., 267

Rather, L., 352n

Reciprocity, 74, 77, 217, 219

Recognition games. See Polite Greeting, Turn Off.

Recreation: and public games, 238, 241, 248, 263, 264, 277, 284, 298, 326

Recuperation, 240

Reich, C., 369n

Relaxation: and Mass Entertainment Dream Machines, 284; and Theater, 249

Renewal: and Revivalism, 373

Repetition, law of, 325

Res publica, 384

Rest, 248

Revivalism, 348, 352, 371–375; characteristics of revivalist's audience, 371, 372n; characteristics of revivalist's message, 373–374; and fraternal gratification, 374–375. See also Healing.

Revolutionary war battle reenactments, 249n

Rex, 290

RFK, 432

Rhetoric games, 229, 237, 238; defined, 234–235, 297, 302–303, 389; and amusement, 302; and "common sense," 345, 346, 349, 351, 362; false or sham art, 307n; five-step formula, 301–302, 308; fraternal quality, 298, 299, 303–304, 305, 306, 307, 308, 341, 345, 376–377, 380, 389; hedonistic appeals, 305, 306, 327; and interpersonal games, 304; and invention, 332; Janus-like quality of rhetorical messages, 298; "mere rhetoric," 302; originated by ancient Greeks, 303–304, 305–307, 327–328, 380; pleasure/pain principle, 299, 300, 301, 302, 305, 306, 307, 345, 380, 389; pragmatic appeals, 305; and Poetic messages, 248–249n; "presence" of the communicator, 299, 305–308, 381, 389; and probable truth, 235, 298, 299, 346, 348, 380; and propaganda, 334; proving tactics, 323, 324; and recreation, 378; rhetorical messages defined, 228, 236, 238, 297, 302; and renewal, 307, 376; and TGIF session, 391–392; threats, 305; and virtuosity, 305, 306, 307, 330, 340, 341, 389; and willful common action, 378. See also Healing, Political Dialog, Pornography, Publicity.

Rhetoric of the Forum: defined, 299, 327, 389. See also Political Dialog.

Rhetoric of the Marketplace: defined, 299, 389. See also Publicity.

Rhetoric of the Sewer: defined, 299, 389. See also Pornography.

Rhetoric of the Soul: defined, 299, 389. See also Healing.

Rich, A., 283n

Riezler, K., 35n

Roberts, O., 372n

Robinson, R., 393n

Rogers, C., 370, 376

Romanticism, 375, 376, 377

Rosenfield, L., 13, 216, 218, 219, 221, 380n, 434n

Rosenmeyer, T., 306n

Ross, W., 311n

Roth, P., 110n

Rough Rock (Arizona) Demonstration School, 348

Rousseau, J., 274, 375

Ruby, J., 351

Rules: defined, 31, 46; cheating, 38, 40, 327; distinguished from natural laws, 32–33. See also Customs, Tactics.

Russia, 412, 434n

Sabine, G., 330n

Sadecky, P., 384n

Said, the, and the Act of Saying, 67–70, 94, 120, 147

Sandburg, C., 267, 272

Santayana, G., 443n

Schickel, R., 289n

Schlesinger, G., 400n
Schlien, J., 79n
Schole, 248n
Schopler, J., 77n
Schulz, C., 261n
Schutz, W., 376
Science: defined, 435; assumptions about reality, 399; dialog between scientist and nature, 398; God as foul ball, 399; hypothesis testing, 401–402; level of experiential data, 398–401; level of mathematical models, 406–407; level of theoretical propositions, 401–406; levels of scientific discourse, 398; meaning and measurement, 400; meaning and sensible effects, 399–400; objective vocabulary, 401; operationalism, 400; pragmatic maxim, 399–400; quasi-sciences and hypothesis testing, 404–406; quasi-sciences and political bias, 405n; and Rhetoric games, 408; strong inference, 404–405; verifiability principle, 400–401; X-rays and "common sense" reality, 399n, 426
Scott, G., 290
Scott, R., 114n
SDS, 384
Sears catalogue, 290
Secret Service, 426
Sensitivity and encounter groups, 348, 375–377. *See also* Healing.
Sentimentality: substitute for human contact, 441
Serendipity, 222
Sesame Street, 293
Shakespeare, W., *As You Like It*, 257; *Hamlet*, 249n, 250, 251–252; *Macbeth*, 266–267; *The Merchant of Venice*, 257; *Romeo and Juliet*, 255; *The Taming of the Shrew*, 256; *Twelfth Night*, 257
Shanghai, 359
Shapiro, A., 366n
Shapiro, K., 386n
Sharp, J., 352n
Shelley, P., 267, 274
Sider, R., 395n
Sidman, J., 382n
Simmel, G., 161, 240n
Skinner, B., 328
Slater, P., 383n
Slogans, *See* Publicity.
Smith, A., 105n, 424
Smith, D., 81n
Smith, F., 70n
Smith, S., 330n
Snell, B., 306n
Sodom, 224n
Solomon, N., 376n
Soma, 306
Sophists, 305, 306, 307, 338
Sophocles, 254–255
Soul, 346n
South, the, 289n, 349
Spectators, 409; and interpersonal games, 80, 245; and public games, 223, 225, 245, 246, 249, 250, 263, 277, 294, 307, 327, 340, 341
Spinoza, B., 328, 394
Spontaneity, 76–77, 217–218, 219
Stafford-Clark, D., 383n
Standard Oil Company, 424
Starr, S., 382n, 383n
Status, 203, 208
Stephenson, W., 285n
Stevens, W., 371n
Stowe, H., 249n
Stranger, 95, 200
Strong inference, 404–405
Subjective needs, 317
Sullivan, H., 75n
Summer, R., 107n
Susskind, D., 291, 293
Syllogistic logic, 413

Symposium, 392
Synergy, 180n
Szasz, T., 84n, 369n, 370

Tabloid newspapers, 283
Tactics: defined, 36, 46; "pseudo-tactics," 38. *See also* Customs, Rules.
Tarbell, Ida, 424
Teleology of a game: defined, 36–37, 39; distinguished from goal directedness, 37; distinguished from motive, 37, 81n
Tennyson, A., 267
Termination: defined, 205, 209–212, 213; and Intensity, 210n; and Turn Off, 212
T-Groups, 375
Theater: defined, 249–250, 253, 263, 294; and carnival, 250; and dramatic literature, 249; and escape, 249; and film, 250, 254n; histrionic quality, 249–250, 253, 294; Impersonal role, 251–252, 263; and interpersonal communication experience, 250; Personal role, 251, 252, 263; and relaxation, 249; Social role, 251, 252, 263; and television, 250, 254n; viewed as concentric rings, 252–253, 262; and virtuosity, 250. *See also* Comedy, Farce, Melodrama, Tragedy.
Theoria, 394
Thompson, V., 77n
Thoughtful (Thoughtfulness), 67, 228, 437, 438; defined, 7–13; and amusement, 248
Thucydides, 423
Tolstoy, L., 122, 123n
Tonight, 288, 293n
Torquemada, 370, 377
Torrey, E., 346n, 370n
Toulmin, S., "Concepts and the Explanation of Human Behavior," 33n; *Human Understanding*, 398n, 401n, 404n
Tragedy: defined, 254–255, 263; and Comedy, 255; and Impersonal role, 254, 255, 263
Trivium, 333
Trojan War, 303, 305, 328
Turnbull, C., 209n
Turn Off: defined, 90, 99–100, 111, 213; defensive tactics, 109–110; offensive tactics, 106–109; played by casual acquaintances, 100–106, 111; played by strangers, 106–111; and Protocol, 206; and Put Down, 161, 162; and Put Off, 114, 128; and Termination, 212
Twenty questions, 398
Two-handed bezique, 435

U.S. Army, 357
U.S. Surgeon General, 286
Unguarait, D., 372n
Utilitarian philosophers, 300n

Valery, P., 421
van der Rohe, M., 287
Van de Vate, D., 216n
Varnhagen, R., 427
Verifiability principle, 400–401
Vernes, J., 29n
Victorian England, 385
Vietnam, 427, 434n
Vincent, Dr., 359–361
Virtuosity, 389; and Rhetoric games, 305, 306, 307, 330, 340, 341; and Theater, 250
Vogt, B., 349n
von Mises, R., 400n

Wallace, K., 441n
Warren Commission, 426
Washington Post, 429
Watergate, 430n
Watzlawick, P., 188n
Weaver, P., 305n, 427n
Weaver, R., 406n, 438

Webster, D., 330
Weed, D., 257–258
Weiss, P. 163n
Welles, C., 289n
White, H., 423n, 424n
Whitefield, G., 372, 373
Whitman, W., 274
Whittemore, E., 183n
Wichelns, H., 411, 413, 415
Wiener, P., 425n
Wilford, J., 348n
Wilkinson, J., 305n
Williams, F., 109n, 149n
Williams, W., 424
Willson, M., 300–302
Winder, A., 376n

Winston, R., 427n
Wolf, S., 366n
Wolff, K., 75n
Wolter, A., 439n
Women's lib, 292, 293
Woodstock rock festival, 376
Wordsworth, W., 267, 274
World War II, 357, 359

Xerox, 432

Young, C., 260–261

Zeno, 394
Ziskind, E., 360n